THE LANGUAGE OF ADVERTISING

THE LANGUAGE OF ADVERTISING

Major Themes in English Studies

Edited by Guy Cook

Volume IV

Routledge
Taylor & Francis Group

LONDON AND NEW YORK

First published 2008
by Routledge
2 Park Square, Milton Park, Abingdon, OX14 4RN

Simultaneously published in the USA and Canada
by Routledge
270 Madison Avenue, New York, NY 10016

Routledge is an imprint of the Taylor & Francis Group, an informa business

Typeset in 10/12pt Times by Graphicraft Limited, Hong Kong
Printed and bound in Great Britain by
MPG Books Ltd, Bodmin, Cornwall

British Library Cataloguing in Publication Data
A catalogue record for this book is available from the British Library

Library of Congress Cataloging in Publication Data
A catalog record for this book has been requested

ISBN10: 0-415-41215-3 (Set)
ISBN10: 0-415-41219-6 (Volume IV)

ISBN13: 978-0-415-41215-5 (Set)
ISBN13: 978-0-415-41219-3 (Volume IV)

Publisher's Note

References within each chapter are as they appear in the original
complete work

CONTENTS

ACKNOWLEDGEMENTS

The publishers would like to thank the following for permission to reprint their material:

Taylor & Francis Books UK for permission to reprint Kevin Moloney, 'PR from Top to Bottom' and 'Markets, Branding, Reputation' in *Rethinking Public Relations: The Spin and the Substance*, 2000, pp. 15–26, pp. 134–149, copyright © 2000.

Common Courage Press for permission to reprint John Stauber and Sheldon Rampton, 'The Art of the Hustle and the Science of Propaganda', in *Toxic Sludge is Good for You: Lies, Damn Lies and the Public Relations Industry*, 1995, pp. 17–25.

Sage Publications for permission to reprint John Swales and Priscilla Rogers, 'Discourse and the Projection of Corporate Culture: The Mission Statement', *Discourse and Society*, 6/2, 1995, pp. 223–240, copyright © 1995, Sage Publications.

Sage Publications for permission to reprint Deborah Cameron, 'Talk as Enterprise: Communication and Culture Change at Work', in *Good to Talk? Living and Working in a Communication Culture*, 2000, pp. 53–90, copyright © Deborah Cameron, 2000.

Taylor & Francis Ltd for permission to reprint Gerlinde Mautner, 'The Entrepreneurial University: A Discursive Profile of the Higher Education Buzzword', *Critical Discourse Studies*, 2, 2, 2005, pp. 95–120. www.tandf.co.uk/journals

Palgrave MacMillan for permission to reprint Guy Cook, ' "This We Have Done": the Vagueness of Poetry and Public Relations', in Joan Cutting (ed.), *Vague Language Explored*, 2007, pp. 21–39.

Taylor & Francis Books UK for permission to reprint Adam Lury, 'Advertising Moving Beyond the Stereotypes', in R. Keat, N. Whiteley and N. Abercrombie (eds.), *The Authority of the Consumer*, 1994, pp. 91–102, copyright © 1994.

Elsevier for permission to reprint J. Wilmshurst and A. Mackay, 'How Advertising is Created', in *The Fundamentals of Advertising*, 1999, pp. 185–202, copyright © 1999.

McGraw Hill for permission to reprint R. White, 'Advertising and Society', in *Advertising* (second edition), 1988, pp. 176–182.

Palgrave MacMillan for permission to reprint Nicholas Ind, 'The Corporate Brand', *The Corporate Brand*, 1997, pp. 1–14.

Taylor & Francis Books UK for permission to reprint Sean Brierley, 'Principles of Persuasion', in *The Advertising Handbook*, (second edition), 2002, pp. 137–150.

HarperCollins Publishers Ltd for permission to reprint Naomi Klein, 'Culture Jamming', in *No Logo: No Space, No Choice, No Jobs, Taking Aim at the Brand Bullies*, 2000, pp. 279–309, copyright © Naomi Klein, 2000.

Disclaimer

INTRODUCTION TO VOLUME IV

This volume (Public Relations and Brands; Insiders and Critics) further broadens our perspective in two ways. The first section (Part 9) widens the subject matter to include discussions of public relations, branding and corporate culture. (All of these have featured in pieces in earlier volumes, though not as the centre of attention.) The next two sections move the debate beyond the confines of the academic world to sample what is said about advertising outside it. The second section (Part 10) presents the highly partisan views of advertising practitioners in defence of their profession. The third section (Part 11) concludes the whole work with two polemical but well informed condemnations of it and an example of the Adbusters website.

Like advertising, public relations (PR) is very difficult to define, and the relationship between the two can be conceived in opposite ways. From one perspective, advertising is the subordinate category, merely a part of the larger superordinate exercises of public relations. Yet, from a historical perspective, PR has emerged out of, and in some ways succeeded, advertising to which, arguably, the consumer has recently become somewhat immune. We begin this volume with one of the clearest approaches to this complex relationship from Kevin Moloney's *Rethinking Public Relations: The Spin and the Substance*. Moloney is concerned to understand the implications for democracy of the growing size and influence of PR, and in the course of his analysis provides excellent insight into its relation to advertising too. He is followed by two of PR's strong critics, John Stauber and Sheldon Rampton (whose views on tobacco advertising we have already encountered in Volume III). In this reading, they tackle the relationship of PR to propaganda (a topic also covered by Moloney elsewhere in *Rethinking Public Relations*).

The ubiquitous mission statement is a PR creation which provides insight into the corporate culture from which it comes. John Swales and Priscilla Rogers analyse examples from two companies. Their work testifies to the fertility of collaboration between experts in linguistics (Swales) and business (Rogers), and the result is a masterful 'synthesis of the textual, cognitive and social perspectives . . . necessary for a comprehensive theory of language'. Not only do they provide a rigorous analysis of the evolving language of the mission statements in question, but also go a long way to achieving their stated aim of 'how mission statements get written and are perceived

1

by their creators and users'. If they do not go all the way, it is only because they encountered some unwillingness by executives to allow access to employees.

In the next reading we return to the relationship of ads to brands in a chapter from one of the wittiest, most approachable and clearly written books on advertising language: Greg Myers' *Ad Worlds*. Like Swales and Rogers, Myers approaches his texts from the senders' perspective, thinking in particular about their need to create product contrasts where there is in fact little difference between competitors. This particular chapter contains close analyses of two advertising campaigns: for Levi's jeans and Daz washing powder.

Mission statements are an aspect of public relations, and so too is the 'styling' of workers in service industries, especially retail outlets and call centres, to speak and act in designated ways, no matter how badly the customer treats them, and no matter what their own personalities, or feelings at the time. This is the topic addressed by Deborah Cameron in her book *Good to Talk?*, from which the next reading is taken. She uses her analysis to make points of broad relevance to language use in contemporary society. She criticises the widespread belief, frequently implied in PR, that 'good communication' and more dialogue will somehow heal disagreements; she shows how the growth of 'language work' and 'emotional labour' has affected the roles of males and females; she argues that communication is debased if language becomes a controlled commodity rather than a medium for speakers themselves. After her, Gerlinde Mautner assesses the coming of business criteria to higher education, relating vocabulary choice to an ideological shift in universities – providing also, in terms of methodology, an exemplary instance of the macro and micro approaches to discourse analysis working together. The section concludes with a piece of my own, contrasting the nature and function of vague language in public relations and poetic discourse. I use a corpus of mission statements from 'embattled' corporations (such as arms, biotechnology and tobacco companies) to provide examples of PR parallelism, and contrast these with similar formal features deployed to very different effect in a Bob Dylan song.

All of the above readings are critical of the PR discourse they examine. They add to the evidence in the first three volumes that academics who analyse advertising also condemn it – almost without exception. The second section of this volume, Insider Views, offers a counterbalance to everything which precedes it, by sampling writing by advertising practitioners. Not surprisingly, theirs is a more positive view, and they defend their profession robustly against its academic critics. Though the inclusion of these defences may well be disapproved of by some opponents, the purpose is to give readers a taste of the opposite view.

We begin with a brief and apparently 'matter-of-fact' statement by Jules Goddard about the nature of advertising, implying a common sense 'seeing off' of critics. Next we have two extracts by one of the industry's gurus, David Ogilvy, from his egocentrically titled *Ogilvy on Advertising*[1]. The first is a chapter entitled 'What's Wrong with Advertising?', the second a confident prophecy called 'I Predict 13 Changes'. As this was written in 1985, it will be amusing for the reader to judge whether Ogilvy's predictions have indeed come to pass. In the next chapter, Adam Lury gives a forthright rebuttal of supercilious establishment attitudes to advertising, including those of academics. He also provides a useful critique of research techniques from the advertisers' point of view, discussing the relative merits of quantitative techniques such as large-scale surveys and qualitative ones such as focus groups. Lury is himself a successful, award-winning 'creative' who in the 1980s brought reality into advertising (more truly than Benetton) by producing ads which included representations of topics such as divorce and racial discrimination, and his plea for realism in 'Advertising: Moving Beyond the Stereotypes' is well argued. However, there is little evidence in the two decades since this piece was written that advertising has in any way followed Lury's lead.

After Lury's atypical thoughtfulness, three brief extracts from standard textbooks are intended to show just how simplistic insider analyses of complex issues can be – though readers can judge for themselves if they agree with my assessment. Wilmshurst and Mackay's 'How Advertising is Created' is a particularly brash example, bristling with unsupported assertions, tautologies ('creative people have vivid imaginations'), platitudes ('Rule One: there are no rules'), and reductionist discussions, notably of art and creativity, and right and left brain processing. Roderick White offers a standard, but to be fair, well-argued, point-by-point rebuttal of critics. Last in this trio, Nicholas Ind gives us his view of the characteristics of the corporate (as opposed to product) brand in a complacent argument larded with highbrow allusions (from Aristotle to Umberto Eco), clichés ('to succeed one needs to become a good communicator') and a naive faith in distinctive company values.

The final reading in this section, from Sean Brierley's *The Advertising Handbook*, is rather unfairly placed in this company, as the author surveys rather than purveys advertisers' 'wisdom'. But what is distinctive about this chapter, and justifies its placement here, is that he approaches advertising from the sender's standpoint, trying to see why advertising creatives make the choices and use the tactics that they do. So far in these volumes we have had mostly analyses of advertising texts, or of audience reactions to them. What we have here, unusually, is an informed commentary on their senders. As we approach the end of these four volumes, the reader who has worked through from beginning to end will find many echoes and cross-references in this piece. Brierley's distinction between 'reason why' and 'atmosphere' ads (memorably summarised in the ad man's adage 'sell the steak not the sizzle') recalls Simpson's discussion of reason and tickle in Volume I or Thompson's contrast of rational core and decorative periphery in Volume II.

I have already expressed my disdain for the arguments (other than Brierley's) in the second section. But for the reader who has been beguiled by them, the concluding section may offer an antidote, containing as it does extracts from two influential polemics against advertising.

The first is from Eric Clark's (1988) *The Want Makers: Lifting the Lid off the World Advertising Industry*. A large part of his analysis and argument is economic, and he quotes many revealing statistics about advertising budgets. His figures are from 1985 but his points about excessive expenditure remain true today. He shows how 'commercials [are] far and away the most expensive items on film' with feature films coming out at around $90,000 an hour and adverts at $140,000 *a minute*. Clark equates branding with advertising, and is concerned with the contrast between the reality of products and the hype of adverts. Quoting an advertising executive who commented on lagers which are 'identical in terms of taste, colour and alcohol delivery . . . so the consumer is literally drinking the advertising, and the advertising is the brand . . .' he concludes that '. . . advertising has now moved on from being the creator of the image that helps sell the product. Today, advertising *is* the product.' Clark's chapter has a wealth of memorable examples, such as an advert for military barbed wire 'in attractive colours'.

The final reading is from Naomi Klein's landmark book *No Logo*, a wide-ranging survey and condemnation of the history and power of the brand in the contemporary globalised world. The chapter presented here deals with the issue of 'culture jamming' – the creative, often very witty, re-creation and subversion of advertising images to give a message undermining the original. To illustrate and amplify Klein's points we conclude with an extract from the Adbusters website: an appropriate sequel, I hope, to the many learnèd disquisitions on advertising in these volumes.

At the end of these volumes the reader will be well informed both about the language of advertising itself and about academic views of it, and thus in a better position to make an independent judgment about advertising's worth and morality. In my own view, there is much to be admired in the creativity and effort which goes into the best advertisements, and certainly much of linguistic interest, but overall it is a sad comment on our times that advertising should absorb and pervert such talent in the service of a corporate capitalism which causes so much personal, social and environmental damage, and in a genre whose goals are – ultimately – always constrainingly commercial rather than truly creative.

Note

1 Ogilvy's book, like advertisements themselves, relies heavily on pictures to create a mood. They have been removed from these extracts, partly for practical reasons, but also to allow the reader to concentrate on the argument – such as it is.

Part 9

PUBLIC RELATIONS
AND BRANDS

PR FROM TOP TO BOTTOM

Kevin Moloney

Source: Kevin Moloney, *Rethinking Public Relations: The Spin and the Substance*, London: Routledge, 2000, pp. 15–26.

Public relations is such a pervasive activity in our society today that it is impossible for a citizen or consumer to avoid. The establishment and the political class have taken to it with enthusiasm. The Queen has had a Communications Secretary since 1998 and the brief for the job was one that puts PR right at the centre of the establishment: 'to devise a PR strategy for the Queen and the other Royals'.[1] The world's richest man, Bill Gates, gives PR a glowing testimonial: 'If I was down to my last dollar, I would spend it on PR.' The Church of England has a media office, as does the Roman Catholic Church, and other faiths.[2] British schools are told that they 'need to be savvy about PR'.[3] Vigilante groups seeking out paedophiles on a housing estate have press officers.[4] The media has feasted on PR's ubiquity and confected up popular sitcoms to laugh it out of respectability – *Absolutely Fabulous* and *Spin City* on television and *Absolute Power*[5] on BBC national radio. Even the more obscure edges of the media have nodded towards PR's existence: there was a 'king of spin' in the University of the M25 satire in *The Times Higher Education Supplement*.[6] Indeed, this weekly house journal for academics urges them to 'work with press officers to ensure their peer-reviewed work is reflected accurately in publicity'.[7] It also tells them how being insulted as 'third rate' can be turned to institutional advantage.[8]

One of the most noticeable features of New Labour governments has been their presentational skills and media management, so much so that in popular language 'New Labour' and 'spin' are synonymous. They have been persistently criticised for 'spinning' policies, for representing them serially in different versions, and condemned for spending between two and three times the amount their predecessor had on special advisers, many of them public relations experts. Peter Mandelson and Alastair Campbell are held to have promoted Tony Blair up to Downing Street through handing out exclusive new stories, favouring some journalists, controlling timing and briefing unattributably – classic PR media relations. The management continued in government; the Prime Minister presented 'state of the nation' reports and held 'big conversations' with the public – classic PR event management. Indeed, to stop digging deeper into the hole of PR's most embarrassing fate, Alastair Campbell resigned from the post of the Prime Minister's Press Secretary in 2003 because he had become the news, not the messenger.

The tabloid and broadsheet newspapers are not far behind in their use of PR. They report and photograph for their front pages the lifestyles of celebrities, those who are famous for being famous, through deals struck with their PR agents. The industry has firms and individuals specialising in 'celebrity PR': Freud Communications for example. But first in this field for over a decade has been the ubiquitous, plainspeaking personage of Max Clifford, famous for engineering the human and animal circumstances in 1986 that led to the *Sun* headline 'Freddie Starr ate my hamster'.[9] Fun and frothy their work may be, but these promoters and protectors of the glitterati carry negotiating clout. It is Max Clifford, as well as libel lawyers, who gets £100,000 plus outcomes for his 'kiss-and-tell' clients.

Well entrenched in royalty, politics, the media and entertainment, PR is now edging towards the domain of individual self-development. It has been personalised and customised as part of the self-improvement culture – *Mastering Public Relations*,[10] *Be Your Own Spin Doctor*[11] and *Public Relations for Dummies*[12] are in the bookshops. Rein *et al.* (1997) see it as the means to high social and public profile for the professional middle classes. Its jargon has spread into everyday language and flourished. The verb 'to spin' is used without flicking apostrophe marks. The verb to 'unspin' has been heard on BBC Radio 4, as has 'spin nurse'. 'Spin dodger' has been uttered.

Indeed, so pervasive is public relations that we can write of the saturation of UK society with PR activity. Ewen (1996) found that state already existing in the USA when he started tracing the intellectual history of corporate PR there: 'Living in a society in which nearly every moment of human attention is exposed to the game plan of spin doctors, image managers, pitchmen, communications consultants, public information officers and public relations specialists, the boundaries of my inquiry appeared seamless' (p. 19). Now there are no boundaries to PR in the UK.

PR as personal behaviour, as organised activity, as attitude, and as language is part of Britain's cultural weather. A forecast in *The Times* has come true:[13]

> Criticise Sophie Wessex for being a poor PR, but not for being a PR. Tony Blair marching through the countryside in a silly yellow plastic suit, the Queen buying the Big Issue, Prince Charles giving to farmers, everyone is in the PR game now.

With this sort of social and political endorsement, the *Spectator*[14] was right in 1989 to proclaim that 'PR is the profession of the decade'. The magazine will be writing the same for decades to come.

If public relations is widely manifest in the UK today, it is also highly organised. Thirty years ago, we would not have talked of it as an 'industry': that word connoted high physical production volumes in mineral extraction and manufacturing. Then, it was still a novelty to hear of services described as industries. Now, the Department of Trade and Industry commissions reports on PR. In 1994 they commissioned one from management consultants BDO Stoy Hayward who found that 'the UK PR sector is one of the most highly developed in Europe'. A decade later, the Department, along with the Chartered Institute of Public Relations, published another entitled *Unlocking the Potential of Public Relations*. It 'highlights that the already significant contribution of the public relations industry to the UK economy can be greatly increased through better understanding by business leaders of what the best of public relations can achieve'.[15]

In the early 1960s, West (1963, pp. 8–9) estimated for the UK that there were some 4,000 PRs (four-fifths of them in London), 300 PR companies and a £50 million expenditure. Kisch (1964, p. 22) also put turnover at £50 million in 1961/2. In 1967, there were 766 PR companies and inhouse departments in the UK, and 9,200 in 1997.[16] In the early 1990s, turnover was estimated at £1 billion. The 1998 figure was £2.3 billion and for 2004 was in excess of £3 billion,[17] with an estimated 40,000 people employed. The figures are from the Chartered Institute of Public Relation (CIPR), the professional development and representative body for PR individuals. By 2005, the CIPR put turnover at £6.5bn and employees at 48,000. A former president of the Institute (2003–4) estimated that the industry was growing at 17 per cent a year and that it employed more people than advertising.[18] The Public Relations Consultants' Association (PRCA) represents the interests of larger PR consultancies. Their fee income grew from £33 million to £220 million between 1984 and 1996, and in 2004 was £400 million. In the same year, these 120 consultancies earned an estimated 70 per cent of the industry's fee income and employed 4,600 people. *PRWeek* (May 2004)[19] reports that the industry is supported by twenty-nine service sectors ranging from fireworks to translators. Moreover, PR producers and their suppliers are comforted by the knowledge that their industry is a good place in which to invest. According to Plimsoll's Industry Investment Index, PR ranks 25th out of 1,000 UK business sectors for investment attractiveness: every £100 invested brings in a profit of £14, compared with an average of £5.[20]

But employment figures underestimate the actual number of people doing PR for they appear to measure only explicit job titles, and persons who self-declare. For example, government PR people never publicly use the term, calling themselves instead information officers. There is also, as detailed below, a flight from the term 'public relations' by many businesses and by some PR agencies because of the negative connotations. Moreover, the methodologies for counting are not clear. A better sense of the saturation of PR is got by looking at it as persuasive communications (excluding advertising) done by people in honorary, voluntary and paid posts in the public, private and voluntary sectors. This would push the total number of people doing PR higher than the 48,000 above.

Young people like PR. *The Times Higher Education Supplement* reports[21] that 'Advertising, public relations and media jobs were the most coveted careers – about one in four students aspire to jobs in these fields'. These aspirants want qualifications to help them get their first job paying between £18,000 and £23,000 in London.[22] The education system has noticed their interest. Since the late 1980s, the subject has been taught at higher education (HE) level in colleges and universities. There are few, if any, estimates of what proportion of business studies courses in further education colleges have an identifiable and separate PR curriculum, but in higher education the subject is taught at diploma, bachelor and masters degree level at, mostly, 'new' universities. PhD students research aspects of PR.[23] An increasingly marketised HE sector wants those extra student numbers and the fee income they bring in. In 2004, there were over 200 PR-related courses on the universities' and colleges' application service website. Twenty universities or colleges offered courses approved by the CIPR, compared with three at the end of the 1980s and before the Chartered Institute offered validation. A PR degree has been offered at Bournemouth University since 1989, once with applications running at ten for every place but dropping since the introduction of tuition fees and more competition from thirteen CIPR approved undergraduate degrees.[24]

The natural response by the British PR industry to these many indicators of expansion is more confidence. The CIPR has developed many of the features of a professional body. It runs a diploma and advanced certificate taught at fifteen centres in the UK and three abroad. It has an 'accredited practitioner' category. It has a training programme. It has 'excellence awards' which acknowledge that work accorded that mark are 'judged the best in Britain, home of the most thriving public relations business in the world'.[25] It gained 'chartered' status in 2005 and said that this 'marks the "coming of age" of the PR profession and is official recognition of the important and influential role that public relations plays in business, government and democratic society'.[26] It has opinions about public policy, e.g. lobbying to stop ministerial special advisers instructing government information officers; and giving evidence to the Phillis committee on how government media relations should be organised after the departure of Alastair Campbell.[27] As the CIPR puts it 'public relations is a flourishing management function'. There is, undoubtedly, a spring in the modern PR person's step.

The public relations of public relations

Yet while it thrives, PR does not enjoy a high reputation with the general public or with some professional groups. Reputation is the social prestige or dislike that a person, job or institution attracts. High reputation can be seen as large amounts of 'credit' in the 'bank' of public opinion. For example, many student readers would give different 'credit ratings' to the reputations of Balliol College Oxford, Bath, Birmingham, Bournemouth, Bradford, Brighton, and Bristol universities. They base their ratings on a combination of experience, surveys, league tables and gossip. When they do this, they are comparing reputations.

There is, however, an irony here. Despite the expansion of PR, the public relations of public relations remains in a poor state: PR generates low opinion about itself. Compare this state of affairs with other activities. The parallel would be if observers of an activity criticised it for not bringing about the outcome it existed to make come about. It would be as if medicine did not increase health, teaching reduced knowledge, or gardening meant fewer flowers. This point is sharper when we remember that the CIPR's double-head definition of public relations focuses on reputation and its management as well as goodwill and mutual understanding. The CIPR president for 2000/1 wrote[28] that 'PR is about reputation and being transparent and open, not about deviousness or manipulation'. The CIPR website states[29] that

> Public Relations is the discipline which looks after reputation, with the aim of earning understanding and support and influencing opinion and behaviour. It is the planned and sustained effort to establish and maintain goodwill and mutual understanding between an organisation and its publics.

That more PR should lead to less of the benefit it promotes for others being available to itself is a rich irony, an irony that was enriched by the infamous 'false sheik' meeting with the Countess of Wessex.[30] This debacle inflicted serious damage to the reputation of PR in a precise way: it revealed how important personal contacts are to many of its operations; how much PR is more about who you know than what you know, or what you do.

The abbreviation 'PR' has entered everyday language, as has some of its jargon (campaign, press release, image, spin doctor, soundbite, on message, off message, prebuttal, rapid rebuttal, minder, positioning, relaunch) – but rarely with positive connotations. It is a fairly safe bet that the proverbial Martian would see that government, business, charities, pressure groups and celebrities 'do PR', and yet be amazed that the public and many non-PR professionals use the term as a mocking colloquial reference. For example, the jibe 'It's a PR job' describes words or actions about which there is a perceived or actual gap between presentation and reality, a gap that is either actively disguised or not owned up to. That is the gap connoted by other commonplace phrases such as 'It's a PR disaster'[31] or 'It's just spin'. For nearly all the media and public, the term 'PR' generally carries a negative charge.

'PR' is what 'spin doctors' do, and people are wary. Max Clifford, who is the *bête noire* of the UK public relations establishment, was in tune with popular perceptions when he talked about his Favourite Hypocrisy:[32] 'I stand up and say that an important part of public relations is lies and deceit. We all know that but they won't ever admit it. It gives me tremendous pleasure to hear PRs say they don't lie.' Max Clifford is right about PR people not admitting to lying; but they are aware of their low reputation. A former editor of *PRWeek*,[33] the industry's trade magazine, wrote at the fiftieth anniversary of the then IPR:[34]

> Part of the problem is that public relations which is all about the 'management of reputation', according to the IPR definition, itself has a reputation which is right off the end of the Ratner scale. In fact, you would be hard pushed to find an industry which is as gleefully vilified as the noble profession of public relations – otherwise known as 'the latrine of parasitic misinformation' as it was dubbed by *The Guardian*.

The more socially sensitive PR people have doubts about reduced status through association with 'PR' and there is evidence of a flight from the term towards substitutes, which usually include 'communications'. Some graduates hesitate to admit that they have a BA Public Relations. It is embarrassing to find a book titled *Public Relations for Dummies* when you have spent three years studying the subject. English, history, architecture and medical students do not face that public scepticism about their subjects' worth. The large agency Burson-Marstellar dropped the term in favour of 'perception management'.[35] Even *PRWeek* noted[36] that 'the term "PR" is giving public relations a bad name' and it wrote of 'anecdotal experience of consultants and in-house practitioners in the UK ... [that] communications is on the up but "public relations" is consistently undervalued as a management asset, and seen instead as a downstream "packaging" function'.[37] When Peter Hehir, a leading PR entrepreneur, said[38] that the term 'has lost its way as a description of what people are doing in the business', he was voicing a common view among senior business people.

Lord McAlpine updated Machiavelli's *The Prince*[39] as a handbook for success in business. He sees the value of PR, but calls those who practise it 'twitchers of image' who use half-truths and convenient words. His advice to employers is never tell PR people more than they need to know. Indeed, the term 'Machiavellian marketing' has been coined[40] to describe what PR people call public affairs and government relations. Some lobbyists publicly distance themselves from 'PR', and most prefer in their literature descriptors such as 'public affairs' and 'government relations'.[41] This bias away from the words 'public relations' is summed up in the titling priorities of two UK textbooks: *Strategic Communications Management: Making Public Relations Work* and *Handbook of Corporate Communication and Public Relations*.[42]

The lecturers who teach PR know about the low status of their subject: when asked if it had a low reputation with the general public, 78 per cent of the academics in a survey of the PR Educators' Forum[43] answered 'yes'. There was a small majority in the same survey who thought PR had a poor reputation with managers and employers. Respondents also felt looked down upon by their peers in traditional disciplines outside of business studies. L'Etang (2004a, p. 346) observes that 'Media academics to varying degrees reflect the prejudices of journalists and may therefore regard PR academics as either nefarious or unthinking functionaries operating in an atheoretical and thus inferior environment.' These academics, therefore, largely dismiss PR as worthy of study but when they do take notice of it, they are heavily critical – which is acceptable – and very dismissive of its significance – which is shortsighted. Typical is Webster[44] who, in his review of 'the information society', sees PR as a pollutant of disinterested, rational and transparent debate in society.

Olasky (1987) is also concerned. A PR man turned academic, he wrote for public relations people 'who want to understand why corporate public relations is sinking deeper into ethical and political quicksand' (preface). He wrote for the conservative, libertarian right; from the neo-Marxist left, Gandy (1982) argued that public relations people used an 'information subsidy' to reduce the cost to politicians, public officials and journalists of access to information favourable to their employers, the large corporations.

The low status of PR is not a new phenomenon. It was noticed by Pimlott (1951) in the USA of the 1940s, the land that Chomsky declares invented public relations.[45] Pimlott was a British observer of the US scene in the early post-war period up to 1950 and he remarked that 'the fact is public relations practitioners have never enjoyed good public relations' (p. 201). He notes that the US 'father' of PR, Ivy Lee, who was an adviser to the Rockefeller business empire, was known as 'Poison Ivy' (p. 202). More generally, public opinion saw PR as a technique favouring the rich. The PR man is a 'plutogogue' (p. 206) used by business to counter attacks on capitalism (p. 207); who identifies with 'unworthy' causes, who is thought to use dis-honest techniques, and who makes claims that are 'eyewash' (p. 205).

Advantages for funders and producers

A rebalancing of the argument, however, is needed at this stage. Whatever the strength of the case against, PR in the UK is a growing activity and a

13

prosperous business with at least 48,000 people turning over £6.5 billion a year, and with plenty of openings for young people. It is a major component of the UK's promotional culture, a pervasive activity done by business, non-business and anti-business groups, by all points of the political compass, and by all classes of material and ideological interests. They use it – as an organisational activity and as a state of mind – because they judge that it will advance their interests. How is that? These are questions for the production supply side of PR. So what value does it return to its paymasters, employers and clients? (See Chs 9–11 for benefits of PR in politics, markets and media). Here is what those who pay for public relations say in advertisements about the needs PR fulfils for them.

A global software company describes the role of its communications manager: 'What we need you to do is to focus on managing our public reputation.' A tobacco company wants a corporate affairs manager for 'close monitoring and guidance of competitive market environment' and 'management of UK legal activity relating to compliance, regulation and commerce' (both from *PRWeek*, 11.6.04, pp. 42, 44). A local authority looks for a principal press officer who will 'proactively shape our reputation with opinion formers locally and nationally' while a university wants a senior press officer 'passionate about delivery of quality communications for a global brand leader' (both in the *Guardian* jobs section, 22.05.04, pp. 50–63). The CIPR wants internal communicators at a conference (June 2004) because they play 'a crucial role in managing change, and motivating and informing the workforce to help organisations to achieve corporate goals and deliver results'. The pressure group Age Concern wants a media relations officer (the *Guardian* jobs section, 31.5.04, p. 7) to join a team that 'creates national headlines that help improve life for older people now'. A headmaster says that 'we do need to drip-feed positive messages all the time' (the *Guardian* education section, 1.6.04, p. 8). A 'fast-moving council' wants a communications manager who will be '. . . spearheading the strategic direction of our e-government and customer services' (the *Guardian* media section, 7.6.04, p. 43). A skills council for the chemical industry wants 'an advocate for the needs of employers in our sector to stakeholders, including Government' (the *Guardian* jobs section, 12.6.04, p. 8) while a police authority wants a communication director 'to develop an innovative communication and marketing strategy, and lead the marketing and publicity team to deliver a media service that gets heard' (the *Sunday Times* appointments section, 13.6.04, p. 9). Those who fund it believe that PR pays back.

Comparisons with advertising and journalism

If these outcomes and advantages are real, why does PR provoke more criticism than advertising? Peter Mandelson is known to his critics as 'Prince of Darkness', but no such soubriquet attaches to Philip Gould, the Labour

14

Party's former advertising specialist and current pollster. Gould has been associated with the advertising side of Labour since 1985, when Mandelson was appointed the party's director of campaigns and communications. He set up the Shadow Communications Agency, an informal agency ready to run election ad campaigns for the party. He advised the 1992 Clinton election campaign on how to avoid the sort of presentational mistakes made by Labour earlier that year in the UK general election. He was as much a party apparatchik as Mandelson, but not as much decried. Advertising has been established longer than PR as an industry and was critiqued by Vance Packard in 1957 in *The Hidden Persuaders*[46] – a title more fitting to PR people than to those who persuade off the page in an eye-catching mixture of visuals and words. Yet high visibility and critical attention have not brought advertising into such low regard.

One explanation is that advertising has been the more established industry and has in the past been subject to obloquy – witness *The Hidden Persuaders*. Grant notes (1994, pp. 28, 31–4) in her review of inter-war UK domestic propaganda that its reputation was low and worse than that of the press. She writes (p. 32):

> If the First World War gave propaganda a bad name, advertising already had one. Long regarded as the purview of quacks and swindlers, it was becoming respectable only slowly, as the industry's attempts to curb abuses, set standards, and organise itself in a profession began to take effect.

If there is a maturation process for the status of new types of work and it matches the cycle of diffusion for an innovation, growing acceptance and reputation awaits PR. But it is taking a long time to arrive; in 1948 Goldman was writing (p. 23) that it 'has so far failed of complete acceptance as a profession'. He noted that because of 'cultural lag', surgeons took more than a century to avoid 'the barber's tag'. On that timetable, PR is coming up to its century.

Another argument is that advertising does not attract low regard precisely because it is so visible. It is very obviously display, where the display is a 'shriek' from the page.[47] It is easy to imagine a PR person smiling at the compliment that their work was subtle: PR often seeks to 'whisper' from the deep background. To an advertising person, the compliment is dubious. More generally, in terms of work prospects and budgets, PR saw itself in the UK as the junior partner to advertising until the later 1980s. It was advertising agencies that had PR sections and not the other way around: these advertising agencies were called 'full service'. Advertising budgets were often in £millions, while PR mostly worked for less than £100,000. Further back in the 1960s, Kisch (1964, pp. 24–5) estimates that PR fees ranged between £1,500 and £8,000. Now, with the spread of integrated marketing communications, it is more difficult to measure separate contributions to total promotional spend but the judgement is that PR is gaining ground because of its lower cost, multiple forms, and because of more editorial space to fill. One estimate is that £400,000 is a medium-sized fee for a large London agency.[48] PR imperialists and loyalists will read with pleasure *The Fall of Advertising and the Rise of PR* (Ries and Ries 2002) and their judgement that 'we see a dramatic shift from advertising-orientated market-ing to public relations-orientated marketing' (p. xi).

The role of the media in the creation of the parlous public reputation of PR needs evaluation. Some PR people believe that it is the determining factor, for journalists seem to have an instinct to label any public presenta-tion malfunction as PR. The *Guardian* reported in summer 2000[49] that the Prime Minister was slow handclapped by the Women's Institute when he addressed their annual conference in the Queen Elizabeth Conference Centre, London. The headline was 'PR disaster as No 10 fails to get the message'. Why not political disaster, speech disaster? Media dislike is not new, for West (1963) reported the existence of a Society for the Discourage-ment of Public Relations, and Tunstall (1964) noted both journalistic resentment towards PR and dependence on it. Today, the bad feeling happens at a time when journalists need PR more than ever: they have so much more space to fill. Satellite, cable and digital television have at the same time finished off the BBC and ITV duopoly. The BBC has eight national TV channels and ITV sixteen national and regional ones.[50] Over 200 local and three national commercial radio stations compete with the BBC's forty local and five national.[51] Many, if not most, PR people blame journalists as their most dangerous bad-mouthers because of their control over the content and tone of public debate. A columnist on *The Times* comment page[52] can write of 'the pseudo-profession that calls itself public relations' and hundreds of thousands of readers will note the put down. PR people also note that, like traffic wardens, journalists are everywhere; moreover that journalists do not deal with advertising agents. Stand back, however, from these inter-professional hostilities and the relationship can be seen as attempts by both sides to gain the most from the supply and demand of information.[53] One survey showed that, on average, editors believed that a quarter of all media coverage is based on PR-sourced material, while PRs believe that the sourcing is 40 per cent. The relationship has been summed up as a choice between 'a partnership or a marriage of convenience?'.[54] 'Relationship in permanent crisis' is another option.

PRs and journalists inside the relationships often find them aggressive and painful. There is a 'love–hate' dimension with strong potential to become 'hate–hate' (see Ch. 11 for a full analysis of PR/media relations).[55] Though they have to deal with them, journalists professionally do not like PR people because they see them as a block, a barrier to facts, figures and people to which the media want access for a 'good' story. The story is usually showing up the fact, figure or person involved in a sensational, critical or false light. PR people tend to offer the less critical fact, figure or person to the journalist for write-up or interview. Journalists complain that this behaviour leads to a blander story than the one that they could get if the PR person was not guarding the gateway to information.

On the other side, the PR person feels that the journalist is usually seeking a critical view of the organisation, cause or person the PR person is representing. It is irritating to be always asked negative questions of an organisation or person one likes or believes in, or which pays one's wages and/or which one fears. The constant stress on the negative grates on the soul of the PR person after a while, but the balance of power in the PR/media relationship does not normally allow this to be shown – another source of negative feeling for the PR person. The supply and demand for information and publicity determines the balance of advantage to both sides, and it is usually the case, given the growth of PR, that there are fewer journalists 'buying' than sources 'selling in' to them. Against that, journalists may weaken their bargaining hand by being pressed for time; under news desk instruction to get a story; or over-worked in an underresourced newsroom. The outcome on both sides is at best formal politeness: minimum information given away by both sides, and a search for more amenable sources or journalists.

Other structural, less personal factors also work their way in to make the relationship tense. There is the journalist's perception that their paper or station carries too many 'puffs'[56] on behalf of advertisers, powerful interests or the editor's cronies. Some journalists go so far as to talk about the 'courtier media'. Second, there is the perception of a dumbing down of content and journalistic standards in the broadsheet press and terrestrial TV. Third, it is believed that PR people are better paid and have an easier professional life than journalists. To these perceptions can be added cuts in journalists' staffing levels occurring at the same time as the growth in media outlets over the last twenty years, culminating in a feeling among journalists that they are being colonised by PR values and behaviour. As Davis (2003, p. 32) puts it: 'Clearly, as British journalism is repeatedly cut and squeezed, so standards drop and the need to cut corners becomes crucial. Journalists must do more with less resources and are becoming out-numbered and out-resourced by their PR counterparts.'

In these circumstances, journalists are likely to be critical of PR and they are in the better position to voice their feelings: they control the words read and heard by their audiences – audiences that PRs want to influence.

It is the (usually private) contention of PR people that journalists continuously bad mouth them out of spite, fear or envy, and that they are the prime builders of their low reputation. The bad mouthing is either mildly derogatory, or acidly insulting. For the latter category, note this: the *Financial Times* carried the headline[57] 'The pioneer of today's spin-doctors'

17

and stated that 'Goebbels was a master manipulator' who 'pioneered the techniques of "news management" and public relations'.

Summary

This chapter has argued that PR is an activity that is noticeable and widespread in our society today – so much so that it is a major pillar of our promotional culture. By volume of activity, it is an industry spread throughout the UK; by social reach, it is done by the establishment and by immigrant groups; by diversity of source, it is done by government, big business, social campaigners, charities, celebrities of all lists, and aggrieved individuals. Its funders and producers spend £6.5 billion on it and employ at least 48,000 people. For them, there are beneficial outcomes and operational advantages for all this money. But despite this pervasiveness, the PR of PR is bad, and through tense relationships with journalists, the low reputation is reported widely. All these factors combine into an unusual asymmetry – a voluntary, legal, universally practised activity, devoted to raising the reputation of what it represents, generating disquiet about itself. This is the starting point for the next chapter. Is this pervasive activity with low reputation linked to other trends in UK society?

Notes

1 *PR Week*, 3.7.98, p. 28.
2 See www.catholic-ew.org.uk/nav/newsandevents.htm for Catholics in England and Wales; and www.bedfordgurdwara.org.uk/pix.htm for Sikhs. Accessed 24.3.05.
3 The *Guardian* education section, 1.6.04, p. 8.
4 The *Observer* notes ('Adults teach hatred as Sarah is mourned', 13.8.00, p. 5) that a leader of a group on the Paulsgrove council estate, Portsmouth 'will only talk in the presence of the self-appointed press officer'.
5 The everyday tale of super-cynical, lobbying folk from the consultancy of Prentice and McCabe.
6 Edition of 30.4.04, p. 20.
7 Edition of 25.6.04, p. 5. Another instance of university involvement with PR is the search by Hertfordshire University for an agency to improve its relations with the local community on a £100,000 two-year contract. Source: 'Herts uni to boost community ties', *PRWeek*, 6.8.04, p. 10.
8 The head of Imperial College calls Luton University 'third rate' in March 2004, and, in October, the head of the university gives a paper on 'reputation management' at the Effective Marketing in Higher Education conference, reporting increases in staff morale, admissions and national profile. The Luton head revealed a good PR tactic when under attack: appear puzzled rather than angry. See 'Insult transforms Luton's fortunes', *The Times Higher Education Supplement*, 29.10.04, p. 1.
9 Edition of 13.3.86.
10 By A. Davis (2004) from Palgrave Macmillan of Basingstoke.
11 By Paul Richards (1998) from Take That Ltd of Harrogate.
12 By E. Yaverbaum and R. Bly (2001), California: IDG Books Worldwide.

13 Jasper Gerard, 'The Dorchester chronicles present us with the regal Bridget Jones', *The Times*, 9.4.01, p. 16.

14 Edition of 10.1.98, p. 8.

15 Foreword, November 2003. See www.ipr.org.uk/unlockpr/Unlocking_Potential_ Report.pdf. Accessed 23.3.05.

16 Source is David Michie (1998), p. 12. Calculated by adding the PR companies' and the in-house departments' sub-totals.

17 Source of the £3 billion figure is head of public affairs, CIPR, in an email to the author of 29.4.04. Turnover and employment figures, however, should be treated with caution, e.g. in 1993, *Public Relations: Journal of the IPR* 11(3), p. 3, gave employment at 48,000 with the comment working 'in some way' in PR.

18 Prof. Anne Gregory at www.anti-spin.com/index.cfm?TERTIARY_ID= O&PRIMARY_ID=21&SECOND/. Accessed on 25.9.03.

19 Website, 30.5.04.

20 Reported by the CIPR on 29.4.04 in an email to the author.

21 Source is 'A post-Blair generation?' *The Times Higher Education Supplement*, 6.8.04, p. 2.

22 Source is 'Career Opportunities', the *Evening Standard*, London, 23.9.04, p. 59.

23 Topics include corporate social responsibility and small businesses; lobbying in Italy; e-communications by MPs; and corporate branding by multinational mobile phone companies competing in the UK.

24 Source is CIPR map on back page of *Behind the Spin* 9, February 2005. There are also eleven postgraduate degrees approved and six postgraduate diplomas.

25 See the brochure *IPR Excellence Awards 2005*, p. 2, from the CIPR.

26 See www.ipr.org.uk/charterspecial/release_170205.htm.

27 *PRWeek*, 23.1.04, p. 1, and IPR annual review (2003), p. 3.

28 Alison Clark's letter to the *Financial Times*, 26.8.02, p. 8, 'No place in PR for manipulation'.

29 See www.ipr.org.uk/Careers/what/definition.htm. Accessed 25.2.05.

30 March/April 2001. See *The Times*, 9.4.01, pp. 1, 4, 5, 16 for a summary.

31 Managing perceptions extends from seeking mundane commercial advantage to avoiding moral guilt. Doreen Lawrence, the mother of the murdered black teenager Stephen Lawrence, rejected the admissions of racism in the London police by their Commissioner Sir Paul Condon as 'That is a PR job', (the *Guardian*, 2.10.98, p. 1).

32 The *Independent* magazine section, 26.10.96, p. 30.

33 Stephen Farish in the commemorative publication *Managing Communication in a Changing World*, London: IPR in 1998, p. 58.

34 It was awarded chartered status in 2005.

35 *PRWeek*, 23.2.96.

36 *PRWeek* supplement, 26.4.96.

37 *PRWeek*, 7.6.98, p. 7.

38 *PRWeek*, 25.6.04, p. 21.

39 As *The New Machiavelli* (1997).

40 By Phil Harris and Andrew Lock (1996).

41 For a review of hired lobbyists, see Moloney (1996).

42 By White and Mazur (1995) and Oliver (ed.) (2004).

43 A survey carried out by the author in spring 1998. The numbers are small because the PR Educators' Forum then had forty-three correspondents in sixteen universities and colleges.

44 Webster (1995, p. 101): argued in relation to the public sphere concept.

45 *Viewing the Century* – Noam Chomsky, BBC Radio 3, 21.6.98.

46 The second edition, published by Penguin, 1981, has some updating.
47 McQuail (1987, p. 293) says about PR and advertising that the 'relevant mode is mainly that of "display-attention"'.
48 Source is a CEO of such an agency visiting Bournemouth University, winter 2004.
49 Edition of 8.6.00, p. 8.
50 Source: *TBI Yearbook* (2004), London: Informa Media Group.
51 Source: *World Radio TV Handbook* (2004), Oxford: WRTH Publications.
52 Matthew Parris in 'Milburn a communicator? No, he's just his master's voice', *The Times*, 11.9.04, p. 26.
53 The effect on journalists of more media space to fill was described in an article by Brian MacArthur (*The Times*, 11.9.98, p. 40) and it is an effect that favours the PR person.

> A journalist quickly learns sharp lessons about the modern media industry when he becomes poacher (journalist) turned gamekeeper (PR person). . . . One of these lessons, now that there are so many local and national radio and TV stations and newspapers have grown so big, is the insatiable appetite of modern news editors. They need to fill all those hours with talk or all those empty editorial pages with new articles.

54 The phrase is the title of *The Media and the PR Industry: A Partnership or a Marriage of Convenience?* (1991), London: Two-Ten Communications.
55 *Journalist* magazine, October 2004, p. 29. 'PRs "proud to be pants"' reported a survey showing that British PRs were the 'worst in the world', and UK journalists the 'most corruptible'. It was produced by a PR firm. More on 'love–hate' relationships in 'Don't call me a spin doctor' by Colin Bryne, CEO of Weber Shandwick, a London PR agency, in the *Independent* media weekly, 28.3.05, p. 19.
56 See p. 137 for origin.
57 *Financial Times* weekend section, 29–30.11.97, p. iv.

Bibliography

Davis, Aeron (2003) 'Public relations and news sources', in S. Cottle (ed.) *News, Public Relations and Power*, London: Sage.
Davis, Anthony (2004) *Mastering Public Relations*, Basingstoke: Palgrave Macmillan.
Ewen, P. (1996) *PR! A Social History of Spin*, New York: Basic Books.
Gandy, O. (1982) *Beyond Agenda Setting: Information Subsidies and Public Policy*, Norwood, USA: Ablex.
Goldman, E. (1948) *Two-Way Street: The Emergence of the Public Relations Counsel*, Boston: Bellman.
Grant, M. (1994) *Propaganda and the Role of the State in Inter-War Years*, Oxford: Oxford University Press.
Harris, P. and Lock, A. (1996) 'Machiavellian marketing: the development of political marketing in the UK', *Journal of Marketing Management* 12(4), pp. 313–28.
Kisch, R. (1964) *The Private Life of Public Relations*, London: Macgibbon & Kee.
L'Etang, J. (2004a) 'Public relations and democracy: historical reflections and implications for practice', in S. Oliver (ed.) *Handbook of Corporate Communications and Public Relations*, London: Routledge, pp. 342–57.
McQuail, D. (1987) *Mass Communication Theory*, London: Sage.

Michie, D. (1998) *The Invisible Persuaders*, London: Transworld Publishers.

Moloney, K. (1996) *Lobbyists for Hire*, Aldershot: Dartmouth Press.

Olasky, M. (1987) *Corporate Public Relations: A New Historical Perspective*, Hove: Lawrence Erlbaum.

Oliver, S. (ed.) (2004) *Handbook of Corporate Communication and Public Relations*, London: Routledge.

Pimlott, J. (1951) *Public Relations and American Democracy*, Princeton: Princeton University Press.

Rein, I., Kotler, P. and Stoller, M. (1997) *High Visibility: The Making and the Marketing of Professionals into Celebrities*, Illinois: NTC Business Books.

Richards, P. (1998) *Be Your Own Spin Doctor*, Harrogate: Take That.

Ries, A. and Ries, L. (2002) *The Fall of Advertising and the Rise of PR*, New York: HarperBusiness.

Tunstall, J. (1964) 'Public relations in advertising', in *The Advertising Man in London Advertising Agencies*, London: Chapman & Hall, pp. 155–92.

Webster, F. (1995) *Theories of the Information Society*, London: Routledge.

West, R. (1963) *PR: The Fifth Estate*, London: Mayflower Books.

White, J. and Mazur, L. (1995) *Strategic Communications Management*, Wokingham: Addison-Wesley Publishing, and London: Economist Intelligence Unit.

Yaverbaum, E. and Bly, R. (2001) *Public Relations for Dummies*, California: IDG Books Worldwide.

71

MARKETS, BRANDING, REPUTATION

Kevin Moloney

Source: Kevin Moloney, *Rethinking Public Relations: The Spin and the Substance*, London: Routledge, 2000, pp. 134–149.

It is hard to conceive of liberal democracy without markets. The rights to have property and to dispose of it ensure that. Markets, one of the oldest human institutions, distribute goods and services from suppliers to buyers via the two media of information and money. It is through information flows that public relations influences markets. The influence is beneficial for consumers and buyers in that PR sends high levels of one-sided, persuasive messages about goods and services onto the market. The messages come from entrepreneurs ready and able to produce PR material. These messages help buyers satisfy their needs. The first reaction of consumers, however, to this Niagara of weak propaganda should be to exercise the '*caveat emptor*' rule of 'buyer beware'.

This flood of PR marketing communications, however, gives rise to three concerns. They arise when people – in their role as consumers instead of citizens – conclude that an economy, which claims to provide value for money through a wide choice of safe products priced in unrigged markets, is exploiting them through flows of inaccurate, misleading or unsourced information. The first concern is the tension between acceptable marketplace values promoted by PR, such as wide publicity, consumer awareness and good reputation for quality producers, and, on the other hand, the deceptive use of PR as 'education' and/or as 'objective' information. Weiss (2003, pp. 168–9) notes similar defects with advertising.

The second concern centres on information flows into markets. It is whether all suppliers use PR equally in markets, and whether all potential consumers are reached by PR messages. In so far as the answer is no, PR in markets puts some consumers at a disadvantage *vis-à-vis* other consumers, and departs from the concept of competition set out in classical economics whereby product information as well as pricing information is evenly distributed throughout markets. In this way, marketing PR (MPR) creates a communicative deficit in markets. The third concern lies in the sheer volume of persuasive communications in our society today: the continuous pumping at citizens and consumers of promotional material – adverts, mail shots, telephone selling, logos, brands, sponsorships, press releases, competitions, exhibitions, road shows, stunts and T shirts with corporate messages. Plastic bags are branded and homepages vibrate with pop-ups. All marketing communications are one-sided and propagandistic, but not all communications into markets should be of the marketing kind (see p. 138, below).

A starting point for an analysis of PR effects on markets is to establish what PR people do in them. In his history of US PR, Cutlip (1995, pp. 174–81) notes that business was turning to advertising and to press agents, an early term for the modern PR person, in the 1870s in order to build up mass demand for mass-produced goods. He quotes the example of meat 'slaughtered weeks earlier and half a continent away' as in need of promotion. Bernays worked for Procter and Gamble for more than thirty years.[1] Large-scale involvement by PR, however, is a much more recent practice (Kitchen and Papasolomou 1997 and Harris 1991) and today MPR is the largest single source of work. One rule of thumb has it that 70 per cent of PR jobs are in MPR.[2]

MPR jobs are often gathered up inside the generic title of marketing communications that, besides PR, includes advertising, direct marketing and relationship marketing. All are ways of sending persuasive, one-sided messages about goods and services to consumers. PR work used to be categorised, in marketing jargon, as 'below the line' work in distinction to 'above the line' activity, such as advertising and personal selling, but that distinction is largely by the wayside now and is replaced by the idea of integrated marketing communications. One powerful reason for dropping this 'above' and 'below' distinction is that modern marketing propositions are more complex than previously and there are more of them. Put together PR and marketing disciplines and they are better able to handle multifaceted propositions. The rise of 'lifestyle' is an example. Fashion marketeers have 150 years' experience of persuading people to buy a suit with an advert alone; it is a complexity beyond a single medium's ability to persuade people to buy all the products of apparel, personal accessory, hitech gadgets, food, drink and domestic surroundings that comprise the 'lifestyle concept'. PR and marketing techniques together offer the marketeer a wide-ranging variety of expressive modes (words, photographs, visuals, sounds) and a multiplicity of message distribution channels (e.g. editorial, paid advertisements, logos, competitions) to communicate the complexity in a persuasive way.[3]

Writing is the major expression of marketing PR (MPR) for 'press release writing often forms the mainstay of the PR executive's role'.[4] Its importance is increasing as the word-based Internet makes language a reinvigorated medium of identity presentation (Morris 2000). To read home pages on a half-competently managed website today is to absorb the style of mid-market journalism electronically. Other PR product forms are exhibitions, roadshows and stunts. Over time, the PR product offered to marketing changes. In the 1970s when sponsorship was a relatively new and under-developed promotional activity, it was relegated to PR by the more powerful marketing departments; now large-scale product sponsorships are con-trolled by marketing departments, or they stand alone. PR today handles small-scale corporate sponsorships. The writing side of marketing PR is twofold: media releases (sent by post or email) about goods and services for the national, local and specialist press; and promotional copy for direct mail, brochures, leaflets, exhibitions, homepages and bulletin boards. The task is to create promotional statements (newsworthy enough to win space in the media or persuasive enough to get attention via non-media channels) that support goods or services on sale. There is also the related work of developing ideas with journalists and visual designers for take-up in feature articles, programmes, brochures, exhibitions and visuals; the organising ability to integrate these activities into campaigns; and the forensic skills to track and counter hostile web activists. Whatever the PR product or chan-nel, the purpose is constant. A phrase has appeared in PR jargon that sums it up – the PR person must 'sell in' their story to the required outlet. The imperative is for the PR message to be published.

MPR and 'soft' selling

Another phrase associated with PR generally, but especially with PR for marketing, is 'soft sell'. Journalists are flown overseas to test drive new cars. The new models are associated with celebrities. 'Advertorials' about them appear in the local papers based on technical superiority and buyer advant-age. Customers are invited to dealer showrooms on Sunday afternoon for wine and an inspection. The cars are on stands at summer shows.

Other common MPR techniques for creating newsworthy copy are through surveys that make a point in an 'independent, scientific' way favourable to the product; second, through association of 'celebrities' and colleagues[5] with products; third, through the creation of 'news events' or stunts (see p. 131); and, fourth, through the invention of front organisations, some of which are highly creative (see Kemp 1988, pp. 127–8, for the rise of the Budgerigar Information Council).[6] Indeed, MPR is the technical term for 'soft' sell.

Cause-related marketing, where a business, its goods and services are linked to a 'good' cause, is a contemporary, common form of 'soft sell'. It is in tune with the mood of business social responsibility and has benefits for a third party. The best-known British example is the scheme of the Tesco supermarket chain that supplied £92 million worth of computer equipment between 1992 and 2004 to schools.[7] The money was funded via coupons from customer purchases (Adkins 1999, p. 142). Business in the Community says cause-related marketing 'provides a win:win:win situation' where success relies on partnership, and when 'communicated in a compelling way and implemented efficiently, [it] offers a unique means of emotionally engaging the consumer'.[8] Business in the Community represents what government and part of the UK big business leadership see as 'best practice' and they have consistently promoted cause-related marketing as an expression of benign corporate citizenship. It talked of emotional engagement in 1997.[9] In 1998, it was a 'commercial activity' to 'market an image, product or service for mutual benefit. It is an additional tool for addressing social issues of the day.' It emphasises goals such as 'enhanced reputation', 'awareness, improved loyalty'.[10] Cause-related marketing lends itself to PR in two ways: it can be promoted via editorial and publishing channels with the aim of corporate and/or product differentiation, and most of its outcomes are those of PR, namely publicity, and more good reputation.[11] Business in the Community says that 'there are a variety of different tools that can be used to implement and leverage Cause Related Marketing programmes. These range from advertising, PR, direct mail and sales promotion.'[12] Adkins sets out benefits for marketing and causes, and when Tesco's Computers for Schools is the example they are substantial for both sides. She writes of mutual respect and balanced benefit (p. 118) as the ways to achieve them. The relationship, however, is at bottom an instrumental one of gain – either financial or affective – for all participants. The sub-title of Adkins book puts the distribution of benefits this way – 'Who Cares Wins'.

The phrase 'cause-related marketing' is a reminder of how integrated promotional methods have become. It is very improbable that a new version of Vance Packard's 1957 book *The Hidden Persuaders* would today focus on advertising. The integration, however, has a minor consequence in that it has put in question the boundary between PR and marketing. Five forms (domination, subordination, separation, equality and identity) have been attributed to the PR/marketing relationship,[13] and Hutton (2001, pp. 205–14) argues that PR is being marginalised within it. Such a conclusion of 'marketing imperialism' energises PR loyalists, and their representative bodies who want to police professional boundaries. Doole (2005, p. 290) ensures a bout of energetic defence from PR lobbyists who will see encroachment of their boundaries by 'mega marketing', which 'is where relationships must be sought with governments, legislators and influential individuals in order to make marketing effective on an operational level'.

Rather than defence, a better response to these boundaries disputes is to note that promotional modes are plastic in form (how different is writing for an advertisement and for a media release?), and that such malleability suits the multiple forms that PR takes.[14] What is clear over and above these conceptual and professional dog fights is that the marketing ideology unleashed by the neo-liberal reforms of the 1980s in the UK will encourage continuous experiment with new promotional forms to 'grow' markets, and that the adaptability of PR is an advantage. To take a long historical view, MPR is a successor to what was known as 'puffery', defined by Chonko (1995, p. 5) as 'sales representations that praise the product or service with subjective opinions, exaggerations, or vague and general statements with no specific facts'. The word is associated with R. B. Sheridan's Mr Puff in his play of 1779, *The Critic*.[15] To take a shorter view of history, MPR is at least 100 years old.[16] It first appeared as press agentry to attract audiences to watch the communication invention known as the 'movies' at the turn of the twentieth century. Today it has the 'digital age' to promote and it is well placed to be the narrative and stylistic platform on which that promotion will happen.

Promotional culture luxuriates in marketing and the effect on the language of marketing PR is lushness. The tone is that unnatural, unsubtle exaggeration, that ceaseless emotional brightness associated with forced enthusiasm for selling the product. Only a PR copywriter could write 'red hot loans'; 'invest with greater success'; 'glorious wood'; 'picture perfect entertainment'; or 'an entertaining advantage'. [17] PR copy is different from advertising copy because it is less compressed, more humourless, and is written in the belief that both banality and exaggeration will conceal its selling intentions. These two examples express its promotional tone. 'A French housewife wouldn't even hang out the washing without wearing a fragrance – in the UK, it's more, "I'm going out, where did I put it".'[18] A revamped Millennium Dome in London will 'provide international acts and sports teams with arena facilities of a standard currently unseen in Europe'.[19] Modern Mr Puff is alive and well and working in PR but his efforts usually fail to persuade for he seeks to narrate an impossibly perfect story (Surma 2005).

PR as marketplace information

There are two mass-mediated sources of communications into markets: MPR (as part of marketing communications), and market information from non-producer sources. The producers of goods and services are the source of marketing communications/MPR, for it is in their economic interest to disseminate data and opinion to consumers. Most communications into markets come from them. They are the originators of MPR for, in the language of marketing, MPR results in more 'informed' consumers who are thus more likely to buy. All these marketing communications by the producers of goods and services are persuasive. Self-interest ensures this.[20]

The second mass-mediated source of communications into markets is from market observers who do not produce goods or services. They are UK government departments, official regulators, consumer groups, market critics and commentators, and business data sources. These observers are either neutral or critical towards the producers of goods and services, but they are active communicators and they use public relations techniques such as press releases, brochures, briefing packs, exhibitions, conferences and lobbying. For example, the UK Treasury 'names and shames' pensions companies for mis-selling and for tardiness on paying compensation; the rail regulator rebukes rail companies for inadequate service; fair trade pressure groups tell supermarket customers about Third World labour practices; and business information services sell company news on the Internet. Information from them can be called *market communications* that are intended to monitor the selling or buying of goods and services, as opposed to *marketing communications* (including MPR) that are designed – with one exception – to aid selling. (The exception is product withdrawal communications, usually for safety reasons.)[21] Market and marketing communications combine to make up the category *mediated marketplace communications*, the sum of all communications in a market, except word of mouth.

Persuasive PR

Taken together, marketing communications and market communications add to the volume and source pluralism of communications flowing to consumers, and so provide data and opinion on which to make purchase choices. But identification of these two communications sources (market producers and market observers) raises the problem of whether all mediated market-place communications are persuasive. Is the message issued by a UK car maker's press office recalling a model because of a mechanical fault persuasive?[22]

The argument here is 'yes', for marketplace communications of both sorts are part of a larger debate about communications. There is an extensive literature on persuasion in communication science. One of its conclusions is accepted here, namely that communications are of their nature persuasive, where persuasion is defined as a communicative process designed to influence others and is a quality embedded in messages for that purpose (Jowett and O'Donnell 1992). This conclusion is fully accepted with regard to PR. Acceptance does not deny that communications are designed for other intents (e.g. commanding, admonishing) held by the PR producer and which are separate from persuasion. Acceptance also allows for debates about the relationship between persuasion and reason in message construction and the ethical balance between them. It also keeps in contention the proposition that reason is persuasion in cognitive rather than affective form. Nor does acceptance rule out the view that persuasion, reason and emotion are all involved in PR messaging.

Debate on all these matters might amend, but would not deny, the general conclusion that all PR communications are persuasive in their intent because they seek advantage for their producers. Miller (1989, p. 47) puts the general point powerfully: 'that persuasion as a chief symbolic resource for exercising environmental control remains an indispensable and irrevocable dimension of human existence'. PR messages seek compliance from their receivers. The point is an important one for the argument in this book, namely that all PR is persuasive, including the fourth part of the Grunigian paradigm, symmetrical PR.

MPR as promotional excess

The argument so far about MPR has been in terms of its commercial effects on markets, principally retail. There is also a powerful aesthetic critique to be made in that MPR has become one of the most pervasive promotional forms aimed at UK citizens in their role as consumers. The overall effect on UK society of this search for more marketing opportunities is more and more 'walls of sound' around consumers. Moore uses that metaphor as a title in *An Introduction to Public Relations* (1996). This book opens instead with the metaphor of a PR Niagara falling on citizens and consumers. Both capture a sense of people being trapped in a rising quantity of communications, more often than not of the marketplace sort. Even street furniture is part of the PR Niagara now, with roundabouts sponsored by Chinese restaurants and by garages. Pay for a parking ticket in a public car park and the reverse side is a special offer for a 'McChicken sandwich and fries'. The public service bus is covered with company logos. Tesco supermarkets will give you a miniature loyalty card, complete with electronic chip, for fixing on to your car key ring. MPR is making a contribution to an excessive marketisation of public spaces in the UK. Pratkanis and Aronson (1992, p. 11) write about a 'message-dense environment', in which the average American will see or hear more than 7 million advertisements in a lifetime. The process is becoming more targeted and refined, and adding to what Gabriel and Lang (1995, p. 2) call 'the final stage of commodification, where all relations between people are finally reduced to usage and exploitation'. Spaces free of messaging for consumption become rarer: the small sponsorship sign on the roundabout is strategically placed just in the eye-line of the oncoming driver. The clifftop walker by the sea puts her fat-free chocolate wrapper in a bin sponsored by the local secondary school. Universities give away plastic pens with their logos on. In these small incremental ways, the citizen/consumer can find fewer and fewer physical or mental spaces where there is no MPR. Such density is evidence of promotional culture sweeping its Niagara of self-interested messages through every nook and cranny of cultural and material life. Indeed this avalanche of messaging suggests that there is a promotional phase being developed beyond commodification. It is one of 'personalisation' and it is exemplified in memorial plaques 'to commemorate your loved ones' that can be purchased for deckchairs on at least one seaside resort.[23]

Corporate branding

One promotional form that PR has taken from marketing with enthusiasm is branding. This is a difficult term to define and there are many verbal clusters proclaiming explanation but not offering clear meaning.[24] It is a term to which is ascribed very complicated social roles; Simmons (2004, p. 16) says, for example, that 'brands are a shorthand we use to make connection with others and to help define our own identities'. He writes about the product and corporate brand of Starbucks coffee. The brand, he claims (p. 175),

> starts with a commodity product – coffee beans – and invests them with extraordinary added value by creating an experience that transcends the simple act of drinking an unnecessary product. And this experience becomes an integral part of the daily lives of millions of people.

The definition of Armstrong and Kotler (2005, p. 234), however, has the virtue of clarity about an important term for PR people: 'A brand is a name, term, sign, symbol, or design or a combination of these, that identifies the maker or seller of a product or service.' They comment that 'building and managing brands is perhaps the marketer's most important task'.[25] Such an ascription would not be true of the PR person in relation to the branding of products where the marketing team would be in charge and would be 'buying in' PR services. Instead, branding comes into its own for PR when the 'building and managing' is for the corporate body, for the organisation or group being communicated about. This activity used to be known as 'corporate identity' work by PR people in the 1990s, and before that in the 1970s, when management was an activity without its own vocabulary, it was known as 'It's what we stand for'.[26] Such, however, is the influence of marketing as the ruling paradigm, even for thinking about non-commercial areas, that it is now referred to as 'corporate branding'. Balmer (2003, p. 300) says that 'a corporate brand may be a company's principal asset'. Schultz (2002) links brands with reputation via storytelling about *The Expressive Organisation* and thus sees organisations as symbolic entities. Constructing such entities amounts to the anthropomorphic exercise of giving to an organisation or group (e.g. to an engineering company, retail chain, school, university, trade union, protest group) human characteristics.[27] In this way, these collectivities become humanoid and the PR message is that they are typically some combination of the following vocabulary: 'modern'; 'caring'; 'quality'; 'friendly'; 'fun'; 'young'; 'sexy'; 'exclusive'; 'traditional'; 'cutting edge'; 'hi-tech'; 'best'; 'responsible'; 'excellent'; 'responsive'; 'fast-moving'; 'safe'; 'wealthcreating'; 'trustworthy'; and 'principled'. Indeed, Olins thinks the process included the sexual. He argues (2003, p. 7) that Virgin is a company which take branding so seriously that it is a 'classic seducer' wanting to 'win share of mind, then share of market'. The anthropomorphic connotation continues when branding is done a second time: 'Rebrands are designed to reinvigorate a marque.'[28] Saul (1993) also notes the PR propaganda advantage of choosing the fitting word. During twentieth-century ideological battles between democracies and totalitarian states, he says (p. 46) that 'The very act of getting the word "free" into the public domain on your side places the other side in a difficult position.' Jackall (1995, pp. 351–99) is one of the few academics who write about PR as work experience. He describes it as the persuasive manipulation of symbols (along with advertising and journalism) with a view to constructing the accounts of social reality wished for by its principals. 'Whether in a corporation or an agency, a public relations practitioner, in addition to meeting the normal bureaucratic fealty requirements of his station, must above all satisfy his clients' desires to construct the world in certain ways' (p. 362). From this follows a process of selective narration, and it is one that presents the PR with the ethics of relative truthfulness: 'In the world of public relations, there is no such thing as a notion of truth: there are only stories, perspectives and opinions. . . . Creating the impression of truth displaces the search for truth' (p. 365). Corporate branding is therefore the constructed presentation, by its dominant coalition, of the group or organisation to its stakeholders for immediate, favourable recognition. Its use is spreading to cities ('Bradford: a surprising place'; see Truman *et al.* 2004), towns, regions and whole countries. It is done through the media of words, phrases, visual design (logos, letterheads, signage), photographs, art, sound, architecture, uniforms and behaviour. Note the last medium for it is not on the list of instruments for product branding; but when the task is presentation of the organisation making the good or service offered, the role of people has to be accommodated. Corporate branding is a clear example of PR as 'self-presentation-for-attention-and-advantage'. It is 'the best foot forward' by the group or the organisation. It is usually associated with businesses but there is growing uptake by other entities. Think of New Labour as an exercise in corporate branding and you understand much about recent UK politics. Think of Friends of the Earth and the UNISON trade union, and you have insight into contemporary British civil society. Their brand is their compressed, self-regarding and comforting narrative about themselves. Its subject is themselves and it tells of betterment for significant others – the stakeholders – through association with them. It is a psychological conceit for the subject as well, in that it is consumed as 'corporate comfort food'[29] by the dominant coalition who put the story in place. If McAlpine (1997, p. xiii) is right about business as the 'most exciting and rewarding of all pursuits open to mankind', commemorative narratives will follow as surely as adventure stories follow war. But these tales are much less listened to by middle management and hardly at all by the shopfloor.

Corporate branding is a social construct to assuage, attract, make compliant shareholders, stakeholders, consumers, clients, employees, government and business regulators. Its 'character' is conceived by the corporate parents, the dominant coalition of the organisation or group, and the design work is passed to PR people. It is work that plays to their skills, for good PR writing is the narration of a story designed to attract attention. It is also related to concepts such as corporate personality, image, reputation and issues management, and when it comes into contact with the first two there is often confusion. At first glance, 'corporate personality' would appear to be the same as 'corporate brand' but it is used in some preceding sense of representing the corporate ideal, the perfect expression of what the organisation or group should be. The sense is that the observable expression of the 'corporate personality' is the 'corporate brand'. More confusion comes when these terms are used alongside 'image'. This latter term has two meanings. In vernacular English, it is used both to describe the corporate brand and perception of this brand by others. The confusion is avoided by not using 'image' in PR technical discussions, and by remembering that the construct 'corporate brand' is the subject that is perceived by others, namely stakeholders and general public. A corporate brand is the biography written about a corporate personality and read by others. It is a PR essay in popular corporate psychology. Corporate perception is what others think of the biography.

Is branding a corporate fashion item? A design accessory not to go without? The questions are answered by trying to think of organisations or groups that do not have a 'corporate brand' or 'identity'. It is a hallmark of military regiments (e.g. Napoleon's Imperial Guard); it has been traditionally cultivated by the better class of university (e.g. Harvard). One hesitates to say that it is part of the phenomenon of religion but think of Salvation Army singing, Buddhist orange, and Roman Catholic purple.[30] Indeed, there is more surety in turning the point around and noting that, historically, dominant institutions have published expressive culture about themselves and their interests[31] (e.g. the monarch's head on coinage; the cardinals' portraits, the queenly speech to soldiers before battle). In modern capitalist, market-orientated, liberal democracy, this expressive urge has become near universal – has been democratised. Businesses, trade unions, charities, cause and interest groups are all branded today. It is hard to imagine any corporate entity that is modest or altruistic enough to eschew the expense of branding. Without a brand, it fears that it would not be distinct enough to attract attention.

Human personality invariably generates both positive and negative reactions, and it is argued here that when businesses and groups anthropomorphise themselves, customers, clients and stakeholders will react in the same mixed way as they do in their personal relations with individuals. It is claimed that the 'caring' company attracts 'loyalty' from its customers:

it can be argued that the feeling switches to 'anger' when the product fails. It is a new area of corporate development for the company to personalise itself and it risks the danger of inflating expectations. By giving itself an affective coating, the company is aligning itself with the changing emotional patterns of those in contact with it. Does this introduce another risk factor into business performance? Is it better to be supplied with goods and services by a company with a stable share price rather than by one with a 'refreshing new concept'?[32] The boundary between market economics and consumer psychology therefore needs careful patrolling by the PR person. Economics and branding are also in conflict when the relationship is focused on pricing goods and services in markets. Klein (2000) argues that marketing by human characteristic (branding) is a change from marketing by price, and is therefore the replacement of use value and exchange value pricing by experiential pricing. Such pricing is leveraged by non-economic factors, namely the emotions appropriated (e.g. 'caring', 'sexy'), store and product design, sponsorships, and community relations. Hannington (2004, p. 9) notes this point about emotional leverage on consumers when he quotes a 'Brand Advisor' to the effect that a brand is 'an entity that is loved so much that people are prepared to pay more for it than the material benefit obtained'. This emotionalisation of price weakens competition by price determined by use or exchange, and therefore the operation of efficient markets as classically defined, and is a strategy favouring oligopoly and monopoly. For consumers, it means paying more. Klein also notes that marketing by human characteristic is a threat to advertising as a prime promotional mode, and that it favours the narrative telling capacity of PR.

Brands, moreover, attract public attention in ways that are not always welcome to their constructors. Sometimes they are connected to popular culture in ironic, creative ways and are transformed into counter-cultural icons. Nike, McDonalds, Esso and Ratners are examples of brands given non-intended meanings. The US cultural jammers Adbusters who call themselves 'a maverick band of social marketers on a shoestring budget' are skilled at this. They invert the meaning of advertisements, mimic their copy and visuals, and publicly launch their creations. Thus they develop the 'black spot sneaker', which is an anti-Nike reference, and they say about the corporation that it has developed a 'bogus corporate cool'.[33] Adbusters also organise a named day with the most unwanted message business could wish on its customers – 'Buy Nothing Day'. They urge shoppers to take 'time to think consumer revolt'. The aim is to develop a popular culture of resistance to globalised companies (Klein 2000).[34] Snow (2003, pp. 151–2) lists cultural jamming, along with 'guerrilla marketing', joining protest groups, challenging the agenda of mainstream media, and reading outside 'your comfort zone', as antidotes to propaganda. The Adbusters also use the concepts of 'memes' in their campaigning. 'Memes' are the communicative version of genes and are described by Dawkins (1989, p. 192) as cultural replicators such as tunes, ideas, catch phrases, fashion that 'propagate themselves . . . by leaping from brain to brain via a process . . . which can be called imitation'. The Adbusters say that they are promoting a 'new lifestyle game . . . by spreading uncooling memes'.[35] This reference leads to the idea that PR can be seen as a distribution system for 'memes' that are propelled through social systems by PR's self-advantaging message system, and which are retained or rejected by the self-interest of the message receivers.[36] The more that they are retained, they have the quality of memorability that Gladwell (2000) called 'stickiness' in his thesis that the spread of some fashions, books, social trends in a society is analogous to the spread of viruses in an epidemic. This line of thinking opens up the possibility that PR is an active element, as a mode of persuasive communication, in cultural evolutionary psychology.

Other critiques of corporate brands are that the process may start with intentions to change not only the narrative and imagery of the organisation but also the behaviour of its employees or members. The latter is the most difficult to alter, and is the least likely area to succeed. Brands may seek to be multi-media expressions of the ideal corporate personality but they often reduce in practice to little more than a new logo and letterhead. Also the current PR paradigm of two-way symmetrical communications does not easily accommodate corporate branding in that the construction process is invariably asymmetrical and assumes acceptance by others. Sometimes this acceptance is not forthcoming and there follows public retractions. The £60 million redesign of the tailfins of British Airways airplanes with 'funky' ethnic art was publicly and famously scoffed at in 1997 by the then-former Prime Minister Mrs Thatcher.[37] The £2 million representation of Britain's Royal Mail as the Consignia brand was the source of much mocking humour and was followed by its withdrawal in 2002 after sixteen months.[38]

Corporate reputation

Corporate reputation has had a rising career over the last decade in British public relations as the master outcome sought by PR people. Coyle (2001) in her panegyric for neo-liberal capitalism has suggested a systemic reason: the new, less regulated 'weightless economy' of service industries needs good reputation as a marketing signal. Since September 1993, the then-Institute of Public Relations (IPR) has emphasised reputation in its definition as much as the traditional values of 'goodwill' and 'mutual understanding'. They were embraced at the foundation of the then-IPR in 1948. Now 'reputation management' has become a much more commonly voiced professional role than the achievement of those older and softer civic virtues. For the contemporary CIPR, 'A good reputation is key to organisational success. In today's competitive market, it can make the difference between success and failure.'[39] A few professionals own up to wanting to be 'perception managers' but while that has accuracy, it also has too much of the Orwellian about it for it to be a popular job description.

Corporate reputation is located in the 'other' (stakeholders, publics) and is the perception of an organisation or group by these other parties after their experiences of it. It is perception with judgement. The judgement may be a comparative, historical or an absolute one (e.g. about standards of customer service from banks, over time, against an ideal). It is a concept that has sources in many areas: stakeholding ideas of reciprocal treatment between self and other; in issues management (see p. 36); reaction to the human attributes embedded in the corporate brand (e.g. reactions by others to claims about modernity or technical efficiency); and in the historical record of an organisation (e.g. attitudes to apartheid in South Africa, and Nestlé and breast feeding). If you feel good about the characteristics claimed, and its behaviour towards issues important to you, you will empathise and judge reputation to be positive.

Corporate reputation is, therefore, like moral virtue and human affection (e.g. honesty and love) in that it is the consequence of other activities. It is, for example, the 'reward' for being a 'value for money' retailer with admired social responsibility programmes. It comes after these behaviours have been experienced by 'significant others'. It is bestowed and it cannot be called up on demand. Indeed, it is unlikely that it can be managed in any technical sense of input/output activity.[40] It is closely allied to trust, which is the strong expectation of others that they will be treated as benignly in the future as they have been in the past. Reputation is, so to speak, the connected-up trust of individuals across a public or a stakeholder group. It constitutes a non-specific, general opinion focused on one entity. It is a subjective phenomenon; it is what stakeholders (and publics) say it is and it changes over time. There are many examples of businesses (e.g. Barings Bank, Ratners) that have suffered disastrous reversals of reputation. The same experience afflicted British trade unions in the 1960s and 1970s. Reputation is also a plural phenomenon: a business may have high repute with City financiers but be held in contempt by employees and trade unions. An environmental group may be despised by farmers but admired by animal welfare people. In PR, the concept of corporate reputation has been very strongly associated with companies, as has corporate social responsibility. These associations are now broadening out to include other corporate entities such as cause and interest groups, and, with it, more scrutiny of their performance. The monitoring of these groups has its origins in the admission by Greenpeace that it published inaccurate information during the Brent Spar incident of 1996.

Corporate reputation, moreover, can be seen as the amount of prestige attached to an organisation or group by its stakeholders and by the general public. It is a positive, 'credit' in the 'bank' of opinion.[41] It is also a negative, a 'debit' in the 'bank'. In more affective terms, we can talk about amounts

of low opinion or dislike in which an entity is held. It is indirectly measured through other indicators such as share price, balance sheet strength,
surveys, membership, successful campaigns, positive media coverage, gossip,
and opinion of influential persons and bodies (e.g. 'the great and the good',
think tanks). The principal PR role in regard to reputation is media
communications about behaviours and events which imply that reputation
is positive and strong; and the publication of surveys and testimonials
that proclaim the same. Ideally this witness is better coming from third
parties: like all boasting, the corporate variety grates. Other PR work is the
projection of corporate brand values, the selection of sponsorships and
community relations that bolster them. These are written up in corporate
brochures, explanatory sections of annual financial reports and accounts,
and in triple-bottom-line audits of monetary, social and environmental
performance. All these narratives are designed for the reader to think better
of their source, to hold it in higher repute. Hannington (2004) sets out how
to make these narratives into an operational plan, driven by the warning
that reputation is 'the most important asset' of business (p. 3), a cliché to
which is frequently added another – reputation is made over decades, and
destroyed in minutes.

Beyond the clichés, the difficult questions about corporate reputation
come when other organisational goals are laid alongside it. Is it the same as
success and how does it rank against survival? Integrating, separating and
ranking goals is a core task of dominant coalitions in organisations
and groups. Official definitions of PR pragmatically avoid the philosophical and political difficulties of a communications mode in its relationship
with the purposes for which it is used. But PR people cannot help but note
that they are asked to communicate about cross-purposes. Organisations
and groups have to – may choose to – behave in ways that achieve other
goals at the price of loss in reputation. Survival is the essential purpose of
entities in the political economy and in civil society: survival may be at the
price of reputation. In politics, it could be said that putting survival first is
normal behaviour. Indeed, it could be offered as a definition of government.
In the marketplace, the choice is a familiar one. Consciously or otherwise,
suppliers of goods and services do trade off their reputations against other
goals.[42] There is no organisational imperative for the reputational goal to be
always protected as conventional PR theorists imply. In 2004, organisational imperative worked against corporate reputation in the case of Shell, a
global business that since the Brent Spar incident in 1996 had worked hard
to improve relations with stakeholders towards open dialogue and human
rights. Yet, Briggs (2004)[43] reveals that 'Shell managers' primary challenges
were not concerned with Shell's reputation but with the more prosaic
need to achieve short-term business targets' and it did so by over-estimating
its oil reserves. For this, it was fined by the UK's finance regulator, the
Financial Services Authority.

Looked at this way, PR people are naïve or disingenuous to make reputation their single, desired outcome for their employers and clients. In so doing, they are loading the gun and pointing it at their own professional feet. The then-IPR took this risk in 1993 when it added the second definition of PR based on reputation. It is not wise for modern PR people to speak in mantra tones about 'reputation, reputation, reputation', and to make themselves the guardians of this important, social asset. They forget that reputation is a consequence of other goals. Their concentration places them at odds with these other goals of their principals and clients, and so puts their organisational role at odds with their declarations of professional purpose. Goals such as profitability, growth, downsizing, diversification, merger, campaigning for policy change often take precedence. Reputation therefore should be seen in a relative relationship with other corporate or group goals.[44] Resolving competition amongst goals is the work of dominant coalitions, and PR 'voices' their decisions.

Finally, it is important to discount any claims of functional imperialism made or implied by public relations and to correct a professional deformation that comes from it. Often in the speech of PR people there is an assumption that it is they, through their communications, who are the producers of reputation. Accountants, engineers, marketeers and reception staff produce reputation as much as PR people, and its production and projection is a state of mind and skills set that is widely accessible. This leads to the startling proposition that all organisational and group members are in public relations and that professional PR is but one way of achieving the goals set for it. PR is the producer of the communications wanted by its principals, and not the producer of the organisational goals of those principals. Public relations is one agency to achieve organisational goals, one of many. It is out of the work of these combined agencies that reputation comes.

Summary

PR has benefits and costs for its producers and its consumers in markets, politics and the media. This chapter reviews relationships connected with marketing and markets. The first is marketing PR (MPR), which spreads out promotional information to consumers, and so brings buyers and sellers together. But consumers should use MPR with caution under the *caveat emptor* rule of buyer beware. There is more MPR by volume than any other type; it is an adaptable PR form, and is an effective promoter of 'lifestyle'. It has higher credibility than advertising with consumers, especially when journalists uncritically publish its messages in their work. It is often called the 'soft sell' and it contributes to promoting the modern form of emotionally engaging customers, known as cause-related marketing. MPR and market PR by government, regulators and pressure groups together constitute the flow of mass-mediated marketplace communications outside of advertising.

MPR creates communicative deficits if not all producers and consumers send and receive it. Its growth is leading to an aesthetic assault on public spaces that are now sites for promotional excess.

The idea of a corporate brand is a marketing form much taken up by PR people. Transferred from products, it is an anthropomorphic exercise to give human characteristics to organisations and groups. It is the construction of a favourable narrative about them. It is corporate biography produced by PR people and, like human biographies, produces negative reactions as well as positive ones. The negative feelings are exploited creatively by cultural jammers such as Adbusters and are turned into popular culture, often against big businesses. Branding is experiential pricing and weakens competition through creating emotional attraction to manufacturers and their products. It is imperfect competition by experience and emotion, and tends towards oligopoly and monopoly.

Corporate reputation is in part created by reaction to corporate branding, and has risen up the British PR agenda as a major professional output. It is perception tempered by judgement and defined most easily as amounts of 'credit' and 'debit' held in the 'bank' of opinion. It is bestowed by stakeholders and the public after experience of the organisation or group. Good reputation is the indirect consequence of other behaviours such as responsive customer care, sensitive issues management, large membership and effective campaigning. It is difficult to manage because it is a consequence of other behaviours. It presents therefore a professional problem for PR people because their principals set goals that run counter to good reputation, for example redundancies or foxhunting. Giving these examples is a reminder that reputation is plural and dynamic: different stakeholders award different reputations over time.

The next chapter looks at PR's relationship with journalism and why these two professions should behave in a more wary relationship.

Notes

1 Also for American Tobacco; New Jersey Telephone; Dodge Brothers Automobile; and Filene's department store. Source is Internet Museum of Public Relations at www.prmuseum.com/bernays/bernays_1931.html. Accessed 4.1.05.
2 Based on Bournemouth University's twelve years of placing PR students in year-long work placements. The other 30 per cent are in corporate PR/public affairs work.
3 A good example of the complexity of modern lifestyle PR messaging and advertising is the 'How to Spend It' supplement of the *Financial Times*.
4 Source is the CIPR brochure *IPR Training Spring and Summer 2005*, p. 3.
5 A record company is reported to use schoolchildren to sell music to their friends in a 'peer group selling initiative'. See 'Lessons in hard sell', the *Guardian* media section, 20.12.04, pp. 2–3.
6 This organisation was born out of one of the most inspired public relations briefs, or, more precisely, one of the most inspired marketing briefs. . . . It was

the Petfoods division of Mars that initiated the Council at a time when the birdseed market had come to an apparent standstill.

> The market was saturated and the solution was 'to expand the budgerigar market'. 'There were endless budgerigar clubs and shows, pamphlets, articles, press conferences, books – a real orchestration of activity designed to start a budgerigar craze. It worked.'

7 See Brassington and Pettitt (2003), p. 827. Figures available at www.tesco.com/everylittlehelps/socialdetail.htm. Accessed 24.2.05.

8 Accessed at www.bitc.org.ik/resources/research/research_publication/game_ plan.htm on 16.12.04.

9 Quoted from *The Game Plan: Cause Related Marketing Qualitative Consumer Research* (1997), published by Business in the Community, London.

10 Quoted from the *Cause Related Marketing Guidelines* (1998), published by Business in the Community, London.

11 Cause-related marketing has a constant, direct outcome that PR has not: it raises funds for causes. PR has an indirect relationship with revenue creation.

12 Quoted from the *The Game Plan* (1997), referenced at Note 9 above.

13 See Heywood (1990, pp. 156–7); Harris (1991, p. 35), Fill (1999, pp. 6, 414) and Kitchen and Papasolomou (1997, pp. 239–71).

14 See p. 1 of this book for multiple forms.

15 See *Brewer's Dictionary* (1999, 16th edn, p. 952).

16 See Moloney (1999) for the view that PR in the service of selling to consumers is as old as PR itself, a conclusion corroborated by a look at the cinema in the early twentieth century.

17 A selection compiled by the author from UK newspapers in autumn 2004.

18 Source is 'Perfume got personal', the *Financial Times* weekend section, 27–8.11.04, p. 1.

19 Source is 'That was then, this is now', the *Observer* review section, 5.12.04, p. 41.

20 Kotler in Harris (1991, introduction) writes about the need to 'win' the consumers' hearts, minds and money. Bell (1991, p. 24) says 'if you are a PR consultant you're in the persuasion business'. Thorson and Moore (1996, p. 1) write of 'integrated marketing communication' that 'its aim is to optimise the impact of persuasive communication on both consumer and non-consumer'.

21 An example is an advertisement in the *Guardian*, 2.4.05, p.13, 'Product recall'. It said that a 'foreign object' had contaminated one carton of orange juice and, as a precaution, a whole batch up to a date code was recalled. The next day, the *Observer*, 3.4.05, p. 4, carried a story headlined 'Police probe factory as a syringe is found in Sainbury's fruit juice'.

22 These press releases are carefully crafted to meet minimum requirements set by the Department of Trade and Industry, and to protect the reputation of the brand. Source is guest lecturers at Bournemouth University.

23 Noted in the newspaper of Bournemouth Borough Council, *Bournemouth Journal*, August/September 2004, p. 2. The price is £10.

24 Jeff Bozos of Amazon offers some clarity about what is a brand: 'It's what people say about you when you are not in the room.' Source is 'And the brand played on', the *Observer* business section, 20.6.04, p. 5.

25 Some business people have a different ranking. For example, Tony Froggatt, CEO of Scottish and Newcastle breweries, said that

> Even though, I come from a marketing background, I view brands as vehicles for driving growth and value. . . . We can talk about the

beauties of brands and all that sort of stuff, but at the end of the day investors just want to know what they are going to get in terms of returns.

Reported in 'The beer necessities', the *Guardian*, 26.1.05, p. 30.

26 Organisational culture, out of which corporate identity grows, was known as 'It's what we are'.

27 After product and corporate branding comes the branding of people. They are called 'celebrities'.

28 See 'Surviving change', *PRWeek*, 11.2.05, p. 29.

29 The author's metaphor.

30 Clergy today debate the difference between marketing and evangelising, the Chaplaincy at Bournemouth University tell the author. The separation of metaphysical and lifestyle aspects of religion are discussed.

31 In the Channel 4 television programme *Who Wrote the Bible?* on the origins of the Christian gospels (25.12.04, 8.30 p.m.), it was noticeable how the pre-senter, theologian Robert Beckford, and expert witnesses referred to 'spin' and 'propaganda' as they explored different views on the sources and meanings of the documents.

32 See *Financial Times* property section, 11.12.04, p. 16, and the advertisement headline 'Introducing a refreshing new concept in the pied-a-terre. You don't actually pay when you're not "a terre"'.

33 Accessed at http://adbusters.org/metas/corpo/backspotsneaker/kickass.html on 8.12.04.

34 It has been well noted that the publisher of Klein's book, Flamingo Harper Collins, is a global company.

35 See 'Communique 12: Reclaiming Public Space', 8.3.05, from jammers <\\> @>lists.adbusters.org.

36 Blackmore (1999) writes that ideas which spread widely through populations do so because they are copyable, capable of imitation. Are PR people the spotters and then the transmitters of such ideas? The reference to memes by the Adbusters on 8.3.05 is the first time that this author has seen the 'memes' term used in a PR operational way. Its use, and the provenance of the term in the biology of genes, raises questions about the sources of the PR paradigm described in this book in Social Darwinism.

37 She famously covered up one of the funky designs with a handkerchief from her handbag. See http://news.bbc.co.uk/1/hi/uk/1335127.stm. Accessed 21.12.04.

38 See pp. 831–2 of Brassington and Pettitt (2003) for a case study.

39 See the CIPR brochure *Managing Reputation*, p. 2, for its conference on 11.4.05 at Copthorne Tara Hotel, London.

40 Patrick Kerr, head of communications at Unilever UK, said at the MORI repu-tation conference, London, on 28.10.04 that 'you cannot manage reputation; rather it is like beauty in the eye of the beholder'. Reported on www.bitc.org.uk/ news/news_directory/mori_rep.html and accessed on 16.12.04.

41 Like most terms in PR, there are many definitions for each entity. Reputation is 'the totality of emotional and intellectual disposition towards an organisa-tion' in the opinion of Stewart Lewis, head of corporate communications research at MORI at their reputation conference, London, 28.10.04. Accessed at www.bitc.org.uk/news/news_directory/mori_rep.html on 16.12.04.

42 For example, Southwest Trains in the UK lowered its reputation with travellers in 1998 when it cancelled services because of the cost reduction policy of sacking drivers. Alstom, the train maintenance company, also reduced its reputation in

the town of Eastleigh, UK, when it announced the loss of 540 jobs with the closure of its depot there in the week before Christmas, 2004. Source is 'Alstom cut 540 jobs at Southampton as orders stall', the *Guardian*, 18.12.04, p. 24.
43 See 'Can Shell survive reserves affair?' *PRWeek*, 3.9.04, p. 15. Paddy Briggs retired from Shell in 2002, after thirty-seven years.
44 Lex the columnist is right. Writing about a struggling engineering company quoted on the London Stock Exchange, 'It is worth risking your reputation as long as the rewards are healthy.' Source is 'Jarvis', the *Financial Times*, 11.10.03, p. 18.

Bibliography

Adkins, S. (1999) *Cause Related Marketing: Who Cares Wins*, London: Butterworth Heinemann.

Armstrong, G. and Kotler, P. (2005) *Marketing: An Introduction*, 7th edn, New Jersey: Pearson Education International.

Balmer, J. (2003) 'Corporate brand management', in J. Balmer and S. Greyser (eds) *Revealing the Corporation: Perspectives on Identity, Image, Reputation, Corporate Branding and Corporate-Level Marketing*, London: Routledge, pp. 299–316.

Bell, Q. (1991) *The PR Business*, London: Kogan Page.

Blackmore, S. (1999) *Meme Machine*, Oxford: Oxford University Press.

Brassington, F. and Pettitt, S. (2003) *Principles of Marketing*, 3rd edn, London: FT Prentice Hall.

Chonko, L. (1995) *Ethical Decision Making in Marketing*, London: Sage.

Coyle, D. (2001) *Paradoxes of Prosperity*, London: Texere.

Cutlip, S. (1995) *Public Relations History: From the 17th to the 20th Century. The Antecedents*, New Jersey: Lawrence Erlbaum.

Dawkins, R. (1989, new edn) *The Selfish Gene*, Oxford: Oxford University Press.

Doole, I. (2005) *Understanding and Managing Customers*, London: Prentice Hall.

Fill, C. (1999) *Marketing Communications*, 2nd edn, Hemel Hempstead: Prentice Hall.

Gabriel, Y. and Lang, T. (1995) *The Unmanageable Consumer*, London: Sage.

Gladwell, M. (2000) *The Tipping Point: How Little Things Can Make a Big Difference*, London: Little Brown.

Hannington, T. (2004) *How to Measure and Manage Your Corporate Reputation*, Aldershot: Gower.

Harris, T. (1991) *The Marketer's Guide to Public Relations*, New York: John Wiley.

Heywood, R. (1990) *All about Public Relations*, 2nd edn, London: McGraw-Hill.

Hutton, J. (2001) 'Defining the relationship between public relations and marketing: public relations' most important challenge', in R. Heath (ed.) *Handbook of Public Relations*, London: Sage, pp. 205–14.

Jackall, R. (ed.) (1995) *Propaganda*, Basingstoke: Macmillan.

Jowett, G. and O'Donnell, V. (1992) *Propaganda and Persuasion*, London: Sage.

Kemp, G. (1988) 'Public relations in marketing', in W. Howard (ed.) *The Practice of Public Relations*, 3rd edn, London: Heinemann, pp. 125–36.

Kitchen, P. and Papasolomou, I. (1997) 'The emergence of marketing PR', in P. Kitchen (ed.) *Public Relations: Principles and Practice*, London: International Thomson Business Press, pp. 239–71.

Klein, N. (2000) *No Logo*, London: Flamingo Harper Collins.

McAlpine, A. (1997) *The New Machiavelli*, London: Aurum Press.

Miller, G. (1989) 'Persuasion and public relations: two "Ps" in a pod', in G. Botan and V. Hazleton (eds) *Public Relations Theory*, Hillsdale: Lawrence Erlbaum Associates, pp. 45–66.

Moloney, K. (1999) 'Publicists – distribution workers in the pleasure economy of the film industry', in J. Bignell (ed.) *Writing and Cinema*, Harlow: Longman.

Moore, S. (1996) *An Introduction to Public Relations*, London: Cassell.

Morris, S. (2000) *Wired PR*, London: FT.com.

Olins, W. (2003) *On Brand*, London: Thames & Hudson.

Packard, V. (1981) *The Hidden Persuaders*, 2nd edn, London: Penguin [1st edn 1957].

Pratkanis, A. and Aronson, E. (1992) *Age of Propaganda*, New York: Freeman.

Saul, J. (1993) *Voltaire's Bastards: The Dictatorship of Reason in the West*, New York: Vintage Books.

Schultz, M. (2002) *The Expressive Organisation*, Oxford: Oxford University Press.

Simmons, T. (2004) *My Sister's A Barista: How They Made Starbucks a Home from Home*, London: Cyan.

Snow, N. (2003) *Information War: American Propaganda, Free Speech And Opinion Control since 9–11*, New York: Severn Stories Press.

Surma, A. (2005) 'Public relations and corporate social responsibility: developing a moral narrative', *Asia Pacific Public Relations Journal* 5(2), pp. 1–12.

Thorson, E. and Moore, J. (1996) *Integrated Communication: Synergy of Persuasive Voices*, New Jersey: Lawrence Erlbaum.

Truman, M., Klemm, M. and Giroud, A. (2004) 'Can a city communicate? Bradford as a corporate brand', *Corporate Communications: An International Journal* 9(4), pp. 317–30.

Weiss, J. (2003) *Business Ethics: A Stakeholder and Issues Management Approach*. 3rd edn, Mason, OH: Thomson South-Western.

THE ART OF THE HUSTLE AND THE SCIENCE OF PROPAGANDA

J. Stauber and S. Rampton

Source: J. Stauber and S. Rampton, *Toxic Sludge is Good for You: Lies, Damn Lies, and the Public Relations Industry*, Monroe ME: Common Courage Press, 1995, pp. 17–25.

A state is bound to be more dangerous if it is not governed openly by the people, but secretly by political forces that are not widely known or understood.

Andrei Sakharov

In 1836 legendary showman P. T. Barnum began his career by buying an old Negro slave woman named Joice Heth and exhibiting her to the public as "George Washington's childhood nursemaid."

Joice Heth claimed to be 160 years old. Was she for real? The man who coined the phrase, "there's a sucker born every minute," kept the public guessing through a clever series of forged letters to the editors of New York newspapers. Written by Barnum himself and signed by various fake names, some of the letters denounced Barnum as a fraud. In other letters, also written by Barnum, he praised himself as a great man who was performing a service by giving the public a chance to see George Washington's "mammy." The letters succeeded in stirring up controversy. Joice Heth was discussed in news reports and editorial columns, and the public turned out in droves to see for themselves. Barnum collected as much as $1500 per week from New Yorkers who came to see the pipe-smoking old Negro woman.

When Joice Heth died, doctors performed an autopsy and estimated her true age at around eighty. Barnum handled the situation like the PR pro that he was. He said he was shocked, *deeply* shocked, at the way this woman had deceived him.[1]

Barnum knew that in his publicity for "the greatest show on earth," it didn't matter whether people called him a scoundrel or a saint. The important thing was that the newspapers spelled his name right, and that they mentioned him often. He was one of the first people to manipulate the news for fun and profit.

The 1830s marked the beginnings of what we now call the "mass media" with the rise of "penny presses" such as the *New York Sun* which used low newsstand prices to draw in a large readership. Because of their larger circulation, they were able to charge enough for ads that advertisers, rather than readers, became their main source of income. This change also gave advertisers more power to influence the news and editorial sections. Newspapers offered "free puff stories" to paying advertisers—a practice which is widely denied but still common today, especially in the business, food and automobile sections of newspapers.[2]

This transformation deepened as the years progressed. According to James Melvin Lee's *History of American Journalism,* it was possible by the end of the 19th century "to insert at a higher cost almost any advertisement disguised as a bit of news. Sometimes these paid reading notices of advertisers were distinguished by star or dagger, but more frequently there was no sign to indicate to the readers that the account had been bought and paid for and was not a regular news item."[3]

By disguising paid notices as "news," companies tried to bypass readers' innate skepticism toward advertising. Then, as now, readers understood that advertisements were "propaganda," and they were more likely to believe a story if it seemed to come from an independent reporter.

The first flacks

Before the public relations industry existed, companies employed "press agents" to feed advertisements and publicity to newspapers. Many early press agents worked for circuses, Broadway shows and other entertainment enterprises. Often they were recruited from the ranks of underpaid reporters anxious for a way to earn more money. They used flattery, pleading and, of course, payments of money to grease the wheels for their clients' publicity. They were colorful, scheming, desperate men, drifters and con artists with bad reputations, constantly scrounging for clients and begging for favors.[4] In 1911, writer Will Irwin described them as "the only group of men proud of being called liars."[5]

Like P. T. Barnum, the early press agents were more interested in generating publicity for their clients than in building "images" or "reputations." The railroads, utility companies and big businesses like Standard Oil were just starting to learn that their profit margins could be affected by the public's opinion of them. When a reporter suggested that the New York Central Railroad should adjust its train schedules to accommodate the public, New York Central President William Vanderbilt angrily replied, "The public be damned!" His remark provoked public outrage, and attacks by the New York legislature forced him to sell off part of his railroad holdings.[6]

At the turn of the century, social movements rose up to challenge the power of big business: the Grange movement, the Socialist Party, the Greenbackers, the Populists and Progressives. The labor movement was growing, and radical agitators were urging exploited farmers to "raise less corn and more hell." President Teddy Roosevelt coined the word "muckrakers" to describe the growing number of journalists who were dedicating themselves to exposing the corruption of business and government.[7] William Randolph Hearst's newspapers attacked privilege, monopoly, corporate power, and the "plunderbund" of banks and trusts. The public-be-damned attitude of "robber barons" like Vanderbilt turned public opinion against the railroads, prompting Congress and state legislatures to enact over 2,000 laws affecting the industry between 1908 and 1913.[8]

Ivy Lee was one of the first consultants to offer the service of corporate image-building. According to PR industry historian Scott Cutlip, Lee worked for J. P. Morgan's International Harvester Company to stave off antitrust action and later for the Pennsylvania Railroad, which hired him in 1906 to "take 'offensive' measures as it were, to place our 'case' before the public."[9] This led in turn to work as personal representative of railroad magnate E. H. Harriman. In 1914, Lee was hired as counsel to John D. Rockefeller, Jr. The Rockefeller family had become widely hated because of the ruthless, monopolistic business tactics of their company, Standard Oil. Lee is widely credited (incorrectly, according to T. J. Ross, his former business partner) for advising John Sr. to soften his image as a cold, sinister tycoon by carrying a pocketful of dimes to give away to children whenever he was seen in public.[10]

Lee invented the public relations specialty that is today known as "crisis management": helping clients put the best possible "spin" on a bad situation. At the time he went to work for the railroads, accidents were common, and the railroad companies dealt with the situation by withholding information and using bribes such as free railroad passes to suppress reports of accidents and their costs in lives and property. Lee had worked previously as a newspaper reporter, and knew that this approach often invited suspicion and bad publicity. As an alternative, he proposed an "open policy" of providing information to the press. Shortly after he went to work for the Pennsylvania Railroad, a wreck occurred. Instead of trying to suppress the story, Lee invited reporters to travel to the scene at the railroad's expense and set up facilities to assist them once they got there. Company executives thought Lee was crazy, but they changed their minds after they discovered that his "open" strategy won them more favorable coverage than the old approach.[11]

To advertise his policy of openness, Lee distributed a "Declaration of Principles" to newspapers across the country which is often quoted today in public relations textbooks:

THE ART OF THE HUSTLE

This is not a secret press bureau. All our work is done in the open. We aim to supply news. This is not an advertising agency; if you think any of our matter ought properly to go to your business office, do not use it. Our matter is accurate. Further details on any subject treated will be supplied promptly, and any editor will be assisted most cheerfully in verifying directly any statement of fact. . . . In brief, our plan is, frankly, and openly, on behalf of business concerns and public institutions, to supply to the press and public of the United States prompt and accurate information concerning subjects which it is of value and interest to the public to know about.[12]

According to Cutlip, Lee's approach to PR was not limited to putting "the most favorable light" on corporate activities. He saw himself as a counselor who studied public opinion and advised companies how to "shape their affairs" so that "when placed before the public they will be approved." His standard prescription was, "Set your house in order, then tell the public you have done so."[13]

In practice, however, Cutlip admits, this "two-way street" approach to public relations was limited by the fact that Lee's clients were engaged in activities that the public would never be likely to approve. In fact, Lee's first job for the Rockefellers was to counter bad publicity following their brutal union-busting tactics in the Ludlow Massacre, in which Colorado state militia and company guards used machine guns to fire on a tent colony of striking mine workers, killing women and children. Lee responded with a series of pro-Rockefeller bulletins titled "The Struggle in Colorado for Industrial Freedom." According to Ray Hiebert, Lee's biographer, "most of the bulletins contained matter which on the surface was true but which presented the facts in such a way as to give a total picture that was false."[14]

The great war

The fledgling publicity industry got a big boost with World War I. Ivy Lee and many other industry pioneers joined the US government's campaign to mobilize public opinion in support of the war effort. The Committee on Public Information, led by George Creel, used posters, billboards, advertising, exhibits, pamphlets and newspapers to promote the "war to end all wars"—to "make the world safe for democracy."

In a history of the war effort titled *Mobilizing Civilian America,* Harold Tobin and Percy Bidwell describe the committee's work as "perhaps the most effective job of large-scale war propaganda which the world had ever witnessed." The committee "bombarded the public unceasingly with enthusiastic reports on the nation's colossal war effort and with contrasts of our war aims and those of our allies, with the war aims of the Central Powers. Dissenting voices were stilled, either by agreement with the press or by the persuasive action of the agents of the Department of Justice."[15] The committee enrolled 75,000 civic leaders as "Four-Minute Men" to deliver war messages to people in churches, theaters and civic groups. Ivy Lee's publicity program for the Red Cross helped it grow from 486,000 to 20 million members and raise $400 million by the time the war ended. The Creel Committee also used the time-tested tactic of feeding wartime hysteria with fantastic atrocity stories depicting the Germans as beasts and Huns.[16]

The war demonstrated the power of propaganda and helped build the reputations of Creel Committee members, who returned to civilian life and offered their services to help business in the transition from a wartime to a peacetime economy. They applied and refined the publicity methods they had learned during the war.

The postwar years saw Ivy Lee's firm defending the Rockefellers again, in a private war between coal mine owners and striking mine workers in West Virginia. Nearly 400,000 miners had gone out on strike to protest dangerous working conditions, low wages, and other abuses such as payment of wages in "company scrip" that could only be used in overpriced company stores. The coal companies hired armed Pinkerton detectives. President Warren G. Harding sent in federal troops. The governor of West Virginia declared martial law. Logan County's corrupt sheriff, Don Chafin, used money from the coal companies to hire "deputy sheriff" strikebreakers. The resulting battles left at least 70 miners dead.

Lee worked to clean up the reputation of the coal companies by publishing bulletins titled *The Miner's Lamp* and *Coal Facts*. The bulletins ran stories praising the charitable works of mine owners, and a "first-hand sketch of Sheriff Don Chafin" which "reveals different traits than the public has been given to understand." They attacked the union's method of organizing and collecting dues, and claimed that "company stores protect mine workers' pocketbooks."[17]

These activities notwithstanding, Ivy Lee was the most widely sought-after advisor of his day to companies seeking to improve their public image. Many historians and industry insiders consider Lee the "father of public relations," an honor he would probably hold without challenge if his reputation had not been tainted by scandal near the end of his career. In 1933, shortly after Adolf Hitler's rise to power, Lee's firm went to work for the German Dye Trust to advise them on ways to improve German-American relations, leading to charges that he was a Nazi propagandist. The *New York Mirror* ran a story in July 1934 headlined: "Rockefeller Aide Nazi Mastermind." In November of that year, with the scandal still hanging over his head, Lee died of a brain tumor. An obituary in the *Jewish Daily Forward* described him as "an agent of the Nazi government."[18]

Bernays and the "engineering of consent"

Ivy Lee's fall from grace enabled another early PR practitioner, Edward Bernays, to claim credit for founding the field of public relations. In his history of the PR industry, Scott Cutlip describes Bernays as "perhaps public relations' most fabulous and fascinating individual, a man who was bright, articulate to excess, and most of all, an innovative thinker and philosopher of this vocation that was in its infancy when he opened his office in New York in June 1919." Much of Bernays's reputation today stems from his persistent public relations campaign to build his own reputation as "America's No. 1 Publicist." During his active years, many of his peers in the industry were offended by Bernays' constant self-promotion. According to Cutlip, "Bernays was a brilliant person who had a spectacular career, but, to use an old-fashioned word, he was a braggart."[19]

Born in Vienna, Bernays was a nephew of Sigmund Freud, the "father of psychoanalysis," and his public relations efforts helped popularize Freud's theories in the United States. Bernays also pioneered the PR industry's use of psychology and other social sciences to design its public persuasion campaigns. "If we understand the mechanism and motives of the group mind, it is now possible to control and regiment the masses according to our will without their knowing it," Bernays argued.[20] He called this scientific technique of opinion molding the "engineering of consent."[21]

One of Bernays's favorite techniques for manipulating public opinion was the indirect use of "third party authorities" to plead for his clients' causes. "If you can influence the leaders, either with or without their conscious cooperation, you automatically influence the group which they sway," he said. In order to promote sales of bacon, for example, he conducted a survey of physicians and reported their recommendation that people eat hearty breakfasts. He sent the results of the survey to 5,000 physicians, along with publicity touting bacon and eggs as a hearty breakfast.[22] His clients included President Calvin Coolidge, Procter & Gamble, CBS, General Electric and Dodge Motors. Beyond his contributions to these famous and powerful clients, Bernays revolutionized public relations by combining traditional press agentry with the techniques of psychology and sociology to create what one author called "the science of ballyhoo."[23]

"When a person would first meet Bernays," noted writer Scott Cutlip, "it would not be long until Uncle Sigmund would be brought into the conversation. His relationship with Freud was always in the forefront of his thinking and his counseling." According to Irwin Ross, another writer, "Bernays liked to think of himself as a kind of psychoanalyst to troubled corporations." In the early 1920s, Bernays arranged for the US publication of an English-language translation of Freud's *General Introduction to Psychoanalysis*. In addition to publicizing Freud's ideas, Bernays used his association with Freud to establish his own reputation as a thinker and theorist—a reputation which was further enhanced when Bernays authored several landmark books of his own, most notably *Crystallizing Public Opinion* and *Propaganda*.[24]

Bernays defined the profession of "counsel on public relations" as a "practicing social scientist" whose "competence is like that of the industrial engineer, the management engineer, or the investment counselor in their respective fields."[25] To assist clients, PR counselors used "understanding of the behavioral sciences and applying them—sociology, social psychology, anthropology, history, etc."[26]

This definition of PR was worlds apart from the old days of press agents and circus handbills. In *Propaganda,* his most important book, Bernays argued that the scientific manipulation of public opinion was necessary to overcome chaos and conflict in society: "The conscious and intelligent manipulation of the organized habits and opinions of the masses is an important element in democratic society. Those who manipulate this unseen mechanism of society constitute an invisible government which is the true ruling power of our country. . . . We are governed, our minds are molded, our tastes formed, our ideas suggested, largely by men we have never heard of. This is a logical result of the way in which our democratic society is organized. Vast numbers of human beings must cooperate in this manner if they are to live together as a smoothly functioning society. . . . In almost every act of our daily lives, whether in the sphere of politics or business, in our social conduct or our ethical thinking, we are dominated by the relatively small number of persons . . . who understand the mental processes and social patterns of the masses. It is they who pull the wires which control the public mind."[27]

Compared to Ivy Lee's claim that "all our work is done in the open," Bernays was audaciously blunt about the secret, manipulative nature of public relations work. His celebration of propaganda helped define public relations, but it didn't win the industry many friends. In a letter to President Franklin Roosevelt, Supreme Court Justice Felix Frankfurter described Bernays and Lee as "professional poisoners of the public mind, exploiters of foolishness, fanaticism and self-interest."[28] And history itself showed the flaw in Bernays' claim that "manipulation of the masses" is natural and necessary in a democratic society. The fascist rise to power in Germany demonstrated that propaganda could be used to subvert democracy as easily as it could be used to "resolve conflict."

In his autobiography, Bernays recalls a dinner at his home in 1933 where "Karl von Weigand, foreign correspondent of the Hearst newspapers, an old hand at interpreting Europe and just returned from Germany, was telling us about Goebbels and his propaganda plans to consolidate Nazi power. Goebbels had shown Weigand his propaganda library, the best Weigand had ever seen. Goebbels, said Weigand, was using my book *Crystallizing Public Opinion* as a basis for his destructive campaign against the Jews of Germany. This shocked me. . . . Obviously the attack on the Jews of Germany was no emotional outburst of the Nazis, but a deliberate, planned campaign."[29]

Notes

1 Edward L. Bernays, *Public Relations* (Norman, OK: University of Oklahoma Press, 1957), pp. 38–39.
2 Ibid., p. 36.
3 Ibid., p. 60.
4 Scott Cutlip, *The Unseen Power: Public Relations: A History* (Hillsdale, NJ: Lawrence Erlbaum Associates, Inc., 1994), p. 51. For a description of press agentry in the early twentieth century, see Neal Gabler, *Winchell: Power and the Culture of Celebrity*, excerpted in *O'Dwyer's PR Services Report,* Dec. 1994, pp. 24–25.
5 Will Irwin, "Press Agent, His Rise and Fall," *Colliers* Vol. 48. Dec. 2, 1991. Quoted in Cutlip, p. 51.
6 Bernays, p. 51.
7 Ibid., pp. 53–55, 63–64.
8 Cutlip, p. 21.
9 Ibid., pp. 47–48.
10 Ibid., p. 58.
11 Ibid., pp. 52–53.
12 Sherman Morse, "An Awakening on Wall Street," *The American Magazine,* Vol. LXII, Sept. 1906.
13 Cutlip, p. 64.
14 Ibid., p. 23.
15 Quoted in Bernays, p. 74.
16 Cutlip, pp. 64–71.
17 Ibid., pp. 121–122.
18 Ibid., p. 144.
19 Ibid., p. 160.
20 Edward L. Bernays, *Propaganda* (New York: 1928), pp. 47–48.
21 Edward L. Bernays, ed., *The Engineering of Consent* (Norman, OK: University of Oklahoma Press), pp. 3–4.
22 Cutlip, pp. 193–214.
23 John T. Flynn, "Edward L. Bernays, The Science of Ballyhoo," *Atlantic Monthly,* May 1932.
24 Cutlip, pp. 170–176.
25 Bernays, *Public Relations,* p. 4.
26 Edward L. Bernays, "What Do the Social Sciences Have to Offer Public Relations?" interview with Howard Penn Hudson for *PR: The Quarterly Journal of Public Relations,* Winter 1956. Reprinted in Edward L. Bernays, *The Later Years: Public Relations Insights, 1956–1986* (Rhinebeck, NY: H&M Publishers, 1986), p. 11.
27 Bernays, *Propaganda,* p. 9.
28 Cutlip, p. 185.
29 Edward L. Bernays, *The Biography of an Idea: Memoirs of Public Relations Counsel Edward L. Bernays* (New York: Simon and Schuster, 1965), p. 652.

DISCOURSE AND THE PROJECTION OF CORPORATE CULTURE: THE MISSION STATEMENT

John M. Swales and Priscilla S. Rogers

Source: *Discourse and Society*, 6:2 (1995), 223–242.

Abstract

This article explores how corporations project their corporate philosophy through 'Mission Statements'. Linguistic and textual analysis of such statements drawn from a sizeable corpus allows us to typify the texts as constituting a non-routine, organizational genre, and one that has recently become of some significance. This discussion serves as a foundation for a contextual and intertextual analysis (cf. Fairclough, 1992) of Mission Statements from two well-known US companies. By detailing the history, rationale and role of these Mission Statements we indicate how the texts are rhetorically designed in order to ensure maximum employee 'buy-in'. Despite linguistic and rhetorical similarities among the texts, an exploration of context reveals startling differences in communicative purpose. In one case the Mission Statement emerges as an empowering historical vision to be protected and nurtured through all vicissitudes; in the other case, the rewriting of the Mission Statement emerges as a collaborative response to crisis. The article ends by discussing the implications of such findings for contemporary approaches to discourse and genre analysis within institutional linguistics.

Communication is almost always an attempt to control change, either by causing it or preventing it.

(Hanna and Wilson, 1984: 21)

Introduction

Management experts, whether writing in scholarly journals or in more popular formats, have consistently recognized the importance of language in business affairs. In a 1991 interview for the *Harvard Business Review*, Raymond Smith, Bell Atlantic's Chief Executive Officer (CEO), was asked, 'What are some tangible signs of change in an organization?' Smith responded simply, 'The language is changing' (Kanter, 1991: 123). On the academic side, Weick (1985: 129) observes that 'Agreement on a label that sticks is as constant a connection as is likely to be found in organizations', thereby illustrating the epigraph's second alternative. This inherent relationship between managing and communicating is further recognized in Eccles and Nohria's statement: 'The basic tool of management . . . is to mobilize action by using language creatively to appeal to the self- and collective identities of individuals' (1992: 37). Likewise, Fairhurst comments, 'chiefly through discourse, a new point of reference is created, meaning is created, and action becomes possible' (1993: 344).

More broadly, discussions of the relationships among vision, leadership and communication abound in the management literature. A brief sampling might include Goia and Chittipeddi's (1991) exposition on the importance of 'sensemaking' and 'sensegiving', Dutton and Duncan's (1987a, 1987b) 'strategic issue diagnosis' model of the change process, and more 'practical' interventions such as Judson's (1991) book on minimizing resistance to change. These and other discussions acknowledge the central role of communication in change management in a variety of ways: Judson (1991) does so explicitly, by advocating the need for face-to-face interactions and effective written communications; Dutton and Duncan do so implicitly by suggesting that their model requires giving 'meaning and definition to an issue' (1987: 291). Czarniawska-Joerges and Joerges (1988) note the importance of searching for the labels, metaphors and platitudes by which organizational changes may be identified, understood and implemented. And Kissler is among those who suggest that effective change efforts require not only a formal communication strategy, but also a 'captivating vision' in order to facilitate the necessary consensus-building (1991: 272).

Such intrinsic connections between management and communication have been documented in ethnographic and case studies by scholars in rhetoric and technical business communication (e.g. Paradis *et al.*, 1985; Brown and Herndl, 1986; Doheny-Farina, 1986; and Cross, 1994). Following pioneering work in the sociology of science by Latour and Woolgar (1979) and Knorr-Cetina (1981), these social constructionist accounts place texts, and the processes of their construction and reception, as central to the working of corporate and institutional life. More recently, with the (belated) discovery of Bakhtin (1986) and Giddens (1979), US studies of organizational discourse have gained strength from more fluid and dynamic conceptions of genre (Devitt, 1993; Swales, 1993) and from identifying genre as one of the key modalities in structuration theory (e.g. Bazerman, 1992). For a more extended illustration, Yates and Orlikowski conclude their argument for the importance of organizational genres with the following:

> . . . our genre approach to organizational communication takes into account the inherently situated and dynamic nature of organizational processes. Adopting a concept from rhetoric and using the premises of structuration, we have interpreted organizational communication, not as the result of isolated, rational actions, but as part of an embedded social process that over time produces, reproduces, and modifies particular genres of communication. We expect that this concept of genre will provide new and productive ways of understanding communicative action in organizations.
>
> (1992: 323)

We too are interested in genre development (or its ossification) as an 'embedded social process', and one which concomitantly both shapes and reflects organizational attitudes and behaviors. In this endeavor, we have followed a corpus survey with close textual analysis of three exemplars of the selected genre plus contextual explorations of their histories, authorships and institutional roles. We find sufficient anomalies between text and context to suggest that any interpretation of discourse that relies principally on only the former is likely to be incomplete, and perhaps suspect. (See Chin, 1994, for a broadly comparable view.) We conclude that discourse analysts need cultural and social strategies for discourse comprehension (van Dijk and Kintsch, 1983) just as much as successful discourse consumers do.

Mission statements

Of the myriad types of documents that consitute the matrix of modern corporate or institutional life, we have deliberately selected a class of genres that primarily act as carriers of ideologies and institutional cultures. Some of the genre-exemplars in this class are short, pithy and mnemonic, such as Ford's 'Quality is Job 1', or one of America's largest insurance company's 'Like a good neighbor, State Farm is there'. These catchphrases, slogans and mottos (whether stand-alone or part of larger messages) are typically institutional, although, in the hands of powerful luminaries, they can occasionally also be individual—none more famously perhaps than President Truman's 'The buck stops here'. They tend to occur and recur in visual form on desks and walls and doors, and may act as spoken 'signature tunes' in radio or television advertising. They perhaps have their origins in domestic samplers and genre-pictures of the 'Patience is a Virtue' type. They give rise, as nearly all well-established genres do, to humor and anti-generic parody, such as in grafitti and in posted variants of Murphy's Law and the like. They also occur in more extended form, especially when used to project the 'captivating vision' (Kissler, 1991) of a corporation. Johnson & Johnson's self-described 'Our Credo' is a well-known example. Here is the first of their five 'responsibilities':

WE BELIEVE THAT OUR FIRST RESPONSIBILITY
is to the doctors, nurses, hospitals, mothers and all others who use our products. Our products must always be of the highest quality. We must constantly strive to reduce the costs of these products. Our orders must be promptly and accurately filled. Our dealers must make a fair profit.

Most such Mission Statements are designed as displayable single-page documents or take the form of a folded flyer or small booklet. Doubtless, there are parallels here with religious synopses like 'The Four Spiritual Laws' or 'The Ten Commandments' and with political ones such as Mao's 'Little Red Book'.

These types of genre act as carriers of culture, ethos and ideology. As a result, they stand a little apart from the normal recursive processes that produce and reproduce everyday social and institutional customs (Giddens, 1979). In other words, they seem less directly integrated into the systems of genres that 'get things done' (Martin, 1985), such as the placing of orders, the negotiating of contracts and the handling of complaints, and thus fall into the category of communications that Lengel and Daft (1988) earmark as 'nonroutine'. Rather, genre-exemplars of this type have a ghostly immanence over and above the plethora of regulations, instructions and procedures. This immanence may be invoked for annual events such as Dana Corporation's yearly pilgrimage of managers to headquarters for 'Hell Week', or in times of crisis, as with the now legendary case of Johnson & Johnson immediately withdrawing all Tylenol in the US (after a few instances of tampering with their product), apparently in response to their 'Our Credo'. Indeed, the Tylenol case can be contrasted with Exxon's procrastinated and legalistic response to the *Exxon Valdez* oil-spill, the tardiness of which has been ascribed to the absence of any such guiding principles. As Tyler concludes, 'Public statements that were prudent for legal and financial reasons nonetheless gave the impression that Exxon was cold, calculating, and ruthlessly capitalistic' (1992: 162).

This particular genre, which we will use to illustrate the creation and projection of corporate culture, encompasses texts that appear under a variety of labels, such as 'Our Mission' (SIEL Corporation), 'Our Commitment' (*New York Times*), 'Fundamental Intercor Values' (Intercor Corporation), 'A View to the Future' (Cargill Corporation), or often some form of 'Vision' (Caltex) and most often 'Mission Statement' (e.g. John

Hancock Insurance Company, Fluor Daniel Corporation, Coopers & Lybrand, George Hyman Construction Company). Although terminology may not yet be fully stabilized, these texts possess similarities sufficient to characterize them as a single genre, and we use Mission Statement as it is the label we have seen used most often.

Our general observations are based on over a hundred individual texts, largely collected from organizations associated with the University of Michigan School of Business Administration. From this corpus, we analyzed more closely a sample of 30 texts submitted by participants in the Fall 1994 Michigan Executive Program. Since these executives were selected to form a diverse group in terms of industry, organizational type and country of operation, there is reason to be believe that the 30 Mission Statements comprise a diverse but representative subset.

The Mission Statements in the sample are pithy and up-beat, and tend to deal with abstractions possessing 'a strategic level of generality and ambiguity' (Fairhurst, 1993: 336), somewhat like inspirational speeches. There is an almost total absence of what Walter (1966) originally called 'support' (i.e. examples, comparisons, quotations, statistics, visuals and the like). Rather, the content of these texts largely consists of general statements, claims and conclusions. It is not surprising then that the verb forms are predominantly the present, the imperative ('Return to underwriting profit'—Chubb & Son) and the purposive infinitive ('To provide a caring environment for staff'— Bank of Ireland; 'To be the safest carrier'—Conrail). If modals occur they are typically of the un-hedged variety such as Kodak's 'We *will* be a globally competitive high growth company . . .' or EID-Perry Farm Products' 'All the business activities *must* maximize satisfaction to customers . . .'. Frequently used nouns are *goals*, *principles* and *values*, and the texts draw their color mostly from a variety of adjectives used to characterize activities in a positive light, such as *competent, creative, enthusiastic, leading* and *profitable*.

If the Mission Statement is one kind of generic constituent of corporate culture, then the Ethical Code or Standard Practice Guide constitutes quite another (even though 'hybrids' may be possible and the distinction not always well maintained, e.g. in Berenbeim, 1987). Ethical Codes and Standard Practice Guides became widespread in the United States about a decade ago as a means of *regulating* behavior or of *disassociating* an organization from employees who engage in unethical practices (Cressey and Moore, 1983), even if there is considerable doubt as to their effectiveness on either the behavioral or legal level (Pitt and Groskaufmanis, 1990). Ethical Codes tend to be bureaucratic, legalistic, non-visionary and instructional; in particular, they stress what employees should *not* do. Further, new employees may be required to sign that they have read and understood their corporation's Ethical Code as part of their contractual obligations. Ethical Codes are often quite long and read as if written by corporate lawyers. The sentence below well illustrates the coercive, legalistic character of this genre:

Loans to employees from customers, suppliers or any other persons with whom contact is made in the course of business are prohibited unless extended by those who engage in lending in the usual course of their business, and then only in accordance with applicable laws and regulations and only on terms offered to others under similar circumstances without special concessions as to interest rates, terms, security, repayment terms and other conditions.

(PNC Financial Corp.: Ethics Statement, p. 4)

As the fragment from Johnson & Johnson (above) and the extracts from Dana and Honeywell (Figure 1 below) illustrate, Mission Statements are very different. They tend to stress values, *positive* behavior and guiding principles within the framework of the corporation's *announced* belief system and ideology. It also appears that these Mission Statements are in most cases engendered by senior management, indeed they may be written by the CEO with his or her most senior colleagues, but not likely by the legal staff. Although, as we shall see, the precise sets of motives and purposes underlying a particular Mission Statement can vary quite widely, perhaps all share the aim of facilitating employee 'buy-in' and of fostering identification with the company. Their proliferation can thus be seen as evidence for Galbraith's argument in *The New Industrial State* (1985) that identification has succeeded financial reward, which in turn replaced compulsion and fear, as the primary motivational force in the modern corporation. If Galbraith is right about this trend in the United States, then the Mission Statement has developed as yet another management tool both for promoting corporate culture and ethos and for tying the workforce to that culture and ethos.

Even so, the value of the Mission Statement as a management tool has not gone entirely unchallenged. In his *Harvard Business Review* article entitled 'The Vision Trap', Gerard Langelar recounts his personal knack for implementing ambitious visions that became powerful enough to *weaken* his company. 'I have come to believe that the sense of vision that initially drove Mentor Graphics forward', he wrote, 'came finally to lead us down a primrose path of self-infatuation that carried us away from our best business interests' (1992: 239). Along similar lines, IBM's Louis Gerstner stated 'the last thing we need right now is a vision', and Robert Eaton, who assumed the chairmanship of Chrysler after the company's much publicized comeback under Lee Iacocca, declared, 'we don't use the word vision . . . I believe in quantifiable short-term results' (*Wall Street Journal*, 4 October 1993). However, a little reflection shows that the trenchant, pithy character of these two last remarks actually makes them sound very much like 'Mission Statements' themselves.

Despite the occasional iconclasts, the Mission Statement seems to be patently a growing, rather than a dying, genre. It has come to represent for the 1990s what the Ethical Code represented in the decade before—a

HONEYWELL PRINCIPLES

Honeywell is an international corporation whose goal is to work together with customers to develop and apply advanced technologies through products, systems and services, which in turn serve primarily to improve productivity, conserve resources and meet aerospace and defense needs. Honeywell adheres to the following principles.

Profits – Profitable operations are necessary to assure the continued health and growth of the company. Honeywell expects profits which equal – or exceed those of leading international companies.

Quality – Quality of product, application and service is essential to continue Honeywell's success. Quality improvement should pervade every job within the company. Honeywell believes quality results from an environment in which people work together to sustain excellence.

THE PHILOSOPHY AND POLICIES OF DANA

EARNINGS

The purpose of the Dana Corporation is to earn money for its shareholders and to increase the value of their investment. We believe the best way to do this is to earn an acceptable return by properly utilizing our assets and controlling our cash.

GROWTH

We believe in steady growth to protect our assets against inflation. We will grow in our selected markets by implementing our market strategies.

PEOPLE

We are dedicated to the belief that our people are our most important asset. Wherever possible, we encourage all Dana people within the entire world organization to become shareholders, or by some other means, own a part of their company.

We believe people respond to recognition, freedom to participate, and the opportunity to develop.

We believe that people should be involved in setting their own goals and judging their own performance. The people who know best how the job should be done are the ones doing it.

We believe Dana people should accept only total quality in all tasks they perform.

We endorse productivity plans which allow people to share in the rewards of productivity gains.

We believe that all Dana people should identify with the company. This identity should carry on after they have left active employment.

We believe facilities with people who have demonstrated a commitment to Dana will be competitive and thus warrant our support.

We believe that wages and benefits are the concern and responsibility of managers. The Management Resource Program is a world-wide matter – it is a tool that should be used in the development of qualified Dana people. We encourage income protection, health programs, and education.

We believe that on-the-job training is an effective method of learning. A Dana manager must prove proficiency in at least one line of our company's work – marketing, engineering, manufacturing, financial services, etc. Additionally, these people must prove their ability as supervisors and be able to get work done through other people. We recognize the importance of gaining experience both internationally and domestically.

We believe our people should move across product, discipline, and organizational lines. These moves should not conflict with operating efficiency.

We believe in promoting from within. Dana people interested in other positions are encouraged to discuss job opportunities with their supervisor.

HONEYWELL STRATEGIC PRIORITIES

Our Mission

Honeywell. We are a publicly owned, global enterprise in business to provide control components, products systems and services. These are for homes and buildings, aviation and space, industrial processes and for application in manufactured goods.

For the future:

We are committed to sustaining our focus on the controls business as we grow and change, and to being the global leader in the markets we serve.

Our Guiding Values

As a business, we have responsibilities to all of our stakeholders: customers, shareholders, employees, suppliers and communities. Balancing these responsibilities requires a value system, and ours comprises the following:

Integrity To practice the highest ethical standards.

Quality To strive for total quality to set the pace for our industry and satisfy our customers' current and future needs.

Performance To achieve and reward outstanding results through continuous improvement, personal and organizational commitment, and accountability.

Figure 1 Extracts from Mission Statements.

management tool for projecting corporate integrity and instilling loyalty and normed behavior in the corporate workforce. The difference is that prohibition has been replaced by exhortation.

Dana and Honeywell and their mission statements

In this section of the paper we examine three Mission Statement documents from two companies:

1. *The Philosophy and Policies of Dana,*
2. *Honeywell Principles,* and
3. *Honeywell Strategic Priorities.*

As we shall attempt to show, the fact that there is but one document from the Dana Corporation, while there are two from Honeywell, will turn out to be a crucial variable in the two case histories. Extracts from these three documents are displayed in a 'collage' in Figure 1 in order to communicate something of their typographic and rhetorical character.

Dana is a world-wide automotive parts supplier with its headquarters in Toledo, Ohio. Its total workforce is around 35,000. It has been widely recognized as an excellently managed company (Peters and Waterman, 1984; Levering *et al.*, 1985). *The Philosophy and Policies of Dana* (henceforth PPD) was first produced and distributed in 1969 and, until recently, remained virtually unchanged, apart from a small addition to cover 'globalization' in 1987. The PPD is in the form of a flyer which opens to a full-page, small-print, single-space document consisting of eight sections and 66 sentences. On the overleaf is a brief introduction concluding with the statement that 'The Policy Committee is responsible for our philosophy and our policies'.

Honeywell is also a world-wide company with a total workforce of around 60,000 at the time of our site-visit. It is perhaps best known for its temperature control systems. The corporation has its world headquarters in Minneapolis, Minnesota, in a building that has come to be known as 'The Fortress'. *Honeywell Principles* (HP) first appeared in 1974, and its seven short paragraphs offer a somewhat unstructured mix of elements: goals (profits, quality), virtues (integrity, citizenship), groups (customers, people) and processes (decision-making). In the middle 1980s Honeywell experienced a financial crisis as a result of extensive diversification, from which it has apparently recovered by refocusing on what it does best—the designing and making of control systems. One important casualty of the crisis was Ed Spencer, who had been CEO since 1974 and had written HP soon after assuming office; he was replaced by Jim Renier. As part of the crisis recovery process, in 1986 Honeywell replaced the HP with another Mission Statement entitled *Honeywell Strategic Priorities* (HSP). This replacement is about four times longer and has a much more developed structure than the earlier HP.

Figure 2 displays the main changes that have occurred as HP was transformed into HSP. We can note, in particular, how four of the original paragraph headings in HP have now become subheads in a new section entitled 'Our Guiding Values', while the notion of 'Customers' has been expanded into another new section entitled 'Our Goals for Stakeholders'. The ordering of elements has also changed. Most noticeably, 'Profits', which appeared in first position in HP, is now tucked under 'For Shareholders' in the second section and, in fact, reappears in more euphemistic guise as

	Honeywell Principles	Strategic Priorities					
Title	"Honeywell Is..."	"Our Mission. For the future . . ."					
Opening							
Body Headings & Subheadings	Profits Integrity Customers People Quality Decision-Making Citizenship	**Our Guiding Values** Integrity Quality Performance Mutual Respect Diversity	**Our Goals for Stakeholders** For Customers For Shareholders For Employees For Suppliers For Communities For All Stakeholders	**Our Unifying Strategies** (summary) Customer Satisfaction Business Focus Employee Motivation Global Leadership Market Focus Shared Resources Technology Business Balance Strategic Alliances Financial Levarage Rewards for Performance	**Our Organizational Philosophy** [Paragraphs describing Strategic Business Unit]	**Management Responsibilities** Senior Management [will]: Provide... Establish... Lead... Allocate... Balance... Establish... Select... Ensure...	**Strategic Priorities and You** [Paragraphs describing personal application]

Figure 2 Honeywell Principles become 'Strategic Priorities'.

'to consistently generate above-average returns'. Whereas the original HP (as well as Dana's PPD) frontloads the profit motive—perhaps as a way of getting certain uncomfortable realities over early—HSP places 'Integrity' first. The value 'Quality', which appeared fifth in HP, also finds promotion to the second spot in the HSP, perhaps reflecting the US response at that time to Japanese use of 'quality' management techniques. Finally, by beginning the entire document with a section entitled 'Our Guiding Values' and by frontloading those elements most associated with virtues (such as 'Integrity'), the HSP Mission Statement can be seen as placing greater emphasis on ethical concerns.

On a micro-level, the three Mission Statements reveal a number of linguistic features also of rhetorical significance. The most interesting of these revolves around attempts to foster affiliation and identification. A classic rhetorical device for doing this is to adopt the first-person-plural pronoun (Rounds, 1987), a decision adopted by many of the Mission Statements in our corpus. Cheney, in a study of 10 in-house company magazines, comments as follows:

> The assumed 'we' is both a subtle and powerful identification strategy because it often goes unnoticed. Uses of this strategy allow a corporation to present similarity and commonality among organizational members as a taken-for-granted assumption. To the extent that employees accept this assumption and its corollaries unquestioningly, they identify with their corporate employer.
>
> (1983: 154)

Table 1 presents the data for sentence-subjects of finite declarative sentences in the three texts. Category B sums the total number of sentence-subjects that refer in some way to employees (as opposed to customers, the environment, the economy and so on), while part C offers a breakdown of the category into its lexical realizations.

Table 1 Sentence-subjects in three Mission Statements.

	PPD	*HP*	*HSP*
A. No. of finite sentences	66	19	29
B. No. of employee-denoting subjects	44 (66%)	15 (79%)	14 (48%)
C. Realizations of B:			
(a) 'We'	33	0	8
(b) 'Our' + NP	0	0	4
(c) Company people (e.g. 'Dana People' or 'Honeywellers')	3	1	1
(d) Company name or 'The company'	2	14	1
(e) Subgroups, e.g. 'Senior management'	6	0	1

If we ignore sentence fragments and imperatives, we can see that in all three cases there is a remarkable percentage of sentences containing subjects that refer to the employees of the corporation (from 48 percent to 79 percent). Fairly consistently then, employees are, in terms of functional linguistics, the *unmarked* themes and thus serve, in the traditional formulation, as the points of departure for the statements (Halliday, 1985). Syntactically at least, the Mission Statements are 'about' the employees. If we now turn to part C, we can see that, in any particular instance, these employees can be referred to in one of a small number of ways. We have displayed them along a cline of congregation–segregation; in other words 'we' is the most affiliative and incorporating of the reader, while some subset of the employees such as 'senior management' is the least (except for uncommon cases when the reader happens to be a member of the subset). Similarly type (c), 'Dana People' or 'Honeywellers', seems a little more identifying and congregating than the type (d) equivalents—'The Dana Corporation' or 'Honeywell'. As can be seen, the PPD and the HSP score strongly on we-identification while the HP does not. On the other hand, the HP has the highest proportion of sentences beginning with employee-denoting subjects. We shall return to these points later.

Elsewhere (Rogers and Swales, 1990) we have discussed in some detail the 11 instances in the Dana text where the authors have chosen something other than 'we' for an employee-denoting subject. In some cases the Policy Committee authoring group decided that the potential advantages of using 'we' were outweighed by an increased possibility that employee-readers would not accept, in Cheney's words, the identity assumption 'unquestioningly'. Compare the original with a possible 'we' alternative (1a):

(1)   The Purpose of the Dana Corporation is to earn money for its shareholders and to increase the value of their investment.
(1a) Our purpose is to earn money for our shareholders and to increase the value of their investment.

The profit motive can be rhetorically problematic for Mission Statements since it can appear to conflict with the high 'ethical' tone and regard for 'human' values that tend to dominate the genre. Like some other Mission Statements (including the HP), Dana's PPD gets this 'bad moment' over with right at the beginning, as a kind of no-nonsense reminder as to what the corporation is ultimately about. However, by associating the company rather than 'we' with profits, the authors wisely refrain from enjoining their workforce to believe that they should *personally* identify with seeing their labor as designed to line the pockets of the shareholders.

In a second illustrative case of 'we' avoidance, the PPD offers the following:

(2)   It is highly desirable to outsource a portion of our production needs.

In fact, this is the only occasion in the whole document where the authors have used an agentless, adjectival structure, and it thus stands out from the surrounding sentences which typically begin with either 'we' or 'Dana people'. Again, the reason becomes apparent if we reformulate (2) in the 'standard' PPD format:

(2a)   We believe in outsourcing a portion of our production needs.

Since outsourcing has been a contentious issue between management and (organized) labor, particularly in the automotive industry, not all employees are likely to 'believe' in the virtues of outsourcing. On the other hand, a managerial *pronunciamento* like:

(2b)   It is Dana policy to outsource a portion of . . .

would run counter to the affiliative and cooperative tone adopted in the Mission Statement as a whole.

At this juncture we seem to be well embarked on a linguistic and textual analysis of the chosen examples of the Mission Statement genre. We have charted the macrostructure of at least two of the texts; we have presented some quantitative data on salient linguistic features; and we have begun to use the standard linguistic technique of substitution to demonstrate the consequences of discoursal choices. There is in fact quite a lot more that could be said: about the order and arrangement of the topics; about contrasts between declaratives and imperatives, and between full sentences and fragments; about the choice of lexis; and about the relative absence of modals (in marked contrast to their heavy use in Ethical Codes). However, as Fairclough (1992) reminds us, such accounting would in the end do little more than underscore the limits and limitations of a purely textual approach to genre analysis. It is time for a contextual turn.

Vision, mission statement and controlling change

Here first is some further information. In 1969, PPD was initiated by Ren McPherson, the legendary CEO of Dana. McPherson's Dana is an unusual automotive parts supply company in which, as retired President Gerald B. Mitchell tells it, 'We worked to develop communication as an art. There is little, if anything, written down; it's all done orally' (*Industry Week*, 13 October 1986). Indeed, when visiting Dana headquarters, we were struck by the fact that there were almost no papers visible anywhere (except in the Accounts Department). Rather, the emphasis was on talking to people, their *own* people, the Dana people, as most strikingly illustrated by their strongly avowed policy of 'promote from within'—a policy which sets them on a collision course with the whole apparatus of management experts, head-hunters and Business School MBA production lines.

As we talked to three of the four executives on the ruling Policy Committee, we began to see what their Mission Statement really was. As Executive Vice President, Borge Reimer remarked, 'What we have here is a belief system . . . It's a bit like when you pledge a commitment, as in church.' It became clear that the four-man Policy Committee, overseeing an extensive international set of business activities, saw themselves as keepers of the McPherson and Mitchell vision. As Reimer observed, 'At Dana, style may change, but vision and belief can only come from the top.' The Mission Statement, signed as written by this Policy Committee, is the instrument for maintaining this vision, and it is therefore not surprising that as many as 22 out of the 66 sentences in the document begin with the credo-like incantation 'We believe . . .'. Further, this vision has been inherited almost intact from the McPherson era, which is today more than 20 years old. The Policy Committee speaks of the PPD, as we have seen, in quasi-religious terms and, at least as far as the Mission Statement is concerned, they see themselves as but disciples of the company's great leaders. The PPD is thus an immanent and inherited guiding philosophy largely impervious to trend, fashion and change.

However, we learnt in 1994 that the Dana Policy Committee was, indeed, for the first time in many years reconsidering the PPD, 'the rock on which Dana has stood'. Moreover, it is quite significant, we think, that the company would not reveal to us the nature of any revisions. As Reimer confided, 'Changes in the PPD are our competitive advantage so we don't want to go public with them just yet.'

The first of the two Honeywell documents, HP, was written by the then CEO, Ed Spencer, in 1974. The one-page document was accompanied by a cover letter which explains Spencer's motives clearly enough:

> These principles have developed naturally as we have grown, and have become the core of the culture of our company. I learned about them from Harold Sweatt, who, along with his father, founded and built Honeywell . . . I felt strongly about the principles and, in 1974, when I became your Chief Executive Officer, I put them into words so that we could all understand them and share them.

In contrast to Dana's McPherson, Spencer saw himself as an annalist and historian orchestrating into a convenient single page the previously unconsolidated cultural traditions of Honeywell. As heir apparent, he stressed his intention to maintain the old ways. Spencer then did not see himself as a charismatic innovator like Dana's McPherson, who, in a widely remembered incident, introduced the PPD by ceremoniously dumping all the old policy manuals into a trash-can. Indeed, Spencer's cover letter introducing the HP is full of positive references to the past and consistently uses the present perfect tense to carry the continuation of tradition. The HP themselves are, of course, in the present tense and the principal subject-entity is Honeywell, as in:

> Honeywell manages its business in ways that are sensitive to the environment and that conserve natural resources.

Thus, the corporate name as theme emphasizes an enduring entity over the variable collectivity of employees constituting its workforce; the HP stands in direct contrast to the personal affirmations of Dana's PPD.

Spencer was replaced by Jim Renier as Honeywell's CEO in 1986 in response to the deep financial crisis the corporation was experiencing at that time. Commenting on leadership during his first year in charge, Renier observed, 'A leader is the person who knows how to deal with the value system of the organization and paint a picture of what we are doing' (quoted in Tichy and Devanna, 1986: 30). Renier painted this picture in part by initiating a revision of the HP, which resulted in the writing of the corporate document we now know as HSP. This Mission Statement rewriting process took on particular significance at Honeywell, not only because of when it took place, but also because of who was involved.

According to Karen Bachman, Honeywell Vice President for Communications, writing the HSP was essentially a 'bottom-up' process extending over several months, involving hundreds of people and several layers of management. Revisiting the old HP in the process of crafting a new statement forced Honeywell employees to examine the current state and future direction of the corporation in a very personal and intense way (cf. Doheny-Farina, 1986, for a comparable case), which would not have been possible if the Mission Statement had been simply 'dropped from on high' by Jim Renier and his most senior officers. In essence, we see here the process of creating a document as a calculated device for driving institutional change (which has now become the bread-and-butter for high-paid consultants with facilitation skills). In this new document, the impregnable 'Honeywell Fortress' of previous years is infiltrated by the much humbler, indeed marginally punning, theme of 'Customers Control Our World'. The change in Mission Statement title itself from 'Principles' to 'Strategic Priorities' reflects a shift from a stable independent value-system to one admitting the possibility of future modification.

Of further note is the fact that, whereas the lead paragraph in the old HP opened with a definitional structure: 'Honeywell is an international corporation whose goal is to . . .', the HSP begins with a topic-comment structure: 'Honeywell. We are a publicly owned, global enterprise in business to provide . . .'. These definitional changes are significant. First, the clever use of the 'Honeywell. We are . . .' rhetorical device in the HSP allows for a *double* identification of the corporate entity and of the people comprising it. Second, 'international' has been replaced by 'global', thus avoiding the 'Uncle Sam-ism' traditionally associated with American multinationals. Third, we can note that 'corporation' as a hierarchical legally embodied entity has been replaced by the racier and more entrepreneurial 'enterprise'. Furthermore, unlike the HP, the style of the new document is punchy and action-oriented. Compare these typical HP and HSP formats:

> HP: Honeywell believes in the highest level of integrity and ethical behavior.
> HSP: To practice the highest ethical standards.

Indeed, at times the punctuation in the HSP is decidedly idiosyncratic since it is used to break sentences into fragments, thus achieving a kind of one–two staccato rhythm which accentuates causes and effects. Below is one HSP example of many:

> To ensure continuous improvements in our productivity and quality.
> By seeking mutually beneficial partnerships with suppliers.

In effect, these textual changes both signal and promote the 'real-world' changes that were requied to make Honeywell profitable again, including reframing long-established values and demonstrating a change in leadership that regularly accompanies them (Bass, 1981).

Discussion

After an introductory survey, this article has centered on the case histories of the three examples of the Mission Statement genre. In doing so, we have gone beyond the surface of the text to explore the framing context. With this aim, we have studied company history, collected a wide range of documents, searched the business press, made site-visits and talked to key players, all in an effort to establish how Mission Statements both get written and are perceived by their creators and users. If all this activity leads to more systematic analysis and a somewhat 'thicker' description of the texts (Cross, 1994), there is one further step that we have been unable to take. Our research plan was to follow the site-visits with interviews of a stratified group of employees, so that we could gain a sense of their attitudes toward and uses of the Mission Statements (if any). In both corporations, we were politely but firmly discouraged from any such ambition. From hints received, we concluded that this was because we ourselves were perceived as being *outsiders* to the particular corporate culture; in effect, we were neither 'Dana People' nor 'Honeywellers'. We mention this 'reverse' because it seems to us to be a significant part of the narrative of the case histories that we have offered.

Table 2 Foci in the three Mission Statements.

	PPD	*HP*	*HSP*
Purpose	Credo	Historical record	Call to action
Theme	Identity	Entity	'Customers'
Self-definition	People	Technology	Business controls
Subjects	We	Honeywell	We/Our customers

The overall picture that emerges from the study offers the profiles of the three Mission Statements, illustrated in Table 2. Beyond these differences in purpose, theme and self-definition, the contextual aspect of the study also reveals that the first two Mission Statements operate to prevent change, while the third, viewed as both product and process, is designed to encourage it. Indeed, the HSP breaks out of the internal, 'fortress' mentality of both the PPD and HP, admitting the assault of external forces, including international rivals vying for marketshare. It is only by learning of these attitudes to change that we can come to fully understand the structural, discoursal and stylistic characteristics of the three texts.

Witte, in a major article entitled 'Context, Text and Intertext', argues for a more embracing theory than we have at present which will 'permit a synthesis of the textual, cognitive, and social perspectives that Halliday suggests would be necessary for a comprehensive theory of language' (1992: 241). One of his principal examples of such a synthesis is his study of the minimalist genre of shopping lists, wherein he is able to show that an understanding of their embryonic structure is only possible after gaining access to the thoughts of their originators. Although there may be value in purely textual studies for cross-cultural or stylistic purposes, we join Witte and Fairclough in arguing that a useful understanding of the role of genres in institutional and community affairs requires more sociocognitive input than the texts themselves provide. Certainly, the rationales for the three Mission Statements did not exactly leap off their pages, but were enmeshed within the context of corporate history, culture and legend.

As we have seen, Mission Statements are largely detached from day-to-day social, economic and administrative events and decisions (and their associated media 'coverage'). Even so, their permanence, provenance and role place them within what van Dijk has recently called 'elitist discourse' (1994a: 6). Like many other kinds of elitist discourse, Mission Statements have the strategic objective of creating allegiance and inspiring commitment within and to a constructed discourse community—and in this genre, communities that may number many thousands of individuals distributed in subcommunities across a good portion of the globe. Further, in these cases, the discoursal means employed by the corporations to encourage this employee commitment can be quite subtle.

As a situated response to an emerging rhetorical need, the Mission Statement is a newly evolved genre of somewhat uncertain origins and with a somewhat uncertain future. Indeed, as we have seen, one or two cautionary tales are emerging about the *dangerous* propensity for visionary Mission Statements to produce 'more poetry than product'. As a CEO from a company outside our case study observed, 'our company vision had become a laboratory creation, built to satisfy us, not our customers' (Langelar, 1992: 52). The further evolution of Mission Statements (or their atrophy), just as much in Europe and elsewhere as in the United States, thus emerges as a viable research topic in the interface between critical linguistics and discourse-based business communication.

Afterword

Purposefully, our illustrative analyses of the Mission Statements have been framed in largely non-technical language; moreover, the analyses have also been presented independently of a general theory of discourse, and without much overt attention to our own ideological stance. At the close of the paper, we would like to explain the thinking behind these decisions.

On the first point, we have tried to make our analyses as accessible as possible in a spirit which supports and encourages multidisciplinary collaboration. More importantly, however, we suggest that this type of study can contribute specifically to our understanding of what Eccles and Nohria identify as 'the rhetorical nature of managerial action' (1992: 50) and, more generally, can serve as an element in educational and social action (Kress, 1985; Martin, 1993). After all, Mission Statements themselves are easily accessible even on a secondary school level. They also represent a type of corporate document that entry-level employees of corporations regularly encounter. We would like to claim that the 'rhetorical consciousness-raising' which the analysis of such texts might engender can help both younger and older people gain a better understanding of the strategies behind the corporate messages and images that are so prevalent in contemporary society. We ourselves have used the case studies in a variety of educational settings to good effect and, in the spirit of critical linguistics and educational genre analysis, we would be happy to supply any interested readers will full-size copies of the complete Dana and Honeywell Mission Statements. As de Beaugrande observes:

> The imperative today is clear enough, however arduous and remote its realization: an integrated, discourse-centered approach to the entire educational experience, placing the language program in the pivotal (and rather daunting) position of training the discourse skills for navigating both in everyday life and in the several domains of schooling itself.
>
> (1993: 444)

Our second decision stems from our experience that initial studies of genres are best conducted *sui generis*, and are not helped by trying to fit those genre exemplars into complex frameworks arising from the study of other text-types (Swales, 1990). This experience is part of our own personal histories. As we began this study, we recognized that we have a greater and more variegated understanding of our own corporate world (the academic) than we did of the 'other' corporate world of business, even if one of us comes into frequent contact with businesspeople on a professional basis. And recall that we were rebuffed from site studies of employee reactions to the texts despite our meticulous preparation for the executive meetings, not excluding discussion of what we should wear!

On the other hand, like presumably most readers of this journal, we have subsisted fairly successfully within our own complex framework of academic culture and its preferred and privileged academic texts (even if those texts may appear uselessly arcane and obtuse to their critics, e.g. Limerick, 1993). However, we suspect we differ from most of the journal's readers in consequence of our own separate roles as individuals in charge of programs in English for Academic Purposes and Management Communication. These responsibilities have involved us extensively in the difficulties of non-native speakers and those who come from various kinds of minority or otherwise less privileged backgrounds. Indeed, much of our *routine* daily activity is devoted to propping up van Dijk's statement that 'Exclusion, marginalization and inferiorization have no place in a universal multicultural academia' (1994b: 276). The irony is, of course, that such efforts at preventing marginalization in others always tend to foster our own marginalization and those of the units within which we work, since the majoritarian culture will view them as more remedial than scholarly. They have also led to the charge (Benesch, 1993) that such efforts should best be construed as 'accommodationist' and the counter-charge that Benesch and others are 'ideologist' (Allison, 1994). We make this brief mention of our own complex engagement with academic institutional discourse (complex at least in the sense of conflicting levels of power and authority) simply to underline the fact that, in more cases than not, our own institutional discursive efforts are compromised and problematized by what they attempt and do not attempt to do. Why then, we asked ourselves, should we assume that another arena of institutional discourse (that of the corporation) should somehow be free of comparable dynamic tensions or competing values and be dismissed as 'Yet More Bad Corporate Statements' or whatever?

It is this question which leads us to the last of our concluding comments—those that deal with discourse and ideology. In our view, much has become clearer about this debate following Pennycook (1994). Pennycook's own preference is obvious enough from this short extract:

To think in terms of discourse in a Foucauldian sense is useful, I believe, because it allows us to understand how meaning is produced not at the will of a unitary humanist subject, not as a quality of a linguistic system, and not as determined by socio-economic relations, but rather through a range of power/knowledge systems that organize texts, create the conditions of possibility for different language acts, and are embedded in social institutions.

(1994: 128)

Indeed, we have deliberately tried to convey, in the previous paragraph, something of our own felt sense of that 'range of power/knowledge systems'. Pennycook contrasts this Foucauldian approach with 'the decontextualized contexts and political quietism of applied linguists and the often reductionist and deterministic frameworks of CDA' (p. 133) and concludes that 'even if these three views cannot be reconciled or merged, they can at least be mutually understood' (p. 134). We would, however, like to suggest that recent studies of genre, as outlined by Yates and Orlikowski at the beginning of this paper and as recently put forward by Devitt (1993), Schryer (1993), Bazerman (1994) and Berkenkotter and Huckin (1995), offer a dialogic middle way of thinking about social control and human agency, reproduction and innovation, coercion and resistance, model and instance, and linguistic form and institutional setting that promises more than a hint of that reconciliation Pennycook finds so elusive. Such studies carefully delineate those forces that, in the words of the opening epigraph, 'attempt to control change, either by causing it or preventing it'. But, of course, transforming this emerging consensus into a Mission Statement may still be some way off...

Acknowledgements

We would like to thank the University of Michigan Business School for underwriting the site-visit costs of this project. We are also particularly grateful to Borge Reimer, Executive Vice President of Dana, and Karen Bachman, Vice President for Communications at Honeywell, for their time and patience, even though neither, we suspect, is likely to agree with all our conclusions.

References

Allison, D. (1994) 'Comments on Sarah Benesch's "ESL, Ideology and the Politics of Pragmatism"', *TESOL Quarterly* 28: 618–23.
Bakhtin, M. M. (1986) *Speech Genres and Other Late Essays*. Austin: University of Texas Press.
Bass, B. M. (1981) *Stodgill's Handbook of Leadership*. New York: Macmillan.

Bazerman, C. (1992) 'The Generic Performance of Ownership: The Patent Claim and Grant'. Paper presented at the 'Re-thinking Genre' Seminar, Carleton University, Ottawa, April.

Bazerman, C. (1994) *Constructing Experience*. Carbondale: Southern Illinois University Press.

Benesch, S. (1993) 'ESL, Ideology and the Politics of Pragmatism', *TESOL Quarterly* 27: 705–17.

Berenbeim, R. E. (1987) *Corporate Ethics*. New York: The Conference Board, Research Report No. 900.

Berkenkotter, C. and Huckin, T. (1995) *Genre Knowledge in Disciplinary Communication: Cognition/Culture/Power*. Hillsdale, NJ: Erlbaum.

Brown, R. L. and Herndl, C. G. (1986) 'An Ethnographic Study of Corporate Writing: Job Status as Reflected in Written Text', in B. Couture (ed.) *Functional Approaches to Writing—Research Perspectives*, pp. 13–28. Norwood, NJ: Ablex.

Cheney, G. (1983) 'The Rhetoric of Identification and the Study of Organizational Communication', *Quarterly Journal of Speech* 69: 143–58.

Chin, E. (1994) 'Redefining "Context" in Research on Writing', *Written Communication* 11: 445–82.

Cressey, D. R. and Moore, C. A. (1983) 'Managerial Values and Corporate Codes of Ethics', *California Management Review* 25: 53–77.

Cross, G. A. (1994) 'Ethnographic Research in Business and Technical Writing', *Journal of Business and Technical Communication* 8: 118–34.

Czarniawska-Joerges, B. and Joerges, B. (1988) 'How to Control Things with Words: Organizational Talk and Control', *Management Communication Quarterly* 2: 170–93.

de Beaugrande, R. (1993) 'Discourse Analysis and Literary Theory: Closing the Gap', *Journal of Advanced Composition* 13: 423–48.

Devitt, A. (1993) 'Generalizing about Genre: New Conceptions of an Old Concept', *College Composition and Communication* 44: 573–86.

Doheny-Farina, S. (1986) 'Writing in an Emerging Organization', *Written Communication* 3: 158–85.

Dutton, J. E. and Duncan, R. B. (1987a) 'The Creation of Momentum for Change through the Process of Strategic Issue Diagnosis', *Strategic Management Journal* 8: 279–95.

Dutton, J. E. and Duncan, R. B. (1987b) 'The Influence of the Strategic Planning Process on Strategic Change', *Strategic Management Journal* 8: 103–16.

Eccles, R. and Nohria, N. with Berkley, J. D. (1992) *Beyond the Hype: Rediscovering the Essence of Management*. Boston, MA: Harvard Business School Press.

Fairclough, N. (1992) 'Discourse and Text: Linguistic and Textual Analysis within Discourse Analysis', *Discourse & Society* 3: 193–218.

Fairhurst, G. T. (1993) 'Echoes of the Vision: When the Rest of the Organization Talks Total Quality', *Management Communication Quarterly* 6: 331–71.

Galbraith, J. K. (1985) *The New Industrial State*. 4th edn. Boston, MA: Houghton Mifflin.

Giddens, A. (1979) *The Constitution of Society: Outlines of the Theory of Structuration*. Cambridge: Polity Press.

Goia, D. A. and Chittipeddi, K. (1991) 'Sensemaking and Sensegiving in Strategic Change Initiation', *Strategic Management Journal* 12: 433–48.

Halliday, M. A. K. (1985) *An Introduction to Functional Grammar*. London: Edward Arnold.

Hanna, M. S. and Wilson, G. L. (1984) *Communicating in Business and Professional Settings*. New York: Random House.

Judson, A. S. (1991) *Changing Behavior in Organizations: Minimizing Resistance to Change*. Cambridge, MA: Blackwell.

Kanter, R. M. (1991) 'Championing Change: An Interview with Bell Atlantic CEO Raymond Smith', *Harvard Business Review* January–February: 118–30.

Kissler, G. D. (1991) *The Change Riders: Managing the Power of Change*. Reading, MA: Addison-Wesley.

Knorr-Cetina, K. D. (1981) *The Manufacture of Knowledge*. Oxford: Pergamon.

Kress, G. (1985) 'Socio-linguistic Development and the Mature Language User: Different Voices for Different Occasions', in G. Wells and J. Nichols (eds) *Language and Learning: An Interactional Perspective*, pp. 135–9. London: Falmer Press.

Langelar, G. H. (1992) 'The Vision Trap', *Harvard Business Review* March–April: 46–55.

Latour, B. and Woolgar, S. (1979) *Laboratory life: The Social Construction of Scientific Facts*. Beverly Hills, CA: Sage.

Lengel, R. H. and Daft, R. L. (1988) 'The Selection of Communicative Media as an Executive Skill', *The Academy of Management Executive* 2: 225–32.

Levering, R., Moskowitz, M. and Katz, M., eds (1985) *The 100 Best Companies to Work for in America*. New York: New American Library.

Limerick, P. M. (1993) 'Dancing with Professors: The Trouble with Academic Prose', *New York Times Book Review* 31 October.

Martin, J. R. (1985) 'Process and Text: Two Aspects of Human Semiosis', in J. D. Benson and W. S. Greaves (eds) *Systemic Perspectives on Discourse*, pp. 248–74. Norwood, NJ: Ablex.

Martin, J. R. (1993) 'Genre and Literacy: Modeling Context in Educational Linguistics', *Annual Review of Applied Linguistics* XIII: 141–72.

Paradis, J., Dobrin, D. and Miller, R. (1985) 'Writing at EXXON ITD: Notes on the Writing Environment of an R & D Organization', in L. Odell and D. Goswami (eds) *Writing in Nonacademic Settings*, pp. 281–307. New York: Guilford Press.

Pennycook, A. (1994) 'Incommensurable Discourses?', *Applied Linguistics* 15: 115–38.

Peters, T. J. and Waterman, R. H. (1984) *In Search of Excellence: Lessons from America's Best-run Companies*. New York: Warner Books.

Pitt, H. L. and Groskaufmanis, K. A. (1990) 'Minimizing Corporate Civil and Criminal Liability: A Second Look at Corporate Codes of Conduct', *The Georgetown Law Journal* 78: 1559–654.

Rogers, P. S. and Swales, J. M. (1990) 'We the People? An Analysis of the Dana Corporation Policies Document', *Jnl of Business Communication* 27: 293–313.

Rounds, P. L. (1987) 'Multifunctional Personal Pronoun Use in an Educational Setting', *English for Specific Purposes* 6: 13–29.

Schryer, C. F. (1993) 'Records as Genre', *Written Communication* 10: 200–34.

Swales, J. M. (1990) *Genre Analysis: English in Academic and Research Settings*. Cambridge: Cambridge University Press.

Swales, J. M. (1993) 'Genre and Engagement', *Revue Belge de Philologie et d'Histoire* 73: 687–98.

Tichy, N. M. and Devanna, M. A. (1986) 'The Transformational Leader', *Training and Development Journal* 40: 27–32.

Tyler, L. (1992) 'Ecological Disaster and Rhetorical Response: Exxon's Communications in the Wake of the *Valdez* Spill', *Journal of Business and Technical Communication* 6: 149–71.

Van Dijk, T. A. (1994a) 'Editorial: The Discourses of "Bosnia"', *Discourse & Society* 5: 5–6.

Van Dijk, T. A. (1994b) 'Editorial: Academic Nationalism', *Discourse & Society* 5: 275–6.

Van Dijk, T. A. and Kintsch, W. (1983) *Strategies of Discourse Comprehension*. New York: Academic Press.

Walter, O. M. (1996) *Speaking to Inform and Persuade*. New York: MacMillan.

Weick, K. (1985) 'Sources of Order in Underorganized Systems: Themes in Recent Organizational Theory', in Y. S. Lincoln, (ed.) *Organizational Theory and Inquiry*, pp. 106–36. Beverly Hills, CA: Sage.

Witte, S. (1992) 'Context, Text and Intertext: Toward a Constructionist Semiotic of Writing', *Written Communication* 9: 237–308.

Yates, J. and Orlikowski, W. J. (1992) 'Genres of Organizational Communication: A Structurational Approach to Studying Communication and Media', *Academy of Management Review* 17: 299–326.

74

PRODUCTS, BRANDS, AND SIGNS

Greg Myers

Source: Greg Myers, *Ad Worlds: Brands, Media, Audience*, London: Arnold, 1999, pp. 17–34.

- A television commercial begins with a scene of a woman in evening dress walking across a polished floor against a Parisian background, with saxophone music, and sitting at her make-up table, applying cream and talking in a soft, husky voice. It seems to be for cosmetics, but it turns out to be for Boddington's bitter.
- A commercial shows documentary-style video footage of a woman stopping to help another woman who is having a dizzy spell – it looks like the ads for charities or Special Constabulary urging us to be Good Samaritans. Only in the last seconds do we see that what has induced the dizziness is her shock at seeing a poster for a Volkswagen Polo at £7990.
- A poster headline says '17-year-olds wanted to serve fast food.' The picture shows relief workers handing out supplies to starving people. In the lower right it says ARMY.
- A bus poster in Seattle shows the masthead of the *Seattle Times* in black and white. Below it, in white on red, the text says 'Great Paper. Lousy Blanket. Give *real* help. Call (206) 722-HOME. Union Gospel Mission.'

Each of these ads depends on our associating a certain visual style and kind of claim with certain categories of products; they can then reverse expectations, make us reflect, and also emphasize something about the product, job, or service actually being advertised (the bitter is creamy, the car is surprisingly inexpensive, the army does humanitarian work, the mission offers an alternative to sleeping rough). These ads depend on our being surrounded by advertising and knowing something about typical ads for cosmetics, charities, job vacancies, and newspapers. I will discuss that knowingness further in Chapter 12.

But why is it funny to sell beer like face cream (or ice-cream or sun cream)? The question is especially important because many analyses of ads focus on just a few categories of products, and apply conclusions drawn from them to advertising in general. In this chapter I want to consider how the product shapes the ad and how the ad shapes the product. First I will consider four factors that marketing textbooks tell us must be considered in selling a brand. But my approach deals with the wider meanings of brands, so I discuss four more factors that constrain the way a brand is reproduced in culture. Then I consider in detail the strategies used in a series of award-winning ads for Levi's jeans, and in a series for Daz detergent, to show how different the strategies, and their realizations in ads, can be.

Products and brands

One of the themes of this book is that brands associate meanings with products. The study of how meanings are associated is a major part of marketing, as branding. It is also a major tradition of academic study, as semiotics, the study of signs. Both marketing and semiotics have been taken up by wider fields, as branding and consumption enter into new areas of our lives; they are no longer of merely specialized interest. Branding, whether of soap or university courses, may seem a simple enough process. An advertiser pays to reproduce their trademark, and associate meanings with it, such as the universality of 'Coke', the genuineness of Levi's, the manliness of Marlboro (see BRAND). Critics point out that these meanings are entirely constructed; Leslie Savan (1994) reminds us that Marlboro was first marketed as a women's cigarette.

The earliest ads just sought to attract attention to the name by repeating it or associating it with some striking visual image: an inflated man made out of tyres for Michelin; the smiling face of a man in an eighteenth-century hat for Quaker Oats; an arm bearing a hammer for Arm & Hammer Baking Soda. These images were chosen to be distinctive and recognizable, not necessarily to evoke the right associations with the brand. Later, as various product areas matured, and a few brands dominated the market, and brands were seen as more and more alike, ads began to use associations with a life the consumer might desire. These associated meanings have become increasingly complex and subtle, and have been translated into the new media of radio, television, and the Internet, but the basic process of associating meanings with brands remains the same. It is a process that is particularly interesting to discourse analysts, because it links particular texts – the ads – to larger systems of meanings, such as what it means to be young (Pepsi), or healthy (BUPA), or a good parent (AT&T), or a Briton (Brooke Bond Tea).

Semiotics is the academic discipline that deals with the ways signs (such as ads, poems, shoes, or cars) take on meanings. In fact, semioticians from Roland Barthes (1977) to Thomas Sebeok (1991) to Gunther Kress and Theo van Leeuwen (1996) have always been particularly interested in ads as examples (and have produced strikingly original readings), because ads use very simple means to convey very complex meanings. However critical these readings are of advertising (and Kress (1987) is critical), I cannot avoid a sneaking admiration for the way that ads achieve some remarkable links, so that the Explorer car stands for the natural environment, Tampax stands for freedom, Häagen-Dazs for sensuality, the Body Shop for political activity, or the Army for humanitarian aid. It may seem that with enough advertising, a product can take on any meaning. This is a common fallacy of both critics and proponents of ads. But these meanings are not infinitely flexible; they have to rely on the way the brand is used, and how it relates to other brands. All the meanings shift when a new sign is introduced or new links are made. To think about those systems, it helps to go back to basic marketing.

The Four Ps

Many introductory marketing courses start with 'the Four Ps' of Product, Placement, Promotion, and Price (Kotler 1983). There are of course other, much more complex models of marketing strategies, but the Four Ps serve to emphasize that marketing is not just a matter of spending more on advertising (included under Promotion) or cutting the price. They are a useful starting point because they lay out factors over which the marketer, for any given product, has some control. Let us think, for example, of a bag of crisps (potato chips, for US readers), and to be very specific, let us say they are Walker's Salt and Vinegar flavour crisps.

Product

It is crucial to have the right thing on offer, and for our example of crisps that means not only ingredients (whole potatoes or reconstituted flakes), processing (what kinds of oils or salt), flavours and cuts, but also the packaging (big bags or small, foil wrapped or plastic), and the presentation (Are most sales in multi-packs or single bags? Can the box turn into a dispenser in pubs?). In what way, however trivial, can the product itself be distinctive? Traditional copywriters were proud of knowing how beans are baked, how beer is bottled, how cars are inspected, or how grains are puffed (see Hopkins 1927/1966; Mayer 1961; Higgins 1965). Advertising may try to make a silk purse out of a sow's ear, but marketers still have to think about the selection of sows and the packaging of ears.

Placement

It is crucial to have the product right there when the consumer wants it. Since crisps are snack foods, so their placement is not just a matter of competitive shelf space for multi-packs at supermarkets, but also displays in newsagents, or at petrol stations, or in vending machines at swimming pools. 'Within an arm's reach of desire' was the goal set for 'Coca-Cola' (Prendergast 1994), and though Walker's hasn't gone that far, they seem to be everywhere. But there may be reasons why a marketer wouldn't want a brand to be sold in some outlets; one might want to keep the image of one's brand as a special treat. We will find in many of the examples in this book that the advertising only makes sense in relation to the distribution network. The Co-operative Bank (Chapter 3) can occupy a market niche without an extensive branch system because of the development of cash machines (ATMs). The expansion of Häagen-Dazs as a premium brand (Chapter 5) required provision of freezer cases to dealers. Benetton (Chapter 11) relies on a chain of franchised retailers, so it has more (though not unlimited) latitude to offend.

Promotion

People have to know about the brand. But there are many ways of promoting a brand besides advertising. The Walker's crisps we have in the house now (not bought for my consumption, I hasten to add) have a Spice Girls tie-in and a chance to win a prize (usually another bag of crisps). The same brand also got lots of publicity with its tie-in with the football player Gary Lineker, and even from complaints about one of the ads (for showing a child talking to a stranger, even if the stranger was Gary Lineker), and went so far as to rename the brand, temporarily, 'Salt 'n' Lineker'. Many of the other brands discussed in this book rely on other forms of promotion, so the Co-operative Bank has various forms of sponsorship to stress its role in the community, and Peugeot 406 has a range of special offers from dealers.

Price

People have to be willing to pay just the amount it says on the packet. Of course lowering prices might increase sales, but it is not always the case that the lowest price is most effective. One of the desired results of branding has always been that people will pay a good price for the branded item, not just the lowest price possible, because of the meanings, the added value, associated with it. Premium crisps are deliberately priced much higher than mass market crisps, to signal higher quality, and it is because of this premium that one can take them, say, to a party as a treat. Pricing was a key issue in a number of the campaigns I discuss; Daz stresses that its price is not much higher than that of store's own brands, while Häagen-Dazs, for instance, starts with the idea of a premium price being part of what identifies it as a high quality product for adults.

Four more Ps

For marketers, the Four Ps are a useful introductory survey of variables; for us as analysts of ads they can serve as a reminder of all the factors involved in marketing besides advertising. What they do not suggest is the way a brand is already constrained by the meanings around it; the marketing strategists are not free to shape the meanings as they might wish (see Schultz 1990 for a treatment of 'Four Cs' from a marketing point of view). To suggest these constraints, I can suggest four other Ps one might derive from cultural studies (and unlike the first list these are just my own list, not a formula memorized by thousands of marketing students), moving from immediate associations with the brand, to its relations with other brands, with consumers, and with the wider system of popular culture.

Past

Brands come with what marketers call 'heritage' and what semioticians might call associative or connotative meanings (Myers 1994). So, for instance, when sales of Adidas shoes were lagging behind those of Nike and Reebok, the UK agency Leagas Delaney knew it still had a powerful starting point in the heritage of the brand. As far as I know, the crisp market doesn't have its classic brands such as Adidas, BMW, Rolex, or Heinz beans, but there are long associations with Lay's in the US or Walker's in the UK. New premium brands like Brick Oven or Phileas Fogg try to project a ready-made heritage, evoking traditional methods and packaging, or a fictional founder. Some companies try cross-branding, carrying the associations of a brand across to a new sector, as Caterpillar has done from heavy construction equipment to clothing, or as Virgin has done from records to air travel to cola and vodka to financial services and now passenger railways. Cross-branding can backfire, as when one is served warm Virgin cola on a delayed Virgin train, and begins to wonder about the airline.

Position

Brands are placed in a competitive position in relation to each other. Walker's crisps must compete, not only with other salt and vinegar crisps, but with other possible snack foods. Being the market leader has its advantages, but many brands (Virgin Air, Motel 6, Co-operative Bank, Holsten Pils lager, Rent-A-Wreck car rental) have built their brands on the basis of not being the market leader, of having instead their own distinctive niche. In a wider sense, the brand is positioned in relation to other brands, most obviously in the car market, but also in soft drinks, beers, or shoes. Some of the most successful advertising campaigns in history owe their success, not to the texts of the ads themselves, but to a carefully planned repositioning. But again the scope for repositioning is not endless. When the agency head who had just won the new Kia car account said that it would be the Volkswagen beetle for the 1990s, he was greeted with guffaws from other agencies. One problem faced by Nike (says the creative director who has the account of a rival brand) is that the ubiquity of the name and the swoosh make it hard to continue to market them in terms of rebellious-ness and street cred (*Campaign* 5/3/98).

Practices

Brands are at the mercy of what people do with the product (see CONSUMPTION). People eat crisps as an indulgence that breaks a diet, or as minimal nourishment in pubs, or as sustenance for an all-night session of work, or as a treat in a child's lunch box (or they rattle them in the cinema, which drives me crazy). Or they stop eating them because they are associ-ated with fat, or sodium, or kids. When a politician can call a critic of the Royal Opera House a 'crisp eater', then there must be some practices that are assumed to go with crisps and don't go with opera. Some brands can shift the practices with which they are associated, as Levi's jeans or Doc Marten boots went from work clothing to fashionable styles, or as Starbuck's coffee moves from a small coffee-house across from the Pike Place Market in Seattle to a national chain of counters found in airports, or as mineral water becomes a style drink rather than a health drink, or as wine replaces spirits at parties, or as personal computers shift from the business market to the home market. Marketers rely on research to inform them of these shifts, so they can counter them or take advantage of them, but one still has a sense that the marketer is not entirely in control of these meanings.

Paradigms

Semioticians tell us that a change in one part of a network of meanings affects the other elements. I have used the much abused term *paradigm* to remind us of the underlying, taken for granted set of relations. Consider the crisps that come unsalted, with a little blue packet of salt to shake on oneself. The ads for these crisps present this packaging as a matter of herit-age, tracing it back to the first, unpackaged crisps in pubs with salt available in twisted paper. (A colleague says the blue packet reminds her of the way the salt always clogged in the damp British homes of the 1960s – a form of nostalgia not yet exploited by the crisp manufacturers.) But the blue packet also relates to a wider sense that additives can be bad as well as good, that having no added salt, or no added sugar, or no colourings, or being lead-free or CFC-free or phosphate-free, are further benefits of the product. The removal of CFCs from aerosol sprays affected the consumers of those sprays, but also introduced a kind of phrasing into the language, and a way of thinking that has affected hundreds of other products. The word paradigm can serve for the very broad cultural frameworks that some theorists might call 'orders of discourse' (Fairclough 1992): examples would be ideas about body shape and health, digitization of information, cloning of identical copies, or citizenship (see DISCOURSE). Changes in signs can ripple through the system in unexpected ways. In the 1950s, the 'Radiation' electric cooker signalled modernity and magical ease, but I doubt that the brand name 'Radiation' would have such favourable associations for any product today.

These further four Ps of Past, Position, Practices, and Paradigm are meant to stimulate our thinking, not as marketing strategists, but as analysts of ads. In particular, they focus our attention on wider changes that may affect the meanings of brands as signs. To show these facts at work, we can consider some of the strategies involved in two series of ads, for Levi's jeans and Daz detergent.

Constructing heritage: Levi's 501 jeans

You might think the advertising agency with the Levi's account had an easy job. After all, though the company had a rather disappointing year for profits last year, there remains a huge demand for jeans around the world. In the US they are still reasonably priced as the basic, non-designer jeans; in the rest of the world they carry a price premium and instant recognition. They also carry all sorts of associations with youth, Americanness, and rebellion. But it is just this status as an institution that makes them something of a challenge to advertise. At the moment their market share is being eroded by designer labels and budget-priced own labels. In terms of the Four Ps, Levi's are considering the product (should they market more or fewer cuts?), the promotion (but ordinary advertising or promotions might actually undermine these core meanings of the brand), and the placement (but wider distribution might have its dangers, so, for instance, Levi's has tried to keep them from being sold in truck stops in the US and Tesco supermarkets in the UK). Cuts in price might not be a possibility, since that would run the risk of their being seen as a cheap alternative.

The brief given to the agency that has the account in the UK, Bartle Bogle Hegarty, was that they get across the idea that Levi's were the original but still contemporary jeans. They had to somehow set them apart from the increasingly fierce competition, and show that design features had a tradition behind them, while the style could change subtly. They have done this in a series of ads since 1986, many of which have won awards in the industry and many of which have been discussed by journalists and academics (Corner 1995). If we look back over five of these ads, from a series of more than 30, we can see the outlines of the campaign underlying the particulars of each ad.

Table 1 is a rigidly schematic representation of some witty and carefully crafted ads, but it is enough to bring out my point, that while they are strikingly different visually, they keep the same structure and strategy.

- All establish a period and a place, typically America in a not too clearly defined past.
- All draw on lighting, colour, clothing, and especially music to establish a style in the first few seconds.
- All tell a story that involves excitement, voyeurism, and surprise.
- None of them suggests the product advertised until the end.
- All end with a product claim focusing on an apparently trivial feature of the product.
- The logo comes with an assurance of the genuineness of the product.

Now let's look in more detail at how these features work within a strategy.

Textual analysis

The most basic level of this analysis is to look at the signs themselves, the physical form in which you get the message. The signs could be spoken words, or written words, or pictures, sounds, music. With this series, there are no spoken words; it is the music that people remember. It can mark a shift in mood, as with 'Creek', where it is part of the building of tension. The ad opens with a long chord. What is the effect? There is a sense of tension, of expectation. The change in style in the middle marks the shift in structure and mood. Similarly, you may take the rock music as indicating sexual excitement, the choral music as indicating purity. But the association of verbal meanings with music is notoriously variable.

Similarly, the choices in the visual style can have a number of functions. 'Creek' is black and white, while most ads and all programmes are in colour. This choice can be used to link the film to an artistic style (here the nature photography of Ansel Adams, or artistic portraits in the press ads for The Gap), or to suggest a kind of stylized plainness (as in the Co-operative Bank ad in Chapter 3), or to suggest documentary style (as in Peugeot 406 in Chapter 4). In any case, we notice it and try to interpret it because it is different from what we expect.

There are no spoken words in these ads – that in itself is a striking deviation from conventional ads, which nearly always have an off-screen or onscreen voice telling you how to interpret the images. Here you are left with the feeling that you are interpreting them yourselves. Another kind of sign is, of course, the written words. They are simple, as in 'Creek':

Table 1 Structure of UK Levi's ads (agency: Bartle Bogle Hegarty).

	Belt Loops	Creek	Fall	Washroom	Escape
Setting	California, 1921	Nineteenth-century Yosemite Valley	American West during WW II	contemporary US city	US South 1950s
Look	sepia colour, missing frames like silent films, projector sound (Little Rascals)	black and white, (Ansel Adams)	aged colour, 1940s film angles (Nicholas Ray)	film noir lighting (Pulp Fiction)	black and white, frantic editing (The Defiant Ones)
Sound	tinkling piano	choral/heavy metal	movie music		metal music
Characters	football players and flappers	Amish family, pioneer hunk, pioneer old fart	oil rig hunk, nurse, doctor and nurse	woman as black/white young black man/old black man	two convicts/ pursuers and dogs
Begins	football players watched by women and boy	girls watch swimmer and take jeans	man falls from oil rig and is taken to hospital	car screeches into gas station and woman runs into men's room	guards chase two escapees
Change	dog pulls off braces and jeans fall	hunk emerges from water	nurse unbuttons jeans rather than cut them	woman sees man sitting with white cane and buttons her fly in front of his face	one escapee just misses jumping onto a railway car
End	woman laughs, man looks sheepish	jeans belong to another swimmer	another nurse observes her and brings doctor	an older man emerges from the stall and the younger man leads him out	the other pulls him on by his jeans
Text	IN 1922 LEVI'S FINALLY INTRODUCED BELT LOOPS Levi's 501. The Original Jean	IN 1873 JEANS ONLY CAME SHRINK-TO-FIT Levi's 501. The Original Jean	1943. LEVI'S WERE IN SHORT SUPPLY Levi's 501. The Original Jean	ORIGINAL BUTTON FLY FOR WOMEN Levi's 501. The Original Jean	RIVETED TOGETHER FOR EXTRA STRENGTH Levi's 501. The Original Jean

IN 1873 LEVI'S JEANS ONLY CAME SHRINK-TO-FIT. LEVI'S 501. THE ORIGINAL JEAN.

How do we interpret 'The original jean'? For one thing, we are used to having 'jeans' in the plural. Also, the world 'Levi's is written in the form of the logo. But otherwise it is not itself a striking slogan. There must be something else going one, at another level.

We have seen that the ads have the same basic story, in which we have no idea at the beginning what the ad is for. We get caught up in teasing revelations, and then there is the surprise in which we see, first, what the images meant, and then, second, apply them to the product. Each ad has some new elements of structure; in 'Creek' there is the tension of parents and the daughters, the contrast of the two young women, the contrast of the two men, the contrast of the sensual pool and the cool, pure mountains. But it is the same basic plot. Within this story there is also a visual structure. At the beginning and end are wide shots of the mountains. Then there are medium shots of the family group. There is a black-out, and then the sequence in which the girls watch the bather. Here the shots come much faster, editing together extreme close-ups of eyes and lips with sensual images of his body. His rising body is paralleled by their pulling the jeans over their mouths. But instead of a pornographic climax, there is the joke of the appearance of the man's wet jeans.

The ads, then, establish a stylized past, and position us as voyeurs, before a final joke emphasizing a product claim. Let's see how this structure relates to the kinds of issues I have raised in branding: the use of the Past, the Position in relation to other brands, the Practices associated with it, and the shifting Paradigms of meaning systems.

Past

The key problem for Levi's is to keep the sense of their being genuine American work clothes, while opening them to contemporary associations. John Hegarty explained that with the first in the series, 'Launderette', he wanted a general sense of a mythical America. But America and Americanization can carry all sorts of negative meanings around the world (as I am only too aware). Here is Hegarty's comment:

> I thought it would be more interesting to do the ad with a period look. The 1950s idea wasn't in the brief. It just happened, and out of that we established a mythical period for Levi's. *Grapevine*, the music that backed the ad, was a 60s not a 50s song – it came to me simultaneously and there was no real logic to it. The aim was to portray the US without the US being boring – a US no-one could object to.
>
> (*Campaign* 20/9/96)

Almost all the later ads were set in this mythical period America, with elements of anachronism. The music may not be from the same period as the pictures, but they work together to suggest a sort of pastness. This past overlaps with a sense of the past as youthfulness. It is suggested by such devices as jerky film, suggesting the older film with fewer frames per second, or with colours reminiscent of those from now faded technicolor, or with references to styles of photographers or film-makers (see Table 2.1).

Position

Up to the last 5 seconds of these ads, many first time watchers are probably puzzled about just what is being advertised ('Washroom' is a particularly good example). But the ads are not at all unrelated to the product, the ways some clever ads seem to be. Levi's can't afford this – it is in a ferociously competitive market where the competitors make clever ads too. In a sense, the whole ad is a product demonstration of just how good the jeans can look, or rather, just how good the body can look that is under the jeans. Only in the last seconds is the erotic tease transferred to Levi's. Given the success of these ads, other brands have tried similar erotic stories. But in doing so they only reinforce the associations with Levi's. A contrasting approach is taken by the cinema ads for Wrangler jeans, which show awkward, home-video-style interviews with real rodeo cowboys, talking about what they go through in the ring. Levi's themselves, in the current commercials for white tab jeans (also from Bartle Bogle Hegarty), has a zany, Monkees-like 1960s film, that maintains the sense of Americanness and heritage without interfering with the 501 branding.

Practices

Where does one wear Levi's? When I was in college, Levi's were student clothes, manual work clothes, counter-culture. Some time after that, and after I stopped wearing them, they entered into other settings. They were able to draw on these associations with counterculture and informality, and yet be accepted as clothes for older people in more formal situations – such as President Clinton. The company tried to adapt to this shift, recognizing that middle-aged men and women, such as most university lecturers, are different shapes from university students (as you will have noticed). So they sold jeans with different cuts, and developed ads aimed at this market, and developed a new brand, Dockers (UK posters for Dockers showed tough middle-aged men in mock news photos, but the TV ads for Dockers feature the same young bodies as in 501 ads). The original Levi's 501s remained undeniably hip, but part of the appeal was that one could do things to personalize them – shrink to fit, cut, patch, bleach, dye. Some jeans have tried to keep up with these alterations, selling jeans already prewashed. But it is in the nature of such alterations that they cannot be entirely brought within the marketing plan. People are making the uniform commodities their own.

Paradigms

These shifts in the uses of jeans go on against larger shifts in meanings. What it means to be American has changed radically throughout the last 50 years, from GIs to the Beats to Vietnam to the Gulf to Friends; that is why John Hegarty is so careful to set his ads in a mythical, timeless America. Notions of the erotic change too; the transvestite in the ad 'Taxi' and the race-changing woman in 'Washroom' mark current fascinations with boundary crossing. Associations with manual work change as most people are employed in services, The uses of tradition have, if anything, expanded in this period of rapid change; paradoxically, Levi's turns to travellers, drifters, and fugitives for its emblems of rootedness. This is not the place to trace the workings of detraditionalization (see Lash and Dillon 1997); my point is just to stress that this timelessness is the product of a particular place and time.

Constructing ordinariness: Daz Automatic Powder

Levi's ads win awards, more than any other UK campaign over the last dozen years. Just a few categories of products and services account for most of the ads that win awards, get journalist comments, and are analysed in books like this one: clothes, cards, athletic shoes, cosmetics, charities, tobacco, and beer would be examples. I realized how little these categories represented ads in general when I watched all the ads from several 24-hour periods of television. I don't recommend you try this experience unless you are writing a book about ads; most ads make dull, repetitive product claims, with the simplest of appeals, usually for frequently purchased household products. (I developed a particular horror of a fabric conditioner ad; its monotonous repetition made me think of its namesake in Poe's poem 'The Raven': 'Nevermore'.) The producers of these ads might argue that the difference between their ads and the award-winners is not in the quality of advertising, but in the kind of appeal one can make in this product category. Would a shopper choose a bottle of fabric conditioner from the many on the shelf just because of a witty, ironic, self-mocking image of a brand like Levi's?

Let's take an ad for the category of products known to marketers as 'fast moving consumer goods', one from a series I have mentioned already, in which the comedian Danny Baker approaches 'real people' on their door-steps or in a shopping mall and asks them about Daz. Daz is a Procter & Gamble product, and in marketing that means something. It means that the brand manager has a very clear strategy for its place in the market, and keeps the ad agency on a very short lead – the agency has to pass a series of tests, and keep to a very restricted range, and is then rewarded with a loyal and highly consistent client. That is why a Procter & Gamble account is considered such a good training ground for other areas of marketing, even though it is unlikely to win any awards for the advertisers.

This particular Daz ad was repeated many times during one of the 24-hour periods I recorded. It could be argued that all it does is repeat the name, like one of those 19th century newspaper ads that filled the whole column with the brand name of a medicine. But I think more is going on, in the way it uses the interaction between Baker and the ordinary people. The ad focuses, not on the results in washing (as does a typical Persil ad) but on the moment of passing through the check-out.

DAZ AUTOMATIC POWDER
(AGENCY: LEO BURNETT)

DB = Danny Baker   OP = Ordinary Person

actions	words	
[supermarket checkout]	DB	You know Daz is good on whites But did you know how good it is on price? Even compared to some shops' own brands.
[puts package through barcode scanner]	DB	We asked people how *they* thought Daz compared.
	OP1	I'd expect Daz to be a lot more expensive.
	OP2	The Daz would be dearer.
	OP3	A lot dearer.
[to checker]	DB	So what is the difference in price Pat? Only 10 pence in some stores.
	OP1	Is that all. 10p.
	OP4	10p.
	OP5	That's a lot cheaper than I thought.
	OP6	10p. You're kidding. I wouldn't have thought it'd be that cheap, honestly.
[tosses coin*]	DB	Check it yourself against shops' own brands. Daz whites cost less* than you think.
Reproduced with permission of Procter & Gamble.		

Textual analysis

How does this ad connect to consumers? It doesn't use the period setting, sexual plots, fancy editing, or catchy music of the Levi's ads. The emphasis is overwhelmingly on the words, and on the way Danny Baker interacts with a range of people.

1. First, it starts with *you*, the pronoun of direct address, the oldest trick in the copywriters' handbook. Instead of telling you Daz is good on whites, it tells you that you already know this. The brand name is used as an adjective ('Daz whites') as if we were familiar with this term of approbation.

2. Then the ad opens with the second oldest trick in the copywriters' handbook – a question. This is to be answered, but only after consulting a version of popular opinion.

3. The strategy of the ad is to reproduce in the vox pop interviews a sense of the kind of talk with 'people' that might go on around a product, outside of ads. The stress on *they* implies, 'Don't trust us, see what *they* say.' This is the main device of the Daz series; they all show apparently ordinary people confronted by the show businessy and confident Danny Baker. How do we know they are ordinary? They are confronted in the shopping mall. They are with other people who look on. They wrestle kids. They don't use the range of intonation in the performer's voice. Most of the ad is spent getting them to seem like ordinary people.

4. Note how the comments are structured. First we start with longer statements, and then we get more and more elliptical comments added to it, as if they were all participating in the same discussion. The effect is to create a sort of universal consensus out of just three responses. Then DB offers the answer (with the rider 'in some stores'). Each of the respondents has to display disbelief: 'Is that all?', 'just', 'cheaper than I thought', 'You're kidding'. Here responses escalate in their incredulity. This is typical of how people state opinions in a conversation, but here the on-going conversation is assembled from several different interviews.

5. Finally DB confronts us, the viewers. Note the last challenge: 'Daz whites cost less . . . than you think.' This is a complex statement that attributes to us beliefs about Daz (it produces white clothes but costs more), then cancels the belief about price – they are not that expensive. (It need not be the case that viewers already do see Daz as expensive). The 10p piece is waved as a symbol of this difference. Then it is used to flip a coin – implying one can't choose between the two alternatives.

6. The name of the competition is 'concealed' with the video technique used to censor obscene pictures or disguise the identities of the guilty – it attracts attention to the competition box. Note that even in this price led ad, the competition is not based on price alone. Instead, Daz is asserted to be not too expensive for what it is, and it is assumed to be a better product.

So here is a different relation of text, brand, and consumer from that in the Levi's ads. The text is not evocatively poetic, but deliberately banal. The ad builds a brand, but it has to build it in a different way, by attributing sceptical responses to people (they would think it costs more) and placing them in a familiar setting, then triumphing over their scepticism. It is a simple but effective little story.

Past, Position, Practices, and Paradigm

The Daz ad might seem to be completely routine, but it shows the same sort of strategic thinking as the Levi's ads.

- Like Levi's, the brand is constrained by its Past: it treats 'Daz whites' as a category already established in people's minds. Brierley (1995) has an account of the kind of disaster that threatened another brand, Persil, when it tried to alter its formula, out of line with its heritage; it was the 'New Coke' story in a box.
- Daz is also constrained by its Position, not only in relation to Persil (from Unilever) and Ariel (also from Proctor & Gamble), but crucially in relation to stores' own brands. As I noted in discussing the ad for 'Coke', these are especially dangerous competition in Britain, where the stores are national, and can serve, in effect, as a powerful brand in themselves. (A much higher percentage of UK purchases are own brand (12 per cent), compared to those in the US (5 per cent).)
- What sorts of Practices are relevant here? Washing powder manu-facturers have to think about shifts to 'green' products, or changes in types of washing machines (it's Daz *Automatic*), or in fabrics (the development of non-iron materials and the need to wash them more gently), or patterns of shopping, and perhaps the rise of network selling (the way Amway sells through local distributors coming to the house).
- Finally, though it may seem odd to say so, this ad takes on a Paradigm, one described by Roland Barthes in his essay on 'Soap Powders and Detergents' (1954/1972); he analyses the system of myths underlying ads for laundry powders and liquids, including fighting dirt, cleaning deeply, purifying fire, luxurious foam, and comparative whiteness. (Whiteness remains a bench-mark even when most of the laundry load is made up of fast-coloured materials.)

These two examples, Levi's and Daz, suggest the constraints on market-ing strategists making products into brands. They also suggest that the constraints are different for different categories of products, whatever the strategies of the marketers. We can see that a fashionable item of cloth-ing like Levi's jeans will be different from a regularly purchased household product like Daz. What sorts of categories are useful to us in thinking about our analyses of ads?

Product categories

The marketing textbooks divide products into categories such as fast-moving consumer goods (fmcgs), white goods such as refrigerators and ovens, and business-to-business products. But the resulting categories follow the traditional divisions of retailing, so they are not general enough to be useful for our analyses of ads. I will draw on the kinds of issues raised in the marketing and advertising literature to suggest some questions as a starting point.

1. *How often does one buy it?* One makes a different sort of decision about fmcgs like Daz (a box every few weeks), from that about Levi's (regular users buy five pairs a year) or about tyres (a set every few years). On the one hand, goods bought frequently would seem to leave room for impulses. On the other hand, they may be matters of habit that are very hard to shift.

2. *Is it new?* Both products in this comparison are well established, and both ads draw on this prior knowledge. A new detergent (as when Radion was introduced in the late 1980s) demands a different, more disruptive advertising (Radion favoured simple, bright, bold layouts); so does a new brand of jeans (such as Guess in the UK) or a new category of casual clothes, such as Dockers. Establishing a new kind of product (for instance, 'green' washing powders) takes much more explanation, as does establishing a new need, such as water purification or computer file back-up. Often these new needs are explained by analogy to accepted needs, so computer utilities, smoke alarms, and credit card protection schemes can all be presented by analogy to household security.

3. *How much is it embedded in one's life?* Consumers tend not to change banks, sanitary protection products, phone companies, or underwear brands, either because they get used to the product or because it is too much hassle to change. At the other extreme, consumers of pain relievers are notoriously fickle (if one doesn't work, try another), and our cats seem to get bored with any flavour of cat food after just a few weeks. Marketers refer to a category of 'high-involvement' products like hi-fi sets, computers, or cars, to the purchase of which consumers give a lot of thought; these are products for which consumers might compare, do some research, ask around, and go some distance to get a good price or selection. At the other extreme would be crisps, which are always bought on impulse from a wide choice, and for which one's commitment lasts about 5 minutes.

4. *Is it visible and significant to others?* Levi's can be sold as an image product because they are part of one's display to the world; one's consumption of washing powder is usually private. In fact, most consumption would seem on the face of it to be private, to have no relation to one's social relations or aspirations. It is the brief of most advertising to convince us otherwise, for instance in ads that try (rather unconvincingly) to convince us that the choice of washing powder can have social consequences for ourselves or our children.

5. *How is it regulated?* Many puzzling features of ads can be traced to regulations; one example is the careful disclaimer that Daz is only about 10p more 'in some stores' (so you cannot complain if you find the difference more at your local store). The rather coy reference to the rival brand is a relic of earlier restrictions on comparative advertising. The sexually suggestive style of the Levi's ads could not be used in US or UK tobacco ads; some Levi's ads are approved only for use in cinemas before 12 or 15 certificate films, or after 9 p.m. on television. As we will see in Chapter 11, the regulations affect not only the obvious categories, such as tobacco and spirits ads, but also toys, pharmaceuticals, cereals making health claims, cars, and financial services.

Summary

The aim of this chapter has been to suggest how products may shape ads and ads may shape products. The key link is the process of branding, the attachment of meanings to labelled products. Two lists can serve as exploratory guides to thinking about how brands are marketed: the marketers 4Ps of Product, Place, Promotion, and Price remind us how much there is to marketing besides advertising, and the further 4Ps I suggested of Past, Position, Practices, and Paradigm, can guide us to ways a brand is constrained by a wider set of meanings in the culture.

I analysed two ads as examples: from Levi's and Daz. In both cases I took approaches that will be used in other analyses in this book:

• Look for similarities and differences across a range of texts.
• Relate choices in various modes: spoken words, writing, pictures, music, etc.
• Look for choices that go against expectations.
• Step back and consider the overall structure.
• Relate details to the overall effect (the transformations in the Levi's ads, the ordinary people in the Daz ad).

I used these ads as a basis for considering what factors might account for some of the differences between ads in different product categories. There may never be a clever, self-mocking, brilliantly shot ad for a toilet cleaner that will sweep Cannes, the British Television Advertising Awards, or the US Clios. But the problem is not a lack of imagination or talent among advertisers winning the toilet bowl cleaner accounts: the marketing manager and advertising team of the toilet bowl cleaner have had to work with a different set of constraints in making their product into a brand.

References

Barthes, R. 1972. *Mythologies* (Annette Lavers, Trans.). New York: Hill and Wang.

Barthes, R. 1977. The rhetoric of the image. In *Image – Music – Text* (pp. 32–51). London: Fontana.

Brierley, S. 1995. *The advertising handbook*. London: Routledge.

Corner, J. 1995. *Television form and public address*. London: Arnold.

Fairclough, N. 1992. *Discourse and social change*. Cambridge: Polity.

Higgins, D. 1965. *The art of writing advertising*. Lincolnwood, IL: NTC Books.

Hopkins, C. 1927/1966. *My life in advertising*, reprinted in *My life in advertising* and *Scientific advertising*. Lincolnwood, IL: NTC Books.

Kotler, P. 1983. *Marketing management* (6th edn.). Englewood Cliffs, NJ: Prentice-Hall.

Kress, G. 1987. Educating readers: language in advertising. In J. Hawthorn (ed.), *Propaganda, persuasion and polemic* (pp. 123–39). London: Arnold.

Kress, G., and van Leeuwen, T. 1996. *Reading images: the grammar of visual design*. London: Routledge.

Lash, S., and Dillon, G. M. 1997. *Detraditionalization*. London: Sage.

Mayer, M. 1961. *Madison Avenue: USA*. Harmondsworth: Penguin.

Myers, G. 1994. *Words in ads*. London: Arnold.

Prendergast, M. 1994. *For God, country, and Coca-Cola*. London: Pheonix.

Savan, L. 1994. *The sponsored life: ads, TV, and American culture*. Philadelphia: Temple University Press.

Schultz, D. 1990. *Strategic Advertising Campaigns* (3rd edn.). Lincolnwood, IL: NTC Books.

Sebeok, T. 1991. *A sign is just a sign*. Bloomington, IN: Indiana University Press.

75

TALK AS ENTERPRISE: COMMUNICATION AND CULTURE CHANGE AT WORK

Deborah Cameron

Source: Deborah Cameron, *Good to Talk? Living and Working in a Communication Culture*, London: Sage, 2000, pp. 53–90.

The softer words of leadership and vision and common purpose will replace the tougher words of control and authority because the tough words won't bite any more
> *– Charles Handy*, Beyond Certainty, 1996.

Every time a customer comes within ten feet of me, I will smile, look him in the eye and greet him. So help me Sam
> *– Oath sworn by new recruits to Wal-Mart*[1]

A smartly dressed young man walks up to a slightly younger woman. He asks: 'how are you feeling today?'. 'Fine', she replies. 'That's good', says the young man, 'but when I ask you how you're feeling I want you to say "*outstanding!*"'. As he utters the last word, his voice rises in pitch and volume; he punches the air with both hands. The young woman looks surprised – evidently she had assumed that 'how are you' was the opening move in an ordinary exchange of greetings – and then uncomfortable. She repeats 'outstanding', but without much enthusiasm. The young man is dissatisfied. He demonstrates what he wants again, emphasizing the air-punching gesture. Then he starts the routine from the beginning: 'how are you feeling today?'. This time she produces a better imitation of his 'outstanding', though her facial expression and a certain bodily stiffness betray her continuing discomfort. They go through the whole thing again. And again. Her performance passes muster. The young man smiles and moves on.

What is going on in this little scene? Is it some kind of political rally, or a religious revival meeting, or a session from one of those 'inspirational' courses about the power of positive thinking? Maybe the young woman is an athlete and the young man is her coach, psyching her up for an important event. Or maybe he is an entertainer, and she a member of the audience reluctantly dragged up on stage. In fact, the scene took place in a McDonald's restaurant at the beginning of a shift. The young man was the shift supervisor, and the young woman a member of his 'crew'. Their encounter was recorded for an Open University television programme about new management practices in British industry.[2] The programme also showed the young man on the receiving end of the same technique, which he learnt on a course at the company's training centre, 'Hamburger University'.

This motivational routine is not the only case in which McDonald's employees are instructed in how to talk. McDonald's is among the organizations that pioneered 'routinized' customer service interactions (Leidner, 1993). In this respect as in many others, McDonald's has attracted legions of imitators; George Ritzer, the author of a book whose self-explanatory title is *The McDonaldization of Society* (1996), suggests that 'pseudo-interaction' is a widespread and striking feature of present-day consumer culture. But why do employers find it necessary to regulate such small linguistic details as what words their employees utter, and in what tone of voice? How does this kind of regulatory practice square with the philosophy of 'empowerment', which is supposed to involve *less* control over the minutiae of employees' behaviour than the traditional model? And what about the employees themselves – how do they feel about being told what to say, and taught how to talk?

Talk at work

There is already an extensive literature on talk in professional or 'institutional' settings (see for instance Boden, 1994; Drew and Heritage, 1992; Drew and Sorjonen, 1997; Gunnarsson, Linell and Nordberg, 1997; Mumby and Clair, 1997; Wodak and Iedema, 1999). Some of the most notable contributions to this literature have been made by scholars in the research tradition of conversation analysis (CA). Before I proceed further, I should clarify the relationship of my own analysis of workplace 'communication' with this body of research; for although I hope I have learned from it, I do not see myself as directly contributing to it.

CA, which has roots in ethnomethodological sociology, regards talk as an important locus for the organization of social life generally. In institutional settings, as Paul Drew and John Heritage observe in their editors' introduction to the influential collection *Talk at Work*, 'Talk-in-interaction is the principal means through which lay persons pursue various practical goals and the central medium through which the daily working activities of many professionals and organizational representatives are conducted' (1992: 3). Studying institutional talk is thus a way of studying the workings of institutions themselves. In addition to this sociological significance, however, institutional talk is of interest more specifically to analysts of language and discourse. Because it is designed to accomplish particular goals, institutional talk has features that distinguish it from 'ordinary' talk. Drew and Heritage characterize them as follows (1992: 22):

1. Institutional interaction involves an orientation by at least one of the participants to some core goal, task or activity (or set of them) conventionally associated with the institution in question. In short, institutional talk is normally informed by *goal orientations* of a relatively restricted conventional form.
2. Institutional interaction may often involve *special and particular constraints* on what one or both of the participants will treat as allowable contributions to the business at hand.
3. Institutional talk may be associated with *inferential frameworks* and procedures that are particular to specific institutional contexts.

Later on, they identify five major 'foci of research into institutional talk' (1992: 28 *et seq.*). These are *lexical choice* – for example the selection of technical or lay vocabulary in institutional encounters; *turn design* – the way turn-taking rules may differ as between institutional and other talk; *sequential organization* – for example the tightly constrained use of question-answer sequences in institutional contexts such as clinics, classrooms and courtrooms; *overall structural organization* – the way many institutional interactions have a pre-determined 'shape'; and *social relations* – which are more apt to be asymmetrical in institutional contexts.

The framework set out by Drew and Heritage is useful, and many of my own observations in this and the next chapter will relate to one or more of their 'research foci'. However, I will be approaching the phenomenon of institutional talk at work from a different angle – one suggested by the McDonald's vignette with which I began this chapter. For a conversation analyst, the 'institutional' nature of talk is not something given in advance, but something accomplished by participants in the course of talking. Ian Hutchby summarizes this position succinctly: 'institutions do not define the kind of talk produced within them: rather participants' ways of designing their talk actually constructs the "institutionality" of such settings' (1999: 41). 'Interaction', say Drew and Heritage, 'is institutional insofar as participants' institutional or professional identities are somehow made relevant to the work activities in which they are engaged' (1992: 4). But without disputing that anything that goes on in talk has in the final analysis to be accomplished by the participants, I think there are cases where institutions (or to be more exact, people with certain kinds of authority in institutions) *do* define the kinds of talk produced within them to a greater extent than the CA formulation suggests. I am especially interested in professional identities and ways of talking that are not so much negotiated by participants 'on the ground' as imposed on them from above by training, scripting and surveillance. It is my contention that many kinds of 'talk at work' are increasingly subject to this explicit codification. Today it is not always left to workers to construct a suitable professional identity and 'somehow' make it relevant in talk; instead, approved forms of interactive discourse are prescribed in advance, and often in detail.

This development has a bearing on how we understand the 'special and particular constraints' mentioned by Drew and Heritage as distinctive features of institutional talk. When institutional interaction becomes subject to detailed codification, it is not only the participants in talk who decide what will count as 'allowable contributions to the business at hand'. Certain decisions on what is 'allowable' (and what is compulsory) are pre-empted by the codifiers, while the agency of the participants is correspondingly curtailed. Prescriptive interventions constrain interaction in two respects particularly, one of which Drew and Heritage mention and one of which they do not.

The one they mention comes under the heading of 'overall structural organization'. Here I will quote more fully from their remarks on this point:

> Many kinds of institutional encounters are characteristically organized into a standard 'shape' or order of phases. Conversations, by contrast, are not. With the exception of the opening and closing stages . . . it does not appear that conversations ordinarily progress through some overarching set of stages. The locally contingent management of 'next moves' in conversation, and the options speakers have even within particular sequences or activities, ensure that there is no 'standard pattern' for the overall organization of conversations. The activities conducted in many kinds of institutional interactions, by contrast, are often implemented through a task-related standard shape. In some instances that order may be prescribed, for instance, by a written schedule or formal agenda of points which an inquirer may be required to answer when requesting a service . . . But equally the order may be the product of locally managed routines.
>
> (Drew and Heritage, 1992: 43)

Prototypical instances of institutional interactions with a 'task-related standard shape' might include examining witnesses in court, taking a patient's history in a medical consultation or eliciting information on the location and nature of an incident when answering a call to the emergency services. Drew and Heritage are obviously right to point out that this sort of 'shaping' marks a significant difference between institutional talk and ordinary conversation. But I would also argue that *within* the 'institutional' category, 'locally managed routines' seem increasingly to be giving way to 'prescribed schedules' and 'formal agendas'. More and more institutional interactions – supermarket checkout transactions, customer enquiries made to a bank or utility company via one of its 'call centres', unsolicited telesales calls, and so on – have not merely a standard 'shape' but a standard *script* covering the sequencing, the content and function, and not uncommonly the actual wording, of every move the institutional participant makes.

This tendency has not been much discussed in the 'talk at work' literature, though it has attracted some attention from critical discourse analysts and sociologists of work (Fairclough, 1992; Goodman, 1996; Leidner, 1993). This relative neglect may partly reflect the fact that so much research on institutional talk has focused on interactions involving professionals like doctors, therapists, lawyers and business executives, whose status protects them from the degree of linguistic regimentation to which many other workers are now commonly subjected. It is also fair to say that the kind and degree of regimentation that interests me has become progressively more salient during the late 1980s and 1990s. The rapid diffusion and intensification of linguistic control strategies (which may have existed before but were less widespread and less efficient than they have since become) has occurred for two interrelated reasons. One is technological change (a point to be explored further in Chapter 4, which deals with call centres), and the other is the increasing influence of new management approaches. The overall effect of these developments has been to place not just linguistic behaviour but many other kinds of on-the-job behaviour under much closer scrutiny and surveillance.

The constraint which Drew and Heritage do not mention, but which will be an important topic in my own analysis, concerns the *manner* in which workers may be required to talk, whether or not the 'shape' and content of their talk has been scripted in advance. Particularly in customer service contexts, politeness phenomena, prosodic, paralinguistic and nonverbal (body language) behaviours, and sometimes lexical choices, are strictly regulated in a process I will refer to later on as *styling*. For instance, announcers at one British rail terminus are expected to perform announcements at a certain rate of words per minute and in 'smiley voice' (an effect which results from holding the lips in the posture of a smile whilst speaking). Assistants at a designer clothes shop are forbidden to approach customers with the conventional salutation 'can I help you' and instructed instead to 'strike up a conversation', resorting if necessary to remarks about the weather. At the same shop, there is a list of words that may be used to describe an outfit: it includes *exquisite* and *glamorous*, but *lovely* and *nice* are proscribed.[3] In the rather less exclusive retail environment that is Wal-Mart, meanwhile, employees swear an 'oath' to smile, make eye contact and utter a greeting 'every time a customer comes within ten feet of me'.

In sum, then, the kinds of observations made here on 'talk at work' will overlap in some respects with the tradition of research on that topic represented by contributors to Drew and Heritage's collection, while departing from that tradition in other respects. The most important difference is that I am interested less in 'locally managed routines' than in the codified and 'styled' forms of talk which, I argue, are increasingly overriding or disrupting the locally managed character of interaction. Since my primary interest is in the phenomenon of codification, and the practices of training and surveillance which are needed to make it 'bite', my primary data here will not be examples of naturally occurring workplace talk, nor will I be undertaking the kind of microanalysis favoured by conversation analysts. Instead I will examine prescriptive texts (including manuals, memoranda, training materials and lists of appraisal criteria) whose function is to spell out what kinds of talk people are expected to produce at work.[4] Of course, my use of these data invites the question: 'but is that what happens in practice?' The short answer is, 'yes and no'. I do not intend to suggest that workers are the 'cultural dopes' whose existence ethnomethodology has famously denied – that they simply follow the rules handed down to them in a passive, unquestioning way. Codification does not in practice eliminate the necessity for talk to be locally managed; what it does do, however, is change what participants have to manage. Workers who are given a script they find unsatisfactory may deviate from it, but in that case the institutional definition of what they are doing as deviant and 'accountable' behaviour becomes one of the factors they must take into consideration. Where codification is backed up by surveillance, institutional interactions begin to resemble 'mediated' discourse – that is, talk has to be designed not only for its immediate recipient, but also for an eavesdropping third party, namely the manager or supervisor who monitors workers' compliance with the rules.

I will return below to the issues raised in this section. First, though, it is necessary to say something about the broader context in which institutional interaction has become subject to increased codification and regimentation, which means returning to one of this book's main themes, the relationship between 'communication' and enterprise culture.

Everybody's business: corporate speak and cultural change

In discussions of the 'new' economy whose character I described in the introduction, much rhetoric centres on so-called 'human capital' – a reference not to people themselves, the innumerable willing 'hands' of the industrial age, but to the skills and knowledge that are today's most valuable assets, and are embodied (or en-minded) in human beings. Governments worry about the level of *technical* knowledge and skill possessed by today's workforce (hence election pledges like 'a computer in every classroom' and ideas like 'the university of industry'). Yet many employers – particularly in the burgeoning service sector – seem more interested in the so-called 'soft skills': they want recruits to be team players, 'good with people', and not least, 'good communicators'. Language, then, looms large among the attributes employers pay attention to when recruiting, training and managing workers. But in addition, it is an *instrument* for managing both individuals and organizations as they struggle with the process of 'culture change' that global competition is believed to necessitate. The point is summed up by management guru Charles Handy in the observation that appears as an epigraph to this chapter: to succeed in new worlds, businesses must adopt new words.

In a book titled *Corporate Speak: the Use of Language in Business*, Fiona Czerniawska, a management consultant, elaborates this point. She argues that given the new emphasis on 'human capital', language, with its power to win hearts and minds, is more important in organizations now than it has ever been before. She suggests that language can be 'a weapon of competitive advantage' for companies who are willing and able to exploit its potential (1998: 13). In business, she says,

> . . . [O]ur preferred mode of communication has been figures . . . [but] more and more companies are finding that some of their most important assets – people, knowledge, commitment – are non-quantifiable. And they are realising that if they cannot express these assets in terms of figures, then they cannot use financial metrics to manage them. It is therefore not surprising that they are turning to something other than figures to fill the gap – words: mission statements, commitments to quality, customer charters, corporate advertising – the list is growing exponentially.
>
> (1998: 2)

'Corporate speak' might seem an odd choice of title for a book whose aim is to make managers appreciate the potential of language as 'a weapon of competitive advantage'. Describing any linguistic register as *X-speak* tends to imply a perception of it as meaningless jargon, at best baffling and at worst sinister – perhaps because the '-*speak*' formulation so readily recalls Orwell's 'Newspeak'. But Fiona Czerniawska's mission is to rehabilitate something she regards as having been misunderstood and unfairly maligned by businesspeople who pride themselves on being doers rather than talkers. She does warn against Orwellian excesses: 'No sane business today would want a workforce of automatons: after all, anything an automaton can do, we can automate. People are needed for dealing with customers, for communication, and for lateral thinking, none of which businesses will get if they attempt to regiment the way people talk too rigidly' (1998: 27). But that does not mean businesses should not attempt to manage the use of words at all. If used judiciously, 'corporate speak' (a phrase that might be glossed as 'managed language-use') is a valuable 'new tool by which to influence collective culture and individual behaviour' (1998: 26). In this chapter I will focus particularly on two features of 'enterprising' corporate cultures which are thought to require the application of this 'new tool': the shift to 'teamwork' and the systematic adoption of 'customer care' policies.

'Teamwork' is one of the buzzwords of the enterprise approach, and the thought behind it is summarized in the aphorism 'None of us is as smart as all of us'. What it usually involves in practice is forms of workplace organization where people, often drawn from different levels of the corporate hierarchy, have to work together in groups to achieve particular outcomes. In a presentation of work she did with a group of colleagues in an Australian food manufacturing plant (Joyce *et al.*, 1995), Hermine Scheeres (1998) provides a table listing the 'spoken and written language demands of the restructured workplace'. Under the heading of 'teamwork' she notes the following spoken language demands:

- Solve problems and negotiate solutions and outcomes
- Initiate and participate in team discussions
- Know how to challenge
- Know how to ask for advice
- Argue for and against a proposition
- Ask a speaker to clarify or explain a point.

Under the heading 'changing role of the manager' Scheeres also lists the new spoken language responsibilities managers acquire in a teamwork culture, as follows:

- Explain and discuss changes in workplace practices
- Explain and negotiate team membership
- Negotiate allocation of tasks
- Listen and discuss openly problems and issues that arise
- Explain section interests and needs to others.

These demands are the linguistic instantiations of the shift away from a 'command and control' culture in which managers give instructions and workers follow them, towards an 'empowerment' culture. Managers are encouraged to 'explain', 'discuss', 'negotiate' and 'listen', while workers are permitted to 'question', 'challenge' and 'argue', and expected to 'solve problems'. Training may be needed to enable both managers and workers to master the more egalitarian and co-operative forms of spoken discourse that constitute 'teamwork'. Another important issue, not explicitly mentioned on Scheeres's list but possibly implied by 'explain and discuss changes in workplace practices', is *motivation*. Motivation matters, because in theory, at least, the 'teamwork' approach puts peer support (and peer pressure) in place of 'external' sticks and carrots. A good team-member is both highly motivated and able to motivate others, which inevitably involves communicating with them. Below I will consider how far the 'ideal' model outlined by Scheeres is reflected in actual practice; and I will look more closely at the particular forms of spoken communication recommended in training for teamwork.

'Customer care' is an approach to service in which an organization systematically sets out to manage the customer's whole experience. A set of training materials in my corpus (developed for a non-profit making arts organization to which I will give the pseudonym 'City Arts') explains the concept by quoting the chief executive of the Scandinavian airline SAS, who once said: 'coffee stains on the flip-down trays mean to the passenger that we do our engine maintenance wrong'.[5] The idea is that the customer's view of the organization is conditioned by a large number of small, and possibly quite trivial, details. 'Customer care' means getting employees to focus consistently on all the details that make a difference to the customer. It is also common for the approach to be extended to employees' dealings with one another: co-workers within the organization are defined as 'internal customers'. Customer care policies overlap here with the philosophy of teamwork, for the point is that everyone should work together for the ultimate good of the customer (and thus, of course, the company). Even those employees who have no contact with 'external' or 'end' customers – the people who actually consume goods and services – are materially affecting those customers' experience through the quality of support they give to colleagues down the line.

The City Arts materials sum up customer care – whether the customers are 'external' or 'internal' – as a matter of 'having the right attitudes and behaviours in place within an organization. In general terms, these attitudes and behaviours can be summarized as *caring, co-operating and communicating*'.[6] In fact, the discussion that follows makes clear that 'communication' in the sense of 'spoken interaction' is relevant to all three of these 'attitudes and behaviours'. What is placed under the heading of 'communicating' is essentially the use of language to convey information ('transmitting information accurately and speedily'). But language is not just a medium for transmitting information, it is also a medium for constructing and maintaining interpersonal relationships. Thus 'caring' and 'co-operating' also turn out to be ways of 'communicating'. 'Caring', for instance, is explained by breaking it down into several more specific behaviours:

- Treating [customers] with courtesy and consideration
- Responding reasonably to their requests and demands
- Showing an interest in them
- Taking time to find out what they feel
- Accepting responsibility, i.e. avoiding blame and helping out when problems occur
- Being aware of how what you do affects them

It is evident that at least the first four of these requirements will depend for their fulfilment largely on the way the employee talks to customers.

Some of the most noticeable reflexes of customer care policies in language-use are aptly described by Norman Fairclough's phrase 'synthetic personalization'. As Fairclough explains:

> One finds techniques for efficiently and nonchalantly 'handling' people wherever one looks in the public institutions of the modern world. Equally, one finds what I shall refer to as *synthetic personalization*, a compensatory tendency to give the impression of treating each of the people 'handled' *en masse* as an individual. Examples would be air travel (*have a nice day!*), restaurants (*Welcome to Wimpy!*) and the simulated conversation (for example, chat shows) and *bonhomie* which litter the media.
>
> (1989: 62)

The City Arts customer care training materials warn against saying things like 'sorry, that's our policy' and 'I don't make the rules' when a customer complains about something. These utterances imply (not inaccurately, in most cases) that the organization has routine procedures that it follows with every customer. The customer care ideal, by contrast, is to give the impression of attending to the needs of each customer as an individual. (A training manager at McDonald's told Robin Leidner: 'we want to treat every customer as an individual in 60 seconds or less' (Leidner, 1993: 221), while according to George Ritzer (1996: 82) some organizations even have 'subscripts' for customers who object to the normal routine as depersonalizing; employees may be told, for instance, to say they will 'bend the rules just this once'.) The City Arts materials ask: 'can you imagine how differently your customers would react if . . . an employee smiled and said, "I'm sorry you've had a problem. I'll take care of it immediately"'.

The behaviour being recommended here has several features of 'synthetic personalization'. The hypothetical employee smiles, apologizes to the customer (using a formula that incorporates both first and second person pronouns – '*I*'m sorry *you*'ve had a problem') and takes personal responsibility for putting things right. One difference between this approach and traditional notions of 'polite' service is the greater attention paid to what politeness theorists like Brown and Levinson (1987) term 'positive face', the desire people have to be liked or approved of by others (in contrast to 'negative face', the desire not to be imposed upon by others). Employees who have internalized the customer care philosophy are supposed to 'show an interest' and 'take time to find out how [customers] feel'. They must communicate not simply respect for the customer as a customer, but a friendly, empathetic attitude towards the customer as a person. Below, I will consider how this expansive definition of 'good service' has been codified in rules and procedures for what employees should say to customers, and how they should say it. I will also consider how employees negotiate, and in some cases resist, the positioning imposed on them by linguistic prescriptions relating to customer care.

The examples I will use in my analysis come from the commercial service sector: not from manufacturing, or 'caring' work, or the work of public institutions like universities and the civil service. That is not because enterprise, empowerment, teamwork and customer care are confined to the service sector. On the contrary, these innovations are by now very widely diffused across different types of workplaces. I have chosen to examine them in the commercial service context because, arguably, the form they take there is their prototypical form. Attempts to integrate ideas borrowed from commerce with the traditional structures and values of other sectors, especially public service and caring, cause complications, including linguistic ones (are sick, disabled and elderly people 'customers'?). These issues are interesting, but beyond my scope here. It is also worth recalling that approximately two thirds of all workers in the economies I've used in my examples are employed in the service sector, and the proportion is expected to grow. That in itself is a reason to be interested in what goes on in their workplaces.

The formal introduction of teamwork or customer care policies into an organization is an example of 'culture change'. Not only do such initiatives change actual work routines – they involve employees in new forms of training and appraisal, new events such as team meetings, and so forth – their effectiveness is thought to depend on whether the organization can bring about a more profound shift in employees' *attitudes*. Reorganizing your workforce into teams, for instance, will succeed only to the extent that people embrace the concept of teamwork and strive to become 'team players'. It is this 'deeper' kind of change that Fiona Czerniawska (1998) has in mind when she characterizes language as a 'tool with which to influence collective culture and individual behaviour' and a means for 'instilling a common outlook and ideology'.

The idea of using language deliberately for the purposes Fiona Czerniawska mentions inevitably raises the issue of Orwellian 'thought control'. I commented above that Czerniawska's phrase 'corporate speak' tends to recall 'Newspeak', the language invented by George Orwell in his novel *Nineteen Eighty-four* (1989 [1949]). Newspeak was deliberately created by the ruling party of a totalitarian state to ensure that only orthodox thoughts could be given expression in words. Indeed, it was intended to abolish not only the words, but also, ultimately, the subversive thoughts themselves. Writing just after World War II, Orwell took his inspiration from the linguistic abuses of fascism and Stalinism. Today, these ideologies are marginal, while another 'ism' – capitalism – has gone from strength to strength. We might be tempted to ask, then, if big business has taken over where Big Brother left off.

In fact, I think this is the wrong way to frame the question. Most linguists would probably agree that the notion of thought control through language is a myth: even those who accept language may influence the way we think acknowledge that this is a complex and variable matter (for one recent discussion of the issue, see Stubbs, 1997). Controlling thought, however, is by no means the only way to achieve certain objectives. It may not be possible to control what goes on in people's minds by prescribing what language they may speak, hear, read or write, but enforcing that prescription is itself a way of controlling people's behaviour. That it falls short of 'brainwashing' does not automatically make it unobjectionable.

Fiona Czerniawska gives a number of examples where companies have set to convey an official 'collective outlook' to employees, using the simple linguistic strategy of renaming things. The Disney Corporation, for instance, renamed its personnel department 'Central Casting' and its employees 'cast members'. The areas where employees can be seen by customers are known as 'on stage'. All this conveys that Disney's business is showbusiness. At one of Britain's leading supermarkets, staff were renamed 'colleagues'. A financial institution renamed meetings 'events'. This strategy underlines the symbolic importance accorded to language, but as Czerniawska herself points out, in isolation it accomplishes very little. Just calling something an 'event' without doing anything else to make it less dull than the 'meetings' it replaces is more likely to engender derision than excitement. Renaming people 'colleagues' without otherwise modifying the previous hierarchical relations among them will provoke cynicism, not enthusiasm. However, it is unusual to find a company using the renaming strategy in isolation. More commonly, the introduction of new vocabulary is part of a more comprehensive strategy for culture change within the organization. At this point it is useful to turn to an example – one which, as it happens, has some strikingly Orwellian features.

'The changes' at John Stephenson Ltd

John Stephenson Ltd is one of the organizations discussed in this book whose language practices were studied by a participant observer, an employee who was also a student in one of my classes (see note 4 and Appendix). The student in question, Gordon Graham, had worked for several years as a member of the company's sales staff (during university vacations he worked full time, otherwise part time). As well as drawing on his observations as a participant in training and work routines, he collected relevant internal documents and carried out interviews. I am indebted to him for the information and some of the analysis presented here.

John Stephenson Ltd is a regionally based retail business selling electrical appliances through a network of shops: founded by John Stephenson, it is still owned and run by the Stephenson family, whose members continue to dominate the board of directors. Until recently, the company had the paternalistic values and culture traditionally associated with family businesses. Relations between managers and staff were not egalitarian but they were 'easy going', in the words of one employee. Workers did not feel they were under undue pressure, and generally 'enjoyed their jobs'. In the mid-1990s, however, the company found itself struggling; turnover and profits declined steadily. Afraid that the business might not survive in an increasingly competitive environment, the board decided to implement major restructuring. This began with 'downsizing' – a significant number of employees lost their jobs – and continued with the involvement of management consultants and the adoption of a more 'enterprising' managerial approach.

In 1997 the Managing Director sent a memo to every department in the company, part of which read:

> This is year one; from this point onward, all that has happened before in the company is to be forgotten. This may take some time, but it is hoped that in five or ten years' time, no one will remember back beyond this year and our new beginning.

It is hardly surprising if this prompts comparisons with Orwell's *Nineteen Eighty-four*. The memo tells its recipients – many of them people who have been with the organization for years – that history is to be abolished ('All that has happened before in the company is to be forgotten'). The developments which led up to this memo and gathered pace after it are now referred to within the company simply as 'the changes'.

Rather like the society depicted in Orwell's novel, John Stephenson contains three major groups: the Management Team (analogous to Orwell's 'Inner Party'), which consists of the directors, the service manager and seven area managers known as 'team leaders'; the office staff, individual shop managers and salespeople (who are rather like Orwell's 'Outer Party'), and the behind-the-scenes workers, such as van-drivers and 'store-boys' who oversee the storage and movement of goods (parallel to the 'proles' in *Nineteen Eighty-four*). 'The changes' directly affected only the first two groups. Managers, office staff and salespeople, but not drivers or storeroom workers, were required to adopt new working routines, and to undergo programmes of training intended to inculcate the skills, attitudes and dispositions associated with 'teamwork'. (Asked about the exclusion of drivers and store-boys, one manager commented that involving them would have been pointless, since they were 'too stupid to realize what's going on, [and] even if they did they're too stupid to do anything about it'. Ben Pimlott remarks in his editor's introduction to the Penguin edition of *Nineteen Eighty-four* (1989: xv) that 'in Oceania the relative freedom of working-class people is merely a symptom of the contempt in which they are held'.)

The architects of 'the changes' believed that language was an important tool for getting employees to consent to new arrangements; in particular, they believed that certain communication practices would be crucial in motivating employees and persuading them to adopt new attitudes and beliefs. In 1997 members of the Management Team attended a training course which was intended to teach this lesson. Those who were interviewed subsequently were invited to talk about their reactions to the course, and particularly to the way the trainer used language. This question elicited the following narrative from one participant:

Manager: Everyone had to do a presentation, including [the trainer], he did his first. He started by asking: 'who is the company?'. We all had to reply: 'We are'. His reply was: 'I can't hear you'. It was like something from an American show.

Interviewer: Were you embarrassed by this?

Manager: At first. But before I knew where I was, I was shouting and screaming the answers back at him, everybody was. By the time he'd gone on for about five minutes, he asked the question again, 'Who is the company?'. It was like I wasn't in control any more. I'd say it was a mixture of him controlling us using language and gestures and probably wanting to fit in with everyone else.

Interviewer: How do you feel about this now?

Manager: Obviously I can see how we were controlled but I don't think it did me or anyone else any harm. I think it brought us together, made us feel part of a team.

Interestingly, most interviewees who were questioned about this event both agreed that they were being 'controlled' by the techniques the trainer used, and at the same time explicitly denied (in some cases with considerable emphasis) that they were being 'brainwashed'. 'Brainwashing' was seen as a disreputable practice, and it was also seen as a sign of personal weakness to be vulnerable to such an extreme form of manipulation. If 'brainwashing' is taken to imply a permanent suspension of one's critical faculties, then clearly the managers' denial that they had been 'brainwashed' was justified: all were able to reflect critically on what had happened after the event. None, however, was willing to express resentment about being 'controlled'.

Another quasi-Orwellian feature of 'the changes' was a requirement that sales staff and managers should write regular reports detailing what they had achieved, and also what their workmates had achieved. The reports would be passed up the line and ultimately analysed at a meeting of the Management Team. This measure was considered controversial, and some people resented it – less because of the time it consumed than because it was seen as a way of getting employees to spy and inform on one another. One team leader commented: 'only the gullible believe anything good can come from these reports, it is all about noting down the negative to use against an individual'. This is a good example of the way 'empowerment' approaches may in practice intensify rather than lessen the surveillance associated with 'command and control' methods. It is also, however, a good illustration of the fact that few employees swallow the rhetoric of empowerment uncritically. If that rhetoric is intended as 'brainwashing', it clearly does not work. But arguably it does not need to: whatever they may think of new practices, employees are in no position to refuse to comply with them. At the time of the interviews, everyone at the company was conscious that 'the changes' had been precipitated in the first place by a crisis in John Stephenson's fortunes, as a result of which many jobs had been lost. Nobody wanted to be first on the list in any new round of layoffs.

A key aspect of 'the changes' was the reorganization of personnel into teams. This required explicit attention to be given to the way employees used interactive spoken language. An internal document, 'Our Five Year Plan', proclaimed: 'We shall make the teaching of good communication, assertiveness and listening skills a priority as these are essential to effective teamwork'. To that end, a programme of communication skills training was designed and delivered by an outside consultancy. I want to look in some detail at what was taught, referring to the training materials given out to participants. (These materials have much in common with other workplace materials in my sample (see Chapter 2), and where appropriate I will compare them with other examples.)

One respect in which the John Stephenson materials are typical is in their eclecticism: they do not adopt a unified approach but draw on various bodies of knowledge or expertise. These range from the clinical/therapeutic precepts of assertiveness training to the anecdotalism of popular how-to-succeed-in-business books like Stephen Covey's *The Seven Habits of Highly Effective People* (1989). Consequently, there is some incoherence in the materials; for instance, two somewhat different accounts may be given of the same phenomenon, or principles may be adduced which conflict with one another. It is seldom explained where the accounts and principles come from – in most cases they are presented as obvious and indisputable pieces of common wisdom. Appeals to experience are more prominent than appeals to scientific authority ('if you're like most of us, positive reinforcement probably increased your desire to participate' rather than, say, 'research has found that . . .'). This kind of training is meant to be practical rather than 'academic'.

It is therefore interesting that one of the first documents in this set of training materials is a lengthy presentation of Eric Berne's Transactional Analysis (TA), which is glossed as 'an important technique in the search for improved communications'. (The materials justify this unusual excursion into theoretical territory by saying: 'The main advantage of TA is that it avoids the usual psychological jargon and so is very easily learned and understood'.) It is explained that TA categorizes every communicative act according to whether it is 'parent', 'adult' or 'child' behaviour. The key to good communication is judging whether a particular utterance ('stimulus') is coming from your interlocutor's 'parent', 'adult' or 'child' and then either designing your own response to complement the stimulus or else responding in such a way as to invite the interlocutor to shift to a more appropriate mode. A sample analysis is provided, using the utterance pair

Fred: John, have you seen the report on the new machinery?
John: Yes, it's here on my desk.

The analysis is: 'Fred asked a straightforward question from his Adult aimed at John's Adult and John responded as expected, from his Adult to Fred's'.
   A less straightforward exchange is then illustrated:

Jim: Call yourself a manager, this whole office is in chaos thanks to your new system.
Boss: Look, I'm the boss around here. If you don't like the system you'll just have to lump it.

Jim has adopted the position of the Critical Parent, and his boss has refused the complementary position of the Child, taking an even more markedly parental role himself. What he should have done, however, was to direct his response to Jim's Adult, by saying something like

Boss: What exactly is causing the problems within the system, perhaps we could modify it to solve them.

This strategy would put pressure on Jim to 'discuss the situation logically' in his Adult persona, and in this way the incipient conflict would be resolved without the boss needing to invoke his status as Jim's superior.
   I noted in Chapter 2 that transactional analysis crops up quite frequently in my sample of training materials. Although it is usually presented as a means for avoiding *communication* problems – 'complementary' transactions are less likely to lead to misunderstanding than 'crossed' ones – the examples given make clear that in practice, TA is seen as particularly useful for avoiding or defusing *conflicts*. These may be expressed or manifested linguistically, but their underlying cause is not linguistic. In the 'call yourself a manager' exchange quoted above, for instance, Jim and his boss are not having trouble because one has misunderstood what the other is saying, but because of a difference of opinion – firstly about the system which Jim alleges is causing chaos, and secondly about Jim's right to challenge a superior in the way he does. The account TA gives of conflict (or perhaps it

would be fairer to say the account training materials give of TA's account of conflict) does not dwell on its causes nor consider its legitimacy in a given situation. Instead it treats conflict as the undesirable result of a failure to act in the appropriate, 'adult' manner. It suggests that conflict can and should be defused, and that this is simply a technical matter. It also suggests that good leadership is about rational persuasion and teamwork: 'how can we solve the problem' rather than 'I'm the boss, so do as I tell you'. In other words, TA is not simply a tool for understanding what is going on in inter-action, but has an ideological agenda – one that fits particularly well with the goals and values of the enterprising organization. This may help to explain the otherwise puzzling phenomenon of time being spent training domestic appliance salespeople to grasp the conceptual apparatus of TA and even draw diagrams of interactions. They are not being instructed only in techniques for effective 'communication', but also, and probably more importantly, in the conduct expected of a mature, responsible, well-balanced person.

In contrast to transactional analysis, which is more about the roles speakers take up than the minutiae of their conversational behaviour, the parts of the John Stephenson training materials devoted to 'active listening' offer more specific guidance. As I noted in Chapter 2, 'active listening' is a common preoccupation in training materials and there are several different approaches to it. The one which appears in these materials focuses on four kinds of behaviour:

1. Non-verbal behaviours, for example, posture, eye contact, gestures, utterances like 'uh-huh'.
2. Paraphrasing – to check accuracy of hearing.
3. Verbal encouragement, for example, 'tell me more', 'mm-hmm', etc.
4. Summarizing.

Advice on non-verbal behaviour or 'body language' is relatively sparse in these materials – other examples in my corpus make much more of it – but what there is, is typical of most guidance on this subject. Essentially trainees are encouraged to do more consciously what they would normally do without reflection, and given a metalanguage with which to reflect on common behaviours. They are also presented with generalizations about what is 'normal' behaviour – for instance, one should make eye contact with an interlocutor for 'about 60–70% of the time'. Here, what is presumably a statistical average derived from research on naturally occurring gaze behaviour is made into a benchmark or standard: the 'normal' becomes the normative. Behaviours which in a descriptive framework would be points on a continuum or normal distribution curve are redefined in a prescriptive framework as 'wrong' and in need of remediation.

As well as making sure that there is some eye contact rather than none, trainees are counselled to avoid a 'fixed stare'. They are told that their posture should be 'relaxed' rather than 'tense' and that their gestures should be natural rather than 'stiff and artificial'. At the same time, it is emphasized that they should 'smile'. (We will see later on that this injunction is ubiquitous, even in materials telling people how to conduct telephone interaction.) It would seem, then, that trainees are being urged to simulate naturalness. They are told to think consciously about gaze, posture, gesture and so forth rather than doing what comes naturally, but at the same time warned that the resulting behaviour should not display any evidence of self-consciousness.

'Paraphrasing' and 'summarizing' – giving the gist of what someone has said in order to get confirmation that you have understood them correctly – are things people sometimes do in ordinary talk, but in the context of a business or service encounter it may be necessary to do them more explicitly and more often than usual. A number of practice exercises aimed at developing these skills are included in the John Stephenson training materials. The paraphrasing task, for example, requires trainees to write out two different paraphrases of the following passage (which handily encapsulates the rationale behind 'active listening' itself):

> Inefficient listening is extraordinarily costly. Listening mistakes have severe repercussions throughout business, however it is often simple everyday occurrences multiplied by many thousand that add up to the greatest costs. Letters have to be retyped, appointments rescheduled, shipments missed, meetings cancelled.

The most obvious peculiarity of this exercise is that it has nothing to do with listening: the passage appears in written form and the paraphrases are also rendered in writing. Another oddity is the amount of space provided in which to write the paraphrases; it is large enough to suggest to the trainee that the point of this task is simply to reformulate the original in full using different words. In conversation this would be bizarre. Someone who insisted on repeating every detail of what their co-conversationalists had said, in different words but at similar length, would quickly be judged communicatively incompetent: the results would be more reminiscent of a 'Garfinkel experiment'[7] than of any normal interaction.

Guidance on 'verbal encouragement' suggests that 'reinforcement' is necessary if people are to remain motivated. Two kinds of 'verbal reinforcers' are recommended: positive ones like 'I'm glad you noticed that' and 'What an interesting thought!', which 'reinforce desirable responses' and neutral ones like 'I see, thanks for your input', which 'discourage undesirable behaviours'. Negative comments like 'no, that won't work' are to be avoided, since they undermine people's motivation. This advice is clearly informed by an old-fashioned behaviourist model of communication and indeed of human behaviour in general, in which stimulus-response chains loom large.

Another way in which trainees are advised to give verbal encouragement is by asking open rather than closed questions. 'For example', the materials suggest, 'instead of asking "did you get our free sample?" ask, "what did you think of our sample?"'. The open/closed question distinction is fetishised in virtually every set of materials I have come across, and it implies a very simple and literal model of how communication works. Form and function are thought to be so intimately locked together that if you ask someone a yes/no question they can only respond with a yes or no answer. The question 'did you get our free sample?' could never elicit an answer like 'yeah, terrific, can I place an order for 400 of them?' but only 'yes, thanks'.

Attempts to prescribe 'standard' ways of performing particular communicative tasks typically take no account of the fact that spoken discourse exhibits a high degree of contextually conditioned variation, which is functional for communication rather than presenting some sort of obstacle to it. Unawareness or intolerance of variation can give rise to some strange and unnatural prescriptions. Variation is not only a question of the presence or absence of a particular variant, but also of its relative frequency and its distribution – a point that goes unacknowledged in most communication training materials, whose assumption seems to be that you can't have too much of a good thing, be it paraphrasing, verbal reinforcement or smiling. So while the materials may offer guidance on the mechanism of, say, paraphrasing, they will not discuss the equally relevant issue of where in an exchange it might be useful to paraphrase or how often it is reasonable to do so in a given context. Paraphrasing itself is not an unnatural strategy, but it can become unnatural if it is done without regard to the demands of the specific context. A service encounter may demand more frequent paraphrasing than a casual conversation between friends, but less frequent paraphrasing than, say, a counselling session.

In some cases, the behaviour prescribed in training materials is unnatural not because it is contextually inappropriate but because it flouts pragmatic principles that apply across contexts. For instance, assertiveness training (or AT, the subject of a later section in the John Stephenson materials), counsels trainees to avoid indirectness, even or especially when performing seriously face-threatening acts. AT believes indirectness to be misleading and 'manipulative'; politeness theory by contrast tells us that indirectness is one conventional strategy for mitigating face-threats (Brown and Levinson, 1987). Consistently refraining from mitigation is not just unnatural, it has considerable potential for giving offence.

The John Stephenson materials are not only eclectic in approach but also unsystematic in structure and content. There is neither an explicit nor an implicit resort to anything like Hermine Scheeres's (1998) list of 'spoken language demands in the restructured workplace', and it is never explained why the materials developer decided to focus on exactly the things he or she did. The statement in 'Our Five Year Plan' that 'good communication, assertiveness and listening skills . . . are essential to effective teamwork' looks at first glance like a plausible enough statement of training priorities, but on reflection its logic is obscure. For one thing, the three items on the list are not all on the same taxonomic level. 'Good communication' is a generic phrase, which might reasonably be taken to subsume 'assertiveness' and 'listening skills'. 'Assertiveness' and 'listening skills' themselves reflect the application of different subcategorizing principles to the general field of 'good communication': 'assertiveness' is an approach that may be brought to bear on all aspects of communication, whereas 'listening skills' apply to only one kind of communicative behaviour, namely listening. It is as if someone had announced their intention of listing three kinds of fruit and then come up with a list containing 'fruit, jam making and lemons'. Why 'effective teamwork', in particular, should demand assertiveness and listening skills training, and not something else, is never made clear.

This might seem an overly pedantic response to a single sentence from an internal memo, but the sentence in question is symptomatic of a very general problem. In my sample, many or most materials have a similar 'ragbag' quality. Some of the advice given on specific points is perfectly sensible, but the whole does not hang together in the way someone used to reading or writing course materials (an applied linguist such as Hermine Scheeres, for instance) might expect. Trainees are exposed, seemingly almost at random, to ideas about 'communication', systems for reflecting upon it and practical tips on how to do it which are not necessarily connected to each other, and which are not presented as interrelated parts of any larger whole.

Whatever the shortcomings of the training programme, however, 'the changes' at John Stephenson provide a good illustration of the foregrounding of language and communication in contemporary management practice. In particular, they illustrate a widespread belief among managers that linguistic regulation can be used systematically as an instrument of culture change and of control over people. Thus the consultant who designed the training package used motivational techniques to induce managers to shout and scream 'we are the company!'; managers used new report-writing formats to keep tabs on the day-to-day performance of their subordinates; those subordinates were instructed in using TA, 'active listening' and assertiveness to produce the desired outcomes in interactions with customers and with one another. From the management team's perspective, this belief in the power of language was vindicated by the outcome of 'the changes': a few months after the introduction of new practices and new training, turnover had increased significantly. Others in the company were more sceptical: they attributed the improvement not to teamwork or communication training, but to increased effort on the part of individuals whose job was to sell the company's products. What lay behind the increased effort was fear: 'the changes' were interpreted as a sign that the company was in trouble, and that unless employees took action they would soon find themselves out of a job. Gordon Graham's interviews elicited at least some negative comments on 'the changes' from every informant, but at the same time, in his words: 'Every employee knows and has been warned that any resistance to "the changes", or any anti-company feeling reported back to the Management Team will result in dismissal'.

This might suggest one final comparison with *Nineteen Eighty-four*. The novel ends with the capitulation of the hero, Winston Smith, but the reason for his capitulation sometimes gets forgotten. Winston's resistance is broken, not by the use of Newspeak to control his thinking, but by conventional torture, and particularly his dread of being eaten alive by rats in Room 101. Obviously, businesses do not use such extreme forms of coercion. Nevertheless, it seems employees' consent to and compliance with new arrangements may depend less on Charles Handy's 'softer words of vision and leadership and common purpose' than on knowing that 'tougher' words (such as, 'you're fired') are being kept in reserve.

Forcing a smile: customer care and 'superior service'

Although John Stephenson Ltd is a retail organization, the explicit rationale it gave for introducing communication training was to ensure employees worked effectively in the teams into which they had been reorganized during 'the changes'. More commonly, however, the primary focus of linguistic training and regulation in retail businesses is the way staff interact with customers. Since the perceived standard of a company's service is a function of its employees' behaviour, the 'customer care' approach means that companies are essentially selling the qualities of their staff. Consequently, they must take a close interest in the qualities staff actually display to customers: in their appearance, their demeanour and, not least, their speech.

In October 1998, the *Washington Post* reported on a controversy that had broken out on the internet[8] around a 'superior service' programme initiated by the Safeway supermarket chain in the USA. Under the title 'Service with a forced smile: Safeway's courtesy campaign also elicits some frowns' (October 18: A1), reporter Kirstin Downey Grimsley explained the background. The rules of 'superior service' required employees to 'make eye contact with the customer, smile, greet him or her, offer samples of products, make suggestions about other possible purchases that could go with the items being purchased, accompany customers to locate items they can't find . . . thank shoppers by name at the checkout using information from their credit, debit or Safeway card'. To monitor compliance, Safeway employed 'mystery shoppers', people who impersonated real customers but were actually in the store to grade staff on a 19-point checklist. These gradings were used in subsequent performance evaluations; good grades could attract bonuses, while poor grades might result in the employee being sent for remedial customer service skills training at what some workers interviewed by the

Post derisively referred to as 'smile school' or 'clown school'. (A spokesperson for Safeway defended the activities of the mystery shoppers by saying: 'sometimes people won't do what you expect, but will do what you inspect' – a telling comment, one might think, on the limits, in practice, of the philosophy of 'empowerment'.) The immediate cause of the furore, which occurred when the programme was already several years old, was that several women Safeway workers in California had complained at a union conference that the company's policy exposed them to sexual harassment. Some male customers interpreted displays of friendliness as signs of 'romantic interest' or as cues to make 'lewd comments'. These complaints sparked off a discussion of the rights and wrongs of the superior service programme.

Much of the behaviour that is regulated by the superior service programme is 'communicative' – in the jargon, verbal, vocal or visual – behaviour. In some cases, regulation takes the form of making speech acts and routines which would be expected to occur in service encounters – such as greetings, thanks and farewells – *categorical*: that is, employees do not choose whether and when to perform these acts, but are required to perform them at every opportunity, and may be 'written up' for any omission. This requirement can have bizarre consequences. The *Post* report begins with a vignette in which a clerk in a Safeway store in Reston, Virginia spots a customer coming down the aisle where he is stacking shelves:

> The clerk sprang into action, making eye contact, smiling and greeting her warmly ... The woman nodded briefly in return and continued shopping. The clerk moved on to another part of the store, going about his duties, and passed her again. Knowing that he might earn a poor grade on the company's 19-point friendliness report card if he failed to acknowledge her fully each time, the clerk again made eye contact and asked her how she was doing. This time she looked quizzical ... But after it happened a third time, the woman's face darkened as he approached. 'That poor lady', the clerk said ruefully. 'You could see her thinking, "what is his problem?"'.

His problem, of course, was that the rules were enforced without regard to such obvious contextual considerations as whether an employee had already greeted a particular shopper. It is only mildly unnatural to be 'warmly greeted' by a store clerk *once*, but it becomes extremely unnatural if the routine is repeated every time the same clerk comes within greeting distance.

Regulation of employees' linguistic behaviour may also take the form of instructing them to do things that would not ordinarily be expected to occur even once in the context of a supermarket. For instance, Safeway staff are exhorted to 'make suggestions about other possible purchases that could go with the items being purchased' – in other words to initiate conversations with people who are in the middle of doing their shopping. Since in context this is a 'marked' action – conversing with staff about what they are buying is not part of most customers' existing schema for visiting a supermarket – it is interactionally quite difficult to 'bring off'. A student of mine, Karen MacGowan, carried out observations in a supermarket in the UK where staff had been furnished with a set of opening gambits for initiating conversation at the checkout (such as 'are you using coupons with your shopping today?'). She noted that although the gambits themselves were perfectly straightforward, some customers appeared to have great difficulty framing a response to them, because they could not fathom the checkout operator's underlying intentions. (Ultimately, of course, the intention both in the Safeway case and in the 'coupons' case is to persuade the customer to buy *more*.)

Finally, employees' behaviour is regulated by instructions to perform all communicative acts in a prescribed manner: smiling, making eye contact, using the customer's name, greeting him or her 'warmly' and selecting personalized formulas like 'how are you doing?' which incorporate direct second person address. These linguistic and paralinguistic preferences are designed to express particular dispositions, notably friendliness and sincere concern for the customer's wellbeing, and thus to construct a particular kind of interpersonal relationship between the customer and the employee.

All these types of regulation, especially the last, exemplify 'synthetic personalization', which as I explained above (following Fairclough, 1989) is a way of designing discourse to give the impression of treating people as individuals within institutions that, in reality, are set up to handle people *en masse*. Supermarkets are obviously institutions of this type. After all, they were founded historically on the concept (novel at the time) of customers serving *themselves* rather than being served by someone else. By comparison with shopping in a traditional neighbourhood grocery, or an upmarket department store, supermarket shopping was a *de*personalized experience, one in which service was minimal and anonymous. Customers understood and accepted this as a concomitant of the advantages offered by the supermarket over other retailing operations, namely speed, convenience and value for money. But customer care programmes like Safeway's are intended to re-personalize the experience by giving the impression that staff relate to each customer as an individual.

As the term '*synthetic* personalization' implies, however, this impression is achieved by interactional sleight-of-hand. It remains a way of handling people *en masse* rather than a genuinely individualized approach: the supposed expressions of personal concern are actually standard formulae, pre-packaged at head office and produced indifferently for every customer. Even the most markedly individualizing strategy, the use of customers' names, is a piece of artifice, and it draws mixed responses from customers. Whereas one customer told the *Post*'s reporter, 'It makes you feel good when you're spending $50 to have them know your name', another said: 'it doesn't make me feel better. I know they are looking me up in the computer. It's not because they know me'. Some people judge Safeway's superior service programme the very opposite of 'personal', because they believe employees are only following a formula: their friendliness is not genuine. A contributor to the internet discussion – not a Safeway employee – suggested that the company was forcing its staff to 'act like androids'. A checkout worker who had resigned in protest after 20 years' service was quoted in the *Post* report describing the behaviour expected of employees as 'so artificial, it's unreal [*sic*]'.

If one problem with 'synthetic personalization' is that people may perceive it as more synthetic than personalized, another is that some find personalization *per se* inappropriate to the context. One customer who was interviewed by the *Post* remarked, for instance, that he was annoyed and embarrassed by staff commenting on what he had bought. He also disliked having his name used at the checkout: 'it's almost too personal, if you don't know the person'. Safeway's corporate spokesperson admitted that the use of names had attracted many complaints – especially from foreign-born customers whose names were invariably mispronounced.

These comments raise the issue of variation. The Safeway spokesperson's assertion that 'in general, people like people to be friendly to them' sounds like a statement of the obvious, but what it conceals is individual, social and cultural differences affecting what behaviours people define as 'friendly' – one person's 'friendliness' may be another's 'over-familiarity' – and what contexts they see as requiring what degree of 'friendliness'. Politeness in general is an area where national and cultural differences can be quite pro-nounced, even when people speak the same language. In Britain, for instance, there are hazards associated with importing signifiers of friendliness from the US – a common practice, since many US-based companies do business in Britain, and in addition there is a widespread belief that service in the US is better than in Britain. (One UK railway company's manual urges employees to 'put American-style friendliness into your voice', as if friendly service were as intrinsically American as Coca-Cola.). Many people are irrit-ated by formulas like 'have a nice day', partly just because they are marked as 'American', and so Americanize public space in ways that offend some British sensibilities,[9] but partly also because they arise from ways of relating to others which are themselves experienced as foreign. Although there is variation in both countries, generally speaking the British have traditionally had a greater distrust of anything that smacks of effusiveness, especially between strangers. Karen MacGowan reported that an initiative whereby shoppers in the Scottish town of Coatbridge were met at the store entrance by a 'greeter' saying 'enjoy your shopping experience' had evoked varying degrees of embarrassment, puzzlement and hilarity: exhortations to 'enjoy' are more Californian than Caledonian. Another difference, crudely stated, is that in Britain polite behaviour between unacquainted equals tends to involve the reciprocal marking of social distance. For people who have internalized this norm, the (increasingly common) practice of workers being identified by their first names only may not connote what it is intended to connote, namely friendliness, but instead may seem to demean the worker by denying her or him the social distance one accords to non-intimates of equal status.

In other parts of the world, where English is not widely spoken or is spoken as a second language, the linguistic and cultural difference issues may be far more extreme. There is much to be said about the implications of the fact that 'globalization' tends to mean 'Americanization'. Though I have neither the space nor the research evidence to take up the subject in detail here, comments made to me when I have presented analyses of service styling in English-speaking countries suggest this is a rich field for future exploration.[10] I have been told, for example, that American English formulas like 'have a nice day' are being rendered by odd-sounding calques in languages like Swedish; that the importation of American-style 'friendly' service into post-communist Hungary is disrupting the complex formal system of address in Hungarian; and that Black South Africans entering service sector jobs previously reserved for white workers have been obliged to learn forms of interpersonal behaviour which are viewed in their community as alien and bizarre. It has also been pointed out to me that some societies have their own highly formalized service styles with which the 'globalized' style is in conflict. An example is Japan, where training for customer service workers has long given considerable attention to their speech and body language. The Japanese style now increasingly coexists, however, with the totally different style favoured by American-owned companies like Disney and McDonald's.

But even within one society, everyone will not necessarily share the same understanding of particular linguistic strategies, nor the same expectations of language-use in service encounters. Making and enforcing invariant rules for 'friendly' behaviour and language-use compels staff to ignore their own readings of what particular customers want or need, and to discard their understanding that, for instance, one might wish to address people differently on the basis of age or gender. An employee quoted in the *Washington Post* pointed out that often someone's body language would tell you that they wanted to be left alone. As she also said, however, if you used your own judgement in such a case and there happened to be a 'mystery shopper' around, you would be 'written up' for poor customer service skills. In this example we see how what employers describe as 'skills' may in fact be no such thing; employees may actually be penalized for making use of their learned ability to interact successfully with others.

The problems staff encounter with the superior service programme do not only arise from being deskilled and required to behave in a way both they and many customers find artificial. There is a deeper problem with the regulation of linguistic and other interpersonal behaviour, and it is essentially a problem of self-identity in the sense Anthony Giddens (1991) uses that term. Workers may be compelled by corporate *fiat* to become, for hours at a time, someone they do not want to be, someone they cannot easily integrate into their ongoing narrative of the self, because it strikes at their self-image and self-esteem.

It is interesting, for example, that some Safeway employees who spoke to the *Washington Post* complained about customers 'abusing' the practice of offering samples. They explained that some people requested an endless succession of samples at the deli counter, knowing that because of the superior service policy the staff would be unable to call a halt: 'they come for lunch. I'm not kidding'. These customers' behaviour does not 'hurt' employees in any material sense (if anything, it gives them more opportunities to gain points on the service score card), and where employees dislike the superior service programme one might expect them to take a grim pleasure in seeing customers exploit Safeway's generosity. But catering with a smile to the customer who 'comes for lunch' makes workers feel stupid. Letting shoppers get away with behaviour that offends against their sense of what is right is experienced as a sort of self-abasement.

A slightly different example of workers 'feeling stupid' comes from a story someone told me about her son's experience of working for a chain of restaurants in the US. Employees were required to send diners on their way with a formulaic 'bye, hope you enjoyed your meal, come again soon', accompanied by a cheery wave. Everyone found this routine artificial, but male employees had a particular problem with the hand gesture: they considered it 'effeminate' and to that extent at odds with an important aspect of their own identity, their (straight) masculinity. They eventually resolved the problem by rendering the wave as a sketchy salute.[11]

A more serious version of the self-abnegation problem appears in the case of the California Safeway employees who complained that their friendliness was misconstrued by male customers. Safeway's response to this complaint was that no increase in sexual harassment claims had been recorded since the inception of the superior service programme. That may be true, but it misses the point. The fundamental problem is that the philosophy and practice of 'customer care' places employees at the customer's disposal, with few well-defined limits on what the customer may expect of them. Their job is no longer just to stack shelves, operate tills and direct shoppers to the deli counter. Their job is also to make the customer feel good. Male customers who treat women staff as sexual objects are unlikely to have 'misinterpreted' friendliness as flirting. Rather they have understood and applied the basic principle of a customer care culture, which is that the staff are there to 'meet and exceed customers' needs'. Even where customers do not take this understanding to the extreme of harassment – sexual or otherwise – it places staff in a subservient position. This marks a difference between the customer service interactions I am focusing on here and the interactions most often studied under the heading of 'institutional' or 'professional' discourse, such as job interviews, medical consultations and classroom discourse. As Drew and Heritage (1992) point out, such interactions are 'asymmetrical': typically it is assumed that the institutional participant will be the more powerful party, as well as (and indeed by virtue of) having more responsibility for the conduct of the interaction. In service interactions structured by the discourse and practice of 'customer care', however, that assumption does not hold: service employees remain responsible for the conduct of talk, but customers are positioned as more powerful. The fact that workers are positioned in this way is a cause of resentment among them. As one recently retired (male) employee told the *Washington Post*: 'I believe in courteous service, but Safeway has taken it to such an extreme that it's torture for most of the employees'.

This remark gestures toward an important distinction: there is, indeed, a difference between 'courteous' service and the kind of service demanded by current philosophies of customer care. The difference is not simply that the latter is insincere and artificial. Old-style professional courtesy could equally involve a degree of artifice: a worker might feel animosity towards a particular customer, or might simply be in a bad mood, but courtesy would require that s/he refrain from showing it. In addition, as Erving Goffman noted in his classic text *The Presentation of Self in Everyday Life*:

> We know that in service occupations practitioners who may other-wise be sincere are sometimes forced to delude their customers because their customers show such a heartfelt demand for it. Doctors who are led into giving placebos, filling station attendants who resignedly check and recheck tire pressures for anxious women motorists, shoe clerks who sell a shoe that fits but tell the customer it is the size she wants to hear – these are cynical performers whose audiences will not allow them to be sincere.
>
> (Goffman, 1959: 18)

This observation, made in the late 1950s, is a useful reminder that insincerity in itself is not a novel feature of service work. In Goffman's account however it is customers who compel service workers to 'delude' them, and the workers are described as 'cynical performers', suggesting they are ultimately in control. In regimes like Safeway's, by contrast, insincerity is less a cynical response to the behaviour of customers and more a matter of complying with rules laid down by those in direct authority over workers. What is demanded, moreover, is a particular kind of insincerity. Both old-fashioned 'courtesy' and the forms of deception instanced by Goffman required workers to suppress negative feelings or judgements – to betray no irritation with people who are vain or recalcitrant or make a fuss about nothing, for example. But the hallmark of many present-day service regimes is the emphasis they place on displaying – which usually entails *simulating* – positive feelings towards customers. This, it has been argued, makes greater demands on workers, and is more likely to be resented by them.

Communication as emotional labour

In her prescient study *The Managed Heart* (1983), Arlie Hochschild elaborated the concept of 'emotional labour' to describe the kind of work that involves making others feel good. Emotional labour involves workers in managing both their own feelings and other people's: the classic example of this duality might be smiling, which signals your intention to make the person you are interacting with happy by displaying to them that you yourself feel happy. The implicit model is the way people behave in personal relationships where the parties have an equal investment – the worker acts like a friend, or a nurturing parent, or a surrogate wife – but in the workplace this behaviour is a commodity with an exchange value: it is part of what the worker gets paid for. Another important contextual feature is that the customer or client does not have reciprocal obligations to the worker.[12] The lack of reciprocity places workers in a subordinate position and compels them to look after the customer's feelings at the expense of their own. Arlie Hochschild studied flight attendants, who reported that they found this aspect of their work particularly stressful. They noted for instance what a strain they found it to smile continually for hours at a stretch, however they were feeling and however the passengers treated them; and how demeaned they felt by the image of subservience and sexual availability they were required to project. The job of a flight attendant is of course one of those 'pink collar' jobs, historically done by women, where emotional labour has always been expected: other examples are secretarial work and nursing. But the codification of 'customer care' has made emotional labour a more prominent part of all kinds of service jobs.

This point is recognized very explicitly in a popular management text titled *What Customers Like About You: Adding Emotional Value for Service Excellence and Competitive Advantage* (Freemantle, 1998). The author David Freemantle (inevitably, a management consultant) argues that:

> Given a range of comparable and competitive products to choose from, in future customers will choose the company they like. In the main this means they will be choosing the *people* they like. . . . Where there is little or no personal contact between the customer and the company, the brand is all important in matters of customer choice. However, competitive advantage can be better secured when a customer's emotional attachment to a brand is reinforced by an

117

emotional attachment to the people who sell and deliver the branded product. This is the essence of added emotional value.

(1998: 6)

From Freemantle's perspective, something like the Safeway superior service programme is an unsuccessful attempt to generate 'added emotional value' or 'e-value'; its rigid prescriptivism inhibits real 'emotional connectivity', which can only be achieved 'if [employees] are sensitive to each customer's individual requirements for emotional value. Sometimes a smile and enthusiasm are totally inappropriate' (Freemantle, 1998: 8). In order to add 'e-value', then, companies must move away from scripted greetings and obligatory smiles, and towards an approach in which workers are trained instead to practise a kind of amateur psychology. What they need to learn is how to 'read' customers in order to decide what kind of emotional response is appropriate for each individual.

Verbal interaction is an important site for this interpretive work, in addition to being the prime site for the actual production of 'e-value'. Thus a later chapter of Freemantle's book titled 'Everyday likeable behaviors' has sections on 'the emotional eye', 'the emotional ear' and 'the emotional voice', all of which deal with aspects of face-to-face communication – gaze, listening and speech (more specifically, the prosodic and paralinguistic aspects of speech). A sample quotation from 'the emotional voice' conveys the flavour of the advice. Readers are instructed first to develop awareness of the emotions they project in their own voices, and then to practice 'modulating' the voice 'to reflect genuine feelings for each customer and to develop their feelings for you'. For example:

- If a customer comes across as cold and diffident, convince yourself that beneath the surface is a warm, caring, loving human being. Try to reach that suppressed warmth by injecting emotional warmth into your own words.
- If a customer comes across as being overpowering and effusive, convince yourself is that beneath the surface is someone who is desperate for recognition and admiration. Therefore in responding to the customer, try to underline your words with a tone of emotional approval.
- If a customer comes across as being kind and caring then respond in the same way, ensuring that your voice is soft, rounded and undulates smoothly to reflect your own feelings of compassion.
  By drawing on your feelings and emotions to fine-tune the way you use your voice, you will be much better able to connect emotionally with customers and become someone they really like. (1998: 109)

Readers are then given a list of emotions that customers' voices might project, and told what emotion they should try to project in response: for instance, if a customer sounds 'worried' you should be 'reassuring', if they sound 'sad' you should be 'compassionate', if they sound 'angry' you should be 'soothing' and so on.

This sort of guidance gives a new meaning to the expression 'retail therapy'. It is a more sophisticated approach to customer care than simply 'writing up' staff every time they fail to smile, but the conduct being recommended nevertheless remains a form of emotional labour, accomplished linguistically through the techniques of synthetic personalization. If it really were spontaneous and natural, an expression of the employee's 'genuine feelings for each customer', presumably there would be no need to spell out the 'correct' responses and exhort workers to practise them consciously. Then again, at times Freemantle appears to be suggesting that people can be trained, not merely to *simulate* the desired emotions but actually to *feel* them. In a chapter titled 'Training people to be liked by your customers', he suggests that training must focus not on 'programmed behavior', but on 'dealing with people's innermost feelings and trying to modify them so that they feel good about the customer and the customer feels good about them' (1998: 229). He adds:

> It is an incredible challenge to teach a person to like a customer as well as develop the necessary attributes to be liked by a customer. To do so you have to teach people how to manage their feelings and emotions; you have to teach them to re-examine some fundamental principles relating to integrity, openness, honesty and trust . . . It is pointless teaching someone to smile at customers unless that person can reach deep down inside themselves to determine the real, genuine reason why they should smile.

Freemantle does not address the possibility that someone might 'reach deep down inside themselves' and discover a real, genuine reason why they should *not* smile. Although his 'big idea' is that customers' choices are not governed exclusively by rational calculation, he does not foresee that *workers* might have some emotional resistance to the kind and degree of re-education he proposes. The hypothetical worker who appears in the pages of management texts is invariably both eager to meet changing corporate expectations and sufficiently plastic to do so easily. By contrast, the real workers whose opinions are reported in, for instance, the *Washington Post* report on Safeway's superior service programme are fully formed persons who bring a certain amount of other baggage to work with them. It would not be surprising if in reality, many workers were reluctant to take on the 'incredible challenge' of becoming a different person – 'someone [customers] really like'.

In fact, though, Freemantle has an alternative suggestion, which is discussed in his chapter 'Recruiting people your customers like'. As that title suggests, the solution is to hire people with the 'right' qualities in the first place, rather than trying to modify them through training later on. 'Too often', Freemantle observes (1998: 211–12), 'the priority in selecting people is technical skills and experience rather than their ability to relate emotionally to customers. . . . subjectivity is essential when selecting the right candidate'. He cites with approval a retail company in New York which recruited workers for a new store by calling applicants in, ostensibly for interview, but then simply watching how they conducted themselves in the waiting room: whether they talked to other candidates, if they offered to get coffee, how they handed the cup. The company took no account of qualifications or previous experience, but selected those whose self-presentation struck observers as most 'likeable'. Such a proceeding is of course antithetical to the current orthodoxy of 'human resources' management with its 'objective' job and person specifications (not to speak of its commitment, at least in theory, to equal opportunities).

After a decade of 'programmed behavior' inculcated by customer care training, it seems there may be something of a backlash, of which Freemantle's book is not the only expression. A 1998 advertisement for the Irish airline Aer Lingus proclaimed, for instance: 'Our people don't need to be trained on how to be nice'. Whereas it has been common for some years to make the thoroughness of your customer care training a selling point, here the selling point is that Aer Lingus staff's niceness is *not* the product of thorough training, but the genuine article. No doubt this exploits a national stereotype of the Irish as particularly friendly people, but it also suggests a more general feeling in the air that consumers have had enough of synthetically personalized service, and are looking for something more 'authentic'.

In early 1999 an industrial dispute – also within the airline industry – provided a dramatic illustration of the increasing tension between managers' wish to present customer care as a natural expression of their staff's sincere desire to please, and workers' experience of it as a form of productive labour. After Cathay Pacific airlines announced that flight attendants must work additional hours in order to qualify for a pay rise, the attendants voted to take industrial action by refusing to smile at passengers for one hour of every flight. Their union chair pointed out that this was essentially a kind of work to rule, given that 'our contracts do not say we have to smile' (Thorpe, 1999). Although the action was reported in newspapers as a humorous story, the reports made it evident that Cathay Pacific's management did not regard it as a joke; it also became evident that management attitudes to the status of smiling on the job were confused and contradictory. On one hand a company spokesman was quoted saying 'I don't think it's fair to the passengers . . . because they are paying good money for a good service' – a comment which suggests that smiling is a recognized part of the service and so part of the attendant's contractual duties. On the other hand, the same spokesman insisted that 'the attendants are not *told* to smile, there is sincerity and genuine meaning in it'. This supports the union's contention that smiling is not compulsory, but at the same time denies the union's implicit argument that it is work; rather it is presented as something that 'comes naturally' to these particular workers. To quote the company spokesman again: 'most Asian carriers, and the region in general, are renowned for their warmth and superior service'. Asian female subservience for Cathay Pacific has the same status as Irish friendliness for Aer Lingus, and also, of course, the same importance for the airline's brand image. The company spokesman conceded that the flight attendants' action would have 'a serious effect on the image of the airline' – presumably not just because passengers would miss the smiles during the hour they were withheld, but because afterwards it would be impossible to maintain the belief that the smiles were authentic expressions of attendants' feelings.

As Robin Leidner (1993) also notes, authenticity is an issue for all organizations that regulate communication in order to personalize service. Despite the ubiquity of synthetic personalization, the idea that a speaker's institutional persona might be wholly constructed, bearing little or no resemblance to their 'real' self, appears to cause many people considerable discomfort. Thus customer care may lose its charm for the customer if it is revealed as 'inauthentic' – coerced or, to echo Goffman, merely cynical. This is the weakness the Cathay Pacific flight attendants exploited, and which some customers pointed out in their comments on Safeway's superior service programme. The Safeway example also illustrates the other dimension of the problem: there is a point beyond which companies are likely to encounter resistance from their own employees to demands for behaviour they perceive as 'so artificial it's unreal'. Generally stated, the problem is that many or most people subscribe to the commonsense view that the way you interact with others in talk is an expression of your individual personality, which is both 'natural' and unique. Certainly, I found this to be the dominant assumption among my informants. Those who objected to the regulation of their spoken interactions at work almost always did so on the ground that it suppressed individuality. The suggestion that regulation imposed, say, a 'white' or 'middle class' or 'southern English' model – that is, that it suppressed *social* differences – was rarely broached, and when I broached it myself it did not elicit such strong reactions as the 'personality' issue. Similarly, when I asked a group of students if they thought it would be a good idea to assess their oral skills in the same way as their writing skills, a majority felt this would be 'unfair' because it would discriminate against people who were 'naturally' quiet or slow to put their thoughts into words. I pointed out that traditional ways of assessing writing might be said to discriminate against bad spellers, nonstandard dialect users and people with writer's block. The students insisted this was quite different: there was not the same close identification between writing style and the individual self.

The idea that the way you speak derives directly from the person you are also underpins a common view, expressed by both managers and workers, that *training* in interpersonal communication is only marginally useful: some people are just not good communicators, and never will be. In a focus group made up of bank employees, for instance, one informant, asked whether he had received training in dealing with complaints (in fact, a very common topic on customer care courses), replied, to general agreement, that such training would be futile. 'You either have it or you don't have it. I mean no one could tell you how to be sympathetic, it's either in your nature or it isn't'. This group made many references to sympathy, confidence, friendliness and other linguistically projected qualities that training often attempts to develop as 'not something you can train into people' and 'something you can't do on a flipchart'.

These views were not shared by everyone I spoke to. Some students saw nothing wrong with assessing oral skills, some managers placed great emphasis on customer care and communication training, and some informants talked about valuable lessons they had learned from the experience of working in service environments where systematic attention was paid to spoken interaction. But the continuing strength of the other point of view shows what the discourse of 'communication skills' is up against. One of the things the 'skills' discourse tries to do is place the ability to interact with others orally on a par with the ability to type, or compose acceptable business letters (or essays), or make arithmetical calculations. The 'skill' is learned, and is taken to be separable from the person; a deficiency of skill is not the same as a personal defect. But persuading people to approach 'communication' in this way is not as easy as persuading them to take a similar approach to numeracy or information technology. One reason why there needs to be so much propagandizing on behalf of 'communication skills' is precisely that many people still do not see the way they talk to others as a form of behaviour which is detachable from their individual personality and, as a corollary, susceptible to modification at will and without limit. This makes criticizing someone's way of talking a more sensitive proceeding than, say, criticizing the speed and accuracy of their typing: judgements on interactional style are easily apprehended as judgements of personal (in)adequacy. A general issue I will return to at various points is how far the idea of talking as artless self-expression is in the process of being displaced by new understandings of communication as a set of skills, which can be improved by the application of expert knowledge, informed constructive criticism and self-conscious practice.

But the foregoing discussion of customer care and emotional labour in service work has raised another question, one which cuts across the 'natural behaviour versus learned skill' debate. Does the sort of linguistic regulation practised by Safeway, or recommended by David Freemantle, really have anything to do with *skilling* people, or would it be better described as *styling* them?

'Skilling' and 'styling'

The term *skill* connotes *practical* expertise, the ability to *do* something, but skills training as traditionally conceived also places emphasis on knowledge, understanding and judgement. A 'skilled' person does not only know how to do certain things, but also understands *why* those things are done the way they are. S/he is acquainted with the general principles of the activity s/he is skilled in, and so is able to modify what s/he does in response to the exigencies of any specific situation. A communication training programme based on Hermine Scheeres's 'spoken language demands of the restructured workplace' (1998) would in these terms be a 'skilling' programme. No doubt it would instruct trainees in specific techniques for 'arguing a point' or 'negotiating', but it would also identify these as linguistic genres or 'activity types' (Levinson, 1992) and explain the general principles in virtue of which some interactional strategies are likely to be more effective than others. Although the execution is inept, the John Stephenson materials examined above are also at least partly about 'skilling' trainees. The advice is mostly of an 'instrumental' kind – it is about using language to do things – and specific recommendations on how to do things are commonly accompanied by reasons and principles (albeit in this case drawn from a manifestly inadequate model of human behaviour).

The word *styling*, on the other hand, connotes a kind of grooming of surface appearances. This, arguably, would be a more accurate description than 'skilling' of what goes on in many regimes of customer care, where there is little engagement with the underlying purposes and principles of verbal interaction, but rather an intense concern to manage what might be called its *aesthetics*. Perhaps the most obvious indication of this preoccupation with the aesthetic is the amount of attention paid to the *voice*, with particular emphasis on prosody and voice quality. Railway announcers are told to perform in smiley voice, Safeway employees are graded on the 'warmth' in their voices, David Freemantle's readers are given pages of instruction on 'the emotional voice'. (As we will see in Chapter 4, call centre operators are subject to a whole set of vocal performance criteria, and in some cases are recruited for the supposed qualities of their voices.) By contrast, Hermine Scheeres says nothing, and the John Stephenson materials very little, about how people should sound.

The phenomenon of 'aesthetic labour' in service economies has been discussed by Witz *et al.*, who point out (1998: 4) that aesthetic 'sense knowledge' has traditionally been distinguished from 'intellectual knowledge', and argue that in the service sector, employers are increasingly prioritizing the former over the latter. Rather than judging people on their knowledge, experience or technical skills, employers now seek 'a supply of embodied capacities possessed by workers at the point of entry into employment' which they can 'mobilise, develop and commodify' in order to 'produce a particular "style" of service encounter' (1998: 4). This 'style' is defined in terms of aesthetics:

> ... a sensory experience through which objects appeal in a special way ... or, more simply, are imbued with expressive form. The concept of aesthetic labour moves beyond the concept of emotional labour because it foregrounds the *sensible* components of the service encounter. In particular, it foregrounds the *embodied* character of service work, and the ways in which distinctive service styles depend as much upon manufactured 'styles of the flesh' ... as they do upon the manufacture of 'feeling'.
>
> (1998: 4)

The notion of workplace regimes seeking to imbue the behaviour of employees with a prescribed 'expressive form' in order that service encounters should conform to a predetermined 'style' nicely captures what I mean by 'styling' communication. The 'styled' communicator uses language less to do things (negotiate, argue, solve problems) than to be, or appear to be things (warm, friendly, enthusiastic, soothing). Expressiveness is valued over instrumentality. The fact that speaking is part of 'aesthetic labour' is underlined by the intense interest taken in employees' accents, their pitch, rate of speech, intonation and voice quality, but it is not just the voice that is 'styled', or 'imbued with expressive form'. There is also an aesthetic dimension to the less obviously 'fleshly' *interactional* style which is valorized by an institution and codified in its instructions to, or scripts for, its embodied representatives. In face-to-face contexts, voice-styles and interactional styles are in addition inseparable from the styling of nonlinguistic elements of the encounter – the employee's appearance and dress, the layout and design of the site where service encounters take place, and so on. The intention is that all these elements should meld into a single, coherent aesthetic experience for the customer.

My use of the term *styling* here is related to the notion of 'linguistic style' elaborated by sociolinguistic researchers such as the California Style Collective and Penelope Eckert (who is also one of the collective's members). Eckert explains:

> Linguistic style is a way of speaking that is peculiar to a community of practice – its linguistic identity ... Briefly put, style is a clustering of resources that has social meaning. The construction of a style is a process of bricolage: a stylistic agent appropriates resources from a broad sociolinguistic landscape, recombining them to make a distinctive style.
>
> (1996: 3)

Eckert and her colleagues are interested in the *self*-styling undertaken by adolescents and pre-adolescents, and particularly in the way they appropriate socially meaningful variation in, say, the pronunciation of vowel sounds. Styling in the workplace operates in a somewhat similar way: a community of practice with a distinctive way of speaking is constructed through bricolage, using resources for meaning among which prosodic, paralinguistic and politeness phenomena are especially prominent. What is different about it is that it is not the speakers themselves who are the 'stylistic agents', deciding what to appropriate from the 'broad sociolinguistic landscape' and how to put elements together. Instead the preferred style is designed by people who will not have to use it themselves, and imposed on those lower down the hierarchy. Like feeling in emotional labour, style in aesthetic labour is a commodity; although they may be encouraged to identify with it, 'styled' workers do not 'own' the style they are obliged to adopt. It is not their own 'cultural capital' but someone else's.

In this discussion of 'styling' and 'skilling' I have invoked a number of distinctions (for example, intellectual knowledge/sense knowledge, instrumental/expressive, acting/appearing) which can hardly fail to recall another culturally salient opposition, masculine/feminine. Commentators on both 'emotional' and 'aesthetic' labour point out that there is a strongly gendered dimension to these forms of work: though increasingly performed by workers of both sexes, they are culturally coded as 'feminine'. It is interesting in this connection that John Stephenson Ltd – a retail business, but one that deals in electrical goods and has traditionally employed men to sell them – emphasizes rational and instrumental aspects of language-use (for instance, problem solving) in its communication training materials, whereas 'feminized' retail environments such as supermarkets and clothes shops seem concerned almost exclusively with styling phraseology and, especially, vocal performance, to project certain attitudes and feelings. This is hardly a watertight distinction, of course: the John Stephenson materials do have an 'emotional' element (they also have some of the hallmarks of 'styling', such as the advice to smile at interlocutors). But it does raise an issue of general interest in relation to 'communication', not only at work but in all the domains to be discussed in this book. That issue is the very widespread perception that women/girls are 'better' communicators than men/boys. In the work domain the postulate of women's superior communication skills underpins the oft-expressed view that women are naturally better suited than men to routine customer service work with its emphasis on the expressive and relational. But the same postulate also underpins a strand of management discourse on enterprise and empowerment, according to which women are well placed to dominate higher status positions too. The thesis is summarized in the title of a piece which the guru of 'excellcnce', Tom Peters, wrote for *Working Woman* magazine in 1990: 'The best new managers will listen, motivate, support: isn't that just like a woman?'. As the 'communication culture' tightens its grip, we hear more and more that the future is female. Conversely we hear more and more about the problem of men and 'the trouble with boys' (Phillips, 1994). I will revisit the issue of gender in later chapters.

Conclusion

As I have tried to show in this chapter, 'communication' – the use of spoken language to interact with others – is at the heart of several important developments in workplaces which have been restructured in line with new managerial approaches. It is both an instrument of organizational 'culture change' and a target for change in its own right; it is implicated, particularly, in the trend towards demanding more and more 'emotional' or 'aesthetic' labour from employees in customer service positions. Discourse about communication at work is also a locus where we may observe some of the contradictions of 'enterprise culture'. The rhetoric of 'empowerment' is in tension with a reality in which the minutiae of linguistic behaviour are obsessively regulated. There is also a contradiction between the rhetoric and the reality of 'skills'. Improving 'communication skills' is the declared aim of numerous workplace training programmes, but at the same time there is debate on whether the ability to communicate in the desired ways really is a teachable 'skill' or whether it is an innate quality of (some) individuals. It is evident, too, that what many employers want, and what they mainly train their employees in, is not communication *skills* but rather a communication *style*. As the Safeway case in particular illustrates, styling employees is not the same thing as skilling them: indeed, one might argue it is often just the opposite.

In the next chapter I will develop these points further, focusing on a kind of workplace where the importance of language and communication is foregrounded even more insistently than it is at John Stephenson or at Safeway: the 'call centre', where standards of service depend entirely on the quality of talk because all customer contact takes place via the telephone. Considering the case of the call centre also allows me to consider a pervasive feature of restructured workplaces that I have not so far mentioned, though it certainly has implications for language and communication: the incorporation of new technology into service routines. The job of the call centre operator illustrates the demands made on workers when service work, and service talk, are subjected to some of the disciplines of the factory production line.

Notes

1 Wal-Mart is a chain of US out-of-town hypermarkets founded by Sam Walton – hence 'so help me Sam' – and in 1997 the *Wall Street Journal* reported it had taken over from General Motors as the largest private employer in the US. The

'oath' is cited by Micklethwait and Wooldridge (1997), who say that new employees are made to raise their right hand and recite it, as if taking the oath in court (see further, Ortega, 1998).

2 The Open University offers degree courses to adults by distance learning (or as the OU calls it, 'supported open learning'). Originally conceived as a 'university of the air', it makes extensive use of BBC radio and television broadcasts. The programme to which this section refers is titled 'Empowerment', and forms part of a course module on 'Managing in Organizations'.

3 This information comes from transcripts of focus group discussions conducted by Dennis Nickson, Chris Warhurst and Anne Witz with the assistance of Anne-Marie Cullen. Participants worked in banks, shops, hotels, bars and restaurants, and were recruited as part of a sociological study of 'aesthetic labour'. All references below to focus group discussions are based on these materials; I am extremely grateful to Anne Witz and her colleagues for making them available to me.

4 These materials were obtained 'unofficially' from employees of the relevant organizations, among which I refer in particular to a non-profit arts organization ('City Arts'), a chain of shops selling electrical goods ('John Stephenson Ltd'), and two major supermarket chains. In all these cases I have participant-observation data as well as documentary materials, and in two cases I have interview data (my thanks to Raymond Bell, Gordon Graham, Samantha Houten and Karen MacGowan). I will also draw on information given in newspapers and on the internet about Safeway supermarkets in the USA.

5 I cannot resist quoting another, less felicitous example from the same materials: it is attributed to a manager from the British Harvester restaurant chain, who allegedly remarked: 'it's amazing how much better our meal tastes to the customer when the toilets are clean'.

6 'Caring, co-operating and communicating' appears to be a standard formula. It reappears in several different sets of training materials in my corpus, including the John Stephenson materials discussed in detail below.

7 The ethnomethodologist Harold Garfinkel used to set his students tasks designed to illustrate the complexity of ordinary social behaviour. For instance, he would instruct them to respond to utterances in casual conversation by asking 'what do you mean?' This was meant to demonstrate that there never comes a point when the meaning of an utterance has been exhausted: asked what they mean, people can always come up with a further layer of explanation. Students carrying out such 'Garfinkel experiments' very frequently found that they provoked a hostile response, until they explained to their baffled and furious interlocutors that they were only doing an assignment for college.

8 The source is an internet discussion group, 'Forced Smiles at Safeway'. For drawing my attention to the *Washington Post* report I am grateful to Scott Kiesling, and for additional assistance I thank Keith Nightenhelser.

9 The offence here may arise from two very different sources. On one hand there is a longstanding tradition of snobbish anti-Americanism in Britain, according to which American expressions are simply 'vulgar' and represent the 'corruption' of a language that originally belongs to 'us'. In complete ideological contrast, however, there is a critique of 'coca-colonialism' which is more concerned to preserve the distinctive linguistic and cultural traditions of other nations in the face of the global dominance of the USA.

10 For the examples given in this paragraph I thank Don Kulick (Swedish), Erika Sólyom (Hungarian), and two delegates to the 44th Annual Meeting of the International Linguistic Association in New York in April 1999, who made comments from the floor regarding post-apartheid South Africa and contemporary Japan.

11 I thank Amanda Harris for this anecdote. Although the issue did not come up in research I did in Britain, while visiting the US I was told more than once by workers in certain sectors (for example, clothes, cosmetics and toiletries retailing, waiting in upmarket restaurants) that male employees perceived the way they had to act as 'effeminate'. One woman reported men in her workplace receiving comments from other men present in the store to the effect that they were 'faggots'. Service scripts and style-rules are officially 'unisex', imposed without regard to the employee's gender, but it can be argued in many cases that they are more consonant with femininity as conventionally understood than with conventional (heterosexual) masculinity (this argument is made in detail in Cameron, 1999b).

12 From a feminist point of view, the same analysis could be made of most heterosexual partnerships: although these relationships are intimate, solidary and in theory egalitarian rather than hierarchical, emotional labour is not equally shared between women and men, but is disproportionately performed by women *for* men.

Bibliography

Boden, Deirdre (1994) *The Business of Talk: Organizations in Action.* Cambridge: Polity.

Brown, Penelope and Levinson, Stephen (1987) *Politeness: Some Universals in Language Usage.* Cambridge: Cambridge University Press.

Cameron, Deborah (1999b) 'Styling the worker: language, gender and emotional labor in new service workplaces (or, you don't have to be nice to work here but it helps to pretend)'. Paper presented to the 44th Annual Meeting of the International Linguistic Association, New York.

Covey, Stephen (1989) *The Seven Habits of Highly Effective People.* New York: Simon & Schuster.

Czerniawska, Fiona (1998) *Corporate Speak: The Use of Language in Business.* London: Macmillan.

Drew, Paul and Heritage, John (eds) (1992) *Talk at Work: Interaction in Institutional Settings.* Cambridge: Cambridge University Press.

Drew, Paul and Sorjonen, Marja-Leena (1997) 'Institutional dialogue', in Teun van Dijk (ed.), *Discourse as Social Interaction: Discourse Studies Vol. II.* Newbury Park: Sage. pp. 92–118.

Eckert, Penelope (1996) 'Vowels and nail polish: the emergence of linguistic style in the preadolescent heterosexual marketplace', Stanford University/Institute for Research on Learning.

Fairclough, Norman (1989) *Language and Power.* London: Longman.

Fairclough, Norman (1992) *Discourse and Social Change.* Cambridge: Polity.

Freemantle, David (1998) *What Customers Like About You: Adding Emotional Value for Service Excellence and Competitive Advantage.* London & Santa Rosa, CA: Nicholas Brealey.

Giddens, Anthony (1991) *Modernity and Self Identity: Self and Society in the Late Modern Age.* Cambridge: Polity.

Goffman, Erving (1959) *The Presentation of Self in Everyday Life.* Garden City, NY: Doubleday.

Goodman, Sharon (1996) 'Market forces speak English', in Sharon Goodman and David Graddol (eds), *Redesigning English: New Texts, New Identities.* London: Routledge. pp. 141–64.

Gunnarsson, Britt-Louise, Linell, Per and Nordberg, Bengt (1997) *The Construction of Professional Discourse*. London: Longman.

Handy, Charles (1996) *Beyond Certainty: The Changing World of Organizations*. London: Hutchinson.

Hochschild, Arlie (1983) *The Managed Heart: The Commercialization of Human Feeling*. Berkeley, CA: University of California Press.

Hutchby, Ian (1999) 'Frame alignment and footing in the organization of talk radio openings', *Journal of Sociolinguistics* 3 (1): 41–63.

Joyce, H., Nesbitt, C., Scheeres, H., Slade, D. and Solomon, N. (1995) *Effective Communication in the Restructured Workplace*. 2 vols. Victoria, Australia: National Food Industry Training Council.

Leidner, Robin (1993) *Fast Food, Fast Talk: Service Work and the Routinization of Everyday Life*. Berkeley, CA: University of California Press.

Levinson, Stephen (1992) 'Activity types and language', in Paul Drew and John Heritage (eds), *Talk At Work*. Cambridge: Cambridge University Press. pp. 66–100.

Micklethwait, John and Wooldridge, Adrian (1997) *The Witch Doctors: What the Management Gurus Are Saying, Why It Matters and How to Make Sense of It*. London: Mandarin Books.

Mumby, D. and Clair, R. D. (1997) 'Organizational Discourse', in Teun van Dijk (ed.), *Discourse as Social Interaction: Discourse Studies Vol II*. Newbury Park: Sage. pp. 181–205.

Ortega, Bob (1998) *In Sam We Trust: The Untold Story of Sam Walton and how Wal-Mart is Devouring America*. New York: Times Business.

Orwell, George (1989 [1949]) *Nineteen Eighty-four*. Harmondsworth: Penguin.

Phillips, Angela (1994) *The Trouble With Boys: A Wise and Sympathetic Guide to the Risky Business of Raising Sons*. New York: Basic Books.

Ritzer, George (1996) *The McDonaldization of Society: An Investigation into the Changing Character of Contemporary Social Life*. Revised edn. Thousand Oaks, CA: Pine Forge Press.

Scheeres, Hermine (1998) 'New workplaces: talk and teamwork'. Paper presented at Sociolinguistics Symposium 12, London.

Stubbs, Michael (1997) 'Language and the mediation of experience: linguistic representation and cognitive orientation', in Florian Coulmas (ed.), *The Handbook of Sociolinguistics*. Oxford: Blackwell. pp. 344–57.

Thorpe, Nick (1999) 'Airline pay offer wipes the smile off staff's faces'. *The Scotsman*, 7 January.

Witz, Anne, Warhurst, Chris, Nickson, Dennis and Cullen, Anne-Marie (1998) '"Human hardware"? Aesthetic labour, the labour of aesthetics and the aesthetics of organization'. Paper presented to the Work, Employment and Society conference, Cambridge.

Wodak, Ruth and Iedema, Rick (1999) 'Introduction: organizational discourses and practices'. Special Issue, 'Discourse in Organizations', *Discourse & Society*, 10 (1): 5–19.

76

THE ENTREPRENEURIAL UNIVERSITY

A discursive profile of a higher education buzzword

Gerlinde Mautner

Source: *Critical Discourse Studies*, 2:2 (2005), 95–120.

The growing orientation of public universities towards the corporate sector has had a significant impact on higher education governance, management, and discourse. The rhetoric of the free market, manifested most tangibly in business-related lexis, is now firmly established in the discursive repertoire employed by academic leaders, politicians, and the media, as well as parts of higher education research. Within this rhetoric, enterprise and enterprising, as well as entrepreneur and entrepreneurial, stand out as keywords carrying significant ideological loads that reflect the colonisation of academia by the market. The organisational and policy-making implications of academic enterprise have received considerable attention from higher education researchers, while discourse analysts have identified general discursive features of the 'marketised' higher education landscape. What the present paper adds to the existing debate is an in-depth study of a set of keywords in which processes of adaptation and appropriation crystallise, thus showing how macro-level social phenomena are mirrored, on the micro-level of linguistic detail, in the collocational behaviour of individual lexical items. The textual data that this paper is based on, gleaned mostly from the Internet, show that entrepreneur, entrepreneurial, enterprise, and enterprising are ambiguous in denotation and rich in connotation, making them susceptible to processes of semantic appropriation to suit particular agendas. Prevailing motifs and representations are identified through a combination of the computer-supported survey of Web-based material and the qualitative analysis of sample texts.

> A university, like all other human institutions ... is not outside, but inside the general social fabric of a given era. It is not something apart, something historic, something that yields as little as possible to forces and influences that are more or less new. It is, on the contrary – so I shall assume – an expression of the age, as well as an influence operating upon both present and future.
>
> (Flexner, 1930, p. 3)

The aim of this paper is to chart the discursive territory round a set of keywords that have come to play a central role in higher education (HE). These keywords are *entrepreneurial, entrepreneurship,* and *entrepreneur(s)*, as well as *enterprise* and *enterprising*. The social, political, and educational context in which they have moved centre-stage is a complex mesh of trends including the reduction of government funding, the consequent necessity to raise money from external, frequently corporate, sources, deregulation, increased competition and internationalisation, and the replacement of collegial by managerial (or, as critics would have it, managerialist) governance structures. More detail on this background will be provided in the section headed 'Socio-political context'. The most significant trend for the matter at hand, however, is the changing relationship between academia and business. Once two separate social domains, the two have been moving closer together and are now melding at various points of contact. What better linguistic expression of this than a previously unthinkable adjective-noun combination: *the entrepreneurial university*.

New ties between universities and business are constantly being established, and existing ones strengthened. They are the result of intensified exchange processes between universities and their commercial environment. These exchange processes generally have both a financial dimension, following a 'money-for-expertise' formula, and an interpersonal one, as businesspeople are appointed to positions in university management or on boards of trustees, for example, or as faculty take on consultancy contracts. Exchange invariably leads to new social and discursive practices, such as 'selling', 'advertising', or 'managing'. They are imported into the academic domain, where previously the prevailing norm was characterised by non-utilitarian knowledge creation and consultative, committee-based governance, as well as by its concomitant non-commercial discourse. While it is true that at various times in the past, and in different ways, reality often diverged from this ideal – witness the traditional role of universities in educating professional cadres (Barnett, 1990) – the extent to which business is now making inroads into academe is quite unprecedented. Within universities, 'manager-academics' (Deem, 2003; Deem & Johnson, 2000; Johnson, 2002) are the key drivers of this development. According to Trowler (1998, p. 32), 'it is among senior higher education managers that the managerialist arguments are articulated in their most unalloyed form.' By way of an example, here are recent comments by the current Vice-Chancellor and Chief Executive (as his full title runs) of the University of Surrey. 'Unalloyed' indeed:

> Modern universities are businesses and, like any business, to achieve sound finances they must develop appropriate services and products for which their customers – the government, business, charities, students and the public – should be prepared to pay a fair price.
>
> (Dowling, 2004, paragraph 2)

'Entrepreneurship', both as activity and discourse, is one of those 'imported' practices. As the corpus and textual analysis will demonstrate, it is deployed by academic leaders and administrators as a carrier of key values that they want their external stakeholders to associate with the organisation, and their internal stakeholders both to believe in and implement. There is no shortage of studies exploring the organisational and policy-making implications of educational entrepreneurialism (Etzkowitz, 1998, 2003; Etzkowitz, Webster, Gebhardt, & Cantisano Terra, 2000; Hay, Butt, & Kirby, 2003; Henkel, 1997; Ozga, 1998; Slaughter & Leslie, 1994; Wasser, 1990). Likewise, key features of 'marketised' discourse have come under scrutiny from discourse analysts (most notably, and seminally, by Fairclough, 1993). The specific contribution that the present paper is making consists in showing how the social, macro-level phenomena identified by higher education research can be traced at the micro-level of lexis and phraseology, through examining the discursive profile of pivotal expressions in which social structures and processes crystallise.

The organisation of this paper is as follows. I shall begin by outlining the sociopolitical context in which the concept of the entrepreneurial university is embedded, drawing on and surveying a wide range of higher education literature as I go along. Next, I shall discuss the concept of keywords as well as the data and method used to build the discursive profile of the keywords in question. Having examined key usages of the term, in both prominent academic texts and a large, computerised reference corpus, the paper then moves on to extract the term's semantic prosodies from the results of a search on the World Wide Web. Following an analysis of key motifs and rhetorical devices used in connection with the 'entrepreneurial university' in three texts, the final section integrates the findings from a critical perspective.

Before proceeding, I would like to declare up-front where I stand on this contested terrain, taking, as van Dijk (1993, p. 252) advises critical discourse analysts to do, 'an explicit sociopolitical stance'. Some of the changes effected under the banner of entrepreneurship I would certainly regard as beneficial. Institutional cultures fostering innovation, for example, strike me as a more than welcome change from the hierarchical overbureaucratisation that used to be (and some would claim still is) the hallmark of so many universities. Other developments, such as research being subjected to commercial pressures, I object to because I regard them as a threat to disinterestedness, independence, and objectivity. The blurring of boundaries between universities and the for-profit sector also jeopardises the freedom of the former to criticise the latter: the hand that feeds is less likely to be bitten. I agree with Ronald Barnett's assessment that 'through the ideology of entrepreneurialism the university's particular place as a critical forum is undermined' (2003, p. 73). Like Trowler (2001, p. 197), I see 'the importance of active resistance to what is becoming an increasingly hegemonic discourse located in managerialist structural roots'. Thus, in unpacking educational enterprise discourse I am hoping to make a contribution to universities' emancipation from these discursive hegemonies.

The socio-political context

The significance of keywords derives crucially from the social, cultural, and political environment in which they are embedded. It is imperative, therefore, that this environment be described and drawn upon as an interpretative resource.

There is widespread agreement in the HE literature that in recent decades universities around the globe have been undergoing substantial changes (though HE researchers disagree in their evaluative stance, an issue I do not have the space to explore further here). These changes have been conceptualised as occurring on three layers, the 'national-structural', 'organizational', and 'professional-subjective' (Parker & Jary, 1995, p. 320). There are repercussions on all elements of the classic triad of teaching, research, and administration, and in various strata of organisational practices. Overarching and elusive concepts like institutional culture, image, professional identities, and academic value systems are affected as much as the more hands-on aspects of governance and financial management. As Barnett puts it, 'all the conceptual and operational underpinnings of the university crumble' (Barnett, 2000, p. 1). Among the various trends and developments that make up this scenario of uncertainty and upheaval (for a succinct overview see Peters & Roberts, 2000, pp. 128–129), the 'incursion by markets' (O'Neill & Solomon, 1996, p. 82) is probably the dominant force. Several interlocking factors combine to make universities more responsive to 'the market'. First, widening access (or, as critics would have it, 'massification') without a matching increase in government funding produces budget shortfalls. Second, because of budgetary constraints, commercial funding streams are becoming more important, whether generated through spin-out companies, consulting contracts, or sponsorship deals, and this leads to 'the spread into universities of norms and institutional forms characteristic of commercial society' (O'Neill & Solomon, 1996, p. 82). Managerialism is one of these norms (Deem, 1998;

Trowler, 2001). Though marketisation and managerialism are not the same thing, they tend to be mutually reinforcing phenomena and have, in fact, been referred to as 'twin strategies' (Blackmore & Sachs, 2003, p. 478).

While there is a trend in higher education towards 'the adoption of a free-market or corporate-business perspective' (Webster, 2003, p. 85), there is a parallel trend in knowledge-intensive industries towards an increased reliance on scientific expertise and 'collegial' forms of organisational control (Kleinman & Vallas, 2001, p. 453). Instead of seeing current changes in the HE/business relationship exclusively as a case of (one-sided) 'colonisation/ appropriation' (Chouliaraki & Fairclough, 1999, p. 93), they are perhaps more adequately conceptualised, as Kleinman & Vallas (2001) argue, as a process of convergence. However, this convergence is 'asymmetrical . . . because although codes and practices circulate in both directions, industry ultimately appears to have an upper hand in this process' (Kleinman & Vallas, 2001, p. 451).

Another contextual factor that must not be ignored is the part played by governments and the parliaments in which they command majorities. They initiate, support, and sustain change in the HE sector not only through creating the requisite regulatory framework and allocating budgets, but also through promulgating a pro-market educational agenda in parliamentary debates, media appearances, and official policy documents.[1] The apposite keywords appear as central nodes in the argument. Witness, for example, the statement by David Blunkett, then UK Secretary of State for Education and Employment, who said, referring to an earlier comment by Prime Minister Tony Blair, that 'in the knowledge economy, entrepreneurial universities will be as important as entrepreneurial businesses, the one fostering the other. The "do nothing" university will not survive – and it will not be the job of government to bail it out' (Blunkett, 2000, paragraph 87). Note the stark dichotomy: universities are tagged as either 'entrepreneurial' or 'do nothing', the former good and fit to live, the latter bad and doomed to die.

There are two other facets of the socio-political environment which ought to be touched upon here. First, one needs to recognise the international scale on which academic entrepreneurship is being promoted. The World Wide Web search that provided input to the present study revealed relevant documents not only from Western Europe, North America, and Australia, but also from Eastern Europe and Asia. They included a speech entitled *Towards an Entrepreneurial University* by the President of the National University of Singapore (Shih, 2002) and accounts from Estonia (Aarna, n.d.), Brazil (Scavarda do Carmo, n.d.), China,[2] and the Philippines,[3] as well as an outline describing an EU Tempus Tacis Project designed to develop a strategic plan for the University of Nizhni Novgorod (Russia) under the heading of *Becoming an Entrepreneurial University*,[4] the latter being a prime example of the deliberate dissemination of the concept, in this case from

West to East. This confirms Etzkowitz *et al.*'s (2000, p. 313) claim that 'it appears that the "entrepreneurial university" is a global phenomenon with an isomorphic development path, despite different starting points and modes of expression.'

Second, in addition to being diffused across regions and cultures, the cluster of phenomena comprising marketisation, managerialism, and entre-preneurialism is by no means restricted to higher eduation, but has affected diverse social domains, including art (Wu, 2002), health care (Poole, 2000), and public services generally (Flynn, 2000). This, in turn, needs to be seen in the still wider context of the 'enterprise culture' (Keat & Abercrombie, 1991), which was identified, in the British context, as a 'central motif in the political thought and practice of the Conservative government' (Keat, 1991, p. 1), but has since also been described as a constitutive element of New Labour's 'Third Way' discourse (Fairclough, 2000). In this respect, the entrepreneurial university is indeed, to use Flexner's (1930, p. 3) phrase, 'an expression of the age'.

The profiling of keywords: data and method

The idea of the discursive profile is a response to two of the hardy perennials of discourse analytic methodology: first, the time-honoured question of how to deal with the relationship between macro-level phenomena, both social and discursive, and their micro-level linguistic manifestations, and second, how to square the restrictions imposed by the essentially qualitative toolbox of critical discourse analysis with larger (and thus, one would hope, more representative) corpora. The approach adopted here is outlined in Hardt-Mautner (1995; re-published in revised form as Koller & Mautner, 2004) and applied, for example, in Mautner (2000), Piper (2000a) and Piper (2000b). It draws on Stubbs (1996), in particular Chapter 7 on 'Keywords, Collocations and Culture', and Stubbs (2001), who demonstrates 'how corpus methods can provide systematic evidence about the significance of . . . such keywords in English' (2001, p. 145). In both books, Stubbs acknowledges the significance of Raymond Williams's book *Keywords: A Vocabulary of Culture and Society* (1976/1983) as well as that of J. R. Firth's work. As early as 1935, Firth called for 'research into the detailed contextual distribution of sociologically important words, what one might call *focal* or *pivotal* words' (Firth 1935/1957, p. 10, original italics).

Teubert's (2000) work on Eurosceptic discourse (summarised, together with studies in a similar vein, in Hunston, 2002, pp. 109–120) stands in the same tradition. Following Hermanns (1994), Teubert (2000) distinguishes between 'stigma keywords' and 'banner keywords'. Significantly, one and the same term can be a stigma word for one group, and a banner word for another, thus effectively functioning as an indicator of group membership and/or ideological affiliation. *Entrepreneurial*, when applied to universities, certainly falls into that category, polarising as it does supporters and detractors, modernisers and traditionalists.

The fundamental rationale for concentrating on keywords, in previous work and this paper, is that they can be seen as 'nodes around which ideological battles are fought' (Stubbs, 2001, p. 188). Naturally, one must not stop at directing the analytic lens narrowly at the keyword as such; it can only ever provide an entry point to a more wide-angle kind of analysis, as indeed Raymond Williams (1976/1983) acknowledges. He also insists, rightly, that 'the words' must be seen as 'elements of the problems' (Williams, 1976/1983, p. 16), and this is what justifies and in fact necessitates this focus on keywords.

Seeing 'words' as 'elements of problems' is, of course, resonant with a core principle underpinning critical discourse analysis, the view that discourse is both socially constituted and constitutive (Fairclough, 1992, p. 64). Because 'a discourse is not merely talk' but 'actually structures conduct' (Webster, 2003, p. 89), taking issue with discursive practices is one way of influencing conduct.

Data collection for this study followed several interconnected paths. The first step was a search of the World Wide Web, using webcorp (http://www.webcorp.org.uk/), a search engine which also produces concordances. The output for the search words *entrepreneurial university/ies* provided initial evidence of who the key voices are in the debate, of the genres involved, and of the dominant semantic prosodies. Semantic prosody, according to Louw (1993, p. 175), is 'the consistent aura of meaning with which a form is imbued by its collocates,' or, as Hunston put it, the 'indication that something is good or bad' (Hunston, 2004, p. 157).[5]

The results of the webcorp search (clickable, with direct links to the original sites, as in google) were then followed up, with texts being downloaded and/or printed out and added to the corpus. In a second step, the 56-million word COBUILD WordbanksOnline corpus (http://www.cobuild.collins.co.uk/) was searched for occurrences of *entrepreneur/s* and *entrepreneurial* in order to establish what collocates the keywords attract outside the specific social domain under investigation, the assumption being that a lexeme's general semantic aura was likely to have some impact on domain-specific usage. To complete the picture, and because quite a few texts turned out to be using *enterprising* and *enterprise* alongside *entrepreneurial*, COBUILD was searched for those terms as well. The third source of data was a systematic trawl through the Web sites of the top 30 British universities, following the ranking published on the Web site of the *Education Guardian* (http://education.guardian.co.uk/higher/).

Drawing up the discursive profile, then, involved: (a) cataloguing key usages; (b) examining frequent and salient collocations of the keywords in question (both in the thematically focussed, purpose-built corpus described above and in large reference corpora), with particular attention being paid to semantic prosody; (c) mapping out the motifs that cluster around the keywords, and (d) identifying the rhetorical devices used to talk the keywords up and down, respectively. The 'motif' is understood as an analytical category capturing content (Mautner, 2000, p. 83). For example, references to a university's contribution to the local economy would constitute a motif, as would independence from state funding. Motifs do evaluative work through their presence/absence and the degree of salience they are awarded in text. Authors signal stance by choosing or foregrounding some motifs while ignoring or backgrounding others. 'Rhetorical device', on the other hand, is used as a cover term to refer to strategic choices among the linguistic forms available on various linguistic levels, from the macro-level of textual organisation to the micro-levels of syntax and lexis, where systems such as modality and transitivity are located and where the persuasive force of semantic 'loads' comes into play.

Entrepreneurial and enterprising: key texts and an overview of usage

The phrase *entrepreneurial university* is generally attributed to Burton R. Clark. His 1998 book, *Creating Entrepreneurial Universities: Organizational Pathways of Transformation*, has become the hub of an intertextual network of cross-references. It is mentioned and quoted from frequently in the British, North American, and Australian higher education literatures, and also worldwide. A google search for it yielded well over 100 results, showing the book to feature in seminar programmes, policy documents, and on reading lists, with the trail of reception reaching far beyond Anglo-Saxon academia. Clark's picture of the entrepreneurial university is rightly said to have 'achieved iconic status among university models for the twenty-first century' (Shattock, 2003, p. 146). Hindle (2001, p. 5) calls Clark's book 'the bible of the [entrepreneurial university] movement'. Although both concept and phrase have since developed a life of their own, the key position and sustained impact of Clark's book make it an obvious starting point for the discursive profile the present paper aims to draw up.

Clark (1998) begins his account by setting out his understanding of *entrepreneurial*:

'Entrepreneurial' is taken in this study as a characteristic of social systems; that is, of entire universities and their internal departments, research centers, faculties, and schools. The concept carries the overtones of 'enterprise' – a willful effort in institution-building that requires much special activity and energy. Taking risks when initiating new practices whose outcome is in doubt is a major factor. An entrepreneurial university, on its own, actively seeks to

137

innovate in how it goes about its business. It seeks to work out a substantial shift in organizational character so as to arrive at a more promising posture for the future. Entrepreneurial universities seek to become 'stand-up' universities that are significant actors on their own terms. Institutional entrepreneurship can be seen as both process and outcome.

(Clark, 1998, pp. 3–4)

He then continues to explain his choice of *entrepreneurial* over *innovative*, conceding that the latter would have been 'gentler in overtone':

Throughout much of the two years and more of the research, the two terms 'entrepreneurial' and 'innovative' were used as loosely synonymous. The concept of 'innovative university' has much appeal. Gentler in overtone, it also casts a wider net. It avoids the negative connotations that many academics attach to individual entrepreneurs as aggressive business-oriented people seeking to maximize profit. . . . I have chosen 'entrepreneurial' over 'innovative' as the organizing conception for this book because it points more powerfully to deliberate local effort, to actions that lead to change in organizational posture. Under its banner I can more appropriately group some processes by which modern universities measurably change themselves.

(Clark, 1998, p. 4)

In this passage, Clark describes a deliberate process of semantic choice, the result of which, given the success of the book, was to prove momentous. In weighing up the options, he shows full awareness of the negative connotations that *entrepreneurial* would have in some quarters, but decides to go for it all the same. The main reason he gives for doing so is of a rhetorical nature – the term, he feels, 'points more powerfully' to what he wishes to get across. This is a point worth noting in the light of subsequent re-contextualisations of Clark's book. Those who support and adopt his ideas also accept his chosen terminology: the concept and the label have become inextricably linked.

A detailed and very telling semantic argument also stands at the beginning of another key book in this debate, Slaughter and Leslie's (1997) *Academic Capitalism*.[6] The subtitle, significantly, reads *Politics, Policies, and the Entrepreneurial University*. Thus, while the *entrepreneurial university* does feature in their title and elsewhere in the book, they choose to overlay it in their main title with another keyword, *capitalism*, which has negative connotations. As a matter of fact, *capitalism* is intended specifically to counteract the persuasive power that *entrepreneurial* is perceived to have:

> We decided to employ *academic capitalism* in part because alternatives – *academic entrepreneurism* or *entrepreneurial activity* – seemed to be euphemisms for *academic capitalism* which failed to capture fully the encroachment of the profit motive into the academy.
>
> (Slaughter & Leslie, 1997, p. 9, original italics)

Their choice is of course no less rhetorical than Clark's, and the lexis they use to defend it is also highly charged with emotion: the 'encroachment of the profit motive into the academy' is decidedly negative, with *encroachment* suggesting unwanted and excessive intrusion. The perspective thus conveyed is distinctly different from the 'partnership' discourse that pro-entrepreneurial authors like to activate when describing universities' relationship with the corporate sector.

In these two seminal academic texts as well as in the other sources I shall examine later on, academic entrepreneurship emerges as a complex, multi-layered concept. Its various meanings fall roughly into three groups: (a) engaging in for-profit activity (i.e., selling goods and services, be they patents, courses, or consulting, at competitive market prices), under the university's own name, through so-called spin-out/spin-off companies, or under contract to for-profit enterprises; (b) restructuring and managing the organisation in ways that facilitate such market-driven behaviour; and (c) aspects of organisational culture, in particular a rallying around values such as efficiency, dynamism, and innovation. Which of these elements are fore-grounded in any given text, and what discursive representation they are subjected to, is a function of the ideological stance of the author. Broadly speaking, sceptics foreground (a), marketisation, whereas believers focus on (c), the somewhat elusive psychological and atmospheric aspects of organisational transformation. Later, we shall examine how these positions are articulated.

In actual discourse, the meaning elements identified above are not neatly separated but intertwined and blurred, with many authors exploiting the fuzziness of the word in question, and selecting certain meaning elements to suit particular political agendas. Semantic malleability is characteristic of keywords, and *entrepreneurial* is no exception.[7]

A discursive profile would be incomplete if we ignored the wider universe of discourse that lies beyond the particular social practice being investigated. We may be interested ultimately only in how a particular keyword functions in some type of discourse – political, media, religious, or, in our case, higher education – but this does not mean that other usages in other types of discourse are irrelevant. The chances are that these other usages have some impact on domain-specific usage, and that there is a certain degree of semantic spillover between them, creating, if not a complete transfer of denotative meaning, then at least interference among various associative meanings.

Interestingly, the general collocational profile of *entrepreneurial* as well as of *entrepreneur/s*, as it emerges from the COBUILD reference corpus, is not exclusively positive. This ought to be food for thought for all those eager to take Clark's terminology on board. Certainly, in the COBUILD corpus, *elites* and *farmers* can be seen to be referred to as *entrepreneurial*, but so can *hucksters* and *inmates in our jails. Entrepreneurial* is co-ordinated with *flexible, outspoken,* and *innovative,* but also with *free-wheeling, unscrupulous,* and *aggressive.* The noun, *entrepreneur(s),* has a similarly mixed semantic prosody. Collocates hint at success stories (*entrepreneurs made small fortunes, could help revitalise the economy,* and *have their sleeves up and really make it* [the American economy] *work*), but also speak repeatedly of failure. Adjectives used to refer to *entrepreneur(s)* include, on the one hand, such positively charged items as *persistent, able, bright, great, savvy, successful, wealthy,* and *young,* but also *criminal, dubious, haphazard, opportunist,* and *slimy.* Perhaps the most interesting adjective-noun combination is the *serial entrepreneur.* There may be nothing negative about *serial* as such, but the fact that it collocates chiefly with *killer* and *monogamist* does suggest that it is meant disparagingly when applied to entrepreneurs, too.

Whether positive or negative, there is never any doubt in the general corpus that commercial success is what entrepreneurship is about. Entrepreneurs *are expecting to reap rich rewards, are leaping to make money,* or may be *down to* [their] *last million.* In view of this evidence, attempts to strip *entrepreneurial* of its commercial connotations, illustrated by one of the texts analysed in the 'Sample analyses' section, are bound to appear rather futile.

Enterprising, by contrast, has an altogether broader semantic range. Like *entrepreneurial,* it can be both positive and negative (*this enterprising and talented little group* vs. *an enterprising slum-trained coward*) and is used to refer to a quality conducive to commercial success (*those enterprising enough to run a business*). However, unlike *entrepreneurial,* there are instances of *enterprising* that come from domains other than business, and refer to more general adventurousness and innovativeness rather than specifically commercial acumen. There are examples from rugby (*The Eagles were more enterprising behind the scrum*) and from high culture (*the London Symphony Orchestra's enterprising Bruckner-Mozart series*). Most telling of all, perhaps, is the fact that *enterprising* can be applied to animals. The concordances included an *enterprising monkey* and an *enterprising starling.* Neither, presumably, would be referred to as *entrepreneurial.*

The entrepreneurial university: dominant semantic prosodies

As explained in the 'Data and method' section, my exploration of the semantic and social territory surrounding the keywords in question began with a Web search using the webcorp search engine.[8] Serving as an entry point to the universe of discourse that orbits around the keywords, the webcorp output revealed, even before complete texts were retrieved, that over half the occurrences (63 out of 121) had a positive semantic prosody, 25 had a negative one, and the remaining 33 could not be classified either way because the 10-word collocational span in those instances happened not to include any evaluative lexis.

Let us see how the positive semantic prosody is constituted. Adjectival collocates to the left of *(a/the) entrepreneurial university/ies* include *strong, modern, dynamic, top, new, innovative, pre-eminent, young, nimble, respons-ive*, and, indeed, *corporate*. The adverbs that co-occur are *highly, distinctively*, and *truly*.[9] Where the search word functions, syntactically, as a complement, characteristic predicates are *renowned for, is proud of being, show itself off as* ('showing off' is negative, but you can only show something off that you consider an essentially positive quality), *showcases us as, establish a reputa-tion as, we intend to remain, we characterise ourselves as, quality outputs apposite to*, and *the pivotal role of*. To the right of the search word, posit-ively loaded lexis also abounds. The entrepreneurial university is described variously as *active and competitive; of high quality; one of the most self-sufficient in the country; with a long-standing track record of working with local businesses; market-driven in partnership with business; meeting the educational needs of learners world-wide; overflowing with talented students, world-class researchers and excellent teaching staff* (Swinburne University of Technology, n.d., paragraph 12); one *that will attract students, researchers/ professors and external research funds* ("Research and Higher Education", paragraph 3); and one *in which the higher quality of its provision for students is nationally and internationally recognised alongside the excellence of its research* (University of East London, 2000, Appendix 1, paragraph 9). It is said to have *quickly become a pioneer in scientific and technological fields* and to be *a place where you can invest in an area and watch it grow*.

Most of these quotes, as one might have guessed from their up-beat promotional tone and the use of *we*, come from universities' own Web sites, from mission statements, vice-chancellors' and presidents' speeches, and so on. There can be no doubt that in those kinds of sources, 'entrepreneurial' is considered a good thing for a university to be, something to aspire to if you aren't, and to hold on to if you are. Even from these restricted textual environments, we can identify key motifs and discursive representations. We can see, among other things, that the university is cast in a 'serving' role, *meeting* and *responding to* needs, rather than actively shaping them, and that the relationship with business is conceptualised as a *partner-ship*. This foregrounds equality, backgrounds the commercial exchange processes involved, and obfuscates dependence. (It is characteristic of pro-entrepreneurial argumentation that independence from government funding is hailed as 'self-sufficiency', whereas in reality it is more likely to be simply a different form of dependence – one on corporate monies that tend to be more short-term and less reliable than budgets allocated by the state.) The reference to *quality outputs* shows academic activity modelled on industrial production. The language of rapid movement (*dynamic, nimble, active, quickly*) ties in with Barnett's characterisation of the entrepreneurial university as being 'restless' and 'always on the move' (Barnett, 2003, p. 66).

What the extracts given above also reveal is the co-presence of a number of other keywords, motifs, and topoi characteristic of contemporary higher education discourse, such as quality, excellence, meeting needs, internationalism, and a general societal pre-occupation with growth.

As I indicated earlier, the first output from the search engine showed up considerably fewer critical voices. They certainly exist, but their main forum is traditional, paper-based academic writing rather than the Internet (Barnett, 2003; Bok, 2003; Slaughter & Leslie, 1997). Notable exceptions include Banja (2000) and Robinson and Tormey (2003). It is not a coincidence, therefore, that what criticism of academic entrepreneurialism does appear on the Web is often contained in book reviews, descriptions of books on the Web sites of publishers or Internet bookshops, and abstracts posted on conference Web sites. Still, looking at the concordance lines with negative semantic prosody, one does get some idea of what the main objections are and the rhetoric with which they are expressed. To the left of the search word *entrepreneurial university/ies* we find *challenge to, limitations of, alternatives to*, and *beyond*. The latter, incidentally, is not entirely negative, indicating as it does that the concept is not being rejected outright, but needs to be developed further. There is also an interesting case of *purely* being used as a modifier before *entrepreneurial university*, suggesting, like *limitations of*, that the concept is felt to be too narrow. There are instances of emotive language, such as *pernicious ideologies* (which is a section heading in Barnett, 2003, and was picked up by webcorp on a publisher's Web site), *capitalist regime*, and *entourage of administrators*,[10] which is linked to *further draining of institutional resources*. To the right of the search word, negatively charged co-texts include a reference to *the psychological contract* having been *breached, with serious consequences for staff morale* (Roberts, 2002). The entrepreneurial university is described as being *seriously at risk for institutional conflict of interest* (though in this example there is a distancing matrix clause on the left, namely *Critics have charged, however, that ...*) (Schafer, 2003), and as having been *very rapidly (and quite uncritically) taken up into South African HE policy* (Subotzky, n.d., paragraph 6). Another source (Banja, 2000) expresses *worries as to how the entrepreneurial research university might violate the 'soul' of academe* and *that the university that insists on charting an entrepreneurial course runs the danger of turning into a business, valuing capital more than talent*. The author then poignantly asserts, *if the university becomes business, then it's no longer a university*.

The concordance output thus gives us an idea of what the argument against the entrepreneurial university rests on: anti-capitalist and anti-bureaucratic critique; concerns about conflicts of interest with traditional academic values; the 'soul' of the university and the profit motive; psychological issues (staff morale); and worries about rash uptake by policy-makers.

Sample analyses: key motifs and rhetorical devices

In this section, I shall examine three texts that show how the motifs that emerged in the analysis of the concordanced Web output are developed in longer stretches of discourse. Although from different national backgrounds (Dutch, British, and Austrian), they share key motifs as well as a self-reflective approach to academic entrepreneurialism. Essentially, echoing one of the distinguishing characteristics identified by Clark, the 'integrated entrepreneurial culture' (Clark, 1998, p. 7), the three sample texts, like many others in the corpus, represent 'going entrepreneurial' as more than just commercialisation. Rather, it is conceptualised as a pervasive institutional transformation targeting staff and students, and aiming to achieve in them not just behavioural, but also cognitive and 'emotional' changes. Texts 1 and 2 were among those picked up by the Web search engine (see 'Data and method' section), with Text 1, significantly, originating from one of the five universities that Clark showcases in his book. The third text is the most overtly self-reflecting of the three, putting into particularly sharp relief how the intricate semantics of *entrepreneurial* are unravelled by a 'manager-academic' (Deem, 2003) in line with his policy agenda.

Example 1

Text 1, from the Web site of the Dutch University of Twente, is an example of a genre familiar on university Web sites on both sides of the Atlantic – the introductory or welcoming message from the Rector/Vice-Chancellor/ Dean, etc. Whether framed explicitly as a 'welcome' or, as is the case here, as a less personal introductory statement, one of the functions of such texts is to demonstrate the senior leader's endorsement of institutional values. At the start of a virtual campus tour, the University of Twente's *rector magnificus* (note how the use of the old Latin title affirms academic traditions) describes his university as follows:

1 UT Campus Tour
2 The University of Twente is a university that offers both technological and
3 social study programmes. We characterise ourselves as an *entrepreneurial*
4 *university*, adapting our research efforts *to the benefit of society in general*. The

143

5 *entrepreneurial attitude permeates* the university: from our students to our

6 professors. It is a *state of mind*, a *mental approach* to science and society, which

7 allows us to respond rapidly to new ideas and challenges. We believe that this

8 approach is *forged* through the nature of our study programmes, in the qualities

9 we seek in appointing new members of staff, and in our research and funding

10 policies.

11 (Prof. Dr. Frans van Vught, rector magnificus)

(van Vught, n.d., paragraph 1, italics added)

The entrepreneurial agenda is metaphorised as a process of material transformation that is all-encompassing (line 5: it *permeates the university*) and requires a good deal of strength (line 8: *is forged*). It is helpful to remind ourselves of the literal meaning of *forging* – 'to form (as metal) by heating and hammering' (Merriam Webster online, http://www.m-w.com) – in order to appreciate the power of the metaphor in suggesting how much determination is required and how solid the resulting new entity will be. The depth of the transformation is emphasised further by psycho-logical vocabulary: being entrepreneurial, we are told (ll. 5–6), is an *attitude, a state of mind*, and a *mental approach* (with *mental* carrying a nice, and presumably unintentional, double-entendre, which would no doubt delight cynical detractors of entrepreneurialism).

The university is positioned in reactive mode, *adapting* and *responding*. It does so *rapidly*, of course, adjusting its pace to that of the market economy. What the university is shown to respond to in this text, though, is not the market or the economy, but rather vague – and uncontroversial – *ideas and challenges*. Indeed, one of the text's significant silences is the absence of any explicit mention of business or the economy. Instead, it is *society* that research is adapted to (line 4) and that enters into the definition of the entrepreneurial state of mind (line 6). As a matter of fact, 'society' will frequently confront universities in the shape of businesses – profit-oriented, market-driven, and competitive – but this is obviously something that this university prefers to downplay.

Example 2

My second example is an extract from a Web site of Sheffield Hallam University which is headed *University Enterprise*. Under a second, smaller heading (*Enterprising University*), an eight-paragraph text appears, the first three of which are reproduced here:

1 Enterprising University . . .
2 Our Enterprise Centre aims to redefine the concept of enterprise in education.
3 Its mission is to *embed an enterprise culture in everything the University does,*
4 benefiting students, clients and partners in new and unusual ways. Founded in
5 2001, the Enterprise Centre is not just a building, but something much more
6 significant – it represents *a state of mind.*
7 We believe that *enterprise ought to be an integral part of education, like the*
8 *lettering through a stick of rock, and that all our students should be enterprising*
9 *students.*
10 Of course not every student will want to go on to start their own business. *In*
11 *its fullest sense enterprise means being imaginative, innovative and bold.*
12 Contributing to other people's welfare, for example in the public and charitable
13 sectors, is just as valuable a way to apply a spirit of enterprise as more obvious
14 wealth creation.
15 Our service to business and industry clients and partners is all about *applied*
16 *creativity and innovation – business solutions, not ivory towers.* Near-market
17 and high tech research, R&D partnerships and applied consultancy are all great
18 strengths and our social and economic research is no less focused and
19 professional.

(Sheffield Hallam University, n.d., paragraphs 1–3, italics added)

In the original, there are two visuals on the page. One, next to the larger headline, shows two coins (one of which, interestingly enough in the British context, is recognisable as a euro cent). No doubt is left in the *visual* mode that 'enterprise' is understood to be about making money. The other image, next to paragraph 2, is a photograph of an unidentified male in front of a computer screen which has some form of map or technical drawing on it.[11]

Example 2 uses keywords deriving from *enterprise* rather than *entrepreneur*, but the message is strikingly similar. Like Example 1, this passage develops the motif of culture (line 3) as well as of psychology (line 6), and it also describes the concept as pervasive (ll. 7–9). Again, the metaphor chosen is one of material transformation, albeit this time not from metal processing but from the production of rock, that quintessentially British sweet. Outlandish though it may seem (and interculturally it would not travel well), the image is a powerful one, depicting enterprise as something that is inextricable from the whole and as a result inescapable. Whichever bit of 'education' offered at that university you 'bite off', it will have *enterprise* in it.

In line 10, an interesting shift occurs. As if to refute a counterargument in an imagined dialogue, *Of course* signals the starting point of an act of clarification and a semantic line of reasoning. Should readers have interpreted *enterprising* to mean 'starting one's own business' – which, given the general usage and political history of the term (see the 'Socio-political context' section), they might be forgiven for doing – they are now told that this is not what Sheffield Hallam University has in mind at all. An act of definition, in categorical mode, follows: *In its fullest sense enterprise means being imaginative, innovative and bold*, and in that sense, the argument continues, it can be applied to a much wider range of activity, including the public and charitable sectors. These are given as examples of *contributing to other people's welfare* and are contrasted with *more obvious wealth creation* (i.e., business).

In the third paragraph, the theme of creativity and innovation is kept up (l. 16), but the argument returns to the domain of *business and industry*. Business buzzwords are poled up (*near-market, high tech, R & D, consultancy*) and are pitted against that most classic and succinct of all denigrations of traditional academe, the *ivory tower*. Following the same strategy as the Education Secretary quoted earlier, this text, too, talks the new 'enterprising' university up by talking the supposedly non-enterprising old university down. The rhetorical device used here is to apply a label (*ivory tower*) which is rich in negative connotations, activating the cliché of academics as otherwordly, unaccountable recluses who pursue interests of no concern or consequence to anyone but themselves.

Although, as a whole, the passage comes over as taking a pro-entrepreneurial stance, we can see how the text oscillates between, on the one hand, a focus on business and money-making – the *obvious wealth creation* that is represented so powerfully by the illustration of the coins at the top of the page – and a more encompassing, non-commercial, and altogether 'softer' interpretation of enterprise on the other, that is, one that includes concepts such as *people's welfare*.

It may be worth stressing at this point that Sheffield Hallam's status as a 'post-1992' university, founded originally as Sheffield City Polytechnic, is quite coincidental to its 'entrepreneurial' ambitions and inconsequential to the analysis presented here. If anything, the oldest and most prestigious universities are more actively engaged in and, because of their prestige, infinitely better placed to pursue entrepreneurial activities. Their self-promotion in this regard follows remarkably similar discursive templates, as the following extract from the University of Oxford's Web site demonstrates.

Bar the reference to its 800-year history, the text could easily be slotted into the descriptions of Twente or Sheffield Hallam, and would blend in quite harmoniously:

> Oxford is one of Europe's most innovative and entrepreneurial universities. Drawing on an 800-year tradition of discovery and invention, modern Oxford leads the way in creating jobs, wealth, skills and innovation for the 21st century.
>
> (University of Oxford, n.d., paragraph 1)

Example 3

My third example is a pair of quotes from two speeches given in German by Christoph Badelt, the Rector of Vienna University of Economics and Business Administration (*Wirtschaftsuniversität Wien*).[12] Crucially, in the speech from which (b) is taken, Badelt himself quotes Burton Clark's (1998) book and confirms the equivalence of *entrepreneurial university* with German *unternehmerische Universität* (which is clearly a prerequisite for including in the present analysis sources that were German originally).[13]

(a)

1 The fact that an organisation, in our case a university, acts in an
2 *'entrepreneurial'* manner says nothing about the goals that are pursued by or
3 within it. . . . I stress this because one is easily tempted to *equate the*
4 *'entrepreneurial university' with a 'for-profit university'*, which renounces
5 genuinely educational aims and replaces them with the goal of profit
6 maximisation. *Yet equating the two is simply wrong!*

(Badelt, 2003, italics added)

(b)

1 1. The WU[14] *must become an entrepreneurial university in the best sense of*
2 *the term.*
3 2. At the same time, the WU ought to remain – and continue to evolve as – a
4 place in which teachers and learners engage cooperatively in *free academic debate,*
5 *in order to provide intellectual stimuli for business and society.* . . .
6 *The WU as an 'entrepreneurial university'*
7 The principle of the *entrepreneurial university does not mean commercialising*
8 *the WU.* A university still has primarily a social and educational remit, and it will

9   engage in commercial activities only in relatively restricted fields of
    activity – such
10 as continuing education . . . – and, even then, above all with a view to
    attaining
11 educational goals.
12 The principle of the *entrepreneurial university*, as I understand it, means
13 acknowledging that **a university is also a place in which services are
    produced,**
14 and in which a certain *'output'* is created in a multi-stage *production
    process.* This
15 output manifests itself, for example, in publications, graduates and similar
16 *'products'* and is to be generated in accordance with *the economic
    principle* – that
17 is, by **maximising productivity.** *Indeed, this idea is to guide the university
    in all its*
18 decisions. Yet, at the same time, the university is also responsible for
    the social
19 impact of these *'products'.*

(Badelt, 2004, italics added, bold face in the original)

As in Example 2, the semantics of the keyword loom large, and its contested
nature once more becomes apparent. It is the *best sense of the term* (b, ll.
1–2) that the Rector wishes to use as the cornerstone of his change initiative. What the passage that follows aims to accomplish is to take issue
with and refute other senses that would be at odds with the agenda the
author pursues. His own interpretation needs to be established as authorit-
ative so as to function as a legitimised foundation for the entrepreneurial
transformation he wishes the institution to embark on. In (b), there is an
act of explicit defining, couched in categorical modality (l. 7: *does not mean*).
In line 12, the speaker appears to concede that it is *his* definition of *entrepreneurial* that forms the basis of his argument; he does not claim at this
point that this is *the* definition. However, his qualifying, subjectivising
insertion (*as I understand it*) is followed by an assertion which, through
the semantics of *acknowledge*, is in fact again categorical (l. 13: *acknowledging that a university is also a place at which services are produced*). To
say that something needs to be acknowledged amounts to a categorical
assertion of the existence of that which is to be acknowledged, and this
at least partly cancels out the apparently self-effacing *as I understand it.*
Extract (a) is even more confident, referring to the equation of entrepreneurialism with profit maximisation not simply as a position which
the speaker does not hold, but as *simply wrong* (l. 6).

A substantial part of (b) is concerned with affirming values that are
not associated with the commercial profit motive, such as *free academic
debate* and *intellectual stimuli* (ll. 4–5). Both *educational* and *social* goals are

foregrounded (l. 8, l. 11, ll. 18–19), even in the context of the one, 'restricted' area that will go commercial, namely continuing education (ll. 9–10). Furthermore, *also* in line 13 (*acknowledging that a university is also a place in which services are produced*), emboldened for emphasis in the manuscript (and, presumably, stressed in oral delivery), indicates that the construction of the university as entrepreneurial is not meant to be exclusive of those other, more traditional, constructions that lines 8–11 elaborate on.

However, in spite of the affirmation that *the principle of the entrepreneurial university does not mean commercialising the WU* (ll. 7–8), that principle is then elaborated exclusively through lexis originating in the economic domain (ll. 12–19), including terms such as *output, production, productivity*, and the *economic principle*. Scare quotes are used as a distancing device, but not consistently; they are around one instance of *output* (l. 14) but not around the other (l. 15), and around *products* (l. 16) but neither around *produced* (l. 13) nor *production process* (l. 14). That the author's own academic specialisation is economics may go some way towards explaining his preference, but it is unlikely to be the whole story. After all, economists can choose when to activate their technical vocabulary (and there are many contexts in which they do not). Whatever the professional socialisation of the author, conceptualising a university in economic terms is invariably also a rhetorical choice.

To sum up, the semantic engineering that (a) and (b) engage in can be seen to accomplish two aims: first, to renounce the 'commercial' and, as the two texts imply, negative connotations of *entrepreneurial*, and second, to substitute a more technical and neutral interpretation, attempting conceptually to divorce entrepreneurial activity from entrepreneurial goals. As an activity, the author contends, it 'simply' means following the economic principle, and this is presented as not necessarily being at variance with educational and social goals.

Summary and critique

In contemporary higher education discourse, the *entrepreneurial university* stands out as an iconic representation of the coming together of business and academia, two hitherto separate but now increasingly intertwined social spheres. That the term is contested can be inferred from the textual residue of controversy over what it means, and how it is to be evaluated. Some (though not all) advocates of the entrepreneurial university reveal that they are aware of the potentially contentious nature of the term, and try to pre-empt resistance by anticipating and refuting counterarguments (along the lines of 'Oh no, it isn't about commercialisation,' or 'Oh yes, we still care about education and society'). Both sides are silent on issues that would not further their cause. Advocates usually disregard the issue of dependence on business, whereas critics tend to ignore the flaws of the traditional university, its inefficiencies, élitist power structures, and lack of accountability.

Thus, *entrepreneurial* and related keywords are focal points around which current discourses of change, both supportive and antagonistic, crystallise. The players on this terrain may not fall neatly into two clearly delineated camps, but there does appear to be a fair degree of polarisation. On the one hand, there is the institutional discourse of self-promotion, which typically supports academic entrepreneurship. On their Web sites, for example, universities flaunt entrepreneurial initiatives as particularly palpable evidence (or so they claim) of the 'real world' relevance of their teaching and research; vice-chancellors integrate *entrepreneurial* and its cognates into leadership discourse in an attempt to encourage staff to 'buy into' changes in organisational culture, and in order to promote an institutional image that is aligned with corporate models. In the rhetoric of neo-liberal governments, too, the entrepreneurial paradigm is firmly established. Schafer (2003, paragraph 3) argues that 'large-scale "scientific entrepreneurship" has moved, almost in one fell swoop, from being an oxymoron to becoming the prevailing norm on university campuses across North America.' On the basis of both higher education literature, which was drawn upon in the 'Socio-political context' section, and primary textual evidence gathered on the Web and discussed in subsequent sections, a case can be made for affirming Schafer's claim also for the European and indeed world-wide context.

In higher education discourse, *being entrepreneurial* can mean both engaging in commercial activity and being innovative (without necessarily pursuing a profit motive). In everyday usage, as evidence from the COBUILD database shows, *entrepreneur* can have a positive as well as a decidedly negative semantic aura. Faced with this varied semantic profile, authors do rhetorical – and, ultimately, ideological – work by foregrounding whichever meaning and sets of collocations best suit their agenda. Put simply, those in favour of academic entrepreneurship emphasise innovation and the positive connotations of *entrepreneurial*, while those against highlight commercial-isation and negative connotations. The symmetry is deceptive, however, because the playing field which the two camps compete on is far from level either socially or discursively. Supporters of academic entrepreneurship tend to be members of university management, holding positions which give them the power to implement entrepreneurial policy as well as promulgate the discourse that goes with it – declaring, for example, that certain connota-tions of entrepreneurial are the only valid ones (and others 'simply wrong'). By contrast, most sceptical and antagonistic voices tend to come from indi-vidual academics who are not in such positions of power as would enable them to translate their anti-entrepreneurial sentiments into transformative action, or promote their preferred selection of connotations. As a result, their polemics are generally as passionate as they are inconsequential, making good reading but poor action plans. By the same token, the critical stance prevalent in the HE research community appears to have no impact outside that community. Article after article and book after book critiquing the 'McUniversity' (Hayes & Wynyard, 2002) and 'academic capitalism' (Slaughter & Leslie, 1997) may be published, but the entrepreneurial juggernaut, propelled by its powerful supporters, rolls on.

It seems hard to understand why universities, with hundreds of years of tradition under their belt and a formidable assemblage of intellect under their roofs, should not be able to pursue a reform agenda independently, without playing to the rules set by economically powerful external constituents, and without deliberately appropriating the language of the commercial sector. In this respect, my position is similar to that of Thrupp and Willmott (2003, p. 4), who proclaim in the introduction to their book about school management, 'We are not against management *per se* but against managerialist conceptions of it.' Like them, I believe that it is possible to develop alternatives to current market-oriented orthodoxies, while also being realistic about the context in which organisations operate (by acknowledging new 'facts of life' such as competition, for example).

As corpus evidence shows, *entrepreneurial* and its cognates come with a heavy load of commercial connotations. If those connotations are unwanted, as some sources are at pains to point out, and increasing commercialisation is not, in fact, the declared aim, then why choose *entrepreneurial* as a central motto and rallying cry? Is it perhaps because, ultimately, this is the sort of language that powerful external constituents – corporate 'partners' and governments – understand and like to hear? Whatever the motive, the dialectic between language and the social needs to be reckoned with, and giving a term such as *entrepreneurial* a salient position in policy and leadership rhetoric will inevitably encourage the modelling of organisational practices, identities, and relationships on commercial templates.

Academic leaders and administrators may well regard some academics' visceral rejection of the entrepreneurial agenda as blinkered and ignorant of economic necessities. Behind the opponents' denigrating rhetoric, however, lie genuine concerns about the future of higher education and very real insecurities and fears about professional roles and identities. The kind of discourse that vice-chancellors, rectors, and deans believe will galvanise faculty into action may in fact alienate them, making it harder to enlist their support, and even harder to garner their active co-operation for institutional reform. It would appear that leaders who want those constituents on board should think twice about borrowing too liberally and naïvely from the linguistic repertoires of the commercial sector. Much as the zeitgeist may seem to dictate discursive alignment with business, it is a strategy that can easily backfire and jeopardise rather than win support.

Acknowledgements

I am grateful to Annabelle Mooney for comments on a draft version of this paper, and to Christoph Badelt for his untiring willingness to engage in critical debate. Thanks are also due to my (entrepreneurial) university, *Wirtschaftsuniversität Wien* (Vienna University of Economics and Business Administration), as well as to the Austrian National Bank for their financial support during a sabbatical I spent at the Centre for Language and Communication Research at Cardiff University, during which this paper was written.

Notes

1 The two most recent examples of such documents in the UK are the White Paper entitled *The Future of Higher Education* (Department for Education and Skills, 2003) and the *Lambert Review of Business-University Collaboration*, commissioned by the Treasury (2003).

2 In the *People's Daily Online*, the president of the Directing Group of the OECD Program on Institutional Management is reported as saying, in a review of Chinese universities, 'that he has seen several examples of areas where they already display the characteristics of successful entrepreneurial universities' ("Chinese universities", 2000, paragraph 3).

3 The description that the Philippine Women's University gives of itself on its Web site reads like a compendium of higher education buzzwords:

> Currently serving both men and women from nursery to graduate school in its Manila, Quezon City, Caliraya and Davao campuses, on its 80th anniversary, the Philippine Women's University System and its Affiliate Schools for Men and Women has laid the foundation for corporate entrepreneurial university [*sic*], market-driven in partnership with business and industry, government and non-government, fully wired, on-line, on the Net, and experimenting on computer-related, internet-assisted teaching and learning where student competencies and skills are achieved through economically gainful hands-on experiences. Its 80th anniversary them [*sic*] QUEST (Quality Universal Education, Science and Technology) for the 21st century speaks for itself.
>
> ("About PWU," paragraph 5)

4 The partners in this project are the London Metropolitan University, the University of Nizhni Novgorod, and the Centre for Strategic Management in European Universities (ESMU) in Brussels. See http://www.londonmet.ac.uk/services/london-office/projects/projects_home.cfm and socis.isras.ru/socisarticles/2003_04/grudzinski.doc, a corresponding text originating from the University of Nizhni Novgorod itself.

5 On semantic prosody see also Sinclair (1987, 1998), Stubbs (2001), and Partington (2004).

6 An exact chronology of how these ideas were developed is hard to establish. Although the publication of Slaughter and Leslie's book (1997) predates that of Clark's (1998), one has to bear in mind that, as Clark states in his Acknowledgements (1998, p. xi), he carried out his research between 1994 and 1996, and his

preface is dated July 1997. Also, Slaughter and Leslie (1997) quote an earlier paper by Clark (1993), in which he already discusses entrepreneurship at European universities.

7 In both the literature on higher education and in universities' own promotional texts, we find *enterprising* alongside *entrepreneurial.* Marginson and Considine's (2000) study on Australian universities has *Enterprise University* in its title and uses it throughout (though not exclusively), as do two separate papers by Marginson (1999) and Considine (2001), as well as an edited volume of British provenance (Williams, 2003). In those works, both *entrepreneurial* and *enterprising* are used without any discernible difference in meaning. The same is true of Bok (2003), who appears to use the two adjectives interchangeably, as if for stylistic variation (e.g., Bok, 2003, p. 191).

Although varied evidence on usage emerged from different sources – some using only *entrepreneurial*, others only *enterprising*, some using them synonymously, others not – a case can be made for putting *entrepreneurial* at the centre of the investigation; hence the title of my paper and the choice of *entrepreneurial* as the primary search word in the computer-supported part of the analysis. The case rests on two interrelated arguments. First, *entrepreneurial* was the expression of choice in Clark (1998), the sustained intertextual impact of which has ensured continuing endorsement of his terminology. Second, and presumably at least partly because of that, *entrepreneurial university/ies* is the more common expression: google produced well over 3600 hits for it, but only 700 for *enterprising university/ies.* The archive of the *Times Higher Education Supplement* contained 24 articles in which *entrepreneurial university/ies* occurred, but only five with *enterprising university/ies.* All things considered, it was *entrepreneurial* that emerged as the lead actor in this particular scene of higher education drama, with *enterprising* playing an important, though less central, role as a member of the supporting cast.

8 Two output formats were chosen, one with 10 words on either side of the keyword, which produces neat, though truncated and thus often semantically obscure, concordance lines, suitable for a rough overview of usage. Set at its 50-word maximum, on the other hand, the collocational span accessible through webcorp amounts to a fairly extended stretch of text (about seven lines in a 10-point font) which allows a reasonably reliable assessment of the author's evaluative stance (essentially, is he/she supportive or critical of the concept in question?), the motifs in which the keyword is embedded (e.g., references to economic growth, to institutional culture, to change processes), and how they go about arguing their case (for example, by piling on positively or negatively loaded attitudinal lexis).

9 Following standard practice in corpus linguistics, I am not giving individual source references for brief citations when corpora are being explored as aggregates of textual data. Appropriate references to institutional and individual authors will be given for longer passages and in all those cases where an in-depth qualitative analysis of coherent stretches of text is carried out.

10 In *the coming of the capitalist regime brings with it a new entourage of administrators to oversee the entrepreneurial university,* from a review of Slaughter and Leslie (1997) by Michael Ryan (1998, paragraph 5).

11 Judged against the many other Web sites that I accessed during this study, this is a fairly typical visualisation of 'research'. Many forms of research are notoriously intangible, and bringing in artefacts such as computers and, in many other cases, laboratory equipment, helps create that visual appeal which reading, thinking, and writing do not have. This introduces a visual bias in favour of technology and science. In addition, photos show considerably more men than women.

12 The translation is my own, but has been authorised by the speaker.
13 The immediate context in which the speeches were held was the start of the Rector's new term of office, which is typically the time at which long-term strategic plans are set out. The wider context is characterised by far-reaching changes in the legal framework which have given Austrian universities greater independence from the state, more freedom in budgetary allocation (though not bigger budgets), and new organisational structures. The newly created supervisory boards consist exclusively of members recruited from outside the university concerned, and include, significantly, representatives of private-sector organisations.
14 WU is short for *Wirtschaftsuniversität Wien*, the German name of the Vienna University of Economics and Business Administration.

References

Aarna, O. (n.d.). *A decade of reforms in higher education management: Estonian case.* Retrieved December 22, 2003, from http://www.cfh.lviv.ua/seminar2/aarna.htm

About PWU. History. Retrieved September 22, 2005, from http://www.pwu.edu.ph/history.htm

Badelt, C. (2003). *Die unternehmerische Universität: Herausforderung oder Widerspruch in sich?* [*The entrepreneurial university: A challenge or a contradiction in terms?*] Public lecture given in Vienna City Hall on November 25, 2003. Retrieved January 10, 2004, from http://www.wu-wien.ac.at/rektorat/mitarbeiter/mitarbeiter_inhalt/badelt_frame.htm

Badelt, C. (2004). *Inaugural speech.* Given January 21, 2004. German original retrieved January 25, 2004, from http://www.wu-wien.ac.at/rektorat/mitarbeiter/mitarbeiter_inhalt/badelt_frame.htm

Banja, J. (2000). *No conflict, no interest. Ethical considerations in technology transfer.* Retrieved December 22, 2003, from http://www.emory.edu/acad_exchange/2000/febmar/banja.html

Barnett, R. (1990). *The idea of higher education.* Buckingham, UK: Society for Research into Higher Education and Open University Press.

Barnett, R. (2000). *Realizing the university in an age of supercomplexity.* Buckingham, UK: Society for Research into Higher Education and Open University Press.

Barnett, R. (2003). *Beyond all reason: Living with ideology in the university.* Buckingham, UK: Society for Research into Higher Education and Open University Press.

Blackmore, J., & Sachs, J. (2003). Zealotry or nostalgic regret? Women leaders in technical and further education in Australia: Agents of change, entrepreneurial educators or corporate citizens? *Gender, Work and Organization, 10*, 478–503.

Blunkett, D. (2000). Speech on Higher Education, 15 February 2000 at Maritime Greenwich University. Retrieved September 22, 2005, from http://cms1.gre.ac.uk/dfee/

Bok, D. (2003). *Universities in the marketplace: The commercialization of higher education.* Princeton, NJ: Princeton University Press.

Chinese universities facing management challenges: Expert (2000, April 13). *People's Daily Online.* Retrieved September 22, 2005, From http://fpeng.peopledaily.com.cn/200004/13/print20000413_38860.html

Chouliaraki, L., & Fairclough, N. (1999). *Discourse in late modernity: Rethinking critical discourse analysis.* Edinburgh, UK: Edinburgh University Press.

Clark, B. R. (1993). The problem of complexity in modern higher education. In S. Rothblatt & B. Wittrock (Eds.), *The European and American university since 1880* (pp. 263–279). Cambridge, UK: Cambridge University Press.

Clark, B. R. (1998). *Creating entrepreneurial universities: Organizational pathways of transformation.* Oxford, UK: Pergamon Press.

Considine, M. (2001). *The enterprise university and its 'new governance' dynamics: A public interest perspective.* Retrieved November 15, 2003, from http://www. fabian.org.au/new%20papers/2001/considin.html

Deem, R. (1998). 'New managerialism' and higher education: The management of performances and cultures in universities in the United Kingdom. *International Studies in Sociology of Education, 8,* 47–70.

Deem, R. (2003). Gender, organizational cultures and the practices of manager-academics in UK universities. *Gender, Work and Organization, 10,* 239–259.

Deem, R., & Johnson, R. J. (2000). Managerialism and university managers: Building new academic communities or disrupting old ones? In I. McNay (Ed.), *Higher education and its communities* (pp. 65–84). Buckingham, UK: Open University Press.

Department for Education and Skills. (2003). *The future of higher education.* London: HMSO.

Dowling, P. (2004, January 12). Free up our enterprise. *The Times Higher Education Supplement.* Retrieved January 15, 2004, from http://www.thes.co.uk

Etzkowitz, H. (1998). The norms of entrepreneurial science: Cognitive effects of the new university – industry linkages. *Research Policy, 27,* 823–833.

Etzkowitz, H. (2003). Research groups as 'quasi-firms': The invention of the entrepreneurial university. *Research Policy, 32,* 109–121.

Etzkowitz, H., Webster, A., Gebhardt, C., & Cantisano Terra, B. R. (2000). The future of the university and the university of the future: Evolution of ivory tower to entrepreneurial paradigm. *Research Policy, 29,* 313–330.

Fairclough, N. (1992). *Discourse and social change.* Cambridge, UK: Polity Press.

Fairclough, N. (1993). Critical discourse analysis and the marketization of public discourse: The universities. *Discourse and Society, 4,* 133–168.

Fairclough, N. (2000). *New Labour, new language?* London: Routledge.

Firth, J. R. (1957). The technique of semantics. In *Papers in Linguistics 1934–1951* (pp. 7–33). London: Oxford University Press. (Original work published 1935)

Flexner, A. (1930). *Universities: American, English, German.* New York: Oxford University Press.

Flynn, N. (2000). Managerialism and public services: Some international trends. In J. Clarke, S. Gewirtz, & E. McLaughlin (Eds.), *New managerialism, new welfare?* (pp. 154–184). London: Sage.

Hardt-Mautner, G. (1995). *Only connect: Critical discourse analysis and corpus linguistics* (Technical Papers No 6). Lancaster, UK: Lancaster University, Unit for Computer Research on the English Language. Retrieved October 15, 2003, from http://www.comp.lancs.ac.uk/computing/research/ucrel/papers/techpaper/vol6.pdf

Hay, D. B., Butt, F., & Kirby D. A. (2003). Academics as entrepreneurs in a UK university. In G. Williams (Ed.), *The enterprising university: Reform, excellence and equity* (pp. 132–187). Buckingham, UK: Society for Research into Higher Education and Open University Press.

Hayes, D., & Wynyard, R. (Eds.). (2002). *The McDonaldization of higher education.* Westport, CT: Bergin and Garvey.

Henkel, M. (1997). Academic values and the university as corporate enterprise. *Higher Education Quarterly, 51,* 134–143.

Hermanns, F. (1994). *Schlüssel-, Schlag- und Fahnenwörter: Zur Begrifflichkeit und Theorie der lexikalischen "politischen Semantik"* [Keywords and buzzwords. On the terminology and theory of a lexical "political semantics"] (Arbeiten aus dem Sonderforschungs-bereich 245, Sprache und Situation, Bericht Nr. 81). Heidelberg: Universität Heidelberg.

Hindle, K. G. (2001). Entrepreneurship education at university: The Plus-Zone challenge. *Small Enterprise Research, 9,* 3–16. Retrieved January 4, 2004, from http://www.swin.edu.au/agse/publications/hindle/educ_pluszone.pdf

Hunston, S. (2002). *Corpora in applied linguistics.* Cambridge, UK: Cambridge University Press.

Hunston, S. (2004). Counting the uncountable: Problems of identifying evaluation in a text and in a corpus. In A. Partington, J. Morley, & L. Haarman (Eds.), *Corpora and discourse* (pp. 157–188). Bern: Peter Lang.

Johnson, R. (2002). Learning to manage the university: Tales of training and experience. *Higher Education Quarterly, 56,* 33–51.

Keat, R. (1991). Introduction. Starship Britain or universal enterprise? In R. Keat & N. Abercrombie (Eds.), *Enterprise culture* (pp. 1–17). London: Routledge.

Keat, R., & Abercrombie, N. (Eds.). (1991). *Enterprise culture.* London & New York: Routledge.

Kleinman, D. L., & Vallas, S. P. (2001). Science, capitalism, and the rise of the 'knowledge worker': The changing structure of knowledge production in the United States. *Theory and Society, 30,* 451–492.

Koller, V., & Mautner, G. (2004). Computer applications in critical discourse analysis. In C. Coffin, A. Hewings, & K. A. O'Halloran (Eds.), *Applying English grammar: Functional and corpus approaches* (pp. 216–228). London: Hodder Arnold.

Lambert Review of Business-University Collaboration. (2003). London: HM Treasury. Retrieved January 2, 2004, from http://www.lambertreview.org.uk

Louw, B. (1993). Irony in the text or insincerity in the writer? – The diagnostic potential of semantic prosodies. In M. Baker, G. Francis, & E. Tognini-Bonelli (Eds.), *Text and technology: In honour of John Sinclair* (pp. 157–176). Amsterdam & Philadelphia: John Benjamins.

Marginson, S. (1999). *The enterprise university comes to Australia.* Paper presented at the Annual Conference of Australian Association for Research in Education. Retrieved November 15, 2003, from http://www.aare.edu.au/99pap/mar99470.htm

Marginson, S., & Considine, M. (2000). *The enterprise university: Power, governance and reinvention in Australia.* Cambridge, UK: Cambridge University Press.

Mautner, G. (2000). *Der britische Europa-Diskurs: Methodenreflexion und Fallstudien zur Berichterstattung in der Tagespresse* [British discourse on Europe: Reflections on methodology and case studies from daily newspapers]. Vienna: Passagenverlag.

O'Neill, J., & Solomon, Y. (1996). Education, élitism and the market. In B. Brecher, O. Fleischman & J. Halliday (Eds.), *The university in a liberal state* (pp. 82–95). Aldershot, UK: Avebury.

Ozga, J. (1998). The entrepreneurial researcher: Re-formations of identity in the research marketplace. *International Studies in Sociology of Education, 8,* 143–153.

Parker, M., & Jary, D. (1995). The McUniversity: Organization, management and academic subjectivity. *Organization, 2*, 319–338.

Partington, A. (2004). Utterly content in each other's company: Semantic prosody and semantic preference. *International Journal of Corpus Linguistics, 9*, 131–156.

Peters, M., & Roberts, P. (2000). Universities, futurology and globalisation. *Discourse: Studies in the Cultural Politics of Education, 21*, 125–139.

Piper, A. (2000a). Lifelong learning, human capital, and the soundbite. *Text, 20*, 109–146.

Piper, A. (2000b). Some have credit cards and others have giro cheques: 'Individuals' and 'people' as lifelong learners in late modernity. *Discourse and Society, 11*, 515–542.

Poole, L. (2000). Health care: New Labour's NHS. In J. Clarke, S. Gewirtz, & E. McLaughlin (Eds.), *New managerialism, new welfare?* (pp. 102–121). London: Sage.

Research and higher education (n.d.). Retrieved September 22, 2005, from http://www.electrum.se/artikel/84/013002/en

Roberts, P. (2002). *The virtual university and ethical problems in downsizing.* Abstract for paper at Ethicomp 2002, Lisbon, Portugal. Retrieved November 24, 2003, from http://www.ccsr.cse.dmu.ac.uk/conferences/ethicomp2002/abstracts/49.html

Robinson, A., & Tormey, S. (2003). *New Labour's neoliberal Gleichschaltung: The case of higher education.* Retrieved January 15, 2004, from http://homepage.ntlworld.com/simon.tormey/articles/new%20labour%20he%20white%20paper.pdf

Ryan, Michael (1998). [Review of the book *Academic capitalism: policies, policies, and the entrepreneurial university*]. *College and Research Libraries, 59*(3). Retrieved September 22, 2005, from http://www.ala.org/ala/acrl/acrlpubs/crljournal/backissues1998b/may98/slaughterbook.htm

Scavarda do Carmo, L. C. (n.d.). *The entrepreneurial engineer: A new paradigm for the reform of engineering education.* Retrieved December 22, 2003, from http://www.siu.edu/~coalctr/paper131.htm

Schafer, A. (2003). *My word!* Retrieved December 5, 2003, from http://www.umanitoba.ca/faculties/arts/deans_office/news/features_articles/Schafer/html

Shattock, M. (2003). *Managing successful universities.* Maidenhead, UK: Society for Research into Higher Education and Open University Press.

Sheffield Hallam University (n.d.). *University Enterprise.* Retrieved September 22, 2005, from http://www.shu.ac.uk/university/enterprise.html

Shih, C. F. (2002). Re-making NUS: Fostering a new organizational culture. Retrieved September 22, 2005, from http://www.nus.edu.sg/president/speeches/soua2002f.htm

Sinclair, J. (1987). *Looking up.* London: Collins.

Sinclair, J. (1998). The lexical item. In E. Weigand (Ed.), *Contrastive lexical semantics* (pp. 1–24). Amsterdam: John Benjamins.

Slaughter, S., & Leslie, L. L. (1994). Entrepreneurial science and intellectual property in Australian universities. In J. Smyth (Ed.), *Academic work: The changing labour process in higher education* (pp. 112–128). Buckingham, UK: Society for Research into Higher Education and Open University Press.

Slaughter, S., & Leslie, L. L. (1997). *Academic capitalism: Politics, policies, and the entrepreneurial university.* Baltimore: Johns Hopkins University Press.

Stubbs, M. (1996). *Text and corpus analysis: Computer-assisted studies of language and culture.* Oxford, UK & Cambridge, MA: Blackwell.

Stubbs, M. (2001). *Words and phrases. Corpus studies of lexical semantics.* Oxford, UK: Blackwell.

Subotzky, G. (n.d.). Globalisation and higher education. Retrieved September 22, 2005, from http://www.chet.org.za/oldsite/debates/SanLameer/subotzky.html

Swinburne University of Technology. (n.d.). *Being an entrepreneurial university. The Swinburne expo.* Retrieved September 22, 2005, from http://www.swinke.com/2003/articles/0015swinexpo.htm

Teubert, W. (2000). A province of a federal superstate, ruled by an unelected bureaucracy: Keywords of the Eurosceptic discourse in Britain. In A. Musolff, C. Good, P. Points, & R. Wittlinger (Eds.), *Attitudes towards Europe: Language in the unification process* (pp. 45–86). Aldershot, UK: Ashgate.

Thrupp, M., & Willmott, R. (2003). *Education management in managerialist times: Beyond the textual apologists.* Maidenhead, UK: Open University Press.

Trowler, P. R. (1998). *Academics responding to change: New higher education frameworks and academic cultures.* Buckingham, UK: Society for Research into Higher Education and Open University Press.

Trowler, P. R. (2001). Captured by the discourse? The socially constitutive power of new higher education discourse in the UK. *Organization, 8,* 183–201.

University of East London (2000). *Quality audit report.* Retrieved September 22, 2005, http://www.qaa.ac.uk/reviews/reports/institutional/eastlondon/eastlondon.asp

University of Oxford. (n.d.). *Innovation.* Retrieved September 22, 2005, from http://www.ox.ac.uk/innovation/

Van Dijk, T. A. (1993). Principles of critical discourse analysis. *Discourse and Society, 4,* 249–283.

van Vught, F. (n.d.). *UT campus tour.* Retrieved December 19, 2003, from http://www.ieo.edte.utwente.nl/pre-module/utcampustour.htm

Wasser, H. (1990). Changes in the European university: From traditional to entrepreneurial. *Higher Education Quarterly, 44,* 110–122.

Webster, G. (2003, April). Corporate discourse and the academy. A polemic. *Industry and Higher Education,* 85–90.

Williams, G. (Ed.). (2003). *The enterprising university: Reform, excellence and equity.* Buckingham, UK: Society for Research into Higher Education and Open University Press.

Williams, R. (1983). *Keywords: A vocabulary of culture and society* (2nd ed.). London: Fontana. (Original work published 1976)

Wu, C.-T. (2002). *Privatising culture: Corporate art intervention since the 1980s.* London: Verso Books.

77

'THIS WE HAVE DONE':
THE VAGUENESS OF POETRY
AND PUBLIC RELATIONS

Guy Cook

Source: Joan Cutting (ed), *Vague Language Explored*, Basingstoke: Palgrave MacMillan, 2007, 21–39.

Introduction

This chapter compares VL in two very different discourses: poetry and public relations. To do this, it considers each one in broad terms, analysing both changing critical approaches to meaning in literary discourse in general, and the growing power and prominence of public relations. But to anchor this general discussion, it also homes in on a particular example, statements beginning with the structure 'FIRST PERSON PRONOUN + have + PAST PARTICIPLE', firstly in the Bob Dylan song *A Hard Rain's Gonna Fall* (which I treat as a poem) and secondly in a corpus of public-relations web-pages by the world's largest food and tobacco companies. There is nothing inherently vague about this structure in itself. Indeed I have chosen it because of its apparent definiteness of reference to what has happened in the past. But its use in my two sources produces vague meanings, though with very different likely effects. The aim is to explore how and why this is, and its significance for the understanding and study of language use in the contemporary world.

Before turning to the quality of being 'vague' in poetry and public relations however, it may be well (in order to rescue the concept itself from vagueness) to define this quality with reference to an antonym: being 'precise'. If we can define what we mean when we say that meaning is 'precise', then we may be able to say that vagueness is the absence of that quality. To this purpose, and to provide a yardstick against which to measure poetic and public-relations discourse when we come to them, I begin by considering a very different kind of language use: emergency procedures.

Emergency procedures

Emergency procedures are instructions about what to do in a crisis such as a fire, an emergency landing, the evacuation of a building, or someone suffering a heart attack, arterial bleeding and such (Lobianco 1999). Their aim is presumably to use language as precisely as possible. But what precisely do we mean by 'precise' in this context?

According to the much maligned conduit metaphor of communication (Reddy 1979), linguistic communication is a means of conducting thoughts and ideas from one mind into another, just as a conduit conducts water between locations. The current vogue is to dismiss this metaphor, as Reddy did, for its failure to take account of the active role of the receiver in constructing an interpretation of a message (for example Thorne 2000).

Nevertheless, it remains true that the transmission of information is part of communication, sought after and substantially achieved, albeit only partially, and in some genres more than others. Consider for example the following emergency procedure, presented as typical by Lobianco (op cit.) in her analysis of a corpus of 125 such texts[1]. This particular one is about what to do if somebody chokes.

Abdominal thrusts

NEVER use this on babies.
1. Stand or kneel behind the person. Put your arms around their abdomen.
2. Make a fist with one hand and grasp it with the other hand. Pull both hands towards you with a quick inward and upward thrust from the elbows to squeeze the upper abdomen. Pull hard enough to push the air out and dislodge the obstruction.
3. Repeat up to five times.

Here it seems reasonable to suppose that the main intention was to convey information known to the writer but not to all readers. Of course this simple characterisation of the text is subject to many qualifications. Some of its linguistic choices may fail to achieve this objective, thus leading to an unintended vagueness. The second sentence of point two is a case in point, being linguistically and semantically complex and difficult to process. Technical terms such as 'upper abdomen' (though precise for those with medical training) and formal phrasing such as 'dislodge the obstruction' puzzled some of the readers in Lobianco's study, and may well have been motivated at least in part by a desire to impress and establish authority. In addition, understanding is, as always, dependent upon pre-existing world knowledge – in this case fairly basic and universal knowledge about the human body. Moreover, emergency texts can fulfil purposes other than giving instructions in an actual emergency: they may be used on training courses, or posted to indemnify an organisation from prosecution. Nevertheless, despite all these caveats, it is very possible that some information is conveyed from one mind to another by this text – the fact that we should not use this technique on babies, for example.

The use of language here aspires to precision, where precision is defined as the choice of linguistic forms which facilitate the effective conveyance of non-linguistic information from one mind to another. And indeed such a text can be evaluated by its success or failure in this transfer.

Literary texts

Here then we have a genre which aims to avoid vagueness even if it sometimes fails. Other genres however do not necessarily share this aspiration, and consequently cannot be judged by the same criteria. They are vague for different reasons. Literary texts are a prime example[2]. Their tendency to lend themselves to different often contradictory interpretations is not a sign of failure. Indeed if it were, the literary cannon would need radical re-evaluation, for it is precisely those texts which are conventionally regarded as the greatest, which also give rise to the most controversy and incompatible readings. Was Hamlet mad? Was Milton on God's side or, as William Blake claimed, 'of the devil's party without knowing it'[3]. Part of the reason for the controversy is that, unlike the emergency text above, there is no extra-linguistic reality to convey. So it is not possible to assess the accuracy of an interpretation by the degree to which is corresponds to something else. Even if we treat the text as conveying information about a fictional world, we may still be unsure which of many competing voices within the text to believe. The text is all we have.

Yet in what can be called traditional 'literary scholarship' (Jefferson and Robey 1982, p.2–15), the task which many literary critics set themselves has been to find the single true meaning of their chosen work, rather than to let it remain either multiple or unclear. Was the governess mad when she reported seeing ghosts in Henry James' (1995) novella *The Turn of the Screw*, or were the ghosts real? Alternatively, they may scour the literary work for an insight into the biography and character of the writer, for example, reading off facts about Alexander Pushkin from the character of the main character in his verse novel *Eugene Onegin*, whose life history shares certain features with his own. Inside the apparent surface message is assumed to be another hidden one. Critics of this persuasion are like the theologian who, faced with a cryptic scriptural passage, assumes the role of interpreter for the word of God. And like some religious exegesists, they can be dogmatic, narrow-minded and fundamentalist.

But this approach raises some curious questions, especially if we think back to the criteria for assessing emergency procedures. If there is a single true meaning, why was it not expressed more directly? Why dress it up or distract from it through literary mechanisms creating vagueness and ambiguity? Are the greatest writers after all not very good at expressing themselves, and therefore in need of paraphrase and explanation? Is there some kind of failure in the great works of literature to say what was meant?

Other critical approaches have by-passed these problems by abandoning a search for spurious precision, content to leave the meanings of a literary text both vague and various. The author and the world portrayed, whether fictional or autobiographical, melt into the background (Barthes 1977; Foucault 1969). Readers, each with a different reading, are brought to the fore. Reader-response theories, of various kinds, and to varying degrees, accept the validity of interpretations determined by the reader's varying identity, purposes and contexts, rather than the author (Freund 1987; Tompkin 1980). Certain types of text are seen as lending themselves to multiple interpretations. Bakhtin's frequently cited distinction between monologic and heteroglossic discourse, used in his analysis of literary works such as Dostoevsky's novels (Bakhtin 1984), portrays the latter as voicing many viewpoints simultaneously. The literary text has many voices, each contending with the other and capable of yielding radically different but valid interpretations.

In all of these views, despite differences between various schools of analysis, the implied virtue of the text is its capacity to yield many meanings, with possibilities increasing in proportion to the degree to which the writer is prepared to let go. If precision is the fixed quality of a single monologic truth (such as the correct procedure when somebody chokes) then we have no alternative but to say that literary texts are among the least precise. In this sense, the greater the vagueness, the greater the text.

Before we get carried away however, it is worth adding three caveats to the sweeping statements with which I concluded the last paragraph. Firstly, there is no reason to suppose that these revolutions in theories of textual meaning have actually changed the way people read literary works. We still interpret in particular ways as we go along, and indeed we may need to do this, if a literary text is to be meaningful for us. However well-versed we may be in post-modern literary theories, we are still likely to argue the case (at least in a non-academic forum) for our own views of 'what it is about'. Indeed reader response theory is premised on just such a view. Readers' interpretations are multiple taken as a whole, but that multiplicity is the sum of many unique interpretations. Secondly, literary works are still universally catalogued by author, suggesting a persistence of the view that they are to be understood by reference to a known individual, and that by reading them we come to understand that individual better. Lastly, to say the literary text yields many interpretations is not to say that it does not delimit the scope of possible interpretations. In the words of Widdowson (1992, p.191), 'the meanings we read into texts are not independent of the texts themselves'. We may argue over whether *Paradise Lost* presents an orthodox Christian view of Satan, but we are less likely to say that the poem is comic.

We have then, in broad terms, two diametrically opposed views of literary discourse. In one it is the repository of a precise but hidden message, as though it were attempting, like our emergency procedures text, to communicate a single message, but somehow clumsily failing in the attempt, and therefore being in need of explication by a critic. In the other it has no single message, but is constructed to yield a variety of ever-changing interpretations whose truth, as they correspond to nothing outside the text, can never be finally resolved. The skill of the writer is in creating (whether intentionally or 'without knowing it') a text which will yield such multiple meanings. It is precisely this richness, and the consequent possibility of new readings always opening in front of us (as we reconsider, as our own experience changes, as we attend to new details, as we listen to the interpretations of others) which makes such texts so rewarding and so full.

A Hard Rain's A-Gonna Fall

Let us make these general points more precise by looking at a particular example: Bob Dylan's *A Hard Rain's A-Gonna Fall* (2004a, p.59–60). The literary standing of Dylan's lyrics is now widely recognised (for example Ricks 2003) and I shall treat it here as uncontroversial. Even for those of an opposite opinion the validity of the points made may still stand. I shall also treat the song as a poem. Further reasons for selecting this particular song will become evident when I turn to public-relations discourse below.

The first stanza is

> Oh, where have you been, my blue-eyed son?
> Oh, where have you been, my darling young one?
> I've stumbled on the side of twelve misty mountains,
> I've walked and I've crawled on six crooked highways,
> I've stepped in the middle of seven sad forests,
> I've been out in front of a dozen dead oceans,
> I've been ten thousand miles in the mouth of a graveyard,
> And it's a hard, and it's a hard, it's a hard, and it's a hard,
> And it's a hard rain's a-gonna fall.

This is anything but precise in the sense defined above. If Dylan's aim were to convey any exact information then he has failed. Given the success and popularity of this song then, precision cannot be the cause of its appeal. We are not told the identity of the two speakers, but only their relationship. The claimed experiences cannot be literally true and therefore must be interpreted metaphorically. Nor can we be sure who is speaking. We can relate these events either to events in the life of the young singer (he was only twenty two when this song was released) and assume he is 'the blue-eyed son', or we can treat what is said as the voices of two characters, or, following a common way of relating to a first-person narrative, adopt it as a description of our own experiences (as either parent or son), but whichever we choose, there is no sure way of pairing up these metaphors with particular events.

This epic landscape of mountains and highways and forests is precise only in the most general terms, that it is difficult and ominous and the individual (whether singer or sung to) feels lost and threatened within it. But it is difficult to be more precise than that. Yet various features of this vague landscape are given with apparent precision, in exact numbers: twelve misty mountains, six crooked highways, seven sad forests, a dozen dead oceans, ten thousand miles. There is certainly too that worse is to come ('a hard rain') even if the precise nature of that rain is unclear too. When an interviewer tried to pin Dylan down on the meaning of this phrase, asking if he meant 'atomic rain', thus trying to limit the meaning of the song to the fears of nuclear war at the time it was written, he answered that no, he meant 'hard rain'[4].

But it is all vague, despite being framed in apparently precise structures ('I have done X'). The limits of interpretation are set very wide. We might agree on some general points: that it is not a flippant or a light song, that it is apocalyptic and prophetic, broad in its description of life, about an individual's experiences and determination to deal with them. But if we try to make it any more precise, either as autobiography or political commentary, we can only interpret it as a catalogue of problems and threats. Which particular ones we make metaphorically equivalent to the oceans and forests and graveyards is up to us. We have almost 'carte blanche'. Personally, I have always heard the 'dozen dead oceans' as a reference to environmental pollution. But in making such an interpretation I have no way of knowing whether these relate to Dylan's own correlations, if he makes any at all. The imagery is so vague as to lend itself to equally valid interpretations by people with political views quite contrary to my own. Rightwing evangelical Christians for example could see the deadness of the ocean as an image of godlessness. It is the very vagueness of these lyrics which is their strength, and very likely the source of their popularity and power. Their achievement is to avoid precise reference, and thus to lend themselves to a greater number of interpretations, notwithstanding the fact that many Dylan fans interpreted the song literally as a commitment by the author to political activism and later held him accountable for not having fulfilled his promise (Dylan 2004b, p.119–122).

There are many other features, typical of literary texts, which enhance this vagueness. There are indeterminate intertextual resonances, varying of course with the reader's knowledge. The song has a vague relation to other songs, especially the traditional ballad *Lord Randall* from which its opening questions are borrowed (Ricks 2004, p.330–335) or poems, such as Allen Ginsberg's declamatory poem *Howl* (1956) perhaps. It also echoes prophetic and apocalyptic Biblical passages. The use of precise numbers for no apparent reason, for example, coupled with the author's statement of what he has seen and done, are a marked feature of the *Book of Revelation* (Chapter 12, verse 3)

> And I stood upon the sand of the sea, and saw a beast rise up out of the sea, having seven heads and ten horns, and upon his horns ten crowns, and upon his heads the name of blasphemy.

In addition, *A Hard Rain's A-Gonna Fall* resonates with other songs by the same author. Analysis of a corpus of all Dylan's songs[5] (hereafter the Dylan Corpus) shows that many of the significant words in this song ('ocean' and 'valley' for example) occur in other songs too, making a reading of their meaning in those songs potentially relevant here. In addition, a layer of ineffable meaning is added by the song's phonological patterns: the rhythm of the caesuraed lines, their parallel structures, the accumulation and release of each stanza, the alliteration ('stumbled'/ 'side', 'misty mountains', 'stepped'/ 'sad, 'dozen'/ 'dead') and assonance ('walked'/ 'crawled'). And all this is without treating it as a song and considering dimensions of meaning imbued by voice quality, accompaniment, and so on. In short, there is much more that could be said, for which we have no space here.

Public-Relations Discourse

Let me recap the argument so far. We have considered two very different types of discourse: one striving to be precise, in which vagueness is a sign of failure; the other systematically imprecise, making vagueness a source of strength. Let us now turn to a third type, public-relations discourse, and try to see where it stands in relation to the other two. But before we do, a word about Public Relations in general.

Recent decades have witnessed an exponential growth in an activity defined by its own practitioners as Public Relations (PR), the major part of which is conducted through language which we may term Public-Relations Discourse (PRD). PR has its own theory, a burgeoning workforce, a growing literature, thriving academic courses. It exerts a disturbing influence over both news reporting (Cottle 2003) and political campaigns (Franklin 2003). And it consumes a growing proportion of the budgets of organisations from businesses (which is where it originated and with which it is associated) to churches, political parties, trade unions, clubs and societies (for example the freemasons) universities and schools, charities and Non-Government Organisations (NGOs), as well as individuals such as royalty, celebrities and high-profile criminals (Moloney 2000, p.17–18). Indeed it is hard to find people or organisations engaged in public life who are not also engaged in PR. This very catholicity makes the term extremely hard to define and therefore vague. Outside the commercial world, it is difficult to draw clear boundaries between 'PR' and 'propaganda', 'public information', and 'campaigns', while within business practice it is hard to distinguish PR from other related activities such as advertising, marketing and promotion, all of which may be defined as constituents but also precedents of PR. Given this, most definitions are very general. Moloney (2000, p.60) regards PR as 'mostly a category of persuasive communications done by interests in the political economy to advance themselves materially and ideologically through markets and public policy making'. Yet, as he acknowledges, any such characterisation is inevitably fuzzy at the edges as almost any organisational communication might come under such a heading.

This indeterminacy as a genre is one of the many features PRD shares with literature, the boundaries of which are also notoriously slippery and difficult to define. PRD employs devices which have traditionally been associated with literary discourse, especially by formalist attempts to characterise a poetic function (Jakobson 1960) and in earlier stylistic work (for example Leech 1969) focusing upon the effects of marked or deviant language choices. At the phonological and grammatical level there are instances of parallelism, not only in advertising (if that is regarded as a sub genre of PRD) where it is well documented (for example, Cook 2001, p.125–147), but in more general promotional prose as well. For example, a McDonald's (burger chain) press release[6] about the launch of a new low-fat salad dressing, begins with two parallel noun phrases with the same premodifier, followed by three words with an internal rhyme and a pun: 'New Year, New Look – Dressing to impress.' On the Imperial Tobacco web-site, under the heading 'We value individuality and hard work'[7], are bullet-pointed sentences each beginning with the structure 'We' + present tense + predicate.

- We value people with good ideas who are willing to engage in constructive debate
- We have created a culture where realism and open communication are valued
- We acknowledge hard work, good cost control and goal achievement
- We place strong emphasis on personal accountability
- We encourage employees to voice their opinions

This parallel grammatical structure occurs under all the other headings on the same page creating a parallelism between different sections. In the section headed 'we work together for the good of the whole company' for example, we find:

We aim to deliver best-in-class financial results by each and every one of us contributing to outstanding business performance. What do we mean?

- We recognise that Group results are more important than individual success
- We encourage co-operation with colleagues for the greater good of the business
- We place strong emphasis on sharing information and resources and building relationships
- We have developed a culture based on openness, trust and integrity where conflicts are managed maturely

This self-answering structure is not unlike that of *A Hard Rain's A-Gonna Fall*. In the song, the question 'where have you been?' is answered with a string of replies in the form 'I have done X'; here 'What do we mean?' is answered by a string of replies in the form 'We do Y'.

At the lexical and semantic levels, PRD can have quasi-literary features too, using innovations whose very newness makes them resistant to precise interpretation. Consider for example the following publicity for the 'Milton Keynes Hub', a university unit offering support for businesses[8]

The Hub is designed exclusively to encourage and support knowledge-based pre-start and start-up companies during the early stages of their development, it provides a flexible easy-in, easy-out hatchery for embryo businesses.

Here we have word-class conversion ('start-up companies'), neologism ('pre-start'), and at the semantic level, a host of metaphors: the 'hub' itself, and a 'hatchery' for 'embryo' businesses, as though they are eggs. Curiously, this farmyard imagery is rather common in British University jargon with its 'new blood' lectureships, 'pump priming' grants, 'seed corn' research, and 'drilling down' assessments. In such intensely metaphoric uses of language, connotational and symbolic meanings are foregrounded at the expense of denotative ones.

At the pragmatic level the voice of the sender in PRD, as in many literary narratives, is often ambiguous. 'Who is speaking thus?' asked Barthes (1977), when trying to disentangle the voices of author, narrator, characters and society in the Balzac short story *Sarrasine*. Looking at the 'we' of corporate web pages, we might well ask the same question. Just as we might ask who is speaking in *A Hard Rain's A-Gonna Fall*: a blue-eyed boy character, or the singer himself?

There are already some very significant studies of aspects of PRD such as service speak (Cameron 2000), mission statements (Swales and Rogers 1995) and educational buzz words (Mautner 2005), as well as more general critiques of obfuscatory institutional language which are relevant to PRD, such as Nash (1993) on jargon and Shuy (1998) on bureaucratic language. Nevertheless, given its growing social and political influence, there is still relatively little work specifically on the language of PRD, in contrast for example to the extensive work on the language of advertising, the press, or the law. It is sometimes assumed in some writing on PR (for example, Stauber and Rampton 1995) that the language of PRD, including its 'literary' devices, tends to provoke derision rather than praise and they are seen as superficial, pretentious, manipulative, and insincere. And there is some research to suggest that PRD is indeed held in low esteem (Moloney 2000, p.75–88). Yet much more research is needed both into the linguistic and textual characteristics of PRD, and into public reactions to them, if these beliefs are to be validated. Detailed understanding of PRD has a contribution to make both to discourse analysis in general, and to language education, where the development of critical and discriminating responses to influential manipulative discourse could be a key component of both first-language and additional-language curricula. The analysis here aims to contribute to the understanding of the linguistic and semantic characteristics of PRD and the kinds of interpretation they may generate – but it should be borne in mind that it is confined to textual analysis, and based upon my own reading, rather than on the responses of other actual audiences[9].

Food and tobacco PRD

One readily available source of PRD is the web pages of large corporations seeking to present a favourable view of themselves, both to the outside world (external PR) and to their own employees (internal PR). All major companies have such sites and they tend to have many features in common.

For the purposes of the following analysis I collected a corpus of web pages from a) fourteen of the world's biggest tobacco companies[10] and b) the world's fourteen biggest food companies[11]. Current PRD from these two industries is interesting for different but related reasons. Tobacco is now recognised as a killer and its promotion in many countries constrained by law, giving its manufacturers a particularly uphill task in presenting their activities in a favourable light. Food in contrast, far from being a killer is necessary to life. Yet food companies selling heavily processed food face similar if less extreme criticisms concerning the bad effects of their products on public health, particularly children's health. They too therefore face a difficult PR task, though not on the same scale as the tobacco industry. The discourse of contemporary food marketing brings together many of the key concerns of modern life: health and nutrition, quality of life, political decision making, the environmental impact of agriculture, the relation of humans to other species, and continuity of tradition in both farming and food production (Cook 2004; Cook, Pieri and Robbins 2004; Cook, Robbins and Pieri 2006). It therefore engenders intense activity by marketing, and public-relations copy writers seek to connect their companies and products with beneficial causes and to influence public opinion and consumer behaviour.

From the websites of these two sets of companies I extracted the pages relating to description of the company (often entitled 'about us'), social and environmental issues (often entitled 'responsibility'), attitude to employees (often entitled 'people'), and its products and services (often entitled 'our products'). The last of these categories is necessarily a sample[12], as product descriptions, especially in companies with numerous brands, can far exceed the other three in quantity of words. The whole amounts to a corpus of over quarter of a million words[13] which, stored in text only format, can be searched using Wordsmith Tools for word frequencies, keywords in comparison with other corpora, collocational patterns. I shall refer to it as FTC (Food and Tobacco Corpus).

Key words are those whose frequency is unusually high in one corpus in comparison with their frequency in another. They provide 'a useful way to characterise a text or a genre' (Scott 2005). Two words which emerge as unusually frequent[14] in the FTC when compared with the written component of the British National Corpus (BNC)[15] are 'our' and 'we'. They may be regarded, depending on how we define the term[16], as part of a single lemma 'we/us/our'. This PR use of the first person plural echoes a similar one with first person singular in the Dylan Corpus where 'I', 'my', 'me' and 'I'm' all rank in the top ten keywords compared with the written component of the BNC[17]. Both then seem obsessed with the first person: 'what I/we think'; 'what I/we have done/will do' and so forth. But there is an important difference. While 'I' is relatively precise, meaning the sender of the message (unless the speaker is adopting a persona or repeating the words of someone else), 'we' has a notorious vagueness. Not only does it slip easily between 'exclusive we' ('us but not you') and 'inclusive we' ('us and you'), a difference which is not encoded in English[18], but even within these two categories there is considerable ambiguity often exploited by politicians (Cook 2004, p.9–19) and advertisers (Cook 2001, p.157–159). In corporate PR 'we' can be either inclusive, meaning perhaps all humanity or all 'ordinary' people, or exclusive, meaning 'we the company' as opposed to 'you the customer'. But in this last case who exactly is included? Does the company mean the shareholders, the employees, some unnamed spokesperson, or all of these?

One manifestation of these frequent first person pronouns is in statements of what the company has done in the past. These are frequent in the FTC. There are 137 instances of the construction 'We have + PAST PARTICIPLE' including one from which I have taken the title of this chapter: 'However, where it makes business sense to seek external verification or auditing of our EHS systems, this we have done and will do.' Table 1 contains twenty randomly selected examples. Contrary to usual practice I begin the line with

Table 1 Twenty Occurrences of 'We have + PAST PARTICIPLE' in FTC.

1. We have implemented an active policy to prevent industrial accidents and to improve working conditions, notably through employee awareness and training programs.
2. We have included our 'Principles of Citizenship' to assist in the understanding of our core values.
3. We have acquired businesses with operations in numerous countries that brought more than 50 manufacturing plants into our system, which we have integrated and aligned with our environmental programs and practices.
4. We have intensified our efforts to increase efficiency and eliminate waste.
5. We have introduced significant improvements in our arrangements with effect from May 2004.
6. We have invested in state-of-the-art equipment, further improving our efficiency and competitiveness.
7. We have invested heavily in advanced techniques in this area with a view to improving quality, cutting waste and speeding production.
8. We have launched Bertolli pasta sauces and dressings.
9. We have listed Frito-Lay products according to specific dietary concerns here.
10. We have located our 24 worldwide processing facilities in proximity to our principal sources of tobacco.
11. We have met consumer demand for healthy foods by launching pro.active, a spread which contains ingredients that can help reduce cholesterol levels.
12. We have been at the forefront in developing and applying product-evaluation methods to assess the relative toxicity of cigarette smoke.
13. We have positioned The Coca-Cola Company for growth, guided by our mission to provide branded beverages that refresh people around the world, anywhere, any time, everyday.
14. We have reduced emissions of ozone depleting substances per tonne of product by 99%.
15. We have been at the forefront in developing and applying methods to assess the relative toxicity of cigarette smoke.
16. We have developed new cigarettes based on tobacco-heating technology.
17. We have set up resource development systems and tools, which work well.
18. We have worked to extend the approach embodied in our Social Responsibility in Tobacco Production programme to all our leaf suppliers, to reach those from whom we buy leaf on the open market.
19. We have focused our efforts thus far on commodities that are of both special importance to our business and associated with critical societal issues.
20. We have spent over $6 billion with women and minority businesses.

the search term as in most cases, the substance of what has been done follows this opening.

If we contrast these PRD 'have dones' with those of Dylan's first stanza, we can see that semantically and pragmatically they are very different indeed. In the song they conveyed a sense of helplessness, of being dwarfed and overpowered by the environment. There are words denoting physical actions (stepped, crawled, stumbled) and objects (mountains, oceans, valleys), but they seem to refer to the speaker's experience of the landscape rather than his influence upon it, and they are vague because we do not know what the objects and actions themselves denote, metaphorically. The PRD 'have dones' on the other hand refer to actions, in which the speaker ('we') has intervened decisively in their environment and claims to have changed it for the better. They are vague in a different way, not because they are metaphorical, but because they are abstract, and because the terms used denote evaluations of actions (for example 'improve') rather than the actions themselves.

Let us take a few examples and in each case ask questions to test how precisely the statement tells us what actually happened.

> We have implemented an active policy to prevent industrial accidents and to improve working conditions, notably through employee awareness and training programs.

Who exactly is 'we': the management, the owners, the workforce? Did the policy actually reduce accidents? 'Improve' is a relative and often subjective term. What was the initial state from which there was an improvement? How much improvement was there and of what kind? Who viewed it as an improvement, the company or the workers, or both? How many training programmes were there? Were they voluntary or compulsory, in workers' own or paid time?

> We have intensified our efforts to increase efficiency and eliminate waste.

By how much? Did the effort yield results? If so, how much did you increase efficiency? How do you define 'efficiency' and from whose perspective? How do you define waste? As waste surely cannot be eliminated in any industrial process, by how much have you actually reduced it?

> We have spent over $6 billion with women and minority businesses.

How much over? What proportion of your total expenditure is it? What do you mean by 'spend. . . . with'? Do you mean firms with female employees or female owners or both? Could a reason for your choice be that female labour tends to be cheaper? How do you define 'minority businesses'?

If there were space I could make similar points for almost all the other 'have dones' in the corpus, with very few exceptions, such as 'We have launched Bertolli pasta sauces and dressings'. As an account of actual actions in the real (as opposed to a metaphorical or fictional world) it is all very vague indeed.

But of course, no such questioning is possible. Though these web pages adopt a dialogic and conversational tone, any implied opportunity for interaction is illusory.

171

Similarity and differences

What then are the similarities and differences between the 'have done' statements in the FTC and those in *A Hard Rain's A-Gonna Fall*? One similarity is merely formal: they deploy the same opening structure. Another is in overall effect: both are vague. But this vagueness seems to be very different in nature and quality and value. Why?

The humble emergency procedure text provides a useful point of comparison with both which may help to answer this question. Its success can be measured against a corresponding reality. We might say that it works if: a) the procedure described is indeed the best one to adopt when confronted by a choking adult and b) the writer succeeds in conveying the details of this procedure from their own mind to the reader's through the conduit of language. So any vagueness in the emergency text is a sign of failure. The song is quite different. Though there may be a reality which the speaker is trying to convey, its success is not to be measured against a preceding reality or successful outcome (Widdowson 1984). And this perhaps points to a profound difference between the discourses of poetry and PRD, which makes it seem absurd to compare them at all except at the formal and most general levels.

Being about the behaviour and impact of organisations in a real literal world, PRD can, like the emergency procedure text but *un*like the song, be measured against reality. 'Smoking', as the packets say, 'kills'. Obesity is rising among children eating processed food. Among US adolescents it has tripled since 1985 (Sperlock 2005, p.11). Food retailers rely on poor labour conditions (Zacune 2005) and environmentally detrimental intensive farming (Carson 2000; Humphrys 2001). Food retail is part of a world of gross injustice, which can be expressed in quite precise statistics (Hart 2004). According to the United Nations Development Report (UNDP 1998, quoted ibid.) the world's 225 richest men then owned more than a trillion dollars, the equivalent of the world's 47 per cent poorest people. According to The Institute for Food and Development Policy in 1999 (quoted in McGarr 2000, p.85)

> The world today produces more food per inhabitant than ever before. Enough is available to provide 4.3 pounds to every person every day: 2.5 pounds of grain, beans and nuts, about a pound of meat, milk and eggs, and another of fruit and vegetables. The real causes of hunger are poverty, inequality and lack of access. Too many people are too poor to buy the food that is available, or lack the land and resources to grow it themselves.

In a real world of this kind, we the readers of PRD can ask questions of its producers such as the following, and educate our students to do the same.

What have these companies done to prevent death and ill health among consumers of their products? What changes did they make in their employees' working conditions? What did they do to diminish environmental pollution by their manufacturing and distribution processes? What have they done to address the injustices of wealth and food distribution? In short 'What have you done' in precise and literal terms? In the FTC it is all very vague. PR writers may measure the success of their words by their aesthetic power as though they were poems, but the public may measure them by their truth as though they were emergency texts. There should be no confusion of the two. Vagueness in PRD should be evaluated in quite a different way from vagueness in literary texts. Despite some literary pretensions, it is its correspondence to the facts which matters.

Notes

1 Lobianco's study is of the texts as multimodal communication and also of readers' understandings of them. This particular procedure is in fact probably better demonstrated than explained, and the original is also accompanied by a picture.
2 The summary of approaches to literature in this section receives much fuller treatment in my book *Discourse and Literature* (Cook 1994, p.125–177)
3 William Blacke's famous assessment of *Paradise Lost* in his *The Marriage of Heaven and Hell*. Quoted by Philip Pullman in Introduction, Milton (2005).
4 Included in the Martin Scorsese's 2005 film *No Direction Home*. The song was released in 1963, the year after the Cuban missile crisis, at a time of intense fear about nuclear war.
5 Part of a larger corpus of song lyrics 1955–2005 held by the author.
6 http://www.mcdonalds.co.uk/pages/global/dressing.html (accessed 17 November 2005)
7 http://www.imperial-tobacco.com/index.asp?pageid=78 (accessed 17 November 2005)
8 http://www.01908.co.uk/business/386?PHPSESSID=ac6d867292ecf941a18d595d 243971da (accessed 29 October 2005)
9 In other work on PRD I have combined textual analysis with interviews and/or focus groups eliciting responses from a range of readers to promotional material such as labels (Cook and O'Halloran 1999; Nyyssönen *et al* 2000), arguments for GM agriculture and food (Cook, Robbins and Pieri 2005) and for organic and non-organic foods (Cook and Robbins 2006).
10 Based on information provided by ASH and on the 'fortune 500' list of the world's largest corporations http://www.fortune.com/fortune/global500
11 Using the ranking given by the journal *Food Engineering*, available online at: http://www.foodengineeringmag.com/FILES/HTML/PDF/Top100chart.pdf (accessed 22 October 2005)
12 An amount taken from the beginning of the product description pages equal in size to each of the other categories.
13 275,434 words in total: 122,875 from tobacco companies; 152,559 from food companies.
14 'Our' ranks first and second, 'we' ranks eighteenth.
15 I used the BNC Baby, a four million word extract from the BNC comprising three million words of written and 1 million words of spoken data.

16 They would be by Francis and Kučera's (1982, p.1) definition of a lemmas 'a set of lexical forms having the same stem and belonging to the same major word class, differing only in inflection and / or spelling'.

17 Caution is needed here, however, as the lemma (I/Me/My) ranks highly as a keyword in comparisons on spoken with written discourse. However, even compared with the spoken component 'My' is the first keyword and 'me' is the second keyword in The Dylan Corpus.

18 As it is in many other languages. In Malay the word 'kita' means 'we-inclusive-of-addressee', while 'kani' means 'we-exclusive-of-addressee.'

References

M. M. Bakhtin, *Problems of Dostoevsky's Poetics*, (Manchester: Manchester University Press, 1984). (Original Russian version published in 1929).

R. Barthes, 'The Death of the Author'. In *Image, Music, Text*, (translated by S. Heath). (London: Fontana, 1977). 142–149 (Original French version published in 1968).

D. Cameron, *Good to talk? Living and Working in a Communication Culture*, (London: Sage, 2000).

R. Carson, *Silent Spring*. (London: Penguin, 2000.) (1st edn published in USA 1962).

G. Cook, *Discourse and Literature: the Interplay of Form and Mind*, (Oxford: Oxford University Press, 1994).

G. Cook, *The Discourse of Advertising*, (2nd edn) (London: Routledge, 2001).

G. Cook, *Genetically Modified Language*, (London: Routledge, 2004).

G. Cook and K. O'Halloran, 'Label Literacy: Factors Affecting the Understanding and Assessment of Baby Food Labels', In T. O'Brien (ed.), *Language and Literacies, BAAL Studies in Applied Linguistics 14*, (British Association for Applied Linguistics in association with Multilingual Matters, 1999) 145–57.

G. Cook, E. Pieri, and P. T. Robbins, '"The Scientists Think and the Public Feels": Expert Perceptions Of The Discourse Of GM Food', *Discourse and Society* 15/4 (2004) 433–49.

G. Cook, P. T. Robbins, and E. Pieri '"Words of Mass Destruction": British Newspaper Coverage of the GM Food Debate, and Expert and Non-expert Reactions', *Public Understanding of Science*, 14/1 (2005) 1–25.

G. Cook and P. T. Robbins, *The Discourse of Organic Food Promotion: Language, Intentions and Effects*, (ESRC Research Project, 000-22-1626, 2006).

S. Cottle, (ed.) *News, Public Relations and Power. Media in Focus*, (London: Sage, 2003).

R. Dylan, *Bob Dylan Lyrics 1962–2001*, (New York: Simon and Schuster, 2004a).

R. Dylan, *Chronicles Volume One*, (New York: Simon and Schuster, 2004b).

M. Foucault, 'What is an Author?' (translated by J. V. Harari), In J. V. Harari (ed.) *Textual Strategies: Perspectives in Post-Structuralism*, (Ithaca NY: Cornell University Press, 1988) (Original French version published in 1969).

W. N. Francis and H. Kučera, *Frequency Analysis of English Usage*, (Boston: Houghton Mifflin, 1982).

B. Franklin, '"A Good Day to Bury Bad News?": Journalists Sources and the Packaging of Politics', In S. Cottle (ed.) *News, Public Relations and Power*, (London: Sage, 2003).

E. Freund, *The Return of the Reader*, (London: Methuen, 1987).

J. Gibbons, *Language and the Law*, (London and New York: Longman, 1994).

A. Ginsberg, *Howl and Other Poems*. (San Francisco, CA: City Lights Books, 1956).

K. Hart, 'The Political Economy of Food in an Unequal World', In M. E. Lien and B. Nerlich (eds.) *The Politics of Food*, (Oxford and New York: Berg, 2004).

K. T. Higgins, 'The World's Top 100 Food and Beverage Companies: Diets Define Profit And Loss', *Food Engineering*, 10 January (2004).

J. Humphrys, *The Great Food Gamble*, (London: Hodder and Stoughton, 2001).

R. Jakobson, 'Closing Statement: Linguistics and Poetics'. In T. A. Sebeok (ed.) *Style in Language*, (Cambridge, Massachusetts: MIT Press, 1960.)

H. James, *The Turn of the Screw and Other Short Novels*, (London: Penguin, 1995) (*The Turn of the Screw* first published in 1898).

A. Jefferson and D. Robey, *Modern Literary Theory: a Comparative Introduction*, London: Batsford, 1982).

G. N. Leech, *A Linguistic Guide to English Poetry*, (London: Longman, 1969).

T. M. F. B. Lobianco, *The Effect of the Interplay of Paralanguage and Language on the Accessibility of Written Texts: a Study of Emergency Procedures*, Unpublished PhD thesis, London University Institute of Education (1999).

G. Mautner, 'The Entrepreneurial University. A Discursive Profile of the Higher-Education Buzzword', *Critical Discourse Studies* 2/2 (2005) 95–120.

P. McGarr, 'Why Green is Red: Marxism and the Threat to the Environment'. In C. Harman (ed.) *Anti-capitalism: Theory and Practice, London: International Socialism Quarterly*, 88. (2000) 61–126.

J. Milton, *Paradise Lost*. (ed. Philip Pullman) (Oxford: Oxford University Press, 2005) (First published in 1667).

K. Moloney, *Rethinking Public Relations: the Spin and the Substance*, (London: Routledge, 2000).

W. Nash, *Jargon: its Uses and Abuses*, (Blackwell: Oxford, 1993).

H. Nyyssönen, A. Björkvall, G. Cook, F. X. Fernandez-Polo, B.-L. Gunnarsson, P. Haddington, K. Maryns, K. O'Halloran, S. Slembrouck, C. Suárez Gómez, A.-M. Vandenbergen, *Design and Accessibility of Baby-food Labels from the Consumer's Point of View*, http://www.ekl.oulu.fi/babyfood/index.html (accessed 5 May 2005).

A. Pushkin, *Eugene Onegin*, (translated by Charles Johnston) (London: Penguin, 2003). (Original Russian version published in 1833).

M. Reddy, 'The Conduit Metaphor', In A. Ortony (ed.) *Metaphor and Thought*, (Cambridge: Cambridge University Press, 1979).

C. Ricks, *Dylan's Vision of Sin*. (London: Penguin, 2003).

M. Scott, 'Help Menu', In *Wordsmith Tools*, http://www.lexically.net/wordsmith/ (Oxford: Oxford University Press, 2005).

R. Shuy, *Bureaucratic Language in Government and Business*, (Washington DC: Georgetown University Press, 1998).

M. Sperlock, *Don't Eat this Book*. (London: Penguin, 2005).

J. Stauber and S. Rampton, *Toxic Sludge is Good for You: Lies, Damn Lies and the Public Relations Industry*, (Monroe ME: Common Courage Press, 1995).

J. Swales and P. Rogers, 'Discourse and the Projection of Corporate Culture: the Mission Statement', *Discourse and Society*, 6/2 (1995) 233–242.

175

S. Thorne, 'Second Language Acquisition Theory and the Truth(s) about Relativity', In J. P. Lantolf (ed.) *Sociocultural Theory and Second Language Learning*, (Oxford: Oxford University Press, 2000).

J. P. Tompkin (ed.) *Reader-Response Criticism: from Formalism to Post-Structuralism*, (Baltimore, MD: The Johns Hopkins University Press, 1980).

United Nations Development Program, *Human Development Report*, (New York: UNDP, 1998).

H. G. Widdowson, *Practical Stylistics*, (Oxford: Oxford University Press, 1992).

H. G. Widdowson 'Reference and Representation as Modes of Meaning'. In *Explorations in Applied Linguistics 2*, (Oxford: Oxford University Press, 1984) 150–60.

J. Zacune, *ASDA WAL-MART: Cutting Costs At Any Cost* Corporate Watch. 19 October http://www.corporatewatch.org.uk/?lid=2102 (accessed 29 October 2005).

Part 10

FOR ADVERTISING.
SOME INSIDER VIEWS

78

EDITORIAL

Jules Goddard

Source: *International Journal of Advertising*, 4:4 (1985), Reprinted in Alvarado, M. and J. Thompson (eds), *The Media Reader*, London: British Film Institute, 1990, pp. 205–207.

Advertising is a commodity. Advertisements are supplied only because the market demands them. The value that consumers place on advertisements is roughly equal to their cost (generally between 1 and 2 per cent of G N P). A *marketing* approach to advertising asks: 'What is it that consumers are buying when they buy advertisements?' and 'Which particular human needs are more economically met by advertising than by any other economic goods?' In some markets, advertising is more highly valued than in others. What characterizes these markets? What sets them apart as heavy demanders of advertising? The orthodox view is that people are buying economies of large-scale production. This is a piece of sophistry. They may *sometimes* be buying a lower price. But, more often than not, they are buying a product, where the product is the meaning of the advertising.

The meaning of an advertisement is the use to which consumers put it. To understand how people make use of advertising is the first step in knowing how best to market the product that advertising embodies. Presumably, advertisements are used in many, many ways. And this is something that merits more research. But, as a first guess, we might want to say that, when people buy *advertising*, they are buying the self-assurance of the manufacturer ('it must be good to merit advertising') and the market share of the brand ('it must sell well to afford advertising'); and when people buy an *advertisement* they are returning a compliment (the creative ad is the ad which makes the consumer creative) and applauding a performance (all creativity demands criticism). Advertisements, then, are products on an equal footing with the things made in factories, and advertising agencies are their manufacturers. This releases them from the misleading notion that they are communicators. They are only communicators in the sense that any manufacturer's product carries significance to a market.

The best advertisements draw attention to themselves as advertisements. Indeed, only by doing so can they be charged with meaning and emotion. We feel emotion when our expectations are not fulfilled; we lend the emotion meaning in trying to interpret it. In both cases, we need to locate an advertisement in a tradition of advertising for it to be potent. Blue, in itself, is almost meaningless; blue-rather-than-green, however, begins to acquire significance. In short, advertisements would be better if they emulated works of art (where meaning derives from their handling of the rules of the game) rather than editorials (where meaning derives from the presentation of an argument). This is because consumers perceive advertisements in aesthetic space and do not make use of ads as though they were salesmen. After a time, as Kant suggested, promises become empty if they are continuously broken.

What are the implications of this marketing view of advertising?

Advertising plans should be different
–   concentrating on positioning the *advertisements*, not the product. The product may even be a red herring.
–   built around responses to the advertisements as products in their own right.

Advertising research should be different
–   concentrating on *intensity* of response rather than *content* of response, relating this to the optimal levels in the collative variables (novelty, ambiguity, surprisingness, change, blurredness, etc.).
–   locating meaning and emotion in the gap between people's expectations and preconceptions on the one hand (the 'background') and the reality of the advertisements on the other (the 'foreground').

Advertisements themselves should be different
–   with writers and art directors released from the need to change the market's perception of the factory product and working instead to satisfy the aesthetic and novelty-seeking needs of the market.
–   with campaigns designed in such a way that each ad in the series sets up expectations that its successor can feed off.

Advertising controls should be different
–   focusing on the sales and consumption of the ads rather than the sales and consumption of the factory product.
–   accepting the possibility that the product may be detracting from the sales of the advertisements.

Agency–client relationships should be different

– founded on the premise that both sides are *fellow-manufacturers*, each trying to live up to the market quality of the other's product.
– recognizing that in some markets the factory product, and in others the advertising product, will yield a higher return.

79

WHAT'S WRONG WITH ADVERTISING?

Toynbee and Galbraith vs. Roosevelt and Churchill

David Ogilvy

Source: David Ogilvy, *Ogilvy on Advertising*, London: Prion, 1985, pp. 206–216.

'Holy smoke, is *that* what I do for a living?'

In my *Confessions* I quoted the classic denunciations of advertising by Arnold Toynbee, John Kenneth Galbraith and a galaxy of earlier economists, and wheeled up Franklin Roosevelt and Winston Churchill as witnesses for the defense.

Twenty years later the dons are still tilting at their old windmill. Thus a professor at the New School of Social Research in New York teaches his students that 'advertising is a profoundly subversive force in American life. It is intellectual and moral pollution. It trivializes, manipulates, is insincere and vulgarizes. It is undermining our faith in our nation and in ourselves'.

Holy smoke, is *that* what I do for a living?

Some of the defenders of advertising are equally guilty of overstating their case. Said Leo Burnett, the great Chicago advertising man: 'Advertising is not the noblest creation of man's mind, as so many of its advocates would like the public to think. It does not, single-handedly, sustain the whole structure of capitalism and democracy and the Free World. It is just as nonsensical to suggest that we are superhuman as to accept the indictment that we are subhuman. We are merely human, trying to do a necessary human job with dignity, with decency and with competence'.

My view is that advertising is no more and no less than a reasonably efficient way to sell. Procter & Gamble spends more than $600,000,000 a year on advertising. Howard Morgens, their former president, is quoted as saying, 'We believe that advertising is the most effective and efficient way to sell to the consumer. If we should ever find better methods of selling our type of products to the consumer, we'll leave advertising and turn to these other methods'.

Few of us admen lie awake nights feeling guilty about the way we earn our living. In Churchill's phrase, we just K.B.O.[1] We don't feel 'subversive' when we write advertisements for toothpaste. If we do it well, children may not have to go to the dentist so often.

I did not feel 'evil' when I wrote advertisements for Puerto Rico. They helped attract industry and tourists to a country which had been living on the edge of starvation for 400 years.

I do not think that I am 'trivializing' when I write advertisements for the World Wildlife Fund.

My children were grateful when I wrote an advertisement which recovered their dog Teddy from dognappers.

Nobody suggests that the printing press is evil because it is used to print pornography. It is also used to print the Bible. Advertising is only evil when it advertises evil things. Nobody I know in advertising would advertise a brothel, and some refuse to advertise booze or cigarettes.

Left-wing economists, ever eager to snatch the scourge from the hand of God, hold that advertising tempts people to squander money on things they don't need. Who are these élitists to decide what you need? Do you *need* a dishwasher? Do you *need* a deodorant? Do you *need* a trip to Rome? I feel no qualms of conscience about persuading you that you do. What the Calvinistic dons don't seem to know is that buying things can be one of life's more innocent pleasures, whether you need them or not. Remember your euphoria when you bought your first car? Most people enjoy window-shopping the ads, whether for bargains or for luxuries. For 40 years I shopped the ads for country houses, and finally saved up enough money to buy one.

It is not unknown for an advertisement in a newspaper to be read by more people than any news item. When all the New York newspapers went on strike for several weeks in 1963, research showed that it was the advertisements which readers missed most.

If advertising were abolished, what would be done with the money? Would it be spent on public works? Or distributed to stock-holders in the form of extra dividends? Or given to the media to compensate them for the loss of their largest source of revenue? Perhaps it could be used to reduce prices to the consumer – *by about 3 per cent.*[2]

Is advertising a pack of lies?

Introducing me at an Asian Advertising Congress in New Delhi the other day, the Vice-President and former Chief Justice of India said that I had 'mastered what Stephen Leacock called the art of arresting the human intelligence long enough to get money from it'.

If there are still any natural-born liars in advertising, we are under control. Every advertisement we write is scrutinized by lawyers, by the National Association of Broadcasters and other such bodies. The Better Business Bureau and the National Advertising Review Board (in Britain, the Advertising Standards Authority) review suspected violations of the various codes, and the Federal Trade Commission stands ready to prosecute us for deception. *Caveat emptor* has given way to *caveat vendor*.

But how odd that the Commission does not monitor the advertising put out by departments of the US Government. Writes Milton Friedman, 'Anyone who has bought government bonds over the past decade has been taken to the cleaners. The amount he received on maturity would buy less in goods and services than the amount he paid for the bond, and he has to pay taxes on the mislabeled "interest". Yet the Treasury continues to advertise the bonds as "building personal security", and a "gift that keeps on growing"'.[3]

'The dirge of our times'

While very little advertising can be convicted of crimes against humanity, exposure to 30,000 TV commercials every year – the average dosage in American homes – suggests that Wilfrid Sheed had a point when he wrote that 'the sound of selling is the dirge of our times'. When I lived in New York, I did not notice it, either because I was too busy to watch for more than half an hour a day (Walter Cronkite), or because I was corrupted by familiarity. But when I went to live in Europe, I grew accustomed to smaller doses of advertising. Today, when I return to the United States, I am enraged by the barrage to which I am subjected. And this does not apply only to television. On Sundays, the *New York Times* often carries 350 pages of advertisements, and some of the radio stations devote 40 minutes in every hour to commercials. I don't know how all this clutter can ever be brought under control; the profit motive is too strong in those who own the media.

In the average American home, the TV is turned on, if not watched, for five hours a day, which adds up to 25 years in the average life. But don't blame the *commercials* for this addiction.

Manipulation?

You may have heard it said that advertising is 'manipulation'. I know of only two examples, and neither of them actually happened. In 1957 a market researcher called James Vicary hypothesized that it might be possible to flash commands on television screens so fast that the viewer would not be conscious of seeing them, but his *unconscious* would see them – and obey them. He called this gimmick 'subliminal' advertising, but he never even got around to testing it, and no advertiser has ever used it. Unfortunately word of his hypothesis found its way into the public prints, and provided grist for the mills of the anti-advertising brigade. The British Institute of Practitioners in Advertising solemnly banned the use of subliminal advertising – which did not exist.

My only other example of manipulation will make you shudder. I myself once came near to doing something so diabolical that I hesitate to confess it even now, 30 years later. Suspecting that *hypnotism* might be an element in successful advertising, I engaged a professional hypnotist to make a commercial. When I saw it in the projection room, it was so powerful that I had visions of millions of suggestible consumers getting up from their armchairs and rushing like zombies through the traffic on their way to buy the product at the nearest store. Had I invented the *ultimate* advertisement? I burned it, and never told my client how close I had come to landing him in a national scandal.

One way and another, the odds against your being manipulated by advertising are now very long indeed. Even if I wanted to manipulate you, I wouldn't know how to circumvent the legal regulations.

Hold your horses – I almost forgot. There is one category of advertising which is totally uncontrolled and flagrantly dishonest: the television commercials for candidates in Presidential elections.

Political chicanery

While statesmen in England, France and Persia have sometimes consulted me, I have never taken political parties as clients of Ogilvy & Mather. First, because they would preoccupy the best brains of the agency, to the detriment of its permanent clients. Second, because they are bad credit risks. Third, because it would be unfair to those people in the agency who pray for the victory of the opposing party. And finally, because it would be difficult to avoid the chicanery which is endemic in all political campaigns.

The first politician to use television was Governor Dewey in his 1950 campaign for the governorship of New York. On one program, Happy Felton, the entertainer, interviewed passers-by under the marquee of the Astor Hotel on 7th Avenue. They would say what interested them in the campaign, and ask questions of the Governor. Dewey watched them on a monitor in the studio, and answered their questions. The day before, his staff had carefully *selected* the passers-by. They had *told* them what they were interested in, and rehearsed their questions. On the last day of the campaign, Dewey was on television from 6 am to midnight. People could telephone the studio. Four women on camera answered the calls and passed along the questions for Dewey to answer. A member of his staff was in a phone booth at the corner drugstore with a pile of nickels.

Dewey, the ex-District Attorney, the battler against corruption, the Governor of the State, thought of himself as an honorable man. It never

185

occurred to him that he was involved in deception. I doubt that it would occur to anyone, honorable or dishonorable, to pull such a play today, thirty years later. Times change.

Dewey was a *scientific* demagogue. Before speaking on major issues, he used research to find out which policies had the widest popular support and then put them forward as if he believed in them.

In his book *The Duping of the American Voter*,[4] my colleague Robert Spero analyzed the commercials used by Kennedy, Johnson, Nixon, Ford and Carter. He concluded that they were 'the most deceptive, misleading, unfair and untruthful of all advertising . . . the sky is the limit with regard to what can be said, what can be promised, what accusations can be made, what lies can be told'.

The nine Federal agencies which regulate advertising for products have no say in political advertising. The broadcasting networks, which turn down half the commercials for products submitted to them because they violate their codes, do not apply any code whatever to political commercials. Why not? Because political advertising is considered 'protected speech' under the First Amendment of the US Constitution. The networks are obliged to broadcast every political commercial submitted to them, however dishonest.

In 1964, Johnson's commercials disparaged Senator Goldwater with a cynical dishonesty which would never be tolerated in commercials for toothpaste. They gave voters to understand that Goldwater was an irresponsible, trigger-happy ogre who would start nuclear wars at the drop of a hat. Johnson was presented as a dove of peace.

What had happened was this. Goldwater, one of the most decent men in public life, had been asked by an interviewer to differentiate between the *reliability* and the *accuracy* of guided missiles. He had replied that they were accurate enough 'to lob one into the men's room at the Kremlin'. And he had told another interviewer that it would be *possible* to destroy the forests in North Vietnam by using low-yield atomic weapons. These were no more than theoretical answers to speculative questions. Goldwater did not *recommend* the use of atomic weapons, and Johnson knew this perfectly well.

Nixon's campaigns against Hubert Humphrey and George McGovern were less dishonest, but they too violated the network code for product advertising.

Jimmy Carter's commercials pictured him as an innocent newcomer to politics, with no political organization – a poor farmer with no money. Nothing could have been further from the truth, but the voting public swallowed it. Gerald Ford, his Republican opponent, used commercials which were relatively honest – and lost the election.

The Kennedys and the Rockefellers have proved that it helps a politician to be *rich*. In his campaign for election to a second term as Democratic Governor of West Virginia, Jay Rockefeller spent $11,000,000 of his own money and defeated his Republican opponent, who spent only $800,000.

Rockefeller's commercials were unusually statesmanlike, and a survey found that the people of West Virginia were not shocked by his expenditure. Even his uncle Nelson Rockefeller had not spent so much in his re-election campaign for Governor of New York.

In a period when television commercials are often the decisive factor in deciding who shall be the next President of the United States, dishonest advertising is as evil as stuffing the ballot box. Perhaps the advertising people who have allowed their talents to be prostituted for this villainy are too naïve to understand the complexity of the issues.

The United States is almost the only country which allows political candidates to *buy* commercial time. In England, France and other democracies, the networks allot free time to serious discussion of the issues.

Could political commercials be banned in the United States? Not without violating the US Constitution. Could they be regulated, like every other kind of advertising? That too would be illegal.

Can you imagine Abraham Lincoln hiring an agency to produce 30-second commercials about slavery?

Down with billboards

Highways with billboards have three times as many accidents as highways without billboards. President Eisenhower said, 'I am against those billboards that mar our scenery, but I don't know what I can do about it'. In California, Governor Pat Brown said, 'When a man throws an empty cigarette package from an automobile, he is liable to a fine of $50. When a man throws a billboard across a view, he is richly rewarded'.

Bob Moses, the illustrious Parks Commissioner of New York State, said that 'effrontery and impudence can go no further. The time for compromise with these stubborn and ruthless people is over'. But the majority of legislators are still ready to compromise with them. Here is how a State Senator explains it:

> 'The billboard lobby shrewdly puts many legislators in its debt by giving them free space during election time. The lobby is savage against the legislator who dares oppose it by favoring anti-billboard laws. It subsidizes his opposition, foments political trouble in his home district, donates billboards to his opponents and sends agents to spread rumours among his constituents'.

Says the *New York Times*, 'the forces of uglification are rampant. The Illinois Democrat and the Florida Republican are united in their determination to protect the financial welfare of the billboard industry at the expense of millions of ordinary tourists who would like to see some scenery as they drive'.

The Highway Beautification Act actually states that it is the purpose of Congress to *promote* outdoor advertising. Some departments of the Federal Government are *users* of billboards. The Internal Revenue Service once accepted the free gift of 4,000 empty billboards and used them to urge taxpayers to make honest returns.

One day Monty Spaght, then President of Shell, asked me, 'We get a lot of letters protesting against our use of billboards. Do we *need* billboards?' I replied, 'If you give up billboards, you can still use newspapers and magazines and radio and television. That ought to be enough'. Shell gave up billboards.

Billboards represent less than 2 per cent of total advertising in the United States. I cannot believe that the free-enterprise system would be irreparably damaged if they were abolished. Who is *in favor* of them? Only the people who make money out of them. What kind of people are they? When President Johnson sent the Highway Beautification Bill to Congress, the head of one billboard company protested that Johnson had 'taken a stand in favor of an abstract concept – *beauty*. Some people like scenery and are interested in it. Others can take it or leave it. *There are times when most people would rather look at posters than scenery*'.

The Roadside Business Association has said, 'We do not believe that everyone is for beauty in all things'.

On a Sunday morning in 1958, vigilantes sawed down seven billboards along a highway in New Mexico. Citizens of surrounding areas expressed support for them. One telephone call complained that the vigilantes had not cut down *enough* billboards, and another that they had frustrated the plan of a large group of citizens who had scheduled a mass burning of billboards for later in the month. The vigilantes were never arrested.

In 1961 the Quebec government sent hundreds of men with axes to chop down billboards. In 1963 the head of the New York State Thruway Authority knocked down 53 billboards in a dawn raid; he was sick of legal bickering. But in June 1982, a judge in Oregon overturned an ordinance that required the removal of billboards on the ground that it was *a denial of free speech*. The battle goes on.

Can advertising sell bad products?

It is often charged that advertising can persuade people to buy inferior products. So it can – *once*. But the consumer perceives that the product is inferior and never buys it again. This causes grave financial loss to the manufacturer, whose profits come from *repeat* purchases.

The best way to increase the sale of a product is to *improve the product*. This is particularly true of food products; the consumer is amazingly quick to notice an improvement in taste and buy the product more often. I have always been irritated by the lack of interest brand managers take in improving their products. One client warned me, 'You are too prone to criticize our products. We could find it easier to accept criticism of our wives'.

Not enough information

Do you think advertising gives you enough information about products? I don't.

Recently, I smashed my car beyond repair and had to buy a new one. For six months I read all the car ads in search of *information*. All I found was fatuous slogans and flatulent generalities. Car manufacturers assume that you are not interested in facts. Indeed, their advertising is not aimed at consumers. Its purpose is to win an ovation when it is projected on the screen at hoopla conventions of dealers. Show-biz commercials have that effect. Sober, factual advertising does not. If their engineering was as incompetent as their advertising, their cars would not run the miles without a breakdown.

When I advertised Rolls-Royce, I gave the *facts* – no hot air, no adjectives. Later, my partner Hank Bernhard used equally factual advertising for Mercedes. In every case sales went up dramatically – on peppercorn budgets.

I have written factual advertising for a bank, for gasoline, for a stockbroker, margarine, foreign travel and many other products. It *always* sells better than empty advertising.

Before I started writing advertisements, I spent three years selling Aga cooking stoves to Scottish housewives, door to door. All I did was give my customers the facts. It took me 40 minutes to make a sale; about 3,000 words. If the people who write Detroit advertising had started *their* careers as door-to-door salesmen, you and I would be able to find the facts we need in their advertisements.

*　*　*　*　*

Summary

1   Whether economists are right or wrong in proclaiming that advertising is an 'economic' waste, manufacturers do not regard it as a *commercial* waste.
2   Apart from political advertising, which is flagrantly dishonest, advertising is now far more honest than consumers realize.
3   The world would be a safer, prettier place without billboards.
4   The majority of campaigns fail to give consumers enough information.

Notes

1 Keep buggering on.
2 Automobile manufacturers spend 1 per cent of their revenue on advertising. Appliance manufacturers 2 per cent. Soft drinks 4 per cent. Food manufacturers and brewers 5 per cent.
3 *Free to Choose*, Harcourt Brace, 1980.
4 *The Duping of the American Voter*, copyright © 1980, by Robert Spero, Harper & Row, NY.

80

I PREDICT 13 CHANGES

David Ogilvy

Source: David Ogilvy, *Ogilvy on Advertising*, London: Prion, 1985, p. 217.

I have never been a futurist, and with every passing year my interest in the future declines. However, my publisher insists that I take a shot at predicting the changes that you, gentle reader, will see in the advertising business. So here goes:

1 The quality of research will improve, and this will generate a bigger corpus of knowledge as to what works and what doesn't. Creative people will learn to exploit this knowledge, thereby improving their strike rate at the cash register.
2 There will be a renaissance in print advertising.
3 Advertising will contain more information and less hot air.
4 Billboards will be abolished.
5 The clutter of commercials on television and radio will be brought under control.
6 There will be a vast increase in the use of advertising by governments for purposes of education, particularly *health* education.
7 Advertising will play a part in bringing the population explosion under control.
8 Candidates for political office will stop using dishonest advertising.
9 The quality and efficiency of advertising overseas will continue to improve – at an accelerating rate. More foreign tortoises will overtake the American hare.
10 Several foreign agencies will open offices in the United States, and will prosper.
11 Multinational manufacturers will increase their market-shares all over the non-Communist world, and will market more of their brands internationally. The advertising campaigns for these brands will emanate from the headquarters of multinational agencies, but will be adapted to respect differences in local culture.

191

12 Direct-response advertising will cease to be a separate speciality, and will be folded into the 'general' agencies.

13 Ways will be found to produce effective television commercials at a more sensible cost.

81

ADVERTISING

Moving beyond the stereotypes

Adam Lury

Source: R. Keat, N. Whiteley and N. Abercrombie (eds), *The Authority of the Consumer*, London: Routledge, 1994, pp. 91–102.

I am writing this from the point of view of a practitioner who believes that, in order to have a real understanding of the dynamics of advertising, it is important to understand the background and motivation of the people involved.

Advertising has a small 'legacy' – there is no formal industry-wide training scheme and very little knowledge is formalized. The most powerful influences are myth and oral history. Any study of advertising and advertising research methodology needs to take this 'invisible history' into account and I intend to outline some of the major forces and show how they affect advertising and how it is produced and measured.

The cultural status of advertising: fear and loathing

Most people who currently hold power in advertising agencies and who are directly involved in the production of advertising are university educated. They will have come through universities when there was a considerable academic contempt for advertising (my philosophy tutor on hearing my choice of career responded with 'I don't care if you sell your body but for God's sake don't sell your mind!') Advertising practitioners have internalized that contempt and feel a deep sense of conflict and shame about their profession. But I believe that this shame will disappear gradually as 'cultural studies' and its attendant interest (and consequent legitimization) continues and its graduates and their peers find their way into media careers.

However, there are two key implications for current advertising of this internalized shame and guilt. The first is that it creates the need for public/ consumer acceptance. The thinking runs along the lines of 'I'll get by if I can make you laugh or entertain you.' The phrase 'The uninvited guest in the living-room' haunts advertising people and the apology or plea for acceptance is the capacity to amuse. The second implication of the internalized shame is that advertising people accept the premise that advertising is not intellectually worthwhile. This underpins the Pilate-like approach to discussion of the social influence of advertising, often expressed as 'Advertising can't change society, it can only reflect it.' Remember that many of these people were not taught the critical constructs that allow them to ask 'Whose view of society?' 'Which part of "society's" view?' or to see that 'reflecting' society is a positive act of reinforcing one particular view of society.

Codes of practice

The second key factor driving the production of advertising is the influence of the voluntary codes of practice set up and monitored by the regulatory bodies. These codes institutionalize a view of society that can be summarized as white, male and middle class: the fundamental precepts are based in a 1950s and 1960s view of mass communication in which advertising was the ultimate brainwash that somehow had to be controlled.

The concepts and conceptual power of feminism and anti-racism were marginal at best when the codes were originally designed. As a result, the codes cannot incorporate the huge and relatively recent change in views about the portrayal of groups of people in the media. This is why so much sexist and racist imagery persists in getting through the approval procedures. The best the codes can do is include clauses such as 'No advertisement may offend against good taste or decency or be offensive to public feeling and no advertisement should prejudice respect for human dignity.' There is no recognition that advertising can serve to perpetrate harmful stereotypes and therefore should be monitored carefully. Yet although the codes themselves are unwieldy and out of date, the people working at the regulatory bodies concerned do their best to move advertising into the nineties; they are always sympathetic and constructive.

The creation of 'quality' and the award system

The advertising industry also has an awards industry within it. The theory is that groups of those at the top of their profession (heavily skewed in favour of the 'creative' skills – copywriting, art directing, TV production) meet and 'judge' ads on the basis of their 'creativity'. Creativity is never defined but has increasingly come to mean 'entertaining' – unsurprising given the factors influencing the production of advertising. As awards are a key determinant of perceived success and salary, the judgement of the award juries can make or break the career of those who write and make advertising. It is not surprising therefore that the 'standards' of juries are internalized and reproduced by those aspiring for their approval. The key point here is that the awards juries do not incorporate market-place effectiveness into their judgements *in any form whatsoever*. The judgements on the 'quality' of an advertisement are made independently of any evaluation of its prime purpose. This can only hold water if it is assumed that a consumer-type evaluation (funniest/best) has a connection with effectiveness in selling what is advertised.

Advertising as aspiration

Advertising practitioners all accept as fundamental the premise that advertising is 'aspirational'. Now, at one level this appears to be obvious – most advertising is about making people want something (a favourite expression is 'advertising doesn't sell, it makes people want to buy'). For most practitioners this leads to the assumption that the values contained in advertising and its portrayal of life-styles must be aspirational – somehow better than those held by the consumer (one of the many paradoxes for a profession that merely 'reflects' society). This belief is the basis for the argument that everything in advertising must be attractive, expensive and exotic.

This is one of the assumptions behind the impression that advertising is a 'glamour' business. Whilst 'aspiration' may in the past have been important for a number of product categories, it is by no means applicable for all product categories. People on the whole quite simply do not 'aspire' to soap powder, canned soup, microwave snacks or a current account that pays interest. Changing economic circumstances and attitudes mean that the target market for such products takes such things for granted. They may look for and appreciate differentiated offerings, but they do not see the purchase of a microwave snack as intrinsically aspirational. Advertising people find this hard to accept, as communication predicated on the consumer as partner would require a radical reappraisal of the dynamics of communication.

Communication as a logical process

The 1950s saw the creation of the 'Unique Selling Proposition (USP)' – the idea that advertising should feature a logical (and tangible) product promise. This theory that advertising is at its core a logical, measurable process can be seen as a product of its time. Manufacturers looked at consumers as a 'mass' of identical consumers – a suitable audience for their mass production of identical units. What mattered was the number of units produced, messages made, and consumers reached. This underpins much of the language of advertising today – 'impacts', 'ratings', 'targets'. This value system assumes that everything in communication can be understood in quantitative terms and is correspondingly measurable. Even attitudes, values and feelings can be isolated and measured with great precision. It is the intellectual legacy of the Ford era, its methodology exclusively quantitative.

Whilst they still predominate, these assumptions have eroded slowly over the last twenty years with the emergence of qualitative research as a marketing tool which can give the consumer more direct input into the production process.

The incorporation of the consumer into the advertising process

A major innovation in the production-consumption cycle was the introduction of the concept of marketing. This is best described in Levitt's article 'Marketing Myopia' and at its core is an astoundingly simple thought. In a world where everyone was selling what they want to make, it made competitive sense to ask your customers what they want to buy and then make that. Marketing is about trying to incorporate the customer into the production process in order better to satisfy them and thereby increase your chances of making a profit. In the jargon of the business it is a shift from being product-led to being consumer-led. In advertising agencies this marketing philosophy found an expression in 'account planning'. Stephen King of JWT and Stanley Pollitt of BMP are both credited with having 'invented, created or introduced' the concept in the late 1960s. Fundamental to the discipline of account planning is the belief that the planner is the 'consumer's representative' within the agency. Again the principle is simple – the planner asks consumers what they feel about a product or service, builds the communication around those feelings, and then helps to construct a message that meets with consumers' approval.

A new concept needs a new methodology and qualitative research (predominantly focus or discussion groups) came into its own. This gave the consumer an active voice and one that was not shaped by the methodological assumptions of quantitative research. The incorporation of this approach led to a long methodological struggle with the result that now most agencies and clients apply a 'bit of both' to their processes – with qualitative research favoured for the development of ideas and quantitative research favoured for the testing and measurement of effect. The 'quant-qual' debate raged in the academic trade press (which has very little effect on mainstream agency behaviour) and has now all but disappeared with a 'different strokes for different folks' attitude.

However, the introduction of account planning was critical in the creation of a whole body of user-friendly advertising. It has led to the production of a body of advertising that is liked and approved by customers – commonly referred to by consumer and producer alike as 'good' advertising. British agencies were the first to incorporate the planning process into their production and it is this lead that has meant that British advertising is generally acknowledged to be the 'best in the world' (for which read 'the most likeable/enjoyable').

It is important to note here that the use of these value judgements – 'good' and 'best' – refers to a (consumer-based) feeling about the advertising. It does not in any way relate to other aspects of advertising such as effectiveness. The assumption is that likeability leads to communication which in turn leads to persuasion.

The end of an era

This then is a brief description of the status quo in advertising today. Advertising, despite all the hype and glamour, is a deeply conservative, angst-ridden business where, despite the presence of a number of clever people, there has been little real thinking done over the last thirty years. Much of the real thinking was done when mass communication was in its infancy. The thinkers of that period – David Ogilvy and Bill Bernbach, for example – dominate because, since then, no one has been able to articulate a world view of equivalent stature.

The consequent amalgam of values, attitudes and beliefs has served the industry reasonably well to date, but I believe that we have reached a point where they are exhausted and where advertising needs to adopt a new approach if it is to continue to provide clients with an effective, competitive marketing weapon.

The result of the pressures I have outlined is that advertising today is *passive* – a series of comic set pieces; *reflective* – reiterating the same old jokes and value systems; *explanatory* – lecturing the consumer on a whole raft of features; and crudely *aspirational* – working to a model that assumes that a consumer's life will be vastly improved with the acquisition of a particular product.

The market of the 1990s is radically different to the market of the 1950s and 1960s. Whilst adaptations of the philosophy of the first two decades moved with the market, in the 1970s and 1980s we needed a new start in order to build a dynamic and effective model for advertising in today's market place. This is as a result of a number of factors that I propose to discuss briefly.

A world of reflecting mirrors: consumer research today

Conducting consumer research is a fascinating business. You can lose yourself in the traditional games of bluff and counter-bluff – are they telling you what they think or what they think you would like them to think? Do they mean what they say or is it the result of group/interviewer/methodological dynamics?

Whilst these are important questions, I am operating as a practitioner who has to make judgements daily in order to progress. So although I recognize the validity of the concerns I have outlined, and incorporate the

197

learning from the study of those issues into my work, I have to let go of the purely theoretical concerns at some time. I start from the assumption that the people I interview are there because they are interested and that they want to help me. The people I talk to are not afraid of advertising or of the processes involved (they have all been interviewed before or know someone who has been interviewed).

What I have found is that the consumer is no longer the 'tabula rasa' that she/he once was. People are no longer passive data bases revealing 'pure' or straightforward feelings about advertising. (The previous system was based on the belief that people's feelings about a particular advertisement are immediate, not premeditated and so are 'pure, direct responses'.)

Today's consumer has *internalized the value system* that I have outlined above. There are a number of reasons for this, including the marketing of advertising itself, evident in newspaper coverage and TV programmes, the widespread experience of the research process and, not least, the experience of thirty years of TV advertising. This means that some of the standard research issues are no longer appropriate. When you access today's consumer – *what they think, and what they think you want them to think, are often one and the same.* If you ask people what makes a 'good' financial services advertisement for example, they will tell you that it is an advertisement that tells you that the organization doing the advertising is 'big, warm, friendly and careful with your money'.

Why is this? Is it because people want financial institutions to project an image of being big, warm, friendly and caring or is it because financial institutions have spent the last ten years telling people that they are big, warm, friendly and caring? The answer is both. Ten years down the line it is impossible to say which came first – the chicken or the egg. We are like Rita Hayworth in Orson Welles' *Lady from Shanghai* – lost in a world of reflecting mirrors. This does not lead to a win–win situation for advertisers but rather a lose–lose situation. Strategic consistency becomes strategic parity, and, if the consumer is incorporated directly into the process, the result is that all advertisements look and sound the same, losing any potential competitiveness. How has this situation come about? The answer lies in the way in which all agencies have incorporated the consumer into their production processes – all in the same way.

The planning hegemony

The importance of being liked

If you believe that you are the consumers' representative and you conduct or commission qualitative research over a long period of time, a strange thing happens – you begin to seek the approval of the consumer you access. Remember that as a traditional practitioner you have (at best) ambivalent feelings about your profession. Consequently being liked by those you feel you are manipulating is attractive – it soothes the conscience. As a planner you feel best about advertisements that are liked the best.

I am arguing that as a result of this desire for approval over the years, an implicit model of advertising has grown up which is: *comprehension and approval (likeability) = persuasion*. Now in the past this held good. In a world of producer-led 'soap powder' advertising, likeable advertising often did communicate better and more persuasively – and as a result gave the client a competitive advantage in the market place. Further, those few agencies that incorporated the consumer into their production processes via planning produced better advertising – advertising that was both likeable *and* effective.

However, what was an innovation twenty-five years ago is now standard practice. All agencies now incorporate the consumer into their production. All agencies aim to produce comprehensible, likeable advertising – often saying exactly the same thing. The result is that the old model no longer holds true. Instead: *comprehension and approval = acceptance*. Increasingly, that is, approval has come to mean 'meets my expectations of a good ad' – a response usually made in a research environment. Reactions, however, in the market place (full of similar advertising) will be very different.

The tyranny of the orthodox

As I have remarked, it is a feature of the industry that there has been no fundamentally different world view of advertising articulated for the last thirty years. This has led to an (unwritten) intellectual orthodoxy that pervades the whole industry. Account planners, clever and sensitive individuals on the whole, have been schooled in the planning orthodoxy and have used the authority of the consumer to gain authority for themselves in the production process. Innovative thinking was stifled in the process of assimilation into the mainstream and of copying by competitors. The innovating agencies failed to innovate further, believing that their competitive advantage was structural. Planning became a process in itself and was not seen or understood for what it originally was – a way of giving an agency's clients a competitive advantage. The planning profession preoccupied itself with 'angels on a pin' questions whilst going through a period of rapid growth. (If planners were so much in demand, why innovate?)

This made sense in an era where a company could enjoy a substantial 'lead time' from an innovation. However, in the world of the 1990s where innovations are copied overnight, the process of innovation has to be constant – no company can afford to rest on its laurels (Tom Peters and Robert Waterman chart this change in their move from *In Search of Excellence* to *Thriving on Chaos* and *The Renewal Factor* – arguing that the company that stands still, however excellent at the time, is dead). Quite simply the planning process is at crisis point because *everyone is doing it in the same way*. It is no longer competitive – it no longer works. Planning needs to adapt to the new market conditions of the 1990s – competition, change and complexity.

The shifting basis of competition: values not products

We live now in an age of product and service parity. The nature of competition has changed radically over the last twenty years. First the *volume* of competition has changed. Twenty years ago IBM was estimated to have 20 competitors – now the number is closer to 5,000! Second the *speed* of competition has changed – what took a competitor a year to copy can be done in some industries in seconds, while in other industries parallel production processes mean that similar products hit the market at the same time. This means that competitive insulation has disappeared. Third, most products in many categories have a surfeit of features. Compare cars, audio equipment or even tomato soup to discover a whole range of features incorporated in what seems to be a basic offering. Comparison becomes a long-winded and extremely difficult basis for making a choice.

The consequence of all this for advertising is that competitive communication can no longer be predicated on a feature-based approach. The Unique Selling Proposition was a tangible, specific product-based claim. This, quite simply, is no longer news and no longer competitive. The basis of competition has to shift – and it is my belief that it will shift further back in the production process. What will become important as a basis for competition is the company value system. It is this that is unique, competitive and sustainable. The how and why of production will be more important than the what. The rise of the importance of 'service-based businesses' also adds impetus to this move.

Competitive advertising based on company values as opposed to product features requires a different model of communication and makes different assumptions about the consumers receiving the messages.

I will now outline five driving forces of the new advertising. As will be apparent, they represent a radically different view of the consumer, and whilst they may mean less direct incorporation of the consumer into the production process, they make key assumptions about the consumer's expertise and experience in the field of advertising.

Future advertising needs to be provocative

Today's consumer is overwhelmed by communication. People receive between 1,300 and 6,000 commercial messages a day depending on which estimate you choose. The *only* survival strategy is to edit – the brain simply cannot process and spend time on all these messages and continue with daily life. The media-literate and experienced consumer of the 1990s can decode and deconstruct the messages she/he receives and is highly familiar with particular selling modes. Advertising that meets expected norms will not evoke a response – it will be coded as normal or expected and dismissed as 'noise'. In order for advertising to be registered and for it to evoke a response it must be provocative – it must be unusual and challenge the standard advertising methods. It must *stimulate* the consumer not *reflect* the consumer.

Future advertising must tackle new areas

Advertising has for too long remained stuck in the middle-class kitchen of the 1950s. It has allowed itself to focus on the 'aspirational' and to play in 'sit-com land'. In the future, advertising will deal with issues that are called 'social' by the critics – such as discrimination, one-parent families, prejudice, conditions of employment. It will no longer be able to claim (disingenuously) that the world it has presented is above social issues. Recent campaigns for Fuji film and Bisto gravy featuring discrimination and one-parent families respectively are leading the way. Advertising will be more about the world the consumer of today lives in and will therefore broaden the range of its subject material.

Future advertising will talk to the consumer on an equal footing

The implicit model in old-fashioned advertising has been parent–child. 'We know what's best for you. Buy this product and improve your life.' The assumption is that passive consumers are sitting there anxiously waiting to be told about ways in which their lives can be transformed. Future advertising will work from a different assumption – that of the consumer as an *equal*. The consumer as equal partner in any communication means that the strategies, approaches and advertising devices will have to change.

A recent campaign for *Exchange and Mart* involves the presenter explaining that he buys goods from *Exchange and Mart* because they're cheaper than in the shops and ends with him saying, 'But you don't have to do that. You can spend as much money as you like. No skin off my nose.' This 'take it or leave it' approach is shocking in advertising as it forgoes any overtly aspirational positioning in favour of a 'we both know what's going on here' approach.

Future advertisers will take on the role of the public persuaders

The whole process of advertising and selling is now a part of contemporary culture. Papers have a regular column on advertising. TV series are made about it and feature films refer continually to it. In addition many workforces now have their company's advertising presented and explained to them. The consumers of today actively seek information on advertising and enjoy talking about it.

Advertising is part of everyday conversation. It is not feared and loathed. Surveys show it is actually respected! All this means that the era of the 'Hidden Persuaders' is well and truly past. In the new era of Public Persuaders advertising people can share their 'games' with a knowing audience. In a recent campaign for Britvic Citrus Spring the presenter is the 'client' who updates the viewer on his difficulties in getting the recalcitrant agency to do his product justice. Another campaign, for the Vauxhall Astra, gives a behind-the-scenes look at the launch of the new car model – including the creation of the end line.

It is standard practice for old-fashioned critics to worry that these are somehow 'in-jokes', understood by only a few. This worry is a legacy from the hidden persuaders era and betrays a blinkered view on the influence of advertising in today's consumer culture.

Future advertising will show more 'real' people

Casting in advertising has always been a problematic issue. In a largely male-dominated industry, working to the maxim 'date her, don't cast her' would change the look of advertising overnight. Working on the 'aspiration' assumption, the principle behind casting has often been one of showing the most attractive people possible. This is one of the main driving forces behind the 'glamour business' myth and, like the world of fashion, can be extremely seductive. It assumes a basic insecurity on the part of the consumer and, by projecting idealized examples, aims to constantly reinforce it.

Today's consumers may still have insecurities but they resent the projection of them on to the small screen. The approach is beginning to become counter-productive. Impossibly attractive models (and sets) are a good reason to ignore a message. Future advertising, in order to ensure a relationship with the consumer, will seek to portray more and more 'real' people. This will mean showing a much greater diversity of people and breaking the WASP stereotypes.

Winston Churchill called television a 'tuppenny ha' penny Punch and Judy Show', Margaret Thatcher called it the 'most powerful medium on earth'. Today's consumer is active and knowledgeable – an expert in communication and selling techniques. She/he is a long way from the passive innocent victim of the 1950s and 1960s mass-production and mass-communication techniques. Most advertising today is produced with the implicit assumptions and beliefs about people that were formed in that era. The market place, and, indeed, the world have changed dramatically and fundamentally. In the 1990s advertising will need to change in order to compete and it must draw its assumptions about competitive and effective work from an understanding of the new experienced and expert consumer.

References

Levitt, T. (1960) 'Marketing myopia' in *Harvard Business Review* July–August.

Peters, T. (1987) *Thriving on Chaos: Handbook for a Management Revolution*, London: Macmillan.

Peters, T. and Waterman, R. H. (1982) *In Search of Excellence*, New York: Harper & Row.

Waterman, R. H. (1987) *The Renewal Factor: How to Get and Keep the Competitive Edge*, London: Bantam Books.

82

HOW ADVERTISING IS CREATED

J. Wilmshurst and A. Mackay

Source: J. Wilmshurst and A. Mackay, *The Fundamentals of Advertising*, Oxford: Butterworth Heinemann, 1999, pp. 185–202.

'The creative advertising man is controlled by a tight brief. It is determined by the nature of the marketing and advertising object-ive – the what, whens, whys and to-whoms. The brief states the proposition – itself a single entity – and requests its interpretation. This discipline is a creative necessity.'

David Bernstein, *Creative Advertising*, Longman, 1974

By the end of this chapter you will:

- Realize the importance of the creative ingredient in effective advertising;
- Be aware of what makes a good creative person and how to get the best from them;
- Be able to brief creative teams;
- Appreciate what makes a good advertisement;
- Understand the significance of the terms USP and brand image.

1 The nature of creativity in advertising

A picture may be painted, a poem written, a symphony composed for no reason apart from the desire or need of the artist to express himself. Success to the artist, writer, composer, may simply consist in getting somewhere near expressing the vision that impelled them to create something. Others may feel that success is only achieved when their audience, their 'public', responds to what they have created. But in any of these cases it is hard to be specific about what a picture, a poem or a symphony is *for*. It does not in the most literal sense have any specific purpose (although we could of course argue that life might often be rather pointless and certainly less rich if none of these things were created). To ask a creative artist what specific objectives his work was intended to achieve is usually irrelevant. If it is beautiful, moving, thought-provoking, exciting, stirring in its own right that is purpose enough.

An advertisement on the other hand can be very beautiful or exciting or amusing and yet fail utterly in its purpose. Conversely it may be banal or ugly and yet do what it set out to do. So 'creativity' must have a rather different meaning or at least a more limited one, in the advertising context than it has in the world of art. Advertising is created with very definite, quite specific aims in view.

2 The 'science' of advertising

One of the most famous and highly regarded books on the creation of advertising carries the title *Scientific Advertising*[1]. It was written in 1923 to promote an American advertising agency called Lord and Thomas, of which the author, Claude Hopkins, was a director.

The book opens with the statement 'The time has come when advertising has in some hands reached the status of a science.' Hopkins was a superb copywriter, much of whose experience was in mail order advertising. His claim to have established a scientific approach was based on such ideas, revolutionary no doubt in the 1920s, as:

> *Do nothing to merely interest, amuse or attract. That is not your province. Do only that which wins the people you are after in the cheapest possible way.*

> *Treat (advertising) as a salesman. Force it to justify itself. Compare it to other salesmen. Figure its cost and result.*

> *Almost any question can be answered, cheaply, quickly and finally, by a test campaign. And that's the way to answer them – not by arguments round a table. Go to the court of the last resort – the buyers of your product.*

> *An ad-writer, to have a chance at success, must gain full information on his subject.*

> *Advertising without this preparation is like a waterfall going to waste. The power may be there, but it is not made effective. We must center the force and direct it in a practical direction.*

It could now be strongly disputed just how 'scientific' advertising really is. For example, a fully scientific body of knowledge enables one to predict precisely what will result from a given set of actions. Advertising can rarely do that. Because at the end of the day the results of advertising depend on human reactions (emotional as well as rational) not on purely mechanistic responses. So prediction of results is often uncertain and developing advertising to achieve desired ends involves judgement as well as facts.

Nonetheless, in essence Hopkins was right. Advertising is not a matter of following the creative man's instinct or whim, not just a question of designing attractive pictures or coming up with bright ideas expressed in clever words. Rather it is a matter of expressing clearly defined ideas in a compelling way so as to attract and interest specified types of people in known situations and motivate them to react in a particular fashion. So the 'creative' writers and designers must operate within a framework of known facts, with set targets and subject to measurement of cost-effectiveness. As the above quotations illustrate, Hopkins caught the essential truth that the creation of effective advertising stems from hard logical thinking based on an assessment of the facts rather than ideas from the blue.

Nowadays there has been a great deal of research into the mechanisms of advertising and most major advertising campaigns are based on highly detailed analyses of the facts of the situation. Still though there is the 'creative' ingredient. Still someone has to turn the bare facts and the bold proposition into a compelling message.

David Bernstein[2], a leading and highly regarded British 'creative man', sums up the paradox like this:

> *The central core of our activities is creative. The basic decisions are judgemental. The results of our work depend on human behaviour. Thus advertising can never be a science. But if you are in advertising and accept our working definition, if you believe in advertising's role in the economy, if at the end of the day you want to feel that you have helped the man who pays your salary (i.e. the client) by at least pointing him in the right direction . . . then you'll have to try to make it a science.*

3 What it takes to create effective advertising

Because the facts and the logic – the science – only take us so far; because there has to be the judgemental contribution and the turning of the dull proposition into the exciting message, 'creative' advertising people – the writers, designers and art directors – have a special contribution to make. What is the nature of that contribution and what are the peculiar characteristics of the people that make it?

3.1 The creative contribution – what is it?

Bernstein[2] offers a model of the creative process (*see* Figure 1) consisting of a double-ended funnel, with a wide entrance into which we pour all the facts and figures, eventually concentrating them into the proposition. (The 'offer' – expressed in basic terms – which the advertisement is making

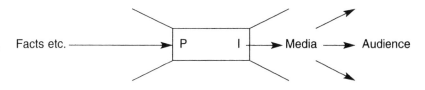

Figure 1

to the reader, listener or viewer.) This goes into the narrow central tube and emerges as the creative idea. The funnel opens up into a second 'mouth' from which the advertising conveying the creative idea spreads out through the media to reach its audience.

The creative process consists of turning the proposition into an idea. So, says Bernstein: 'The proposition is arrived at through *reason* and P becomes I through *imagination*. The idea becomes an advertisement largely as a result of *craft*'. The creative department in an agency typically supplies both the imagination and the craft, although sometimes the functions are separated with a creative department supplying the imagination and an art department supplying the craft. At the latter stage the development of the form and shape of the advertisement consists of the hard graft of applying special skills to the mechanics of layout, detailed copywriting, typography, etc. But, says Bernstein, '. . . though the final execution is important and demands hard work, talent and imagination, it calls for none of that white hot intensity which brings into being something which wasn't there before.'

3.2 The creative contribution – who makes it?

The essential core of a good advertisement then is that it is an accurate but also an imaginative interpretation of the whole marketing strategy and in particular of the advertising proposition which has been developed from that strategy. At its height this imaginative leap can transform an ordinary product into an extraordinary one, or express a perfectly straightforward claim in a striking and dramatic way. For example, Oxo is a well-established brand of gravy flavouring, whose advertising claims it 'Gives a meal man appeal'. KitKat chocolate coated wafer is used by many people to accompany their morning coffee or afternoon tea so the advertising suggests, 'have a break, have a KitKat'. The ability to create dramatic and extraordinary expressions of ordinary statements is what makes a good creative person.

David Ogilvy, one of the 'father-figures' of modern advertising,[3] quotes research carried out at the Institute of California's Institute of Personality Assessment. They found creative individuals to have the following characteristics:

'Creative people are especially observant, and they value accurate observation (telling themselves the truth) more than other people do.

They often express part-truths, but this they do vividly; the part they express is the generally unrecognized; by displacement of accent and apparent disproportion in statement they seek to point to the usually unobserved.

They see things as others do, but also as others do not.

They are born with greater brain capacity; they have more ability to hold many ideas at once, and to compare more ideas with one another – hence to make a richer synthesis.

They are by constitution more vigorous, and have available to them an exceptional fund of psychic and physical energy.

Their universe is thus more complex, and in addition they usually lead more complex lives.

They have more contact than most people do with the life of the unconscious – with fantasy, reverie, the world of imagination.'

Ogilvy[3] describes his own experience of the creative process and creative people in the following terms:

The creative process requires more than reason. Most original thinking isn't even verbal. It requires 'a groping experimentation with ideas, governed by intuitive hunches and inspired by the unconscious.' The majority of business men are incapable of original thinking, because they are unable to escape from the tyranny of reason. Their imaginations are blocked.

I am almost incapable of logical thought, but I have developed techniques for keeping open the telephone line to my unconscious, in case that disorderly repository has anything to tell me. I hear a great deal of music. I am on friendly terms with John Barleycorn. I take long hot baths. I garden. I go into retreat among the Amish. I watch birds. I go for long walks in the country. And I take frequent vacations, so that my brain can lie fallow – no golf, no cocktail parties, no tennis, no bridge, no concentration; only a bicycle.

While thus employed in doing nothing, I receive a constant stream of telegrams from my unconscious, and these become the raw material for my advertisements. But more is required: hard work, an open mind, and ungovernable curiosity.

3.3 Can creativity be taught?

The creative input is the most vital ingredient in many advertising campaigns, if only because most of the other ingredients can be arrived at through careful analysis which is 90 per cent hard work (although even there the other 10 per cent of imaginative insight into the situation can make all the difference). With the creative aspect of things it is the other way round – imagination is the major part of it. We then have to ask where does it come from – do we have to look for people who 'just have it' or can it be taught? Referring back to Bernstein's analysis (*see* Section 3.1) it is probably true to say that the craft aspect of 'making a good ad' can be taught but the imagination aspect can only be encouraged. As is clear from the University of California studies quoted by Ogilvy (*see* Section 3.2) many of the ingredients of a good creative person are in-born characteristics.

Modern jargon would stress that they are predominantly 'right brain' people i.e. good at visualizing rather than verbalizing, strong on seeing patterns, remembering music, tending to the poetical as distinct from 'left brain' people who tend to be rational rather than intuitive, disciplined rather than individualistic. Since (*see* Section 16.6) 'right brain' activity is an important ingredient in how purchasing decisions are made, it is easy to see how vital this aspect may be. Of course all people have both left and right brain characteristics and differences between them are a matter of emphasis. So creativity is something that can certainly be encouraged (by producing the right working conditions and by removing some of the traditionally rigid attitudes toward properly 'disciplined' working). But it would be difficult to teach a predominantly 'left brain' person to become an outstanding creative person – in advertising or elsewhere. His destiny probably lies in some other direction.

When Ted Bell, Creative Director of the Leo Burnett agency in Chicago, started building his creative team he took on unseasoned school-leavers. 'I was looking for punks', he said. 'I wanted kids who had no experience in the business, who didn't have a clue how to create ads. Kids who didn't know the rules and just wanted to do great ads. They had to have talent, excitement and raw energy about them. And a great love of great advertising.' (Quoted in *How to Succeed in Advertising, when all you have is Talent*, NTC Business Books, 1994.)

In *The Brothers – the Rise and Rise of Saatchi and Saatchi* by Ivan Fallon (Hutchinson, 1988), John Hegarty, one of the Saatchi creative team, says: 'Creativity is I believe an expression of insecurity, a desire to win approval. It is in a climate of self-doubt that the creative spark is forced and cajoled into fire.' (See the Bernstein reference in Section 6.)

Thus the creativity aspect is a wayward and difficult to define 'divine spark', perhaps not totally different from that which produces the visual arts or literature. The difference is that we always have to revert to the insistence on working within a clear brief, to achieve a clearly-defined objective. Creative people have to work in one way as free spirits but also within disciplines. As John McKeil puts it (*The Creative Mystique*, John Wiley and Sons, 1985), good creative people, as well as having great ideas, must '. . . have a few other things:

They can take criticism
They can take pressure
They can work wherever they have to
They can work on more than one thing at a time.

Not a very common combination, which is why really good creative people are so sought after and (if they are lucky) so well paid'.

So we come back, to the importance of the creative brief discussed in Section 4. As Garry Duckworth says (*Excellence in Advertising – the IPA Guide to Best Practice*, Butterworth-Heinemann 1997):

> '*Creative briefing is pivotal because it represents the stage in the advertising development process where the strategic understanding developed by the account team reaches the people whose job it is to really crack the creative problem.*'

3.4 Characteristics of creative people

Kenneth Longman[4] lists the following characteristics as being 'common to highly creative people':

> *Perhaps the most important characteristic of creative people is an avid curiosity. There is very little in the world that does not interest them. They may be as interested in the ecology of the North Woods as in the behaviour of teenagers in a discotheque. They read books on a great variety of topics, they are always seeking to understand things in new ways, and they are not fussy about whether the data they receive are completely accurate.*
>
> *Along with this curiosity, creative people have vivid imaginations. They can generate a large number of ideas rapidly. They might, for instance, be able to think of seventeen words that rhyme with 'syntax' and do it in a minute or two. Of greater importance, their imagination enables them to see new relationships between the things their curiosity has led them to discover. They habitually come up with unusual answers to questions and original interpretations of events (a quality that has not always endeared them to their educators).*
>
> *This combination of curiosity and imagination leads highly creative people to make fewer black and white distinctions than other people. With more data on hand and more of an ability to conjecture, they can see almost any issue in shades of grey. Their particular talents also lead them to prefer complex situations to simple ones, things that are easily understood bore them.*
>
> *Creative people are also characterized by the ability to emphathize. They find it easy to 'feel the way it feels to feel that way', whether they are concerned with other people, animals, or inanimate objects. Their*

warmth shows up in their sense of humor, and they will often inject humor into situations where most people consider it inappropriate.

Creative people are also enthusiastic. In fact, enthusiasm is the driving force behind their curiosity and imagination. It gives them a strong sense of mission and its frequent concomitant, a feeling of loneliness. It also leads them to trust in their own abilities. They generally feel less dependent on authority, less anxious about what they produce, and less concerned about salary and status than other people. Accordingly, they look for jobs that provide stimulation and challenge, a fact that probably has more to do with the high turnover of personnel in advertising agencies than anything else. When a very creative person changes jobs, it is less likely to be for the sake of money (though the change may be accompanied by a substantial raise) than for the sake of finding more interesting challenges and opportunities.

Finally, creative people are flexible. They find it easy to shift gears and try a new approach to a problem. They delight in new challenges. They can relate isolated experiences to one another with facility. They are quick to separate the source of information and opinion from the content. They form their own judgements about any information received and are much less influenced than others by attitudes toward the source of the information. In their flexibility, however, they are intellectually honest, and they are likely to stick to their guns when disagreement arises. Highly creative people are not prone to yield to group pressure except as a matter of expediency.

These qualities that creative people share are invaluable in designing both good and great advertisements. Without them, the odds are very much against success.

4 The importance of the creative brief

As well as highlighting the essential role of management on the advertising process (see Section 3.1) David Bernstein insists that 'discipline is a creative necessity' (*see* quote at head of chapter). Chapter 3 presented a model of the advertising process which indicated the importance of a brief based on a detailed analysis of a wide range of information, together with decisions on such things as segmentation and positioning. From this brief the creative people must draw both the information on which their imagination can work and the guidelines within which it must be disciplined to operate.

Maurice Drake, another leading British creative director, suggests[5] the following ingredients in what he refers to as the creative strategy:

Let one thing be clear. The discipline of a creative strategy is not a straitjacket to creative thinking. A good strategy – and there are many useless and unexecutable ones – allows the creative person to direct his thinking into the correct channels instead of just trying to pluck an idea out of the air.

It is important that the strategy should be written by the creative people, naturally in consultation with the client contact and marketing departments. There is a good reason for this; the act of writing the strategy down means that the creative team fully understands the product, the marketing environment in which it must compete and the potential consumer. In addition, a strategy written in the creative department can be executed in an advertisement. That may seem a strange point, but many strategies written outside the creative departments are simply tidy documents that contain far too many elements and could never be executed within the confines of anything other than a documentary film or a leading article!

So what should the strategy contain? In the main the contents fall under the following headings:

Why we are advertising

This sums up, as succinctly as possible, why the client is advertising at all. It may be to launch a new product. It could be to change the positioning of a well-established product, or to take advantage of a seasonal sales peak or extra use of the product in an area that varies from the national norm, or perhaps to achieve a fast rate of trial and sampling. In other words, that situation or circumstance upon which advertising can act and achieve results must be evident.

What the advertising must achieve

This is not a rephrased reiteration of the above, but a statement of what end result the advertising must have on the consumer. There lies the key difference between the general objective and the advertising objective. The latter is a means of achieving the former.

For instance, a general objective to raise brand share may be accomplished by an advertising objective to change a consumer attitude or misconception. The former is to sell more, and the latter is to convince consumers to desire more.

Prospect definition

This is the key to any good strategy. No product can be all things to all people. It is far more profitable to have a motivating effect on a specific group of consumers than to give a blunt-edged promise to an indifferent mass. This principle of consumer segmentation, which is so much part of modern advertising and marketing, throws great responsibility on the correctness and clearness of the prospect definition.

For that important reason it must be so much more than just a bald statement of the prospect's socio-economic grouping. This is part of it, but by no means all of it. Socioeconomic grouping gives you some traditional guide to the prospect's habits, attitudes and disposable income. But imagine

212

if you were asked to go out in the street and find a man in the C2–DE socio-economic group. You might find dozens with that description. But which one would you choose?

This is why the prospect definition must be so much more. It must be like a police identi-kit picture and description, so that the advertising can pin-point the most potential consumer.

Another factor is age, and in clearly defined limits – not something vague like '16–45', for the strata of appeal between those ages are infinite. Obviously the sex of the consumer is important, and whether married or single, and number in family. As far as possible the prospect definition should also cover consumers' aspirations, hates, loves, habits, anything that can help the creative people not only to identify them but to understand them.

Promise

This is the 'reason for being' of the product, which singles it out from competition in the teeming market place. This is 'why to buy'. Remember the famous Charles Atlas advertising: this did not just sell a body-building course on bigger muscles. All the others said that. It was the one that offered weak people the chance to be strong people, and in that promise reposed the seeds of its success.

Above all, the promise must be consumer-orientated not product-orientated. In one example an underarm spray that was a powder in an aerosol stated 'It's surprising what a little powder does for an underarm spray'. That was product-orientated. It was changed to 'Now you don't have to get wet to be dry'. See the difference – that's a consumer promise. And research proved it right to change it.

Reason Why

Obviously evidence as to why a promise is possible will strengthen the promise. It is not always possible to have an exclusive product difference, in formula, engineering, speed of experience. But one reason why, for instance, can be the number of people who have tried the product and found it to be all it promised.

In any case, the consumer must be given some firm basis for believing that the product will keep its promise. If the strategy is properly written and based on known facts, in whatever form a particular agency may choose, and if it contains this kind of information, it can only lead to better, more effective advertising.

Of the creative task Drake writes:

So the creative task can be described as gift-packaging the truth. We have to make the product news interesting enough to stand out and be seen among all its competitors.

Working from the strategy, it is the creative person's aim to find new language, both in words and visuals, to present the product and its benefits to the consumer. For it is saying something that may not be unique, but in a unique manner, that marks the great campaigns.

Let's take some examples. 'Palmolive makes skin look young again!' A good promise, but hardly a new thought. But the creative man said 'Palmolive brings back that schoolgirl complexion' – a visual imagination-provoking set of words, and a campaign that made history. 'More people eat Heinz Beans than any other'. This could just have sounded like a successful manufacturer patting his own back. But 'Beanz Meanz Heinz' said exactly the same thing, but so memorably that it went into the language, and the new spelling of 'Beanz' is now used more often than the standard dictionary version.

The task that faces every creative person says Drake is 'turning information into communication'. The creative 'inspiration' must be firmly based on hard information and must have communication not 'artistic' merit as its aim.

4.1 The influence of media choice

Advertising creativity is all about effective communication. But this has another aspect – the media through which the communications will take place. So although they each need to be considered in detail, they also have to be thought of as part of a whole. Whilst the central creative idea (Beanz Meanz Heinz or Palmolive's 'Schoolgirl complexion') does not change, the way it is expressed may have to vary considerably depending on whether the media schedule provides for a massive TV expenditure, posters, or some small black and white spaces in newspapers. Some creative ideas lend themselves to immediate impact whereas others (such as the classic Benson & Hedges cigarettes campaign which featured the distinctive gold pack in a wide range of increasingly surrealistic settings) achieve their full impact by a gradual build-up over a long period of time.

It may of course work the other way round. If a creative treatment is developed which is seen to have enormous potential but calls for specific media treatment (e.g. large or unusual shaped spaces in newspapers for example) then the media people may be required to plan accordingly.

Ideally the media and creative planning goes step-by-step and hand-in-hand so that each can draw on and influence the other as necessary.

5 What makes a good advertisement?

The short but unhelpful answer is 'one that communicates the necessary message effectively.' It is unhelpful because there are often many different ways of achieving the end results. This means it is very difficult to produce good advertising ideas 'by the rule book'. Indeed Roderick White[6] quotes an American agency as claiming that it has the following rules for producing good advertising:

rule 1 There are no rules.
rule 2 There may be exceptions to rule 1.

White then goes on to suggest some rules of his own (a compendium in fact of guidelines put forward by various advertising pundits down the ages):

1 Every advert should embody a clear, straightforward proposition.
2 Say what you have to say in as few words as possible.
3 There is no place for humour in advertising.
4 Give the consumer credit for some intelligence.
5 Be original.

Some of these guidelines embody the thinking of David Ogilvy[3] who lists his own rules for 'How to Build Great Campaigns'. They run:

1 What you say is more important than how you say it.
2 Unless your campaign is built round a great idea it will flop.
3 Give the facts.
4 You cannot *bore* people into buying.
5 Be well-mannered but don't clown.
6 Make your advertising contemporary.
7 Committees can criticize advertisements, but they can't write them.
8 If you are lucky enough to write a good advertisement; run it until it stops pulling.
9 Never write an advertisement which you wouldn't want your own family to read.
10 The image and the brand – every advertisement should be thought of as a contribution to the complex symbol which is the *brand image*. If you take that long view, a great many day-to-day problems resolve themselves.
11 Don't be a copy-cat.

None of these 'rules' are universally agreed. For example, White points out that humour (his rule 3 and Ogilvy's rule 5) is often successfully used in advertising. He also comments on the fact that the strict application of his rule 1 – the so-called USP approach (*see* Section 5.1) – can be very limiting.

White's own first thought is probably correct, 'There are no rules'.

5.1 USP and brand image

The first of Roderick White's rules quoted in Section 5 refers to a 'clear, straightforward proposition'. The classic embodiment of this approach was propounded by one of the outstanding figures in advertising, Rosser Reeves. In his book *Reality in Advertising*[7] he discussed at length the idea of the Unique Selling Proposition or USP, developed at his New York agency Ted Bates & Company in the early 1940s.

The USP, says Reeves, is 'like Gaul, divided into three parts:

1   Each advertisement must make a proposition to the consumer. Not just words, not just product puffery, not just show-window advertising. Each advertisement must say to each reader: 'Buy *this* product, and you will get *this specific benefit'*.

This admonition, of course, has been on page one of almost every advertising textbook for the past 60 years; but as you will see, it is becoming almost a lost art, and more honoured in the breach than in the observance.

2   The proposition must be one that the competition either cannot, or does not, offer. It must be unique – either a uniqueness of the brand or a claim not otherwise made in that particular field of advertising.

One might assume that a unique proposition, in itself, would be a strong theoretical base for an advertisement. However, there are thousands of unique propositions that do not sell. Witness, a famous toothpaste once advertised: '*it comes out like a ribbon and lies flat on your brush'*. This was a proposition, and it was unique. However, it did not move the public, because it apparently was not of importance to them. So we come to the third part:

3   The proposition must be so strong that it can move the mass millions, i.e. pull over new customers to your product.

These three points are summed up in the phrase: *unique selling proposition.* This is a USP.'

Ever since there has been endless discussion about whether all good advertising has to have a USP. David Ogilvy's 'brand image' approach is sometimes held up as an alternative – almost an opposite – theory. Says Ogilvy[3]: 'Build sharply defined personalities for their (your clients') brands and stick to those personalities, year after year. It is the total personality of a brand rather than any trivial product difference which decides its ultimate position in the market.'

In fact, 'brand image' and 'USP' advertising approaches are equally valid, depending on the situation. Nor are they mutually exclusive, a product may be advertised on the strength of a USP such as 'Persil washes whiter' and *also* have a strong brand image, which Persil for example undoubtedly has.

6 How creative departments work

David Bernstein[2] describes creative departments as 'disciplined anarchy'. On the one hand like any other business activity it needs some degree of structure and control to ensure that things get done and that deadlines are met. On the other hand the production of good advertising ideas comes from imaginations being given free rein (although within the discipline provided by the brief).

Says Bernstein, 'It is the creative director's job to maintain that state of disciplined anarchy. He has to institute controls and procedures while simultaneously encouraging the utmost flexibility'.

The argument has raged for years about the actual procedure by which advertising ideas develop. Do the words come first or the pictures – or the intrinsic idea or 'copy platform'. Do the writers lead the way and then ask the art directors to provide illustrations for their words? Or does design lead and copywriting as it were provide the captions? The answer is both and all possible combinations. Ideas can come from anywhere (even from outside the creative department). The normal practice now is for writers and designers to work as teams, often known as 'creative groups'. Jointly (if it is a two-person team) or collectively they absorb the brief, 'kick ideas around' until one or more useful ideas emerge, and then concentrate on one or more until they begin to take shape as viable creative ideas.

7 The craft of copywriting

Again, the records abound with 'rules' and probably few great copywriters consciously follow any or if so have their own set. Thus there are many examples of defective advertisements that break 'the rules'. Quoted here the ones listed by David Ogilvy, partly because he is in any case one of the great copywriters of all time, but also because his 'rules' (in a chapter[3] headed 'How to write potent copy') are redolent with important basic principles for successful advertising, quite apart from any immediate practical value.

Headlines

1 *The headline is the 'ticket on the meat'. Use it to flag down the readers who are prospects for the kind of product you are advertising.*
2 *Every headline should appeal to the readers' self-interest.*

217

3 *Always try to inject news into your headlines (*free *and* new *are the most powerful words you can use in a headline).*

4 *Use words such as* how to, suddenly, now, announcing, introduce, it's here, just arrived, important development, improvement, amazing, sensational, remarkable, revolutionary, startling, miracle, magic, offer, quick, easy, wanted, challenge, advice to, the truth about, compare, bargain, hurry, last chance.

5 *Always include the brand name in your headline.*

6 *Include your selling promise in your headline.*

7 *End your headline with a lure to read on.*

8 *Avoid tricky headlines (puns, literary allusions, etc.)*

9 *Avoid negative headlines.*

10 *Avoid blind headlines (the kind which mean nothing unless you read the body copy underneath them).*

These rules of Ogilvy's emphasize the important functions of headlines to:

(a) attract attention

(b) win the reader's interest and involvement

(c) make them want to read on because they feel it will be worth their while to do so

Body Copy

1 *Don't beat about the bush – go straight to the point.*

2 *Avoid superlatives, generalisations and platitudes. Be specific and factual. Be enthusiastic, friendly and memorable. Don't be a bore. Tell the truth but make the truth fascinating.*

3 *Always include testimonials in your copy.*

4 *Give the reader helpful advice or service.*

5 *(Quoting Claude Hopkins) 'fine writing is a distinct disadvantage'. So is unique literary style. They take attention away from the subject.*

6 *Avoid bombast.*

7 *Write your copy in the colloquial language which your customers use in everyday conversation.*

8 *Resist the temptation to write the kind of copy which wins awards.*

9 *Resist the temptation to entertain.*

Most of this could be summed up by saying that good copy must be clear, simple, direct, appropriately expressed and relevant. Note that all these attributes can be learned and practised. That is why copywriting can be described as a craft whereas it may take near genius to produce an outstanding advertising idea.

8 The craft of advertising design

Wherever the basic idea comes from (*see* Section 6), sooner or later it will usually (unless it is for radio) have to take visual form. This frequently begins as a very rough pencil or felt pen scribble (known as a 'scamp') on a layout pad – or sometimes on whatever surface is at hand (blackboard, envelope, menu card . . .)

This will be developed, perhaps through various stages, to a 'finished visual' which will be detailed and accurate enough to convey a good impression of the end result. The finished visual accompanied by a typescript of the copy will normally be used for presentation, discussion and approval of the advertisement or campaign and will be used as a reference in preparing finished artwork.

8.1 The principles of good design

As with copywriting (*see* Section 7) the main rule is that there are no rules. A good designer may break all the rules and yet succeed, a bad one can follow the rules and produce something so mundane and uninspired as to be valueless.

Various attempts have been made, however, to express at least some of the elements commonly found in a good layout. Richard E. Stanley[8] for example suggests that it will include:

1 *Balance* 'gives stability to the ad so that it does not seem to "lean" one way or the other.'
2 *Contrast* 'makes the most important parts of the ad stand out'.
3 *Proportion* 'proper proportion avoids sameness and monotony.'
4 *Unity* 'makes the ad appear to be a unified whole rather than a series of disconnected parts.'
5 *Gaze Motion* '. . . positioning ad elements to suggest a certain viewing sequence.'

Kenneth A. Longman[4] states:

> *Studies conducted during the 1930s by George Gallup and others conducted by Daniel Starch beginning in the 1920s, have demonstrated that one of the main requirements for an advertising layout is simplicity. The layout should have a minimum number of elements and should display symmetry and balance. Ads with many different elements, lengthy headlines, and a great deal of scattered copy tend to be poorly noted.*
>
> *More recently, studies of television commercials have produced analogous results. Here too, the basic principle is to keep the advertisement simple. The television commercial with a large number of changes of scene is not very successful.*

219

Longman quotes Fairfax Cone (one of the founders of the Foote, Cone & Belding agency) as summarizing this principle with the words, 'It is the primary requirement of advertising to be clear, clear as to exactly what the proposition is. If it isn't clear, and clear at a glance or a whisper, very few people will take the time or effort to figure it out.'

It couldn't be better put.

8.2 Typography

An important aspect of the clarity referred to by Fairfax Cone is the ability to understand quickly the import of the headlines and body copy of an advertisement. The selection of the best size and style of lettering – the typography – can therefore be crucial. This may be decided by the designer or art director but frequently it will be the specialist task of the typographer – a designer who specializes in this highly important aspect of design.

9. Summary

1   Creativity in advertising is not concerned with producing a work of art, except by accident, but with very specific aims in view – to communicate a particular message to a particular audience as effectively as possible.

2   Although claims have been made that the creation of advertising is a science it is probably best regarded as a craft.

3   The function of 'the creative people' is to turn a possibly banal proposition, arrived at through reason, into a dramatic expression arrived at through the imagination.

4   Up to a point creativity can be taught or at any rate encouraged, but it does seem as though highly creative people tend to be strong in such personal characteristics as avid curiosity, vivid imagination, empathy and flexibility.

5   The useful exercise of the creative ability is very dependent on it being correctly channelled through a good creative brief.

6   Although guidelines can be offered as to what makes a good advertisement, a good layout or good copy, there are certainly no hard and fast rules.

7   The guidelines themselves can be summed up in the statement that advertising 'must be clear as to what the proposition is'.

10. References

1 Hopkins, Claude, *Scientific Advertising*, Crown Publishers, Inc., 1966.
2 Bernstein, David, *Creative Advertising*, Longman, 1974.
3 Ogilvy, David, *Confessions of an Advertising Man*, Atheneum, New York, 1963.
4 Longman, Kenneth A., *Advertising*, Harcourt, Brace, Jovanovich, Inc., 1971.

5 Hart, Norman A. and O'Connor, James [Ed], *The Practice of Advertising*, William Heinemann, 1978.
6 White, Roderick, *Advertising: What it is and how to do it*, McGraw-Hill, 1980 (third edition, 1993).
7 Reeves, Rosser, *Reality in Advertising*, MacGibbon and Kee, 1961.
8 Stanley, Richard E., *Promotion*, Prentice-Hall, 1977.

83

ADVERTISING AND SOCIETY

R. White

Source: R. White, *Advertising* (2nd edition), London: McGraw Hill, 1988, pp. 176–182.

The demon advertising

Advertising, as anyone who works in the industry or is responsible for advertising for his or her employers will find, is blamed for many of the ills of society. Significantly, the word used when a politician—or judge, or social worker, or member of the clergy, or the person next door—accuses advertising of some heinous crime against humanity is always 'advertising'. It is rarely, if ever, 'advertisements', far less 'that advertisement'. The only accusations specifically against individual ads that you are likely to meet are the neat little stickers—themselves a nearly perfect piece of advertising—which appear from time to time on the swimwear and lingerie ads on London Transport escalators saying 'This advertisement exploits women'. (This is arguably true: certainly, a growing number of women feel that this is the case, and that these ads present women as sexual objects in a public place. The fact remains, however, that these products are being advertised *to* women, and the products are—I assume—being bought: the advertisers are presumably not deliberately wasting their money. Of course, if you see the whole capitalist system as exploitation, or women as universally exploited, there's no argument.)

The point, of course, is that if you talk about 'advertising' as a nice vague, amorphous something, you can conjure up fearsome visions of an organized conspiracy, presumably composed of international bankers, multinational corporations, the International League for Cruelty to Children, the Ku Klux Klan, Robert Maxwell and Saatchi and Saatchi, pointing a dagger at the trembling bosom of the poor down-trodden British family. It is good, vivid stuff, if a little lacking in focus or logic. But it is jolly difficult to see how you could conjure up a vision remotely like that if for 'advertising' you substitute 'that ad for Hovis with the theme from the New World' or even 'that amazing Levi jeans commercial in which Nick Kamen strips to his underpants in a laundrette'.

222

The most sinister version of course, in the sense that it can send a nasty shiver down your spine, is the sort of 'mad scientist' vision of brilliant psychologists having discovered all the secret springs of our motivations, and all the necessary tricks of parapsychology and thought transference, so that an apparently innocent ad can be invested with some altogether incredible potency—usually of a rather despicable sexual nature. I could quote a passage from a book that does this *in extenso*, but I cannot really see why I should encourage anyone to read it. So I shall not.

By this stage, you may be beginning to think that I protest too much. I must be hiding something. I have, however, to admit that I am too human for that. If I had anything so powerful to hide, I would be extremely rich, and have long ago retired to Mustique or Mauritius to enjoy my ill-gotten gains. Regrettably (for anyone who hopes to make a fortune in advertising) it is not as easy as that. Nobody in advertising that I know of has any magic insight into human psychology that makes it possible to move human mountains against their will. All that even the most successful people in the business have is an instinct—a salesperson's instinct, on the whole— for what people want to hear. This instinct can, to be sure, be sharpened and refined by market research, but there is nothing magic and effective available to do more than this.

Through the looking glass

Far from turning society upside down, the majority of advertisements, I would suggest, mirror society. It is, however, generally a distorting mirror. As a result, society looks at what it sees in the glass, does not like it, and with a certain justification blames the mirror. Ads are distorting mirrors for two main reasons. Firstly, advertisers, though part of society, are *only* part of it, and not a typical part. The clients, who are usually very normal business-people from the AB or possibly C1 classes—with a dash of upward-mobile ex-C2s—are not 'typical'; nor, far more, are the young people (whom I would not dream of trying to categorize in any way at all) who create the ads.

Then, secondly, once an advertisement has struggled through this initial set of distortions, it gets hit by a massive dose of doublethink. Nearly everyone in advertising believes that an ad ought to be something that the target audience can relate to, or perhaps aspire to. There must be some rapport between ad and audience. But if it is too 'ordinary', people will ignore it. So you find people who are already atypical trying to produce typical ads and then to make them a bit less typical. . . .

Nonetheless, the distorted picture usually has something in common with observable reality, even if the people in the ad are too good, or too nasty, to be true. Understandably, though, the world's critics will react in a jaundiced way if they see a world in which housewives worry endlessly about whether they are using the right washing powder, or spotty kids rush around saying 'gimme this' and 'gimme that' all the time, and words like 'Pinta' keep coming out of the woodwork. This, surely, is what advertising has done to society? And what you see in the ads is merely reflecting what the ads have achieved?

It is, in fact, quite difficult for many people to accept that advertisements are, individually, merely attempts by individual firms to sell their goods; that they do this by presenting them in ways which, they hope, will strike a responsive chord with their target audience; and that no ulterior motive is in their minds beyond the profit figure on the bottom line. Only a politician or perhaps an Ayatollah would seek to change the world with advertisements, and both Dr Goebbels and Khomeini had to resort to arms eventually—though I must admit that they had got some way with publicity first.

The problem faced by the COI and the Department of Health in getting people to adopt sensible measures to prevent the spread of AIDS is a clear indication of the difficulties involved in changing people's behaviour, even where there is very widespread associated publicity in the media, and great public concern. In spite of heavy and intensive advertising—both to the public at large and to high-risk groups such as drug users (a difficult market to reach!), gays and young people in general—evidence of widely changed sexual habits and, in particular, of increased use of condoms, is hard to find.

Servant or seducer?

Advertisements are, of course, a means of separating people from their money. Judging from the relative cost per thousand of a 30-second national commercial and a good in-store demonstrator, I am bound to say that the public has probably gained a substantial degree of safety for its collective purse from the substitution of Patrick Allen's voice on the telly for the blandishments of the snake-oil salesman. The vast majority of ads are at a substantial distance from the actual point of sale, both in physical yardage and in time. What is more, they are clearly and recognizably trying to sell something. And they have to obey the rules (see Chapter 15).

To be sure, much of what the ads display is very enticing. That is what selling is—and always has been—about. There are, of course, plenty of defences against enticements. There is, for example, the good, simple two-letter word 'no', which appears to be much under-rated these days. There is also the rather simple expedient of running out of money—though admittedly sources of credit are so easy to find these days that that is no longer reliable.

The fact is, of course, that salespeople and sales devices have always had a bad name.

It remains true, however, that people do, in fact, want to buy things. They actually do have needs to be met, and sometimes they have to seek quite hard for ways to meet them. One important source of information in this search is advertising. As soon as one talks about ads as information, one runs the risk of raising another philosophical argument—the extent to which ads do, or should, 'persuade' rather than 'inform'. This is an argument which quite misses the point that one person's information is another's persuasion. In this particular area madness lies. The fact remains that advertisements *are* sources of information, at one level or another.

It is actually very difficult to assess how useful ads *are* as information—not least because if you ask people where they heard of something they bought, they rarely say 'advertising'. Nonetheless, if you ask people how they go about looking for, say, a new washing machine, a very substantial proportion will mention ads as one source of information; and if you ask questions obliquely, about—say—the relative merits of ads in different media as sources of information, it is abundantly clear that they have this use very widely. (In fact, I believe you can legitimately argue that even most 'reminder' ads for mass-market grocery products are in fact information more than anything else.)

The brutal persuaders

So, if ads are useful as information—almost regardless of their content—but are also enticers and seducers, what can we make of this? If you put to people in a survey on attitudes to aspects of marketing and advertising the proposition that 'Ads make people buy things they do not need', you will get massive agreement. This is a view which has been picked up by politicians—and moralists—who have painted Dickensian pictures of old age pensioners being forced by compelling ads to waste their hard-earned pensions, meagre as they are, on skateboards and replicas of 18th century carriage clocks. It is, you will find, always other people who are 'forced' by ads to buy things they do not need. As for me, or you, we have our wits about us.

I suppose, in the last resort, all we actually *need* is a roof over our heads—even a cave—some sort of coarse clothing, and a diet of locusts and wild honey. For better or worse, however, most of us live in, and have worked hard for, a rather more elaborately stocked world than that. What people lucky enough to live in the so-called developed world have achieved is a situation of material *choice*. And that choice includes, yet again, the choice not to buy. Advertisements, to be sure, put forward the buying choices: but that is their job, and everyone knows it.

There is, perhaps, an argument which says that you should not dangle diamond necklaces before old age pensioners with low incomes: but it is moderately rare to find such things advertised in media that really poor pensioners see. If the media selection is realistic, the products advertised will rarely be beyond the means of the vast majority of the audience. (Somewhere down this path lies a very complex argument about equality and social justice: but that is really not what we are arguing about. As I said, advertising reacts to and reflects society, and cannot hope to change it.)

In the last resort, there is one very simple refutation (in the proper sense of the word, for once) of the argument that ads force people to buy. Very simply, no ad *could* ever force anyone to buy anything, in any meaningful sense of the word 'force'.

But, of course, ads could lead people into crime by constantly putting before them things they cannot afford, could they not? Yes, of course, they could, in a society where morals do not appear to be very high in anyone's priorities. But is it really the ads that cause all these robberies? If you look at what gets knocked off in the average theft, it is not often heavily advertised goods, except, perhaps, cars, and it is easy to spot the fallacy there: a car is its own advertisement.

Suffer little children

Children, of course, are extremely vulnerable beings, and this includes vulnerability to commercial pressures. As a result, the Code of Practice has an extensive section on advertising to children, and it is a field where there has been considerable discussion over the years by the OFT, consumer bodies and the advertising industry. Children, with regard to ads, are among those classed as 'they'—who are forced by ads, etc. . . . . They are also widely believed, with some justification, to drive their parents mad by wanting 'The one I saw on telly'.

Therefore, say some, ads aimed at children, or screened during children's viewing times, or printed in children's comics, should be banned.

It is a nice simple solution, but difficult to carry through—how do you prevent a child from seeing a poster? How do you define children's viewing times? How do you define an ad aimed at children? More importantly, though, would it do any good in the long run?

Clearly the short-term results could be less over-spending of pocket money and fewer persecuted parents. In the longer term, however, is anything gained? One of the best controls over dishonest advertising, and one of the best pressures for responsible advertising, is an educated consumer. A process has certainly started, some years ago now, by which children have been learning, at least in school, how to deal with advertisements. This learning process is, surely, considerably assisted by exposure to ads. It would be a pity if this were to be halted. Whatever you may think about our materialistic society, it is the one we have to live in, and learning to deal with one of the more conspicuous aspects of that society seems to me to be a useful part of any child's education. A gullible public is a dangerous public, on any terms, and gullibility in the face of ads is just one aspect of a possibly far wider susceptibility to being taken in.

I do believe, therefore, that while advertisements directed to children should be closely controlled—more closely than other ads—it would actually be counterproductive to ban them. I *want* an educated public that can use ads on its own terms: that way ads can be more responsible—because they have to be. I also believe that if parents let themselves be bullied by their kids into buying things they have seen in the ads, they have only themselves to blame. Once again, 'no' is a very useful word, whether it is used directly with respect to buying something for a child, or indirectly as a refusal to replace squandered pocket money.

Prostitution of the arts

In the world of the artist, commercialism devalues most things. The lofty ideal of artistic integrity is above considerations of pounds and pence. So the fact that advertising uses the language of several arts—writing, illustration, photography, music—is in itself an affront. The further, generally observable, fact that most ads contain neither good writing, nor good illustration, nor good photography, nor good music is merely extra evidence of the parasitism of the industry on the fair face of culture. *Ars gratia artis*, but Ads *gratia* Addis, in fact.

Now there is, obviously, something in this, but I do not think it goes very far. In general, advertisements do not masquerade as works of art, though some come very near it: you have only to look through a magazine like *Graphis*, or collections of DADA award-winners, to see extremely 'artistic' ads. Much advertising photography is of an extremely high standard, and TV commercial techniques have contributed much to film. It is less easy —to put it mildly—to claim much positive benefit to the language from advertising copy.

Quite apart, however, from a very positive contribution to visual arts— and, I suspect, to the visual awareness of the public—there is no doubt that the advertising industry provides an essential social service to much of the artistic world. The majority of students from art colleges go into commercial work of one kind or another, and many artists pay for their 'genuine' art by working for advertising. Similarly, there is a significant list of writers, both of prose and poetry, who earn their living in advertising—in spite of the constraints of advertising copy.

Thus, although advertising may ape art, and the objectives of art used in advertising are not the objectives of 'pure' art, the advertising industry's contribution to art (or 'the arts') is, on the whole, a positive one.

The environment

Once the idea of pollution became widely accepted, it quickly became applied, more or less metaphorically, to a vast variety of aspects of the world we live in. Quite apart from pollution of air or water or food, we now have aural pollution, visual pollution, even spiritual pollution. Advertisements, naturally, have become pollution—of several kinds—in these terms.

This is a view with which I have some sympathy. There is little doubt, as one finds only too often when trying to devise and place advertising for a client, that the sheer volume of advertisements, in all media, makes it very difficult—increasingly difficult—to find a way of standing out and getting attention. For many advertisers, the only solution has been to increase the volume of their efforts, and so increase the amount of 'noise' their own and others' ads have to penetrate in order to communicate.

The number of ads to which we are potentially exposed every day is vast. If you live in a town, have you ever counted the number of posters you pass as you go about your daily business? The average newspaper or magazine may be 60 per cent or 70 per cent ads. On television, about three minutes of every hour watched in the UK consists of commercials.[1] Naturally, we attend to only a limited proportion of these ads.

The question of whether ads add to, or detract from, the environment in which we live is, I think, rather more complex than simply to dismiss them as 'pollution', of whatever kind. There is little doubt that our eyes are, in general, accustomed to the presence of posters, and that they do actually tend to enhance the look of a town if they are suitably placed and controlled. The drabness of most Eastern European cities and, indeed, of many small country towns is due, to an extent, to the absence of posters. (The countryside is another thing: the poet who wrote 'I think that I shall never see a billboard lovely as a tree' was, surely, right.)

In television, the old joke that the commercials are better entertainment than the programmes has more than a little truth in it—most commercials are produced with more technical skill and more imaginative thought than most programmes. In the press, as is well known, the publications could not survive without their advertising revenue. Either you have ads or you have no papers—at least not at prices you can afford. In other words, the ads are not pollution of the environment: they actually *are* the environment.

True pollution, I would suggest, is something which actively damages the environment, and the removal of which would result in a positive benefit. Unless you believe that newspapers and magazines are unnecessary luxuries, or that a reasonable choice of TV programmes is not a desirable thing to have, especially if someone else pays, or that towns really are somehow better without posters, I do not think the pollution charge really stands up. You do not *need* to remove the ads. Nearly always, you can ignore them: the human brain is a marvellous machine for excluding unwanted communications—that is another of advertising's problems.

The ethnic problem

Advertising, as so often, reflects society in its unwillingness to recognize the presence of racial minorities. There are very, very few British ads with West Indian, let alone Indian or Pakistani actors in them. Correspondingly, the specifically ethnic market, represented in media terms by (for example) the *Daily Fang* or *Al Arab*, the *Caribbean Times* and the *Fanomot Bengali News Weekly*, is an unknown quantity to most people in the advertising business.

In the USA, various pressure groups have succeeded in achieving both recognition and participation for 'blacks' in US advertising. In the UK, there is a substantial element of Asian staff in most large agencies, but little reflection of this in ads—even on a local basis in cities such as Slough and Bradford.

As in the USA, this is likely to change more as a response to the recognition of significant market segments than in response to political militancy. Andrew Young's ill-informed complaint that the England football team had only one black member was, in these terms, totally counter-productive— anyone with a knowledge of UK population statistics would know that this was 50 per cent more than was justified! The fact is that the ethnic market is very under-recognized, and that, correspondingly, ethnic minorities are under-represented in UK ads. This will, I think, change, and a change would help enhance the standing of the minorities—but not, I suspect, if it were forced into existence by legislation.

A benefit to society?

This chapter has discussed, briefly, the main charges laid against advertising for doing some form of damage to society. They are all more or less common, and some are firmly believed by many people. Most of them, on inspection, turn out to be criticisms of society itself—its materialism, its immorality, its indiscipline, its dishonesty—rather than of advertisements. We happen to live in an advanced industrial society, with a particular economic structure which will change only slowly. As it changes, advertising will change, too: it will not change society. It cannot.

There seem to me to be good reasons to dismiss these charges against advertising as being sweeping, generalized, inaccurate, and wrongly directed. I do not believe advertising is Simon Pure, but people recognize this: there is plenty of research evidence to prove it.

I am not so naive, either, as to argue that advertising is a positive benefit to society in these general social terms—there are some clear benefits, but mostly it seems to me pretty neutral. I do believe, however, that advertising is able to provide at least some economic benefits. These are discussed in the next chapter.

Note

1 Seven minutes of commercials on ITV per hour, and ITV has half the audience.

84

THE CORPORATE BRAND

N. Ind

Source: N. Ind, *The Corporate Brand*, Basingstoke: Macmillan Business, 1997, pp. 1–14.

Why are there so many television programmes, books, newspapers and magazines devoted to business? Partly it is because as consumers, employees, managers and shareholders, companies define, enrich and nurture (and occasionally damage) our lives. Business may not offer us the depth of experience of religion or family, but its influence is all-pervasive. Partly it is because business is a spectacle; it has drama and excitement and adventure. It's like the characters from the *Commedia dell' Arte* 'who display in their costumes and attitudes, the future contents of their parts'.[1] The actors do not just interact with each other, they get the audience on their side, or against them, by their willingness to fight fairly, by their integrity as individuals and by their gestures. We can 'read' the character of an actor, such as the Harlequin, from his actions and his looks. Similarly we 'read' a company by its outward signs, such as its advertising, its brochures and its reported performance. What interests us as an audience is the unfolding of the action; the posturing; the personifications of good and evil. It's IBM versus Apple, Boeing versus Airbus, British Airways versus Virgin, Coca-Cola versus Pepsi. Depending on our experience and image of the adversaries, and indeed our own sense of self, we identify with one or the other. For example, when Apple ran its 1984 campaign which presented IBM as Big Brother and Apple as the iconoclasts out to empower computer users, it was clear, at least to some, that IBM was the personification of evil. However, 'good' doesn't always triumph. IBM came to dominate the personal computer market and Microsoft the software market. Similarly British Airways is the big bruiser who wants to be liked, while Virgin is the underdog – the people's champion. Of course these judgements are simplistic and may not be based on reality. But this is also exactly the way that consumers and other audiences categorise organisations. There is a game you can play in research groups, when you ask the participants to associate organisations with animals or cars or people. The participants have no problems at all –

even on very limited knowledge of making linkages; they read the signs, just as a theatre audience does. Companies that get categorised as rats or snakes tend not to have positive images.

So what can business learn from the *Commedia dell' Arte?* First, images determine people's attitudes and behaviour; a positive image can help create support for a company and its products. Second, that image is a mixture of appearance and action – the one needs to endorse the other. Third, to succeed one needs to be a good communicator. Last, it's not the transient ebbs and flows of the action that matter – it's having the skill and the resources to triumph in the end. It is the combination of performance and image that defines the successful corporate brand.

Definitions

Corporate branding is one of those things that everyone believes is important, yet there is very little consensus as to what it means. Words such as 'values', 'identity', 'image' and 'communication' swirl around. It is undoubtedly related to all these things. Some writers, such as John Balmer equate it with corporate identity: 'the strategic importance of corporate brand management (or what is more appropriately called strategic corporate identity management) would appear to be irrefutable.'[2] However the danger with linking corporate branding to the idea of corporate identity, even when it is prefixed by 'strategic' is that most audiences begin to think design and see logos. Therefore a distinct and clear definition of the corporate brand is required. Both the words 'corporate' and 'brand' carry certain connotations. 'Corporate' implies organisations – both profit and non-profit making – in their totality. It encompasses everything from the small family-run firm to the largest multinational. What defines it as corporate is its cohesion: the idea of people coming together and working towards a common goal. Thus, a corporate body has strategic decision making potential. In this definition, branch offices and divisions of a larger body are not corporate, unless they are responsible for determining strategy or have goals that are distinctively different from the parent company. However things – least of all definitions – are rarely this concise, and there are factors that serve to diffuse the meaning of 'corporate'. First, in many organisations, the common goal is not clearly defined and as a result sub-groups can develop their own, often contradictory, directions. In this context, trying to define what a particular corporation stands for can be very difficult. Second, organisations are not static objects, rooted in time and space. They evolve in response to the environment and as a consequence of the decisions they take. What may be our idea of an organisation at one point may prove to be erroneous later. Last, it is important to remember that no matter how the organisation defines itself and its decision making, there is still the potential for consumers and other stakeholders to see it differently. It is possible for the corporate definition of self and how it is perceived to be out of kilter, either because of deliberate policy or mismanagement. Although these caveats temper the definition of 'corporate', they do not undermine it. Rather it suggests that we need to understand an organisation and its structure in depth, before making judgements about it. Traditionally a 'brand' is a descriptor applied to the sort of fast-moving consumer goods one buys from a supermarket. It is distinct from the simple idea of a product in that there is a suggestion in the notion of a brand of values that go beyond mere functional performance. As Stephen King says, in the preface to his book *Developing New Brands*, 'a product is something that is made, in a factory; a brand is something that is bought, by a customer.[3] A product can be copied by a competitor; a brand is unique.'

It is the joining together of these two words – corporate and brand – that suggests a new way of looking at organisations. There is still the temptation to think of the visual presentation and the immediate reaction is to see company names and logos. These are the most overt signs of an organisation and this indicates why the management of a company's visual identity is so important. Nonetheless we should not mistake the sign for the substance. For example, Apple Computers is more than its name and its Garden of Eden apple. It is a company with a history, a set of values, a reputation and a strategy for the future, managed and worked for by people. In Stephen King's terminology, the Apple is something that is 'bought' by a wide variety of audiences: everyone from shareholders to employees to consumers.

Historically the marketing of brands has dominated marketing literature and thinking. This has been because most academic marketing courses have been focused on brands, as have the texts to support them. Consequently, all too often the enterprise behind the brand has been in the shadows. Now there are good reasons why the enterprise should be in the sun. However, before we blindly accept the pre-eminence of corporate marketing, we need to understand what it is and to recognise there are subtle differences between it and brand marketing. There are three core attributes that define the corporate brand as a distinct area:

- intangibility
- complexity
- responsibility.

Intangibility

The writer Iris Murdoch notes:

> We see parts of things, we intuit whole things. We seem to know a great deal on the basis of very little . . . We fear plurality, diffusion, senseless accident, chaos, we want to transform what we cannot dominate or understand into something reassuring and familiar.[4]

When we buy a consumer brand, such as a shampoo, we can touch, feel and smell it. We may not know or understand its chemical make-up, but we can describe its attributes with a fair degree of certainty. Although a brand will have some intangible elements a company is far more remote. Unless we work for a company, we rarely know much about its history, strategy, values and culture. We glean information from its communications, its people and its products and we make judgements. We decide that Shell is a good company and BP is not, or vice versa. Similarly our ideas change. When Shell is funding the revitalisation of our inland waterways it's a good company, but when it is planning to sink the Brent Spar oil platform out at sea, it's a bad company. Both judgements are simplistic. Shell like all companies makes good and bad decisions, but because we lack an intimate understanding of the company, our attitudes alter depending on the information we have available. (Shell's reputation declined noticeably following Brent Spar. The researcher, MORI, asked people if the company took its social responsibilities seriously. The measure which had been consistent for a number of years fell by nearly 10 percentage points as a direct result of its confrontation with Greenpeace.) In market research into companies, consumer assumptions and beliefs rarely withstand scrutiny. If a respondent claims a certain image for a company, the basis of the view is often shallow and deeply influenced by media coverage. Nonetheless, in spite of this superficiality, people can be deeply motivated by corporate actions – certainly the boycotting of Shell and attacks on petrol stations over Brent Spar was vociferous. It is, as Murdoch suggests, our need to transform plurality into order and familiarity that encourages us to construct the information we receive whatever its validity into something we can understand in our own terms. This echoes Sartre's view that we feel alien in a world without meaning, so therefore we have to create meaning ourselves. We select what is relevant to our lives and interpret it from our own perspective. Our views are determined by our culture, society, upbringing and plain self-interest. When the former Governor of Hong Kong, Chris Patten, was a Conservative MP and member of the Cabinet, he was against the idea of providing citizenship rights to 3 million Hong Kong Chinese. After resigning his parliamentary seat and becoming Governor, his allegiances switched and he announced himself in favour of granting citizenry. A duplicitous or a genuine turnaround? Being generous, one might judge that the same problem viewed from several thousand miles apart looks rather different.

There is, then, an important difference between the reality of an organisation and its image. We see and hear a company's messages and experience its products or people and out of this miasma we construct an image that may, or may not, bear a close relationship to what the organisation actually is. Image then is a personal experience, but it is also collective. Although our deeper views about a specific organisation may vary, what can be observed from quantitative research is the collective view. When an organisation says

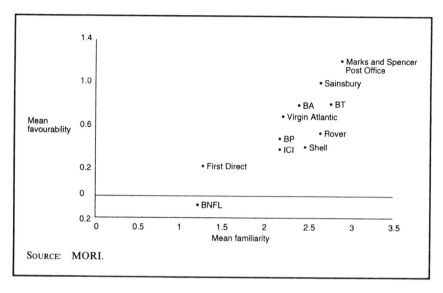

Figure 1 Company familiarity and favourability, general public, November 1995.

it has an image as professional, innovative and dynamic, what it means is that a majority of external audiences subscribe to this view. It will still be possible to find people who believe exactly the opposite. There is a general truism that familiarity equates to favourability (Figure 1), but within that truism there are a great variety of viewpoints. There are then no absolutes, merely a collection of messages that form together in our minds to create an idea of an organisation and what it does.

Getting to grips with a corporate brand is a difficult task and requires relevant communication. To create tangibility, communication should work at two levels. First, while accepting that each individual will have a unique idea of the organisation, there is still the need to try to build a consensual image that is both an accurate representation and also helps the fulfilment of corporate strategy. This requires consistency of communication to all stakeholders. Second, at the micro level, the organisation needs to build interactive relationships on a one-to-one basis with each individual stakeholder, whether they be customer, supplier or investor.

Building relationships

For a small business the idea of tangible relationships is axiomatic. A good high street butcher, for example, will know the names of his customers and their requirements. He will get special orders for them and tell them about special cuts of meat. He will know his suppliers and discuss his requirements with them. If he is sensible he will know his bank manager, provide him

234

with information on the business and seek advice when he needs to. He will probably know and talk to his main competitors and he may belong to a trade association. For the butcher, knowing his stakeholders and understanding their needs allows him to compete with the buying power of the large supermarket groups. However, there is no reason why the supermarket groups and other large companies should not pursue a similar strategy. Historically they have not done so because as with all large businesses they have become complex organisms with bureaucracies that have put up barriers between the strategy and its implementation. Unlike the high street butcher it has not been viable for the Chief Executive of a national supermarket chain to have a relationship with all the company's stakeholders. The process has been delegated and in its delegation diluted. Also the dictates of mass marketing and the concern with market share have dictated that companies have been focused on volume, based essentially on selling fairly standardised products to large numbers of undifferentiated people. In reality consumers have always wanted products tailored to their needs, but apart from the few who could afford bespoke products, the reality of production, since the introduction of the machine age and Henry Ford's Model T, has been standardisation. Now the technology exists to create individual products for individual people. It exists to tailor the process of production and it exists to monitor and interact with consumers. For example, in automotive engineering, developments in electronics means that a car can be tailored by the customer to determine such aspects as the ride height, steering, gear change points, brakes, aerodynamics and performance:

> What makes a Chevrolet a Chevrolet will no longer be defined by a preconception of the engineers, but by an individual's expression of what it should be. This in turn means that auto makers will stop trying to outguess groups of consumers about what they really want the steering to feel like. Their goal instead will be to enlarge the range of choices from which customers can themselves select what they want.[5]

The ability of companies to tailor products has the potential to attract new customers but, more importantly, it has the power to retain and develop existing customers. In certain markets, where since the 1970s capacity has been outstripping demand (cars, steel, trucks, airlines, shipbuilding, textiles), the value of keeping the customers you already have is paramount. This has heralded a boom in loyalty cards, bonus schemes and direct marketing initiatives, aimed at what Don Peppers and Martha Rogers in their book *The One to One Future*[6] call 'share of customer'. They and others argue that it is the potential long-term value of a customer that is important, not a one-off purchase, which is often expensive to obtain. The value to Ford of a first-time Fiesta buyer is not the cost of the car, but the potential lifetime spend and the benefit of word of mouth endorsement if the product performs. The challenge for the company is to spot the best potential source of long-term customer relationships and, having acquired them, to nurture them. Inevitably there are costs and rewards involved in building a relationship and companies need to determine the value exchange:

> the relationship between the financial investment a company makes in particular customer relationships and the return that customers generate by the specific way in which they choose to respond to the company's offer.[7]

In most businesses, the long-established idea of the Pareto effect – that 20% of your customers provide 80% of your business – applies. The primary task for business should be to retain and develop that 20% through specific and relevant offers. The negative aspect of this concentration on core customers is that certain customers become effectively disenfranchised; they lose their ability to consume. This has already started to happen within the insurance industry, whereby insurers will not cover home contents in certain inner-city locations in the UK. Although this may make commercial sense, in other markets, such as retail and air travel, it has the potential to exclude the 20%ers of the future. Loyalty rewarders therefore need to think carefully about the attitudes and behaviour patterns they encourage.

The idea of making an organisation tangible through relationships – as with the high street butcher – can and should go beyond consumers. The Royal Society of Arts (RSA) (1995) research project into British Business, *Tomorrow's Company*, which involved face to face consultations with 8000 business leaders and opinion formers, stated as its overall vision that:

> The companies which will sustain competitive success in the future are those which focus less exclusively on shareholders and on financial measures of success – and instead include all their stakeholder relationships.

It goes on to recommend that 'tomorrow's company',

> Works actively to build reciprocal relationships with customers, suppliers and other key stakeholders through a partnership approach.

The reality is that the RSA report found that very few companies in Britain are truly world class (although most think they are), and that part of the reason for this is the failure to build relationships with all of a company's stakeholders. This is partly a British cultural legacy, but it is also due to the failure of businesses everywhere to integrate all their business relationships in a company-wide strategy based on a common vision. In other words although the technology may now exist to enable organisations to build relationships with all stakeholders, the enabling culture does not. Yet it is only through a relationship-based approach to all of a company's activities that an organisation can achieve meaning for the individual, can communicate in a way that is uniquely relevant to each person.

Complexity

The second key differential between brands and corporate brands is the issue of complexity. Companies can include several decision making bodies, numerous operating divisions, large numbers of products and thousands of people. This makes control very difficult. With a physical brand and to a lesser extent a service brand, continuity of experience is achievable. Within a corporate brand it is much harder to attain. A company can contain several different cultures. David Potter, Chairman of laptop computer manufacturer, Psion says:

> the people within Psion are quite a broad church . . . the psychology and culture of the software nerd is utterly different from corporate sales. I'm not even sure they speak the same language. The one is a vulcan, the other is an earthling. The classic sales person needs a BMW, needs the money to look elegant and his main weapon in his personal armoury is charm. This is total anathema to the software person: he is not driven by money, he is driven by self-esteem and peer group esteem and the excitement at being at the front of something.[8]

The individual who buys a Psion product will probably not appreciate this diversity, but buyers and suppliers, depending on their point of contact with the organisation, will have different perceptions. In addition to the problems of cultural diversity, corporate brand complexity develops through the naming structures that companies use to either link business units or products together under one banner (Sony, Yamaha) or not, as in the case of Procter & Gamble, which sells a number of seemingly unrelated brands. The latter is fairly typical of fast-moving consumer goods companies that often want to put competing products on to the market without the consumer knowing they come from the same stable. However, in the face of competition from own-label, some manufacturers such as Unilever have started to defend their corner through the use of corporate naming on packs. This has two potential benefits. It achieves economies of communication, in that all of a company's products support each other through a common endorsement, in much the same way that the Sony brand name adds value to its full product range. Second, the use of corporate naming helps to communicate to professional audiences, such as investors, the strength of the company's brand portfolio. But, if nothing is done to establish the corporate brand behind the name – the sum of values that represents the organisation – the addition of the company name to a product in itself achieves very little. This is a much more complex area and involves communication to all of a company's audiences.

Just as corporate branding is more complex than traditional brand marketing, so is communications. The way an audience builds up an awareness of a company is multifaceted. It occurs through the overt means of communication, such as advertising, literature, press coverage and direct marketing as well as the actions and behaviour of individuals. If the company name is used on products, such as BMW or Apple, the direct experience – or at least sight – of the product will be a key factor in our attitude towards the organisation. In most contexts where we buy the product will impinge on our views of it. As will the after sales service and support. Finally, but probably most importantly, the leaders and employees who represent the company will colour our beliefs about it – and the latter will also be recipients of many of the above forms of communication. This suggests that if the picture we have of an organisation is to have clarity, all of these forms of communication need to work cohesively together. Recipients of communication, by and large, will not differentiate the source of information. They may admire the advertising in its own right, but generally the messages a company emits are combined in an unconscious way to form an image. This is as true for the consumer as for the institutional investor and for the journalist. Indeed although one tends to separate out all of the audiences of a company for analytical purposes there will be overlap – the journalist may also be a consumer, the employee an investor.

The problem for many organisations is that communications are compartmentalised: corporate affairs talks to financial audiences; marketing talks to consumers; and human relations talks to employees. Even within marketing in large organisations different people will commission direct marketing activity, public relations, design and advertising. Unless there is a powerful integrative force the possibilities for fragmentation are enormous. It needs glue to hold it together. That can come only through structures and systems that encourage convergence and most importantly through a powerful, shared vision, that helps to achieve a degree of uniformity in attitudes and behaviour. Without turning employees into the sort of automatons found in Fritz Lang's *Metropolis*, the organisation has to try to build a set of values that creates consistency. This is the problem of variability of performance that service industries all have to confront in their relationships with consumers. For the corporate brand, variability has to be managed. In his introduction to the RSA *Tomorrow's Company* study (1995), Sir Anthony Cleaver, notes:

> Far too many companies are nowhere near as good as they like to believe, and far too few can support their claims with progress measured and

reviewed at board level. I believe this is fundamentally a leadership issue ... Leadership that has the courage to put across a consistent message which is relevant to all stakeholders – giving the same vision for the company to shareholder and employee, to investor and supplier, to customer and to the community at large.

The sort of vision that Cleaver is referring to is not the banality of most corporate mission statements, but a true and heartfelt belief that is fundamental to the organisation and steers everything it says and does. To achieve this takes courage, because a vision often flies in the face of accepted norms. Visions that tend towards a middle of the road view are unlikely to engender the sort of devotion needed to coalesce the organisation. The Italian writer, Umberto Eco, has noted that in Italian politics, Socialist, Communist and Christian Democrat arguments become more similar the broader the audience. Corporate visions in their desire not to offend anyone or exclude any opportunity all too often achieve a similar effect. Contrast this with the distinct and impassioned beliefs that steered the development of the British housewares retailer, Habitat, founded in 1964 by Terence Conran. For 25 years, his desire to make things accessible, derived from his socialist, egalitarian education, drove the company. His vision permeated everything Habitat did and inspired the people who worked there:

His [Conran's] aim was always to deliver to the customer his view of what was right. He would never sell something he didn't think was good, and largely he sold what he personally liked. There was a sincerity and honesty in this that most of the staff wholeheartedly shared ... Employees quickly got to understand his ideas on products and presentation and, because they were appealingly humanistic, adopted them as their own.[9]

Responsibility

In addition to interacting effectively with all its audiences and balancing their often countervailing needs, the corporate brand also has a broader social responsibility, an ethical imperative. Some organisations such as The Body Shop and Ben and Jerry's Homemade Ice Cream compete in part on their ethical stance towards the environment and employment. Consumers, investors and suppliers who believe in these companies' ethics are not only buying products, but a set of values. Jon Entine, writing in *Dollars and Sense* notes that some of the supposedly ethical stances of companies are more to do with 1960s' liberal ideas of right and wrong, rather than more fundamental truths:

At best, the relatively small number of consumers with a high tolerance for high priced goods – most of the products [green] in question command a heafty premium over ordinary brands – play a modest role in raising awareness of social problems. (And even so, it's just a prosperous sliver of baby boomers affected.) At worst, cause-related marketing, as it is called, is little more than baby-boom agitprop, masking serious ethical lapses.[10]

Whatever the position of the green marketers, ethics is an issue that confronts all companies. A company does not exist independently of the society within which it operates. It relies on the goodwill of the people who work for it, the local communities within which it is located, the governments that determine legislation and the consumers who buy its products. Support from these groups is not automatic, it requires approval of their activities. As George Bull, Chief Executive, Grand Metropolitan, puts it:[11]

Increasingly business people are recognising that their prosperity is directly linked to the prosperity of the whole community. The community is the source of customers, employees, their suppliers, and with the wider spread of share ownership, their investors.

Ethics is not a short-term option, but a long-term necessity. More companies now realise this and have clearly stated ethical positions. This is a sensible business stance, not least because the pressures from consumers and legislators have determined that companies that do not abide by the rules that society defines will be punished either through the withdrawal of their consumer franchise or through fines. As an example of this, human rights protests in Burma against the military dictatorship has led to withdrawals from the country by Heineken, Carlsberg, Levi Strauss, Reebok and Pepsi-Cola. The chairman of Heineken was quoted as saying:[12]

the public opinion and issues surrounding this market have changed to a degree that could have an adverse effect on our brand and corporate reputation.

The glare of publicity that accompanies misdemeanours and miscalculations is extremely damaging. It is all too easy for a company that has a narrow focus on its shareholders and meeting their needs to forget that it has wider responsibilities. As E. F. Schumacher argued in his influential book, *Small is Beautiful – A Study of Economics as if People Mattered* (1974),

What is the meaning of democracy, freedom, human dignity, standard of living, self realisation, fulfilment? Is it a matter of goods, or of people? Of course it is a matter of people.

Businesses are operated by people for people in the context of the society within which we all live. For some organisations, this has been a function of their religious heritage, such as the Quaker companies, Cadbury's and Rowntree's while for others it is derived from a founder's belief, such as the British retailer, The John Lewis Partnership or the American department store chain, Nordstrom. To be credible an ethical position has to be a fundamental part of an organisation's make-up. Aristotle believed that ethical behaviour was the result of habituation. Acting ethically should become automatic and pleasurable, if it is learned and repeated. This implies that business ethics cannot simply be a veneer that in difficult times is stripped away in the pursuit of short-term gain. It must be an inherent part of the company's being.

Summary

A corporate brand is more than just the outward manifestation of an organisation – its name, logo, visual presentation. Rather it is the core of values that defines it. The communication of those values is of course an important part of what an organisation is, for as this chapter has shown, knowledge is often partial. The company that can communicate effectively helps ensure that its various audiences know what it does and what it stands for. It can and should achieve this through understanding the perspectives of its various stakeholders and then building relationships with them that benefit both parties. The important thing to recognise is that communications cannot be based on myth or wishful thinking. Communications must be based on substance. If they are not, inconsistency creeps in and confusion follows shortly thereafter. Employees, for example, can all too easily contradict what is being said in advertising; the reality then fails to match the image. What defines the corporation, in comparison to the brand, is the degree of complexity. It is larger, more diverse and has several audiences that it must interact with. The corporate brand must be able to meet the needs of the often competing claims of its stakeholders. To achieve that it must have clarity of vision, of values and of leadership.

Notes

1 R. Barthes, *Mythologies* (Paladin, 1989 edn), p. 18.
2 J. Balmer, 'Corporate Branding and Connoisseurship', *Journal of General Management*, 21(1) (Autumn 1995), p. 24.
3 S. King, *Developing New Brands* (JWT, 1984 edn), p. iii.
4 I. Murdoch, *Metaphysics as a Guide to Morals* (Penguin, 1992). pp. 1, 2.
5 L. Early and G. Mercer, 'The showroom as an assembly line', *EIU International Motor Business* (January 1993).
6 D. Peppers and M. Rogers, *The One to One Future: Building Business Relationships One Customer at a Time* (Piatkus, 1994).

7 W. H. Grant and L. A. Schlesinger, 'Realise Your Customers' Full Potential', *Harvard Business Review* (September/October 1995), p. 60.
8 Interview with author, May 1996.
9 N. Ind, *Terence Conran – The Authorized Biography* (Sidgwick & Jackson, 1995), pp. 160–1.
10 J. Entine, 'Let Them Eat Brazil Nuts', *Dollars and Sense* (March/April 1996), p. 35.
11 RSA, *Tomorrow's Company* (1995), p. 22.
12 D. Usborne, 'Heineken bows out of £20m Burma deal', *The Independent* (11 July 1996).

85

PRINCIPLES OF PERSUASION

S. Brierley

Source: S. Brierley, *The Advertising Handbook* (second ed.), London: Routledge, 2002, pp. 137–150.

> Advertising is neither a science, art, nor manufacture. It has no general standard, no root principles, no hard and fast rules, no precedents, no foolproof machinery. What man can be expert in a subject without end or beginning, a subject as full of controversy today as it was fifty years back?
>
> (W. A. Alexander of Nash and
> Alexander in Bradshaw 1927: 140)

> Successful advertising appeals both to the head and to the heart, to reason and emotions.
>
> (Beatson 1986: 265)

By the early twentieth century key consumer markets such as confectionery, soap and tobacco had already become saturated. Though advertisers had developed strategies such as expanding consumer spending through increasing credit, they also turned to advertising messages to help increase sales. As early as 1908, when *The Psychology of Advertising* by Professor Walter Dill Scott was published, advertisers began to turn to psychological theories to try to unlock the consumer's mind (Leiss *et al.* 1990: 138). Agencies began to formulate theories of human behaviour and motivation which could be unlocked by persuasive treatments. New approaches to persuasiveness were categorised and systematised in the 1920s into 'reason-why' and 'atmosphere' advertising techniques.

'Reason-why' was designed to stimulate demand by constructing a reason for purchase, such as helping to save time, being modern, or being socially acceptable. Reason-why ads were used to differentiate the product from others on the market, as in an example from the 1960s: 'Make sure it's Cadbury's. Because no other chocolate can possibly give you the proper, creamy, Cadbury taste.' The premise was that consumers were essentially rational and made consuming decisions based upon reason. In an expanding market, there is no other reason to try to make appeals other than reason-why, because consumers continue to buy, but once competition rises and the market flattens, advertisers need to find new appeals. 'Atmosphere' advertising, on the other hand, appealed to the emotional side and was meant to evoke non-rational responses such as sexual desire and patriotism from consumers. Irrationality became an issue when the market became saturated and advertisers needed a competitive advantage.

The debate illustrated that advertising was trying to set up a professional, rational, discipline. It was the first sign of agencies trying to maintain social control over the discipline – that they 'knew' or had the knowledge about ads, and that amateurs did not.

These approaches tried to get to the essence of what advertising is all about and consequently solve all of the problems of advertising. In reality, advertisers used combinations of the two. New products, for example, at the turn of the century had to be explained and the reasons for using them developed in the advertising. However, new inventions could not rely just on reason-why ads, they also used suggestion and atmosphere. One technique of advertisers of new products was to associate the new brand with traditional and familiar settings such as nature, nationhood and the family.

A later version of the reason-why advertisement of the 1920s was the Unique Selling Proposition (USP) developed by US agency boss Rosser Reeves in the 1950s. This too was based on 'rational' consumer decisions, but more explicitly tried to find an essence to advertising. Rosser Reeves specified that 'Each advertisement must make a proposition to the consumer . . . Each advertisement must say to each reader: "Buy this product, and you will get this specific benefit . . . one that the competition either cannot, or does not, offer." It must be unique – either a uniqueness of the brand or a claim not otherwise made in that particular field of advertising . . . The proposition must be so strong that it can move the mass millions, i.e., pull over the new customers to your product' (Reeves 1961: 51–52). A USP has to be original, differentiating a product from the competition. It is determined purely by market imperatives, the need of the advertiser to compete.

A USP can be achieved through the packaging, such as a unique bottle shape, or a lime segment in the top of a beer bottle (Sol). These differences in the product (the look, shape, size, colour and market position (the biggest/best/leading) are less to do with the advertising and more to do with the manufacturer. The manufacturer may decide to design the product in a certain way to provide the USP, such as an unusual pack design. Creatives in agencies would go through the different benefits of the product until they could find something that was different about it – 'melts in your mouth not in your hands' (Minstrels), and, for a boiled sweet, 'double-wrapped to keep in the freshness'. Whether the consumers were interested enough in these USPs to make them want to buy the product was of little relevance. This imperative for differentiation came from the companies and the competitive market, not from any predilection towards the consumer. The greatest strength of the approach was that it re-emphasised the basic communications principle that to be effective advertising of brands must emphasise difference; it did not matter for what rational or irrational reason it was differentiated, just that it was differentiated. The only element of 'rationality' in some of the classic USP advertising was the fact that there was a 'reason' for it, it did not rationally matter which reason it was. It was therefore the discourse of rationality, rather than actual rationality, that motivated it.

In the 1960s advertisers attacked the reason-why approach of rational persuasion. One of the reasons for this was 'the purely technical one of the vast shift to the TV medium, which, of its nature, is better able to communicate in pictures than words, images than arguments; biased, some would say, against understanding' (Tuck 1976: 40). The shift from the perception of rational consumer to one of an irrational consumer came hand in hand with the development of the broadcast medium, at first radio then TV.

Reason-why and USP are still used today in different settings, especially for new products. However, the speed with which goods lose their difference means that the straightforward explanation of the goods' use, and the appeal of product difference is lost and other ways are needed to differentiate the product, such as the emotional sell and the advertising brand image.

If there is a new product to launch and the advertiser needs to explain to the consumer how the product or service works, and why it is better than the traditional way you did things – such as the convenience and ease of using a dishwasher versus scrubbing lasagne off cooking pots – then the next brand that comes into that market is wasting its time telling people the same reason for using the product. The new brand has to differentiate through a separate and distinct product feature or benefit, or, more usually (if there is no difference), to develop a separate personality so that the brand is remembered as quite distinct. It is not so much the appropriateness of the brand's personality to the consumer market as the distinction and therefore memorable nature of the brand's personality that is important.

David Ogilvy asserted that products could be differentiated on the basis of brand image and advertising, though the term 'brand image' had been used for decades before (1983: 15). The distinction for the product is made on brand attributes (softness, strength, German engineering, Australian macho culture), its Emotional Selling Proposition. The personality of a brand is used to replace the selling proposition. If advertisers were convinced that consumers bought goods on the basis of the brand image and values, rather than because it was simply the cheapest or most available, advertising agencies would maintain a powerful position in the communications efforts of firms. Ogilvy was one of the biggest exponents of the power of the brand to influence consumer buying decisions. The attributes are formed by making associations, which provide an identity, which engage with the fantasies or aspirations of the target market. Building brands is as much about establishing familiarity, authority and legitimacy as it is about establishing difference. Any new brand that comes on the market has the weight of this to fight against. What Ogilvy may ascribe to the power of persuasive brand advertising may equally be ascribed to the size, scale and familiarity of the brand's campaign, its availability and product-led modifications. Even if you are not a Coke addict, you may turn to Coke in a store because you are so familiar with its design and its names and packaging. One of the reasons why the brand leaders do not need so much brand advertising is because they have already established that credibility and legitimacy.

The rise of lifestyle advertising in the UK in the 1980s was also a response to the saturation of markets: it has also been attributed to the success of the account planning discipline in advertising agencies. This type of advertising 'draws on the planners' interpretation of the nature of the target audience but fails to talk about the product' (Skorah in Cowley 1989: 9). It focuses on an activity engaged in by the target 'type'. It may be set in a club, at tennis courts, at an exclusive country club or golf club, on a type of holiday. People don't have to be using the product, just doing the kinds of things that people who use this product do such as driving fast cars, or ice skating. The product became secondary, something to be emphasised at the end of the story. Gold Blend was like this: the stories focused more on the story or narrative than on mentioning the product. One ad combines the function of the brand with the lifestyle, Tampax's 'It's My Life', which shows women roller skating, wearing short skirts and doing sports, the idea being that you aren't constrained by your period, and when you aren't constrained the kind of people who use Tampax do all these interesting things.

The brand image, the USP and lifestyle are basically about the same thing; differentiating the brand. The USP differentiated through the product itself, the brand image emphasises the unique values and attributes of the brand, and lifestyle ads differentiate the product on the basis of consumer lifestyles and psychographics.

Research and creativity

Creatives often conflict with the rational and scientific authority of planners and researchers in the advertising industry, especially when their creative ideas are rejected on the basis of empirical tests. However, research findings inform a great deal of creative decisions. Research is conducted to suggest to copywriters, layout artists, photographers and film-makers what the most effective form and content of messages are. Many assumptions about effective communication come from such research, which includes attention research, eye movement, memorability, comprehension and persuasion shift research. This kind of research deals with the most effective use of colour, layouts, typeface, sound effects, use of techniques of suspense and tension. Creatives are told that the first thing readers are supposed to look at is the picture, then the headline, and then the bottom right-hand corner to see who the ad is for. Emboldened quotes, captions, drawings, graphs and charts all attract the eye. When constructing a page, creatives traditionally designed the ad to gain attention and impact by following eye movements from top left to bottom right. Creatives also work on the fact that the average reader spends around 1.5 seconds on most newspaper and magazine advertisements (Crompton 1987: 62).

According to research from the USA, the average US child will have seen around 350,000 commercials by the age of 18 (Law 1994: 28). Research has also suggested that of the 1,500 opportunities to see advertisements that people have each day, only between seven and ten are remembered by a consumer. Advertisers try to increase opportunities to see (using a selection of media, PR, sponsorship), to grab the attention and raise the awareness of the reader; to stand out against editorial matter, against competitors in their own market, and against all the other advertising messages from many other different markets that the target consumer has the opportunity to see. This is in addition to trying to break down the defences of the consumer. Creatives also use psychological research findings from planners to inform creative work. In an article in *Admap* Judie Lannon pointed to research from the British Association which showed that 'young children will eat all manner of foods like spinach and broccoli, providing the authority behind them is someone they admire rather than mother' (Lannon 1993: 19).

The creative target

At the creative briefing stage, the planner gives the creative person information about the aims and objectives of the advertising (such as stimulating trial, reminding or reassuring), whom the ads are aimed at, a breakdown of the targets and their demographic or lifestyle patterns and attitudes. Who uses the brand? Who buys it? Who influences the purchasing decision (parents, friends, scientists, doctors, dentists, pharmacists and hairdressers)? The 'desired' consumer response, or the preferred reading of the text, may include an immediate response: 'a credit card is really handy in emergencies', followed up with 'I need one that is reliable and can be used abroad', 'Barclaycard is widely accepted' or 'I'll go to the bank tomorrow'. Statements and detail of the competitors' work are also outlined, and a phrase pointing to the main proposition of the ad: 'Carlsberg. Probably the best lager in the world'. The briefing also includes a rational reason for buying the product such as providing information on the benefits of using it, and an emotional reason, possibly to do with family or status which involves a role for the brand such as bringing people together. The form and style of the advertising, such as a challenge, demonstration, image or atmosphere or lifestyle, also has to be considered.

The first thing that creatives have to know is how much time they have to make the commercials, the commercials' time length: 10, 15, 30 or 60 seconds, where the commercials will appear (which slots), which magazines and newspapers and the sizes and shapes of ads. The creatives should also familiarise themselves with the editorial environment in which their ads will appear. They may want to stand out from a particular environment or feature somebody who would work best with a specific magazine. The ad may run in a section appropriate to the product market (car section, fashion, beauty). The date the ad will appear is also important: if it is two days before Valentine's Day or Easter or Bonfire night, it might mean a special anniversary for the target consumers; or it might be timed to coincide with an exhibition for the target consumers. Though these may all be important factors, very often ads are created to run for longer periods than the immediate booking time. It may not always be appropriate to tailor the ad to a specific environment.

The creative person then uses information and research people to find out as much as possible about the product: details of how it works, previous ad campaigns, who the competitors are, what campaigns they have run, what the Unique Selling Proposition is: whether it is the biggest, smallest, slimmest, widest, cheapest, most expensive, the same as all the other products. Most importantly, how is the product used, and what do people use it for? What is the purpose of its use, what is the ultimate objective (the satisfaction) that consumers who may use this product are looking for? What are the most desirable brand values and image that differentiate it from others on the market? Account planners and creatives develop a brand personality which is intended first to differentiate it from other brands on the market and second to attach attributes that the target consumers find appealing and desirable. If designing a lifestyle ad, the lifestyles, values and attitudes of the target market are important.

Some creatives use the findings of qualitative research to look for the language and imagery used by the target market. The creative target is the fourth main target in the marketing process: this is a much tighter definition of the target market. Some creatives try to narrow the field even further by constructing a mythic individual to personalise the evidence provided by the researchers. Creatives try to get closer to the consumers to understand the way they supposedly think, their loves, hates, prejudices and aspirations. They construct 'typical' consumers, such as a 'typical' coalminer's housewife: 'she has always voted Labour, believes in capital punishment, and thinks multinational firms are manipulating the world; likes reading romances, does the pools regularly, and watches *Coronation Street* every week' (White 1988: 65).

Modes of address

Two basic modes of address are the direct address – talking directly to you the consumer – and the indirect address, in which the consumer eavesdrops either on a conversation in a TV commercial or on a print image of a slice-of-life advertisement. Direct address often takes the form of a presenter or personality (testimonial) talking directly to you, like a salesperson. You are positioned as the potential sales customer, either in the shop or about to use the service, and the advertisement tries to place you in the right frame of mind for the sale.

Indirect address includes monologue and dialogue. A monologue does not address the consumer directly but usually represents the thoughts of a person in the ad. In the Werther's Original ad, grandad sits on the chair and reminisces in a voice-over, 'I remember when my grandfather gave me my first Werther's Original . . .'. You are invited to eavesdrop on his private thoughts; although you are not mentioned, you are brought into the story as privileged observer. The person delivering the testimonial monologue often appears in the commercial as a personality, an expert, or an 'average' consumer (Leech 1966: 45–46). Celebrities endorsing a product are supposed to sign a form saying that they actually do prefer it, before the ad can pass the ITC, though there are probably numerous cases where they don't. In a dialogue situation, the activities in the commercial or the print ad are taken from 'real life' (Oxo, Nescafé Gold Blend). Indirect address can also be without dialogue, but with a sound track over it, such as the Levi's ads, or Wrigley's gum.

The common denominator is direct address. Pure indirect address advertising, which focuses only on an event, or sets of images, is very rare. The Daz commercials with Julian Clary move from indirect dialogue (Julian interviewing a 'typical housewife'), to Julian Clary talking to you ('So there you have it, Daz really does . . .'). All ads need to talk directly to the consumer, even the 'indirect' slice of life ones; there is usually a narrator, or actor's voice and/or a piece of text with the slogan and brand which delivers the endline to the consumer. Though this may not often say 'buy X' or 'get Y' the intervention of the actor's voice at the end anchors the meaning of the text and relates the story directly to the consumer. Endlines are often spoken and accompanied by text on the film (also called 'supers') to add emphasis, as well as the pack shot and/or logo. Indirect commercials have to use an endline, to bring the viewer into the advertisement. Because advertisers are struggling to stand out amid all of the information clutter, direct advertising demands your attention, involving you in the ad. When someone says, 'Hey you!', you cannot avert your attention. So, when Julian Clary turns to camera and says, 'So there you have it . . .', you are now involved in the ad; previously you were merely a spectator watching an incident. This is a basic method of sales technique.

People are supposed to be much more susceptible once their attention has been raised and a dialogue established.

Because mass communications involves one medium talking to many people, and advertisers need to talk to people individually, advertisers employ the beliefs, prejudices, fears and anxieties of the group to which you are supposed to belong. Hailing the consumer involves recognising the language, classifications and metaphors of the 'target' or positioned group of consumers. Rather than describe the working of the internal combustion engine, the wheels, interior and metal surround, we simply say car; to describe different categories of car we talk about sports, saloons, hatchbacks; and to talk of different features we can say fuel injection, turbo, catalytic converters. As our classifications get more specific we close meanings off to more people. Often the commercial may use language that speaks only to people who are meant to understand, such as the Audi commercials which include references to Sigmund Freud and Coco Chanel.

Metaphors and stereotypes

Metaphors are the common denominators of advertising. 'The skill of the agency ... lies in doing two things: finding a metaphor that is appropriate for the brand; and ensuring that the metaphor means what it is intended to mean to buyers' (Ring 1993: 160). One of the reasons why advertisers use metaphors, apart from the fact that it is an easier method of quick communication, is that we use and understand metaphors in everyday language. Metaphors are part of our everyday speech. We 'chew over' and 'iron out' problems. Metaphors also work by bestowing meanings on goods. In this culture, sending red roses to somebody on Valentine's Day can mean only one thing. At some point red roses came to mean love and passion. Once this was established, advertisers could play upon the metaphor.

Advertisers also try to establish their products and brands as metaphors. A high-performance car can become a metaphor for success. Advertisers try to make their brands omnipotent. In doing so advertisers try not only to attach meanings to the brands, but to attach brands to meanings, so that when you think of softness and strength, you think Andrex, when you think sex you think Häagen Dazs ice cream, and when you think sunshine you think Kellogg's corn flakes. Advertisers want to get consumers to think in these metaphorical ways, to think in images and pictures in which their brands play a leading role (Williamson 1978: 9–14). Williamson argues that the association of the product with the cultural references causes a transfer in meanings and that the cultural reference becomes the product. Love and sharing mean Rolos rather than Rolos mean love and sharing. The problem is that with all of these brands competing for metaphorical status, many things come to mean love, power, status and passion.

Metaphors work by transferring the feelings, emotions and images from one set of objects, such as things that go fast (trains and weapons), and adding them to, for instance, fast food chains, Pizza Express and Chicken Bazooka. Or they work by associating certain objects with the brand: milk chocolate and silk and bread 'morphing' into a wooden log in a lozenge commercial. Advertisers place different things together to suggest that a connection exists. It is not obvious that Roses chocolates should be given to someone in gratitude.

Saying 'Thank you' with Roses chocolates is an attribute added to the brand. The same could be said for Lucozade, which repositioned its added values in the mid-1980s from a drink to revive the sick to an energy-provider for athletes and club ravers. Associating qualities and settings with products and services is the oldest metaphorical device: ads for nuclear energy, petrol and cars tie in with the countryside and the environment; shampoo ads such as Timotei, with a woman washing her hair in a stream, tie in with natural herb extracts.

Often advertisers will create puzzles and metaphors that people will recognise, and the joke will be that we understand it but others do not; it reinforces social cohesion. A TV ad for Carling Black Label shows an English tourist beating a group of German tourists to the sunbeds by throwing his Union Jack towel down to the swimming pool; after bouncing on the water a couple of times the towel unfolds on a sunbed, beating the clutch of German holidaymakers who are running to the pool. This ad plays on a number of metaphors which English people are meant to share in a common bonding. The most obvious is the holidaying myth that German tourists always get up early to claim the sunbeds around the hotel pool. This has been a popular anti-German joke in Britain for some time. Second there is a metaphor about British war films, specifically the bouncing bomb (dambusters), and third there is a reference to a previous commercial by Carling Black Label which copied the war film and had two well-known comedians in an aeroplane dropping bouncing bombs and a German sentry parrying the bombs like a goalkeeper (references to the 1966 World Cup final). At the same time music from the film *The Dambusters* played in the background.

These metaphors and cross-references are meant to indulge viewers around consensual values, to make them share in a communality, a shared understanding of the meanings.

Analogies are sometimes used when the message cannot be realistically portrayed. One ad which appeared in the UK was a hammer going through a peach, which was trying to represent what a car hitting a child is like.

Advertisers who use people in advertisements often face problems with the interpretations of meaning by different groups in society. Our understanding of human categories of gender, ethnicity, age, class and sexuality makes it more difficult for the advertiser to convey a simple linear message to the viewer. An advertiser could not simply grab any teenager off the street to be in a jeans commercial, because the person would have to conform to certain sets of meanings and metaphors that would not alienate, put off or offend sections of the target audience. The meanings we attach to each other are overdetermined, they overlap. Gender, ethnicity, religion, class, education, hobbies, age and sexuality may all contribute to our identities. All these elements contribute to the construction of our identities and carry complex cultural meanings. Representations of people convey many more meanings than objects, animals or pets because people are much more culturally overdetermined. Advertisers, especially mass market advertisers, get round the problem by avoiding including people altogether. They often include animals instead, for instance PG Tips and Pepsi use chimpanzees, Sunkist used an orang-utan, Andrex use the puppy, and Esso a tiger. Guinness also excluded people from their ads from the 1930s to the 1950s (Schudson 1993: 213–214).

Metonymy involves the substitution of an aspect of a product, thing or person for the thing itself, such as crown representing the Queen. To say, in trying to establish the brand, 'The *Sunday Times* is the Sunday Papers' is a form of metonymy, trying to get the brand to stand for and represent the entire product group. Metonymic ads often feature a specific product attribute: Benson & Hedges the gold cigarette box, Silk Cut the use of purple, Marlboro the use of red, Cadbury the use of purple for the wrapper, Body Shop the use of green, McDonald's red and gold.

In 1993 Marlboro ran an advertising campaign which showed black and white pictures of the American West but with red for different symbols of America, such as Harley Davidson bikes, and the lights on an American police car. The ads were playing on two sets of metaphors: first metaphors that we in Britain are familiar with from US films and TV series, and second the metaphor of Marlboro cigarettes being represented simply by the colour red. There was no reference whatsoever to the brand, apart from the government health warning at the bottom which was intended to give the reader an indication of the product area. The reader was left to deduce that this was a cigarette ad, and that the most familiar brand on the market for cigarettes associated with red is Marlboro. The other connections with America, part of the global campaign (with cowboy, etc.), were also meant to resonate with the readers. The main aim of the campaign was to appeal to existing users of Marlboro, who would make the connections with the brand more easily than others.

When a creative director chooses a personality or an actor for a commercial or a photograph, they are chosen to best match the brand, or the message as it arises. The part stands for the whole, some signs stand for authority, others for pleasure. A particular pen may stand for a certain type of person, clothes also stand for the type of job. The creative has to calculate whether the meanings surrounding that person, hair colour, eyes lips, body shape and size are appropriate for the market the ad is aimed at, or whether it may alienate some consumers; or if the extra meanings of a familiar face or personality are also appropriate. For example Jack Dee's age, sex and appearance were judged to fit with the brand for the John Smith's commercial, as his image was as a sarcastic, cynical comedian. A feminist comedian like Jo Brand might not have worked with this brand. Stars no longer have to endorse a brand: they have only to appear with it or use it to help create meaning.

Stereotypes that we construct about other people, places and cultures are convenient ways of understanding things which we are distant or remote from. When advertisers use stereotypes, they are using our shorthand notions of what people and places are in order to communicate. Mothers are always strong metaphors for homeliness, warmth and strength, and are usually worldly-wise (an important part of self-image: look at the Oxo Mum, where mother knows best). They are always positioned as practical and knowledgeable; this helps to reinforce their role in the domestic sphere and also to establish them as the centre or the heart of familial relations. Just as advertisers stereotype people, so they also stereotype settings, such as people's homes and workplaces – for example a Levi's ad set in a garage where a mechanic is sweating carrying a tyre. Each object must fit in with the stereotype and use elements of the setting which we can all understand (all of us who are not mechanics, in this case). Our culture is composed of thousands of stereotypes and metaphors: the advertiser selects those which will anchor the meaning of the texts. Stereotyping is a convenient and inadequate way of understanding. Unlike the original definition of stereotyping, however, it is not permanently fixed. Stereotypes do change over time.

There is a gap between the world of commodities, products, industry and commerce, and the world of real-life consumption. However, as Davidson (1991: 28) points out, 'Advertising bridges the gap; it communicates not just an airline, but global mobility; not an anti-perspirant, but a release from the anxieties of body odour. This is the source of that particular breed of corporate speak that IBM uses when they sell us "not computers but solutions". This is a continuation of a traditional advertising dictum; "sell the sizzle, not the steak" – selling feelings, emotions and cultural values, rather than simply the product – is carried on in many areas of advertising. Though the original dictum may be true of some brands, most advertisers try to "sell the steak and the sizzle".' This is largely because the added cultural meanings are not fixed and are much more highly contested and constantly changing. It was selling the cultural meanings over and above the product which was seen as a primary problem of lifestyle advertising in the 1980s.

Examples

Coca-Cola

As the market for soft drinks in the USA started to mature, Coca-Cola changed its advertising sales messages from reason-why to atmosphere. By 1916 it was running full-colour posters with two women (one with a tennis racket, the other with golf clubs), drinking Coca-Cola, lots of white space and little copy (Prendergrast 1993: 148). By the 1920s Coke had to reposition to try to target the take-home market. It also tried to encourage consumers to drink Coca-Cola in the winter months, with the 1922 slogan 'Thirst knows no season' (ibid.). Ads from December to February used this slogan and portrayed the drink in snow scenes. The unique selling personality of the brand was pleasure and enjoyment, consumed by good-looking, contented and active people.

Oxo

In 1959 Oxo launched a new TV campaign featuring a 'housewife' called Katie. The intention was to shift attitudes towards the brand to get rid of the view following the war that Oxo was a cheap and poor substitute for beef stock. The campaign had given it a more modern feel as well as associating it with aspirational groups (Katie's husband wore a tie and was constructed as a bank clerk). The packaging change had also played a role: Oxo was available in tins before then, and the new individual foil-wrapped packaging stressed convenience and freshness. The ads were primarily lifestyle commercials intended to reflect the kind of people who use Oxo, rather than the product itself: the persuasion was implicit, rather than explicit.

Nike

In 1992 Nike ran an ad campaign on TV for its brand, with Arsenal striker Ian Wright performing on the field with slow-motion action shots and a popular song 'Can you kick it' playing over the top. The ad not only associated the brand with him as a top-class footballer but also played on racial stereotypes of black men as 'cool', stylish and athletic: associating black American soul and street music with a black British footballer helped to reinforce the racial stereotype that all black men share the same characteristics. The meanings associated with the brand are meant to associate with those meanings – not Ian Wright's footballing prowess but the extra meanings that Ian Wright stands for: black, cool, stylish, masculine and desirable. The ad managed to select-out those metaphors of black masculinity and football which would be most usefully associated with the brand. The ad also shows him being successful on the field, conveying obvious messages about success, competitions and winning.

Summary

The persuasiveness of advertising became an issue only when markets became saturated in the 1920s and advertisers wanted to know why sales did not increase. Agencies began to develop theories of advertising persuasiveness to provide a rational basis for creative treatment. Though they all have a different focus, all the theories attempt to differentiate the brand. The Unique Selling Proposition differentiates through a unique feature of the product (packaging, shape, smell, taste), brand image through the distinct emotional values of the brand; and lifestyle, which takes its cue from the marketing concept, focuses on distinct lifestyles of its consumers. Though these approaches claim to be distinct, in reality advertisers often mix appeals. Creatives employ industry folklore and past research when determining the style, design and content of ads. Creatives use familiar metaphors to target consumers, which can deliberately include or exclude certain groups. Most creative treatments try to involve consumers in the ad by hailing them with a direct mode of address.

Bibliography

Beatson, R. (1986) 'Address by the Director General of European Association of Advertising Agencies', *International Journal of Advertising*, vol. 5, pp. 261–266

Bradshaw, P. V. (1927) *Art in Advertising*, London: The Press Art School

Cowley, D. (ed.), (1989) *How to Plan Advertising*, London: Cassell in Association with the Account Planning Group

Crompton, A. (1987) *The Craft of Copywriting*, London: Century Business

Davidson, M. (1991) *The Consumerist Manifesto*, London: Routledge

Lannon, J. (1993) 'Branding Essentials and the New Environment', *Admap*, June, vol. 28, no. 6, issue 330

Law, A. (1994) 'How to Ride the Wave of Change', *Admap*, January, vol. 29, no. 1, issue 336

Leech, G. N. (1966) *English in Advertising: A Linguistic Study of Advertising in Great Britain*, London: Longmans

Leiss, W., Kline, S. and Jhally, S. (1990) *Social Communication in Advertising*, 2nd edn, London: Routledge

Ogilvy, D. (1983) *Ogilvy on Advertising*, London: Pan Books

Prendergrast, M. (1993) *For God, Country and Coca-Cola*, London: Weidenfeld & Nicolson

Reeves, R. (1961) *Reality in Advertising*, London: Macgibbon & Kee

Ring, J. (1993) *Advertising on Trial*, London: Financial Times Pitman Publishing

Schudson, M. (1993) *Advertising: The Uneasy Persuasion*, London: Routledge

Tuck, M. (1976) *How Do We Choose?*, London: Methuen

White, R. (1988) *Advertising: What It is and How To Do It*, London: McGraw-Hill Advertising Association
Williamson, J. (1978) *Decoding Advertisements: Ideology and Meaning in Advertising*, London: Marion Boyars

Part 11

AGAINST ADVERTISING

86

THE ADVERTISING
INDUSTRY

E. Clark

Source: E. Clark, *The Want Makers: Lifting the Lid off the World Advertising Industry*, London: Hodder & Stoughton, 1988, pp. 23–58.

'If I were starting my life over again, I am inclined to think I would go into the advertising business in preference to almost any other.'

President Franklin D. Roosevelt

In the spring of 1986 Pepsi-Cola concluded what by any standards was an extraordinary business deal. The company agreed to pay the twenty-seven-year-old pop singer Michael Jackson nearly $15 million to appear in two of its television commercials and to provide creative consultancy on a third. For 180 seconds of screen time, plus the advice, Jackson was to earn five times as much as Marlon Brando could command for a full-length movie. Furthermore, Jackson would not be shown holding, let alone drinking, Pepsi. It is widely known that, as a Jehovah's Witness, he would never touch a drop of the product.

The $15 million was just a starter. Production added something over another $2 million a commercial (nearly twice as much as it cost to make the award-winning *My Beautiful Laundrette* and almost three times as much as the equally highly acclaimed *Letter to Brezhnev*). Then there was the cost of television time, perhaps another $50 million worldwide. In total, over $65 million. All to sell a carbonated soft drink that, whatever its merits, millions of its customers probably cannot tell from rival colas but for the name on the bottle.

But *that*, in fact, was the point. Pepsi-Cola, like its arch rival Coca-Cola, is primarily its image. It is what millions of customers *think* it is, or what they associate it with. There may be little that is rational about it (although the decision to spend that kind of money is made on very logical grounds: the carbonated soft drink market is worth an estimated

259

$65 *billion*), but the decision to buy something or to choose 'A' rather than 'B' is rarely made on grounds of reason. That, in itself, is not new. Anyone selling anything has known, and acted upon it, since the first sale. What is new is that advertising has now moved on from being the creator of the image that *helps* sell the product. Today, advertising *is* the product. What people are buying, whether it's drink, jeans, medicines, or electronic gadgets, is the perception of the product they have absorbed from advertising and it is that perception that can make the difference between success and failure in the market place.

Mike Detsiny is managing director of The Creative Business, a London advertising agency, and former group marketing director for Allied Breweries where he had four lagers under his control. He says, 'The many competitive brands are virtually identical in terms of taste, colour and alcohol delivery, and after two or three pints even an expert couldn't tell them apart. *So the consumer is literally drinking the advertising, and the advertising is the brand.*' (My italics.)

Such an approach extends beyond products between which there is little or no real difference. Often, even where such differences exist, it is better to sell the image. The reason for this is simple: the product can easily lose its real edge if a competitor comes up with something better; it cannot lose its image because it is not dependent on any actuality.

Dr Stuart Agres, director of strategic planning at Marschalk, New York, explained, 'With rapid technological advances in manufacturing methods, a product doesn't hold its advantage for very long. Any product advantage can be ripped off very quickly. If you sell purely on rational needs, the next manufacturer can not only duplicate those factors, but can make a feature of one upmanship. In the fifties and sixties detergents got clothes white. Then it was white and bright. Then it was white, bright and fresh. Then it was white, bright, fresh and soft . . .'

Today's advertiser tries to make his product timeless in its appeal. Scotch Videotape, from 3M, the $8.5 billion US conglomerate, provides a striking example. With a booming video recorder market in the UK, a number of major brands battle for tape sales. They would all like to be able to say that their tape has a quality not found elsewhere.

Wight Collins Rutherford Scott, the agency given the task of advertising Scotch Videotape, found that the tape could re-record more than 500 times without losing picture quality. There was, however, a slight problem. All quality tapes can do the same thing. In the agency's own words, 'the risk with this proposition was obvious – it wasn't unique. Competitors could easily upstage us'. 3M also had a policy of replacing all tapes with no quibbles, but so too did many of its competitors. The agency's solution: give the tape a lifetime guarantee, illustrating it with ads that showed a 'cuddly and nice' skeleton called Archie still using the same tape he bought back in the 1980s. Thus consumers gained the *feeling* that Scotch offered something no other manufacturer did. As the case history went on to point out, the beauty of the advertising was that once customers were aware of Scotch's message, 'Any competitive activity would only enhance the position as the first, the original and the best'. Scotch quickly spent £1.9 million to get over its new message. It succeeded spectacularly. Within two months of the launch the tape became the brand leader.

3M's advertising was fun to watch, often a sign that what is being sold hasn't very much special to offer. 'A lot of the more entertaining advertising is produced for products that don't have any particularly distinguishing characteristics,' said John Salmon, chairman of Collett Dickenson Pearce, a London agency. It handles Heineken beer, where the tongue-in-cheek advertising has a theme that the beer 'refreshes the parts other beers cannot reach'. It is, says Salmon, 'based on the idea of Heineken being unusually refreshing. There is no basis for this. It is just as refreshing as any other lager.'

Advertisers have long sought to attach special auras to brands, thus giving them an added undefinable value. Charles Revson, founder of Revlon, is often quoted as saying, 'In the laboratory I make cosmetics, in the store I sell dreams'. Products that are mundane and prosaic may become imbued with colour, glamour, imagery: a sweet carbonated British drink made out of apples (Babycham) turns girls into Cinderella at the ball; chocolate mints (After Eights), mass produced and cheap enough for children to buy with their pocket-money, speak volumes of luxury.

Advertising men call it 'the brand property'. Barry Day, vice-chairman of McCann-Erickson Worldwide, defines it as the element that is 'unique, memorable and indissolubly linked to that brand and no other'. The 'brand property', he says, 'lies not in what the product *is* but what it does and what the advertising suggests'. Thus Martini's 'brand property' is the teen and twenties fantasy world created in its slick, jet-set commercials. Coca-Cola's starts with the bottle shape; the basic feeling of the advertising conveys that this is *the* American soft drink.

The brand image may be priceless. Carl Hixon, a consultant, formerly of the agency Leo Burnett in Chicago, told a conference of a fantasy he has in which he asks to buy the Philip Morris Company and is told the price is $850 million. He then makes an offer to buy one part of the Morris empire, the rights to manufacture his own cigarette with the name Marlboro and to use a cowboy to market the brand. This time the price is $45 billion! When Ronson, a company famous for cigarette lighters, shavers and electrical products, collapsed, its name was acquired by others who then licensed it to manufacturers of various products. One was a cigarette; 'Ronson has fantastic recognition as a brand name,' said the cigarette company's managing director. In the United States, Fruit of the Loom and Stetson are two companies that do not make anything. They allow the use of their image-laden names in return for royalty payments. In such a way products are endowed with some *apparent* difference.

Keeping brands thriving has always meant constant modification: in the thirty years after it was launched Tide soap powder received fifty-five significant changes. But today, when a brand *is* its advertising, modifications are frequently made not so much to content but to image.

In 1983, Guinness, probably the world's most famous brewery name, had problems, not the corporate difficulties that were to erupt later but the more specific ones of the famous drink itself. Although the dark stout was still selling 7 million glasses a day in 140 countries, its sales had been falling for a decade. Some felt that Guinness's problem was very simple: the drink was out of date in an age of lighter or less potent tasting drinks. As one trade magazine, *Drinks Marketing*, put it, 'The cynics still claim that the famous stout, which has been brewed for some 220 years, has been overtaken by changes in consumer taste and should be allowed to die gracefully.'

That, of course, is all right unless you own the brewery. What Guinness did, with the aid of psychological research, was to mount a new campaign to try to change the image from something drunk by old ladies in stale-smelling bars to a drink fit for macho young men. The commercials, playlets revolving around the word 'Guinnless' (someone who hasn't had a Guinness) were hardly the stuff of Oscars, but the decline was halted and sales actually began to rise. The product was the same; the image was different.

Cars have always had image as an important selling ingredient but real differences have also been stressed. According to automobile marketing men, those differences are vanishing because of global sharing of technology and management techniques. The National Automobile Dealers' Association meeting in Las Vegas in 1987 were told by one expert, 'The quality difference is closing, and in another five years all [car makers] will have to be over the threshold of world-class value in order to compete.' Product quality was thus ceasing to provide a major, real difference. The expert's advice to the executives, therefore, was 'spend time creating an image that will carry you through the 1990s'.

This and other factors – such as a deluge of new products and the need to open new markets as ones at home become saturated – make advertising one of the great growth industries of our time. To build demand for a product, the amount spent on advertising may equal the anticipated income from sales. Seemingly ridiculous sums are spent to develop markets for tomorrow – Victor Kiam (the entrepreneur who so liked the razor he bought the company) ploughed $4 million into his advertising in Germany in 1984, twice as much as the total sales revenues of the previous year. All this means more, and even more skilled, advertising. This, in turn, requires vast sums of money and an enormous amount of talent. Advertising can call on both in abundance: for money from the product and service suppliers; for talent from the agency men, the professional persuaders.

Advertising is an expensive business. Between them the rival soap powder giants Procter and Gamble and Lever Brothers spend nearly £80 million a year in the UK alone battling to convince us to use their products. Pedigree spent over £30 million persuading us to feed our pets with its brands, Imperial Tobacco over £25 million encouraging us to smoke Embassy and John Player rather than Silk Cut or Senior Service.[1]

In America, with its bigger market-place, figures are even more startling. General Motors and Ford spend nearly $1.4 billion each year in their advertising battles, Pepsi and Coke over $860 million in theirs. McDonald's earmarks $550 million to advertise its hamburgers, and Anheuser-Busch just a little less to promote its beers.[1]

The money spent on actually *making* the advertisements may seem small compared with such astronomic figures, but it is hardly small change. Set beside the money, time, energy and talent that goes into the thirty-second commercial, most major feature films pale in comparison. 'By screen time per pound commercials' productions on the whole still make *Heaven's Gate* look positively cheapskate,' declared Alan Parker, who turned from making commercials to such films as *Midnight Express* and *Fame*.

British Airways' Manhattan Landing commercial – in which a symbolised New York flies – is reputed to have cost £600,000 to make. The Apple 1984 commercial, from Chiat/Day, cost $500,000 and (at the time of writing) has been shown only once. A Diet Coke commercial shot at Radio City Music Hall was reputed to have cost $1.5 million. In the UK, a 1986 Barclays Bank commercial from the trendy advertising agency, Yellowhammer, cost a reported £750,000.

All of this makes commercials far and away the most expensive items on film. Figures quoted by Miner Raymond, a consultant, showed that at the time that an average TV feature film was costing $90,000 an *hour*, the average 30-second commercial was costing $140,000 a *minute*. By 1985 the average cost of producing an American TV commercial was $200,000. In Britain, it was widely accepted to be 'only' £50,000. Mike Townsin, media director of Young and Rubicam, London, estimated it could cost as much to make one commercial as the commercial television companies were spending on ninety minutes of programmes. 'If they spent money at the same rate we really would have the best television in the world.' It is little wonder that directors like making commercials and that the medium has attracted a host of famous names from Joseph Losey to Federico Fellini. It is not just the fees, but the opportunity it allows for achieving perfection, albeit in a small – some would say trivial – world.

Soaring costs are a perennial source of conversation among clients who swap horror stories with all the morbid curiosity of hospital patients exchanging details of their operations. Miner Raymond tells of an art director who rejected a dining-room table scheduled to be used in a commercial.

Reminded that the table would be covered by a cloth, he responded, 'But *I* would know what's under the cloth and it wouldn't be right.' Anne Birnhak, an English woman who models her hands, tells of a two-day shoot (at £35 an hour) for Marigold rubber gloves. 'I wore the gloves for the entire two days. They might as well have used a gorilla.'

To the ad maker, though, it's all – or mostly all – necessary. Peter Levelle, head of television at the London agency Collett Dickenson Pearce, said:

> Everything has to be perfect. In a feature film you might have a scene of two men talking in a bar over a glass of beer. If you turn that glass of beer into a product the approach is different. What does the beer look like? Is it being shown to its best advantage? Is it the right colour and is there the right amount of head on it? Does it look fresh? It must be the perfectly pulled pint.

If, as the cliché claims, genius is the capacity for taking infinite pains, then the making of a commercial must surely be such an act. Take just two examples. The commercials for Heineken lager have become an English institution. With the aid of a glass of Heineken miraculous things happen. In one commercial Heineken makes it possible for Wordsworth to write the poem 'Daffodils' after several earlier attempts fail. The finished film shows the poet surrounded by daffodils. There are, in fact, 6,000 of them, and they were all shipped from London to the Lake District in two pantechnicons and planted on the hillsides especially for the film. Or take a French commercial designed to sell HOM sportswear. In this ad a helicopter flies over Greenland. A man strips and leaps from it, clad only in his briefs, hitting the water between the towering ice floes. He swims to a dinghy, clambers inside, the camera goes into close-up on his face and the words 'Sportswear HOM' come onto the screen, the first indication of the product. Many things are possible in film, but it does not look faked. I sat beside Jacques Séguéla, whose Paris agency made the commercial, at a presentation he was giving to fellow advertising men from all over the world. 'Did he actually do that, Jacques?' whispered a fellow adman as the film faded. 'Yes, he risked his life.' Later, on the rostrum, Séguéla reiterated the point: 'For the first time in the history of advertising a man risked his life to promote a product,' he proclaimed.

The ingenuity and effort that does go into ads is truly awesome. Cars are shipped from the UK to Canada to recreate scenes meant to depict winter in Yorkshire; Bordeaux, France, is combed in the search for just the right wine cellar in which to photograph a wine box (this one was finally shot in Britain after the searches were regarded as having failed); innumerable commercials are photographed in Venice or the Greek Islands or the Bahamas to get just the 'right light'. In an attempt to film wolves baying at the moon for a British cigarette commercial, a film crew camped out for three weeks in a heavy duty wire mesh 'hide' in a Scottish wildlife park that held six Canadian wolves. (That attempt also failed. The scene was finally shot in Slough, using 'pet' wolves belonging to the wife of a stockbroker; sky shots were done separately; everything was then reassembled in the studio.)

For those who believe with Raymond Chandler that advertising is the great waster of human talent, the shooting of the Renault Alliance commercial for Grey Advertising, New York, must rank as a classic.[2] It is impossible not to be impressed with the logistics of the operation. The final film showed New York's Park Avenue with cars flooding out from cross streets, leaving Park Avenue deserted but for 300 cars, each of them a Renault Alliance.

As a first stage in putting together the commercial the agency and the production company plotted cars on a model of the avenue. It was decided that thirty cars would be enough to achieve the effect: the thirty could be turned into 300 in the processing room afterwards. The city of New York was then approached and permission was given for four blocks of Park Avenue and all the side streets off to be closed for ten-minute shooting intervals between 10 a.m. and 3 p.m. for three days. Scaffolding, for a camera, was erected at the junction of park Avenue and 92nd Street; a guard was mounted to make sure it wasn't moved. Precision drivers were recruited in California and flown in from the West Coast. Parking was found for the thirty cars (and six spares) and they were then wrapped in plastic and also placed under guard. During the actual shooting, drivers, directors and the cameraman kept in contact through walkie-talkies. The cars had to be driven at exactly the same speed as each other so that the film could later be doctored to give the effect of 300 vehicles. People living and working in Park Avenue were asked not to use their front entrances; other people were asked not to walk across the street.

The number of companies that can provide the money for such extravanganzas is comparatively small. Although vast numbers of companies advertise, just a few industries and some individual corporations dominate, often across the world. A breakdown of the top 100 advertisers in the US in 1985 shows that ten groups spent over $1 billion: the automobile industry, food, alcohol, confectionery and soft drinks, drugs and remedies, entertainment and amusements, retail, toiletries and cosmetics, travel and hotels and resorts, and business services.

Throughout the world kinds of advertisers and even specific names are remarkably constant. Eighty-seven of America's largest 100 advertisers are multinationals. The main advertisers in Australia include Unilever and Philip Morris; in Brazil, BAT and Ford; in Canada, the Government and Procter and Gamble; in France, IBM and Renault; in Japan, Toyota and Matsushita; in Germany, Volkswagen, Procter and Gamble and Henkel; in the UK, Procter and Gamble, Mars and Kellogg; in Italy, Fiat and Alfa Romeo.

It is not necessary to be very cynical to conclude after a look through the names of major advertisers and products that the less obvious the need for any item the greater its dependence on advertising. As Norman Goluskin, of the New York agency Smith/Greenland, put it, 'If I discovered a cure for cancer I could say it in a ten-second commercial. If I don't have anything exciting or important to say I have to beat you over the head a few times.'

Traditionally, the big advertisers are the producers of what are known as FMCGs – Fast Moving Consumer Goods, in other words smallish items that frequently have to be rebought such as cigarettes, confectionery, crisps, and soap powder. A dozen of Britain's top twenty advertisers are such companies, top among them Procter and Gamble, Kellogg, Nestlé, Imperial Tobacco, Lever Brothers and Pedigree Petfoods.

However, advertising has spread beyond its historic users. Today the list includes more and more disparate groups. It embraces companies trying to sell political philosophies, unions recruiting workers, Jews persuading the Russians to 'Let my people go', and the beleaguered Austrian wine industry attempting to recapture its markets after the scandal of anti-freeze being found in some wines. The Boy Scouts Association of America uses advertising. So does the Dow Chemical Company to polish an image battered by its manufacture of napalm and the defoliant Agent Orange: in one of that company's advertisements a proud father can barely stifle his tears of happiness when he learns his son is going to work for the company. In its attempt to turn American public opinion against President Reagan's 'Star Wars' plans, the Soviet Union has advertised in the *New York Times*, reproducing a *Pravda* editorial. In spring 1986 Britain's largest union, the Transport and General Workers' Union, became the first in the country to advertise its services on television. Even the BBC in its fight to stave off having to take advertisements to solve its financial problems chose an advertising campaign to proclaim itself 'The finest broadcasting service in the world'.

The range of those advertising their commercial wares has grown to take in not only doctors and lawyers and other professional men to whom advertising was once an anathema, but also those selling cemetery plots and even coffins. The unlikeliest products are given the adman's full treatment. Razor Ribbon, a barbed wire 'designed to inflict maximum injury', from the American Security Fence Corporation, is advertised as being available 'in several attractive colours'.

Companies advertise not only to sell their products but to persuade people how wonderful they are. Shell presents itself as caring of the environment: tough and efficient IBM tries to convince that it also has a human face. Advertising has become an integral part of takeover battles; in one three-month period in 1986 the *Financial Times* carried 100 pages of such ads, compared with three to four pages a year before. Charities, in competition for money just like makers of products, use the same techniques and professionals. The Church of England Children's Society even changed its name to the Children's Society on the advice of its new advertising agency, Yellowhammer, which felt the name was 'a stumbling block – it smacked of the wrong Victorian values'.

Government is a major, and growing, advertiser. The British government's spending in 1986 was over £81 million, ranging from £80,000 spent by the Northern Ireland Department of the Environment to over £6 million for the Department of Health and Social Security. In Britain and France vast sums have been spent selling state-owned industries. In three months in 1986 British Gas put enough into its share-offer campaign (£21 million) to outspend all other advertised brands for the whole of the year. In the United States, government in 1986 spent over $300 million, making it the twenty-ninth largest advertiser. In the three-year period to 1986 spending on advertising by the Spanish government rose from 1.5 billion pesetas to 6 billion pesetas.

Governments urge their citizens not to drink and drive, to use state-owned railways, to buy government bonds, not to use drugs and to help prevent the spread of AIDS. The South Africans, arguing they need to counter 'unfair' media coverage, have run image-improving campaigns in Britain and the United States. One typical ad devoted about a third of its space to a picture of happy and prosperous-looking blacks shopping, the rest to text detailing the 'facts'.

Advertising is attractive to both the government and the agencies. For the government it allows it to project the image it wants. Whether an advertising campaign against heroin use is the best way of spending the money is debatable, but it allows the government to be *seen* caring. As for agencies, there's the money, of course, but even more, it is high profile, and because normal checks as to effectiveness (via extra sales) don't apply, agencies are often allowed their creative heads.

Despite these developments, the world's largest advertiser remains a traditional FMCG company, Procter and Gamble. The scale of its advertising, and its consequent impact throughout the world, is truly awesome. During 1986 it spent $1.4 billion on advertising and promotion in the United States alone. It is also the biggest advertiser in other countries, including Britain.

P & G's main businesses are detergents, dentifrice and diapers and, since the takeovers of Richardson-Vicks and G. D. Searle, it is also America's leading marketer of over-the-counter pharmaceuticals. It markets eighty-three brand name items in thirty-eight product categories in the US and 140 foreign countries. Among them are Camay, Ivory and Zest soaps, Pampers diapers, Head and Shoulders shampoo, Crest toothpaste, Jif peanut butter, Duncan Hines mixes and cookies, Vicks cold remedies and Vidal Sassoon products. Its brand names are so great a part of modern international currency that in Singapore plants have been set up to manufacture and market to Arab countries products with names like Tibe, Tike, Tile and Tipe, all designed to fool buyers into believing that they're getting genuine Tide.

Procter and Gamble recognised the importance of advertising almost from the beginning and in 1913 the company was the US's top advertiser.

It was Harley Procter, the son of one of the co-founders, who brought the first marketing brilliance to the firm. In 1878, after years of experimenting, Procter and Gamble developed a white soap, to be called P & G White Soap. Harley argued that scores of companies were marketing a white soap; what the company's new product needed was a distinctive name, well advertised.

Thomas Barratt, of Pears Soap in Britain, reportedly said, 'Any fool can make soap. It takes a clever man to sell it.' Harley Procter knew how to *sell* soap. The right name came to him as he listened to the minister reading a psalm at the Mount Auburen Episcopal Church one Sunday morning: 'All thy garments smell of myrrh and aloes and cassia, out of the ivory palaces whereby they have made thee glad.'

In the words of *Eyes on Tomorrow*, a company-blessed history: 'There Harley abruptly stopped following the minister's reading. His eyes and thoughts focused on the phrase, "out of the ivory palaces". *Ivory!* Ivory was white and hard and long lasting. The word evoked an image of purity and luxury. Harley left church that Sunday morning excited and exuberant. *Ivory soap!*'

Harley then decided to have the soap analysed for purity and to advertise it as '99 and 44/100ths pure', a slogan still thriving a hundred years later. And much was made of the fact that Ivory Soap floated. Advertising can, without malice, be defined as the art of speaking the part-truth, and Ivory's floating ability is a near-perfect illustration. The reason that it floats is that it contains a lot of air. (The legend is that a workman went to lunch forgetting to switch off the soap stirring-machine.) The customer, it might be argued, is paying for more air, less soap. But he gets a product that pleases him and which is different.

Over the years, other products have followed, and so has the advertising. By the beginning of the eighties, Procter and Gamble was already buying anything from 18,000 to 20,000 thirty-second commercial spots on American TV alone. But Procter and Gamble's influence does not stop there. The wrapping around its messages is as important as the messages themselves and the company also produces 1,000 daytime hours of its own TV each year plus mini-series such as *The Holocaust* and *Marco Polo* that have filled screens throughout the world. In the words of the *Cincinnati Enquirer*, 'For better or worse, Procter and Gamble . . . has spent more money and more time on the air injecting itself into the American consciousness than anyone else'. And because both Procter and Gamble and television are universal, that statement can be applied to a lot of other countries.

By coincidence I experienced such an injection the night before I visited the company. Settled in my room at the Westin – built thanks to a $2.6 million loan from Procter and Gamble, repayments not to start until profits are made – I found myself watching the first part of *A.D.*, starring Ava Gardner and James Mason. At a cost of $30 million, it is the largest advertiser-supported mini-series since television began. This twelve-hour-long series is a part of Procter and Gamble's plan to be a major player in network prime time programming. The following morning the programme attracted good reviews. More crucially it also registered a thirty-two Nielsen share of the audience. Later, analysts explained to me that once again P & G had got things right.

Procter and Gamble makes television programmes for the same reason it does everything else – to sell more of its products in the most cost-efficient way. *A.D.* is (in the words of a trade magazine) 'a lean, expertly tailored marketing machine' for forty-one of the company's brands. The mini-series contains space for eighty-four minutes of commercials. Procter and Gamble takes sixty-eight minutes of that time itself. The analysts explained that it then becomes a matter of simple arithmetic. If Procter and Gamble were advertising on NBC in prime time that week, the average cost would be around $130,000 for each thirty seconds. Because of its enormous clout, P & G would not have to pay this much,[3] but it would have had to hand out considerably more than *these* commercial breaks cost them – below $100,000 each. NBC, however, has guaranteed to rerun *A.D.* within two years. On that occasion, P & G's cost for showing its commercials will really fall.

None of this will be known to the millions of people who will later watch the series abroad. What they will see is a highly professional, handsomely produced, mildly entertaining slice of historical hokum that should help pass a few evenings relatively contentedly but which will certainly not offend, stimulate or excite anyone. It is bland communication out of the *Reader's Digest* school, with all the virtues and vices of such. When Stephen is stoned to death, the only sign on his body of the enormous hail of rocks that we have watched hurled at him is a few discreet spots of blood on his face.[4] It is the world according to the advertising needs and values of the American Midwest.

Procter and Gamble's involvement with programme content is far from new. The company invented the soap opera as a vehicle for its commercials. 'Procter and Gamble virtually built daytime radio for the networks,' wrote Oscar Schisgall in *Eyes on Tomorrow*. 'Women listened while they did their housework. According to the letters they sent, they sometimes wept for the characters. When they went to the grocery stores they remembered what they had heard in commercial messages, and for Procter and Gamble business boomed.'

Procter and Gamble's headquarters lie in Cincinnati, one hour fifty minutes' flying time from New York, and, perhaps appropriately, in the heartland of the United States. The company has been attacked for its arrogance and insularity, praised for its fierce loyalty and dedication to getting everything right. It is said to be so loaded in talent that the overflow, according to Hercules Segalas, an analyst, had in 1982 provided the presidents or chief executive officers of forty-seven major US corporations. Personalities, though, are played down. Gordon Wade, a management and marketing consultant in Cincinnati, said, 'the whole theory is that when people die, the corporation lives on'.

It is also one of the most secretive companies in the world. Reportedly, office managers conduct regular checks to ensure desk drawers are locked. Outside, staff are warned not to talk business in aeroplanes or trains, restaurants, elevators or other public places. The company expects such security to extend to its advertising agencies. When Procter and Gamble parted company with Young and Rubicam, their agency for thirty-four years, four men were sent immediately to the agency's London offices to remove the thousands of papers relating to company business. Fifty packing cases of files, letters, and research documents were taken away in an operation that took most of a day.

The vice-president in charge of the company's advertising is Robert V. Goldstein, and as such one of the most powerful men in the business, his name known wherever there is a major agency or media company. He never worked for anyone other than P & G. He began as a brand assistant (P & G started the practice of what is known as 'brand management' whereby managers take overall responsibility for individual brands just as though they are companies in their own rights), rose steadily and took his present job in 1979.

We met on his forty-ninth birthday. At 8.30 a.m. he was already at work, standing jacketless near his eleventh-storey window against the backdrop of the glaring concrete of the new and not very beautiful Cincinnati. The eleventh floor is high-executive land. The corridor carpet was expensive soft green, the panelling dark wood. The walls were hung with portraits of former chairmen and presidents. Open doors showed executives silently at work in large offices. All of them seemed to have computer consoles. There was one in Goldstein's office, accommodated on a second desk behind his main one. Facing the desks were shelves of memorabilia including photographs of his family – the wife he married when he was twenty-one, and three sons.

A cut-out of the 'Mr Clean' liquid detergent character stood in a corner – the brand was twenty-five years old that year. There was also a framed sign which said, 'The eye will remember what the ear will forget.' Goldstein explained that he heard it spoken by a consumer during a research session: 'It really encapsulates what will make a TV commercial work.'

He was welcoming. I had been told that, like Procter and Gamble itself, there were those who 'hate and fear' him. For several hours he answered my questions courteously, only occasionally showing (controlled) anger when the talk turned to such arguments as advertisers as pre-empters of competition or manipulators of media values.

Procter and Gamble's philosophy about advertising, he said, was very simple:

> If you make a better product for meeting consumer needs you ought to tell them about it. Over the years we have found that the most efficient and effective way to do that is mass advertising for the kind of goods we sell. The average-cost TV commercial in the most expensive part of the day in the United States will deliver a message for under one and a half cents a household. You certainly couldn't mail a letter or postcard for that . . . When you get down to looking at it, it is a very efficient method of selling. If there was a better or cheaper way we would not be advertising.

Nor, despite the vast money and talent employed and the wide use of research techniques, did Goldstein believe that the basic practice had changed much in over 100 years. 'I don't think the advertising creation process is dramatically different from when the first Ivory Soap ad was made in eighteen-something or other. The advertisements today look a lot more glamorous and fitting to our eye. My sense is that if I look at an ad today versus an ad of thirty years ago, it is more pleasing. But that's simply because my eye has changed. It's all relative to what else is going on.' He added later, 'The role of advertising is to sell the product. There is a great variety of ways, but basically only one objective.'

Goldstein pointed out that less than 10 per cent of all new products launched in America are still around three years later. 'If we were so damn smart, we wouldn't have any failures.' Nevertheless, the research backup both for products and for the way to advertise them is staggering. The company claims that to learn what consumers think of products they use and what kind of improvements they seek, it has over 2 million contacts with them every year. The research set-up is one of the world's largest. Goldstein said that he 'figures that if it was a separate company it would be the fifth or sixth largest market research company in the world. We spend a lot of money, an unbelievable amount, which is just plain talking to the consumer. Asking questions and getting answers.' Procter and Gamble has been computerising its data for twenty-five years. 'Obviously we can get a lot more out of the data. I think we can profile them [consumers] more accurately – but I have to say, "More accurately than what?" More than the man in the store where they talk every day? No! More than we could twenty years ago? Yeah – I think it's possible.'

Procter and Gamble works closely, very closely, with its advertising agencies. Goldstein said there is daily contact with all of them. Periodically,

271

agency executives are flown into Cincinnati for conferences that have been likened to 'indoctrination' sessions. All agencies who work for Procter and Gamble know they will have to work within close confines and under constant scrutiny. But, in return, the rewards are very real: big budgets, new product assignments and a rare loyalty. The magazine *Marketing Week* estimated that the *average* tenure of a Procter and Gamble agency was thirty-seven years. Five of P & G's dozen agencies in the US each had over $100 million worth of P & G business in the fiscal year 1985–6: Leo Burnett; Grey; Wells Rich Greene; Saatchi and Saatchi Compton; and (a staggering $197 million) D'Arcy Masius Benton and Bowles.

Goldstein said that in relations with agencies there were 'no holds barred, no secrets'. He detailed a 'typical situation'. 'We agree there's a need [for a new campaign] – say a new product. Say we come up with an idea for a Duncan Hines cookie made out of bananas and oatmeal.' The product is developed and tested (with researchers getting reactions of potential buyers). An advertising strategy is conceived. The agency puts together ads. They are discussed with Procter and Gamble, and also tested on consumers. 'They then come in with the results and say, "These look like the two best." We might pick one.' The product and the advertising are tried out in a test market-place – 'That's a miniature version of the world.' While the product is being evaluated as to how well it sells and how people regard it, so is the advertising: people will be asked whether they remember it, how they react to it. Then, unless it is all a failure, the product – and the advertising – will become national.

Advertising agencies who work on Procter and Gamble business may be very well off financially but they have to face the sneers of their 'creative' brothers. Procter and Gamble style advertising, with its reliance on safety and research testing (such as Day-After Recall where an ad is judged by whether people *remember* it) may help sell products but it is hardly admired. In Procter and Gamble formula ads, women demonstrate cleansers or laundry detergents to neighbours, tell simpering small daughters that washing-up liquids are mild to their hands, and stand-up presenters deliver capsules of advice. Detractors in advertising say it is such ads that give the business some of its odium. It is an area where Goldstein became sensitive, and it is true that the company's advertising has recently become – comparatively – more adventurous. 'We don't have a single style of advertising,' he protested. 'We have advertising that's musical and advertising that's not. We have real people and glamorous celebrities. Advertising that is basically heavily demonstration and advertising that is very cosmetic and selling dreams. That is contrary to public impressions but it is true.' He slipped a video into the machine so we could watch the latest batch of commercials made by different agencies for different brands. In the Pampers ad real women are being recorded by a hidden camera; Wondra has a hard-sell testimonial; Downy has a slice of life (it looks pure Americana but it was made in Germany); Jif has children and singing; Bounce shows towels in a washing machine ('This one I hate but it's hard sell'); Duncan Hines muffins shows close-ups of children eating ('charming'); New Hope shows a woman washing her hair; there are lots of bubbles ('Here we are selling sex appeal and dreams . . .').

At the end, he said, 'The point is fairly evident. There is not one style. If I hired a salesman to sell a product to hundreds of different clients, would you expect him to use the same selling everywhere?'

Procter and Gamble is a jealous client, expecting total loyalty from its agencies. Goldstein volunteered he had 'lost or fired more [agencies] than anyone in the history of the company. Until five years ago the only ones we ever lost had been agencies that went out of business. I have parted company with three in the last five years.'

The reason in each case was that Procter and Gamble saw a conflict of interest with another account its agency was handling. The company line on conflict is a hard one. 'Conflict means *conflict of interest*,' said Goldstein, stressing the last three words hard.

> Do you want a lawyer who represents you also to represent the other party in a lawsuit? Do you want a business adviser who is working with you with long-range-plans information if he is also advising a competitor? I am asking rhetorical questions. I don't think anyone would. Would you want the manager of your buying department to be also the owner of the firm selling materials to you? I would say you wouldn't want those things.

After a spate of big mergers among agencies, Procter and Gamble reassigned millions of dollars' worth of business to avoid conflict but also, according to agency observers, as a sharp reminder to its agencies of its power as the holder of the purse. The company even studied the possibility of buying its own agency, but discounted it. Despite the problems of conflict and management changes as agencies merged and merged again, Procter and Gamble had obviously concluded that there was no substitute for the advertising professionals.

As the English adman David Bernstein has pointed out, it is the ability to create ideas that differentiates the agency from the advertiser. Clients may think they know all about advertising, but at the end of the day it's the people from the agencies who come up with the ideas.

Advertisers and their agencies are staffed by people who could be from different planets. They may need each other, but theirs is rarely a love match. 'The average advertiser,' says Geoffrey Palmer-Moore, who runs a London company that helps clients choose an agency, 'is a pretty sensible, level-headed, commercial-orientated businessman.' Many agency people, in fact, see them as dull, solid and boring. For their part clients regard agencies as strange places staffed by odd characters. 'For many chairmen, the world of advertising is an enigma,' said Michael Cox, marketing director of Matthew Clark, the UK drink distributor. 'Advertising is a necessary evil, an expensive waste, or, alternatively, an opportunity to boost the corporate ego. But if the world of advertising is a mystery, the agencies that create this world are peopled by the bizarrest of creatures pretending to be what they are not.'

Many clients watch the cavorting and the continuous flux of the agency world with bemusement. They stare upon agency births and deaths, acquisitions and mergers, breakaways. Names of companies change and change again. Thus a footnote to an agency listing: 'Pritchard Wood and Erwin Wasey Ruthraef merged to become Wasey Pritchard Wood. Later became Wasey Campbell-Ewald. Then taken over by Lowe Howard-Spink to become Lowe Howard-Spink Campbell-Ewald.' (It has changed again since!) One London agency, circa 1987, boasts the name Still Price Court Twivy D'Souza.

As for individuals, 'The agency world, as we all know, is a world of gypsies,' said Keith Monk, advertising adviser to Nestlé. 'They come and go as quickly as you can change shirts.' Fred Turner, chairman of McDonald's hamburger chain, described advertising and marketing executives in general as 'bullshitters'. In England, Malcolm Parkinson, marketing director of B & Q, the country's leading DIY chain of stores, accused agencies attempting to gain the company's £4.6 million advertising business of 'trying to treat us like hayseeds, up from our offices in Southampton. They think they will bamboozle us with the bright lights.' Agency salaries frequently stun them. John Harvey-Jones, the former head of ICI, was once quoted as saying that he earned less than the chairman of one of his smaller advertising agencies.

Nevertheless, need them they do. The United States has about 10,000 advertising agencies, Japan has nearly 3,000, France 2,500, Brazil 1,400, and the UK just under 1,600. It is a truly global industry. 'I don't think there's a country on earth where there's not an advertising business,' said Robert Jenkins, a much-travelled advertising man now with his own agency in London. 'Even in places like Papua, New Guinea, there are advertising agencies.'

If there is business of any size, the international agencies will be there too. Ed Ney, chairman of Young and Rubicam, New York, explained, 'All you have to do is look out for a middle-class economy. Whenever you see one, you know there's an amount of advertising going on. We follow it. Sometimes we try to go ahead. The great interest now is China. The ramifications are just beyond belief in terms of advertising.'

Agencies vary in size from the small like Jenkins' (five staff and freelance help) to the huge like Young and Rubicam (4,000 employees in New York alone, and handling over $4 billion worth of business a year).

The professional advertising man owes his existence to the Industrial Revolution. Manufacturers needed to create national sales for their goods; furthermore, advertising was a way of shifting power from the seller to the manufacturer – it encouraged people to demand specific items that retailers were thus forced to stock.

Early advertising agents were media brokers. The American agency, N. W. Ayer, founded in 1869 and still very much active today, revolution-ised the business by acting as the representative not of the media selling space but of the advertiser buying it. In return it took a fixed commission, 15 per cent of the media budget, a system that remains in use today (although increasingly lower percentages or set fees are now charged instead, much depending on the clout of the client).

The next major development was for agencies to become involved in actually putting together the ads, something at first undertaken only on sufferance. Fulltime copywriters did not emerge until the end of the century. One of them, John E. Kennedy, a former Royal Canadian mounted policeman, changed the direction of advertising. The story goes that Albert Lasker, one of the giants of advertising (he built up a fortune of $52 million), was handed a note in the office one day which read, 'I am downstairs in the saloon, and I can tell you what advertising is. I know that you don't know. It will mean much to me to have you know what it is and it will mean much to you. If you wish to know what advertising is, send the word "yes" down by messenger.' The note was from Kennedy, by then a copywriter for Dr Shoop's Restorative.

Until that time advertising was designed to keep a name before the public. Kennedy changed this. His definition was 'Advertising is sales-manship in print'. Lasker hired Kennedy for the staggering salary of $28,000 a year. Within two years he was earning $75,000.

John O'Toole, who went on to head Lasker's agency, has written:

> It seems so simple and obvious today. But what this definition did in 1904 was to change the course of advertising completely and make possible the enormous role it now plays in our economy. For, by equating the function of an advertisement with the func-tion of a salesman who calls on a prospect personally, it revealed the true nature of advertising. For the first time, the concept of per-suasion, which is the prime role of a salesman, was applied to the creation of advertising.

Although the advertising industry was hit by the depression of the early thirties it recovered quickly and grew steadily from 1935. The real growth came after World War II when US companies began to move aggressively into foreign markets. By the early 1960s most large agencies were 'full service' agencies, that is they offered a whole range of services including research, media analysis and placement, and areas relating to developing new products including packaging and brand name advice.

Like many industries, advertising has gone through its phases. Today, it is the age of the mega-agency and (conversely) the small, breakaway 'creative' agency, determined to offer something different from the 'faceless' products of the big. The big get bigger and the medium size get squeezed harder. New giant companies have been formed by mergers and takeovers. Three major American agencies, BBDO, Doyle Dane Bernbach and Needham Harper, joined in 1986 to become the world's biggest, to be displaced only a month later when Britain's Saatchi and Saatchi took over the Ted Bates agency, creating a company with $7.5 billion worth of business.

The mega-agencies have operations spanning the world. The American Interpublic Group, (a holding company which includes the agencies McCann-Erickson Worldwide and Lintas: Worldwide), has a world map on which outposts are marked with green circles, red triangles and black squares depending on the individual agency involved. Green circles run through Central America like stepping stones, black squares decorate India. An alphabetical list underneath runs from Argentina to Zimbabwe. Both Taiwan and mainland China are included. It reminds me of another map I was once given, that of the US State Department showing diplomatic and consular posts. Or, but for its modern graphics, it could be a page from an old English school atlas, showing the British Empire at its height.

Other agency maps could be drawn and would look as impressive: the world according to Young and Rubicam with its forty-one American and 125 overseas offices; or Ogilvy and Mather (sixty US and 209 foreign); or J. Walter Thompson (seventy-three and 130). 'JWT colonised South America shortly after Columbus,' goes an industry saying.

As business expands and becomes more international, the march goes on. In the three years to 1986, Foote, Cone and Belding (Lasker's old agency), made seventeen acquisitions outside the United States increasing by sixteen the countries in which it operates and so making it 'larger, stronger and truly international'.

As with the advertisers (whom they usually follow), the same names recur constantly, J. Walter Thompson is the top agency in Argentina, Chile, Ecuador, Greece, India, Spain and Venezuela; second in Britain, Columbia and Malaysia; third in Canada; fourth in the Dominican Republic, Hong Kong and Italy. McCann-Erickson is first in Italy, second in Chile, the Dominican Republic, Ecuador, Finland, Mexico, and Singapore.

By 1987 over a fifth of the world's advertising was being handled by the top seven agencies. Of the ten largest agencies in the world in 1986 eight were American, one Japanese, and one British. The largest agency holding company in the world was Saatchi and Saatchi.[5]

The story of the Saatchi brothers, Charles and Maurice, is well known. They started their empire with a stake of £25,000 and a tiny operation in a rented office when they were twenty-seven and twenty-four respectively. They have always shown a flair for gaining publicity, not least by the well-used gambit of embracing personal seclusion Howard Hughes style. One of the agency's key developments was the reverse takeover of an old-established public agency, Garland-Compton, cautious and traditional but twice Saatchi's size, and with blue-chip clients including Procter and Gamble. The other, in 1978, was when the agency was chosen to handle advertising for the Conservative Party. When the Tories won the election, the advertising was given much of the credit. Suddenly everyone had heard of Saatchi and Saatchi.

The agency attracts strong admirers and detractors. Both agree that it has a pragmatic approach to the business. John Salmon, chairman of Collett Dickenson Pearce, told me that, 'Charles Saatchi once said to me, "If our clients don't like our work, I show them some of the rubbish and say, Would you like that?"'

In 1979 it became the largest agency in Britain, overtaking J. Walter Thompson. Three years later acquisitions were being made at the rate of one a month. Its method of financing takeovers is brilliantly simple. An initial downpayment is followed by years of deferred payments linked to meeting future profit targets. Buying agencies gives Saatchi new accounts. Assuming that these accounts grow, the agency is soon covered for its extra outgoings.

Saatchi's takeover of the American agency, Ted Bates, stunned the American advertising business. Ted Bates fills a very special place in US advertising. First, right from its start, in the late 1940s, it has been involved in mass-market products, the kind everyone buys. It was the agency which talked to Mrs Iowa. It also gave advertising the most famous letters in the business – USP, Unique Selling Proposition, coined by Rosser Reeves, co-founder of the agency with Bates. During the fifties Reeves hammered out a disciplined approach to advertising which, he claimed, could result in the creation of a USP for every product, company or service. Thus out of Bates and USP came Anadin's 'Fast, fast, fast relief', which Reeves boasted increased sales from $17 million to $54 million. For Mars' M & M Candies, 'Melts in your mouth, not in your hands'. For the Navy recruiting, 'It's not just a job, it's an adventure'. And for Bic, 'It writes the first time, every time'. Its takeover had considerable emotional significance but, more importantly, confirmed Saatchi's to be right at the forefront of the age of global advertising.

Ever-increasing internationalism is one of the dominant features of the advertising world in the eighties. It is possible to step off an aeroplane in any nation in the world and see the effect. Pick up a paper in Turkey, say, and odds are that there will be an ad for Marlboro or Lowenbrau; switch on the TV and the commercial may feature Mercedes or Mitsubishi.

Such a development is being driven by many factors. With markets at home sated, manufacturers are forced into more and more new areas to sustain growth. If products can be internationalised, there are economies of scale (including ones to be made in advertising). These developments go hand in hand with some in the media. The *International Herald Tribune*, for example, publishes in Paris but by 1986 was printing in eight centres around the world; satellite beams the same TV programmes across continents.

A drinks advertiser ran through products that were now 'international': jeans, T-shirts, sports shoes, soft drinks, power tools, credit cards, fast food . . . He suggested to me that we noted down as many individual brands as came to mind in five minutes. The list was formidable: Colgate toothpaste, American Express cards, Ariel washing powder, Bacardi, Ballantine's whisky, Canada Club, British Airways, Canon Cameras, Coke and Pepsi, Ford Escort, Heineken beer, IBM computers, Kellogg's Corn Flakes, Kodak film, Marlboro cigarettes, Mars bars, Nescafé instant coffee, Persil, Philips, the Fiat Uno, the Volkswagen Golf, Lego Toys, McDonald's hamburgers . . . You could walk into any town certainly anywhere in Europe and find such words were part of the everyday currency, and their advertising part of the routine advertising.

Companies operating internationally have the choice of three approaches. They can standardise, adapt, or produce something different for overseas customers. The same choices apply with regard to advertising.

There has been a trend for major international companies to consolidate their advertising in the hands of fewer and fewer companies. Kodak cut the number of agencies handling its business from fifty to just two. The leading American adman, Ed Ney, said, 'The truth is that world advertisers are choosing agencies of some size, some structure and geographically pretty much cover. They are going to be the winners. It's easier to manage for huge companies. And they have much more leverage against two or three agencies. When something goes wrong in Caracas, they call me up or Bill Phillips [chairman/CEO of Ogilvy and Mather] or Bill McKay [of J. Walter Thompson], and say, "Hey, we are working with you in twenty-five countries; you are screwing up; get it fixed." And, believe me, you get it fixed.'

Agencies without an international network have found themselves increasingly vulnerable. In defence, they argue that although the world may be shrinking, differences are real and vital, and therefore mega-agency advertising is lowest common-denominator advertising. David Bernstein recalls being one of thirty middle management men from the Interpublic empire being called to New York to watch a presentation for Coca-Cola. 'The fast talking presenter screened pictures of ten pretty girls, each a Coke model from a different country. We had to guess which was from which.

None of us did very well. This pleased the presenter, but the prospect of lowest common-denominator womanhood saddened a few Europeans.'

Jacques Séguéla further argues that that denominator will be American:

> Now there is no democracy in advertising because America is dominating. The English play a bad game in this battle. They fight first for themselves. Saatchi and Saatchi became an American [style] agency, not a European one. Advertising is our roots because our children learn life with advertising. They spend more time with television than with school. In ten years we will be not the centres of Bordeaux and of beer, but of Coca-Cola. For me the third world war has begun; it is not a missile war but a communications war on TV, newspapers, cinema and signs.

The anti-globalists have ready stores of anecdotes to illustrate cultural differences that, allegedly, negate trans-border advertising. Séguéla tells of an African advertisement for a brand of battery. The opening sequence showed it being placed in an aquarium. The second scene a week later: the battery was withdrawn from the water and placed in a radio which worked first time. Sales of batteries were a fiasco. Researchers found out why. Potential customers had read the ad as meaning that the battery *only* worked if it was submerged in water first.

In Taiwan, Pepsi's 'Come Alive with the Pepsi Generation' was reportedly translated on billboards as 'Pepsi will bring your ancestors back from the dead'. In Brazil, an American airline advertised that its planes had 'rendezvous' lounges, not knowing that 'rendezvous' in Portuguese means a place to have sex. In French Canada, Hunt-Wesson attempted to use its 'Big John' brand name by translating it into French as '*Gros Jos*', a colloquial French phrase that denotes a woman with huge breasts.

Dr Jean-Bruno Bouée, a Frenchman who applies Jungian psychology to advice on international trading, tells of a Western shampoo that was advertised on Japanese television. The commercial showed a man's hand caressing a girl's hair. A sample of thirty Japanese men and women were asked to imagine what happened next. All but one said that the man produced a sword and severed the girl's head! The ad was withdrawn.

The globalists like the stories as much as anyone, but say that all they really show is that the people devising the ads didn't do their homework properly.

Ads *can* cross borders, they say. With Impulse, a perfumed all-over deodorant from Elida Gibbs, the basic scenario is used everywhere from South Africa to South America: a man rushes to bestow flowers on a girl wearing the spray. (The actual men may differ, however: in South America and Italy older men are used; women in the UK, it is said, would find such men 'too threatening'.) The campaign for Ballantine's whisky appears unchanged in forty-six markets. Henry Pomeroy, the director of advertising for Hiram Walker, explained, 'Wherever a consumer goes he sees Ballantine's positioned with the same message. He boards a plane in Hong Kong and sees a Ballantine's message that is consistent in the departure hall, the duty free shop, on board, in the international magazines that he reads on board and on posters when he arrives at his destination.'

A commission set up by the International Advertising Association had no doubts as to how the future would go: 'It [global marketing] is the breakthrough marketing look of the eighties,' it concluded, 'and it's going to transform the advertising and television industries in the decades to come.' Why now? it asked, answering: because of television developments such as cable and satellite.

Believers point to other factors. People's desires and needs are the same. Erik Elinder argued twenty years ago in the *Journal of Marketing*, 'The desire to be beautiful is universal. Such appeals as "mother and child", "freedom from pain", "glow of health", know no boundaries.' Today there is an increasing convergence of tastes, habits, activities, and lifestyles. Even food tastes, always regarded as among the most national of characteristics, are said to be taking on some uniformity. Nestlé sells frozen mousaka in France, muesli is widely eaten in the UK, the Italians are buying tomato ketchup, and yoghurt and mineral water are found everywhere. 'We're moving towards uniformity in food tastes, if not across the globe, then certainly in Europe,' said Michèle Pougny, of the Research Institute for Social Change in Paris.

Advertising agency men who don't like the mega-world of the big agencies have a solution, of course: they can quit and set up their own operations. Constant start-ups is one of the features of the agency business that makes it exciting – today, a telephone and a room, tomorrow . . . In one recent boom period new agencies were opening in London at the rate of almost one a week. (They can close just as quickly. In the US, six out of every ten are estimated to go out of business within five years.) Starting a new agency is easy. All it needs (given a talented individual or two) is an office, a telephone and enough money to operate until the cash comes in. Small agencies draw a disproportionately large number of the most talented creatives who see the big agencies as advertising machines.

One factor that should prevent any single agency becoming too big a presence, and thus ensure the continuation of a wide variety of agencies, is that issue of clients not wanting their agency to handle the work of a rival. This means, in practice, that the biggest agencies can only take a finite amount of the market available. A conflict of interest may not be immediately apparent to the outsider. Hallmark Cards moved its $40 million worth of business from Young and Rubicam because the agency had won the business of AT & T Communications international long-distance account. The conflict: that on 'special' days, like Mother's Day and Christmas, there was a clash between telephoning and deciding to send a card from Hallmark.

Whatever happens, the situation can only help the smaller agencies (though probably not the medium size). It can also, especially in Britain, lead to the bizarre situation where the big agencies sometimes clash head on with the very small for the same account. It is almost as though the Bechtel Corporation and a group of Irish navvies were fighting for the same contract to build a new stadium. The difference is that in the world of advertising the Irish navvies sometimes win.

Today there are three major centres of advertising in the world: New York, London (generally regarded as the centre of 'creativity' in advertising) and Tokyo (home of Dentsu, the most powerful advertising agency in the world).

No one could deny that New York is the spiritual home of advertising. In many ways, it still dominates. The United States absorbs almost half the world's advertising expenditure, spends the greatest percentage of its GNP on it,[6] and the largest number of big agencies still operate from its shores. To many people, Madison Avenue is New York advertising. In reality, agencies are now strung out over the city. The American Association of Advertising Agencies has well over 100 members in New York but not many more than a dozen with a Madison Avenue address. Many big names are elsewhere. J. Walter Thompson is on Lexington, Ayer on Sixth, Ted Bates on Broadway, Grey on Third. A number of agencies have moved completely away from midtown Manhattan to downtown. The areas they chose, around lower Park and Fifth Avenues, they dubbed 'Madison Avenue South'. The prime motive for moving here and even further south to Hudson Square was price, but the areas became more than a cheaper alternative to Madison Avenue. They began to represent an escape, a freedom from the suit, tie and calculator environment of the traditional Madison. They were colourful, artistic, the stuff of a creative business. But Madison as a symbol remains. 'If Wall Street is one image of American capitalism – dark, grey, granite-cold, calculating,' wrote Michael Schudson, an American sociologist, 'Madison Avenue is its upbeat counterpart – steel and glass, jazzy and fast talking, more cynical than serious, more pressed than pressurising, grinning but terse.'

London has no equivalent to Madison Avenue. Many flocked to Covent Garden in the seventies; a decade later the area was written off as 'too establishment' and new agencies began to nest in Soho. Many of the best-known names, however, are located elsewhere: Boase Massimi Pollitt (probably London's most admired all-round agency, voted both the adman's and the client's favourite shop) in converted warehouses at the rear of Paddington station; J. Walter Thompson in solid, respectable eighteenth-century Berkeley Square, as befits an agency that has been described as the Ministry of Advertising; Lowe Howard-Spink in Knightsbridge.

Unlike New York, London's agency world has a closeness that verges on the claustrophobic. There's a trade magazine, *Campaign*, that thrives on chat and gossip: 'In America, advertising is business-business, here it's show business,' said its ex-editor, Bernard Barnett.

Outside America, London is now the major advertising centre of the world. Nine of the largest London agencies in 1986 were American but the US agencies have been steadily losing out both in real terms and status within the business. An *Advertising Age* survey showed that in the four years up to 1984 their share of the British market fell from 43 to 36 per cent. *Campaign* has commented, 'The facts are that the Americans just aren't cutting it any more; no one in the first division wants to work for them.'

London regards itself as the centre of creativity in advertising. Martin Boase says, 'There's no question that the Athens of advertising was New York throughout the sixties. There's also no doubt that it shifted here in the seventies and is still here.' The view is not insularly British. Jacques Séguéla jokes that the happiest man in the world is one with 'an English advertising agency, an American salary, a French cook and a Chinese wife'. Vincent Daddiego, a writer at Young and Rubicam, New York, also teaches advertising and shows English ads to students. 'English commercials are the Grail,' he says.

Boase believes there are a number of reasons for Britain's pre-eminence. First, there is the British attitude to salesmanship: 'We find it embarrassing to indulge in overt salesmanship. Persuasion has to be covert.' Second, there is more scepticism about the power of advertising from the advertisers themselves. And, third, says Boase, Britain as a country is just the right size, big enough to have budgets large enough to enable agencies to employ reasonable people, but not like the US, 'so gigantic that it can only lead to a master-servant relationship'. The way commercials in the UK and the US have developed historically is also a factor. In the US, the earliest commercials aped radio and repetition of brand names was the central feature. In Britain, on the other hand, TV commercials became smaller versions of cinema commercials. Many were short films.

Britain's class system and rigid union structures have also, more surprisingly, contributed to the country's high advertising creativity. Jay Chiat of Chiat/Day, one of America's most creative agencies, believes that advertising has attracted good young people in England because it provides a way for them to break out of the 'caste system. It's a glamorous, well-paying career. And one does not have to be high born or go to the right school to get in. As a result, young people come in young and hungry, bringing a passion to their work that doesn't seem to exist any more in the young creative people here – at least not in the ones we've been interviewing.' Robin Wight, in London, agrees. 'Young working-class talent is finding its outlet in advertising,' he says. 'It is a great class accelerator. Many professions cut themselves off from the whole of this talent – think of banks and lawyers.'

The single most powerful advertising agency in the world, however, is neither in New York nor London, but in Tokyo, Its position within Japan is illustrated every New Year's Eve when Dentsu throws the country's most spectacular party for 5,000 guests. Competition for invitations is heavy; armies of highly paid Ginza girls wander through elaborate sets spread over two floors of reception rooms at the Imperial Hotel.

As an advertising market, Japan is second in size only to the USA; annual gross advertising expenditure by 1986 was over Y 3.5 trillion ($22 billion). Dentsu spends about a quarter of this (and the second largest agency, Hakuhodo, about 9 per cent). Japan is a market-place controlled by the Japanese agencies. The situation is a unique one. Japanese agencies were originally and primarily media-selling agencies. There are complex interlocking shareholdings between agencies, newspapers and television stations in Japan. Most of the agencies either own a section of the media or are substantially owned by them. What it all means in practice is that agencies, and in particular Dentsu, hold important chunks of newspaper space and television time to hand out as they feel fit. Advertisers thus need to have several agencies. They have to go to a certain agency to gain access to particular TV time slots or newspaper pages.

Enormous power thus resides within the agency. Dentsu claims to work for almost every motor manufacturer, for example. Dentsu's views on programmes are thus very important: when it likes one it can buy a great deal of advertising. The agency has also bailed out faltering newspapers by giving them ads.

Dentsu claims to be able to avoid conflict between its various clients by operating in fifteen separate account divisions, all physically divided and each with its own director. The main headquarters building is an imposing grey-colour twenty-storey block in Tokyo's Ginza district. Significantly, Dentsu's art directors and copywriters are located in another block a short walk away. Creativity isn't a major internal function at Japanese agencies: much work is farmed out to local 'hot shops' and many big advertisers, such as Suntory, the drinks giant, handle their own. The two big functions are media, and account direction; the account executives are expected to keep in *daily* contact with the clients they handle.

Training is then formal by Western standards. At Hakuhodo newcomers go to the company's school of advertising for lessons in marketing, copywriting and running accounts. After three months they are posted to a division.

Dentsu's staff are exhorted to work to 'Dentsu's Ten Spartan Rules' that were laid down by Hideo Yoshida who took over as president two years after the end of the war and built Dentsu up into a true power. They include: 'Once you start a task, never give up – complete it, no matter what . . .' And 'Don't be afraid of friction. Friction is the mother of progress and the stimulus for aggressiveness. If you fear friction, you will become servile and timid.'

Television is the biggest advertising medium in Japan, with newspapers next. Commercials are short – fifteen seconds – and they occur every ten minutes. The pressure, therefore, is insidious. There is no escaping an advertiser. Major advertisers will use all five commercial channels simultaneously. The commercials themselves, perversely, are the softest of soft sell, appearing sometimes, in fact, to be selling nothing at all. Junji Imaki, of Hakuhodo, showed me a series of his agency's commercials. Many were charming and calculated to make you feel nice for having watched them, a feeling meant to be remembered when you shop. In one especially striking one, a toy fireman painstakingly climbs a ladder to the top of a skyscraper where he extinguishes a cigarette. The ad is for National batteries. I'm not sure whether they are any better than other batteries but I suspect faced with a choice of batteries when I needed one I'd feel a heel if I didn't reach out for the National brand. 'The approach to the consumer is very emotional,' explained Mr Imaki. 'People in Japan want commercials first to be beautiful. I think some from abroad are not beautiful. They explain the product rationally. There's no excitement for the audience . . .'

There is one in which a naked woman swims in a pool. The water is yellow at one end, purple at the other. She briefly reveals one breast. A voice intones, 'Water is gentler than men. Parco.' Parco is the name of a fashionable department store. In a Suntory spot for whisky, a puppy is shown having various small adventures as it wanders around the city in the rain. The commercial switches to a closing scene of one hand passing a tumbler of whisky on ice to another hand. The voice-over says, 'There are all kinds of ways of living. Take care. Anyhow, take care. Everyone take care.'

Wherever they are, whether they are enormous international agencies or small, local ones, agencies have much in common. They employ the same sort of people with the same kind of talent, they're organised in roughly the same way, and they're offering the same kind of product. 'When you get down to brass tacks, at the end of the day we're selling ads to clients that they hope to sell to punters,' Bert de Vos, chairman of D'Arcy Masius Benton and Bowles' London operation told me.

Agencies grow and live or wither and die on whether or not they win new business. Louis Hagopian, chairman of N. W. Ayer, New York, said, 'The way you get an account is to convince a client that you've performed some magic for others, and he'll give you the stage to do it for him.' Not surprisingly, agencies pursue clients assiduously. An advertiser can find he is wooed as ardently as any desirable woman. One advertiser who agreed to visit the offices of Allen, Brady and Marsh, a UK agency known for its showbiz downmarket approach, told me he was met at a railway station by a chauffeur who had memorised his face from photographs. Then, as lunch unfolded, it became obvious that the agency had researched his every taste in food with infinite care.

Agency executives swarm to conferences at which clients will be present. Potential clients are targeted and pursued over years if necessary. Account executives are said to join clubs and organisations whose members include target clients. One of the largest agencies is said to have encouraged an executive in England to move into a village where his normal activities would bring him into regular contact with a major advertiser who was of the same, minority, religious faith.

A hint that a client is unhappy will produce a flurry of activity. When Woolworths in the UK fired its agency, another agency, Gold Greenlees Trott, placed a forty-eight-sheet poster where the store's marketing director would see it on his way to work each day. It carried his name in huge letters with under it the words 'Don't just go to the same old shops' together with the agency's logo and telephone number.

In choosing a new agency advertisers often ask agencies to take part in what is known on Madison Avenue as 'the creative shootout', more prosaically called 'speculative presentations'. Selected agencies are 'invited' by the advertiser to prepare ads as though they already had the account. The industry has mixed views about them. Advertisers, in the main, like them. Most of the large, coveted clients insist on them. Agencies, with exceptions, are against them as unfair, costly (in staff, time and cash) and demeaning. However, they are a fact of life. In the UK alone there are 500 or more each year, involving between 1,500 and 2,000 competitive presentations. Money gambled by the agencies taking part can be large: those competing in America for the Hallmark account were said to have spent over $500,000 each in putting together commercials. In Britain especially, small compete against large. The owner of one confessed that entering creative shootouts with the big agencies was like 'sitting down to play poker with $50 and having to bluff all the way'. But small agencies usually welcome them – after all, they've the chance to make an impact.

New agencies, of course, are lean and hungry. 'Obviously you get fanatical enthusiasm from people building a new business,' said Peter Kirvan, soon after he and two partners opened a new London agency. 'The only way you can make your way in this market is to attack.' In the previous three months, Kirvan's company had pitched nine times, winning four accounts and losing two. It was still waiting for the results of the other three. It is a pace that he says could not be continued indefinitely. 'We couldn't pitch thirty-six times a year. It means working from eight in the morning until eight at night and weekends, and hoping that you won't have to do it next year.' Next year, of course, some other new agency will be there, willing and keen to work just those hours.

Chasing new business brings out the show-biz side of advertising. Stars are paraded: during the fight to win Hallmark in which Ogilvy and Mather were competing against Young and Rubicam, Foote Cone and Belding, and Leo Burnett, David Ogilvy himself happened to turn up in Kansas City. Boase Massimi Pollitt dressed up people in yellow page-boy outfits to pitch for Yellow Pages. Geer, DuBois hired Liv Ullman to be the agency receptionist for the arrival of important executives from *People* magazine whose account was up for grabs. Young and Rubicam preceded its bid for the Kentucky Fried Chicken account by sending out executives to work in fast-food restaurants. The chairman of British Rail arriving at the offices of Allen, Brady and Marsh was, according to adland legend, met by staff who parked him in a dirty room and took no notice of him until, finally, someone deigned to serve him tea in a cracked cup. About to walk out, he was stopped by Peter Marsh who appeared like an actor on cue and explained the whole thing was a charade, meant to show the railway chairman the image the public had of British Rail.

Admen occasionally help perpetuate the image many businessmen have of them. Jerry della Femina, long dubbed the wildman of Madison Avenue, reportedly presented for the Alitalia account much against his will. At the presentation he apparently disliked the airline men as much as he had hated the whole idea. The highlight was a demonstration of how well the agency had handled the account for a vaginal deodorant called Feminique. The client interrupted and said, 'You must understand, Mr della Femina, Alitalia is not another Feminique.' 'Yes,' della Femina replied, 'but it's got a better destination.' He said later, 'That remark cost me the account. But given the choice between getting millions in billing and saying that, I'd prefer to say that. It proved to me that I was still me, and not influenced by the kind of billing that was at stake.'

In London, David Abbott, about to present for the Metropolitan Police account, apparently muttered loudly 'Hello, hello, hello' as Sir Robert Mark, the commissioner, entered the room. Mark, never noted for a sense of humour, turned and left.

There is no way of knowing how rarely or how frequently dirty tricks occur. A few surface. Attempts were made to prevent Grey Advertising winning the Saudi Airlines account by 'reminding' the airline that the agency in New York was run by Jews. On a different level, but with the same end in view, Leyland Trucks was apparently fed false information about the British agency Cogent Elliott after it got onto a shortlist. Bernard Barnett, editor of *Campaign*, claimed in 1983 to know of one case when an agency left a pile of cash in the back of a prospective client's car for him to find after the presentation. 'To those who suggest that such things are part of the bad old days of advertising patronage, I can only say that the incident happened two weeks ago.'

One agency's gain, of course, is usually another's loss: they've been fired for some reason. The American Association of Advertising Agencies has said that the average relationship between an agency and client is eight years, with ten years the norm at the largest agencies. However, a lot of breakups do take place. *Advertising Age* figures showed that in just one year a staggering $1.4 billion worth of advertising moved from one agency to another. In the UK, a five-year survey, published in *Campaign*, looked at accounts spending £100,000 and over, and found that 53 per cent of those established during the period had switched agencies, some of them as many as three times. Ironically, perhaps, there seems to be wide agreement in advertising that when accounts are lost, when the divorce does come along, 'bad work' is much less a factor than a host of minor irritations. That is why so much stress is placed on maintaining a good relationship with the client. Whatever the size, agencies usually have three basic divisions: creative (made up of the people who devise the ads), media (which places them) and the account men, who deal with the clients and are responsible for keeping them happy.

Known as 'the suits', the account men are 'the business types' of the industry. They can (and frequently do) cross over to the client side. Historically they are the men in grey-flannel suits, the archetypal gladhanders in button-down shirts. They act as the bridge between the advertiser and the men who create the ads, explaining one side to the other. They are well versed in the special language of advertising, which is constantly changing. ('Let's run it up the flagpole and see if it salutes' is 1950s). There is much military terminology: 'target' audiences, 'shotgun approaches', 'breakthrough campaigns', a 'blitz' on competitors. And sporting: 'game plan', 'touch base', 'run with it', 'see if it'll fly'. Ideas are not good, they're 'big', and if an advertising campaign lasts it 'has legs'. What account executives like to see is a 'cash cow' that the client can 'milk' for years. If he has nothing to say, it can be disguised with phrases like 'we're hitting the norms'.

Until about twenty years ago the account man was generally king. Vincent Daddiego, a Young and Rubicam creative, recalls entering the business about that time: 'In many cases the account guys used to create the advertising.' The top people at the largest agencies have mostly (but not entirely) risen from the ranks of account men. As a breed they are strongest when advertising is most client dominated. Clients and account executives often play tennis or golf together, even share holidays.

Today an upsurge in 'creative'[7] ads – ones that intrigue and entertain to beguile viewers into watching – has given the 'creative teams' of copywriter plus art director more power within agencies. Throughout its modern history, advertising has alternated between periods in which the creative or the hard-sell approach has predominated. Hard-sell may be an actor/salesman waving his arms and delivering his patter, or an actress/housewife holding up a garment to show her neighbour that her washing is whiter. Creative is more likely to be a piece of mini-entertainment – humorous, like Pepsi's archaeological dig set in the future where no one knows what a Coca-Cola bottle is, or intriguing, like Chanel No 5 where a garden becomes piano keys which in turn become sky.

At present creativity – and, thus, 'creative' admen – is 'in' because, in an age of too many ads chasing customers, it seems to work. Even agencies not known for their creativity have rushed to embrace it, with varying degrees of success.

'It is easier to write ten passably effective sonnets than one effective advertisement,' Aldous Huxley, a former copywriter, once said. Those who can write – or scheme or direct – the ads have seen their worth increase, as agencies compete for the best talent. Reuben Mark, head of Colgate-Palmolive, is said to have urged all his staff who deal with agencies to make the admen *want* to work on the Colgate account. 'He said to me that he knew the best creative people can choose what they want to work on,' said Len Sugerman, of Foote Cone and Belding, one of the Colgate agencies. 'That's true. In the end creative people is what this agency is about. It takes a very special kind of talent to come up with a breakthrough idea to order and then have the craftmanship to make it work. People who can do it are in very short supply, earn a lot of money and are in great demand. If you force them into something the danger is that they will leave.'

The creatives are often regarded even by their fellow advertising men as strange creatures. All agencies give them some latitude. An (anonymous) agency chairman told *Campaign*, 'They are like babies, all totally naïve. They have to be because they are talking to other babies [the rest of the creative department] about what is essentially trivia. Can you imagine anyone remotely adult composing, "Hey, Tosh, Gotta Toshiba?"'

A creative team does not start with just a completely blank piece of paper and a rough set of thoughts (like, say, a novelist or scriptwriter). They are presented with what is known as 'a strategy'. This is a document derived from research which spells out in some detail what the advertising is meant to achieve, including just what is being sold and to whom. The team are expected to produce within these confines.

What creatives do at that stage is read, interview, talk, think. They become experts on subjects for brief periods. David Abbott has written sixty print ads for Sainsbury, the British grocery supermarket chain. 'For two weeks,' he told me, 'I am an expert on cheese or pink champagne. I write the advert and move on to the next thing.' Like many creative men, he likes 'the fact that it is a comparatively short attention span'. Neil Patterson, as creative director of TBWA in London, 'piled into medical bookshops and libraries', visited hospitals and special units to research anorexia for nursing recruitment ads – 'I even took an anorexic to lunch'.

Vincent Daddiego reckons that there is a breed of admen who create instinctively. He recalls the first assignment he ever handled. He was twenty-three, and it was to create a series of spot commercials for Playtex's '18-Hour' Girdle. 'What in the name of bleeding Jesus do I know about girdles?' he asked himself. But he says that he knew that whenever the family came home from visiting, his mother would invariably say, 'My girdle is killing me!' He worked his campaign around that cry. One showed an opera soprano and tenor taking their curtain call. Both were smiling broadly and as the camera moved in viewers heard the soprano mutter through her smile, 'My girdle is killing me!' Another portrayed a very attractive woman in an evening gown playing a beautiful melody. She turned to camera, smiled and whispered the same phrase. Daddiego says that his campaign 'was responsible for increasing sales of products faster than the girdles could be manufactured'. In devising it, he says, he only did 'what the old huckster will do. A huckster is just an individual who senses what will turn consumers on to a product.'

Bob Pritikin, a San Francisco writer, fits Daddiego's definition of 'huckster'. He wrote his favourite advertisement early in his career for a company called the Pureta Sausage Co. Trying to find his Big Idea for advertising the company's hot dog, he was told on a plant tour that the whole cow – except 'scuzzy parts like the eyeballs and nostrils' – went into the mincer. The headline, he recalled, came to him like a bolt of lightning: 'Pureta – there's a T-bone steak in every frank'.[8]

In the 1930s, an advertising man called Obie Winters solved the problems of a manufacturer of a horse linament named Absorbine whose sales were falling. Winters had the linament laboratory tested and found it worked on ringworm of the foot. His genius, though, lay in creating a wholly new name for ringworm that would sell his newly-targeted product to the general public – 'athlete's foot', a term that is now in the dictionary and in such wide usage that its derivation has been forgotten.

The legendary Claude Hopkins, described as 'the greatest copywriter who ever lived', noticed grains for puffed wheat and puffed rice being steam exploded in containers resembling cannons when he toured Quaker Oats, and immediately coined the phrase, 'Food shot from guns'. Some thought it 'the idea of an imbecile' but it increased sales and was still being used seventy years later. For Pepsodent toothpaste he invented the term 'film' (for plaque) in ads that appeared in seventeen languages. Hopkins' agency, Lord and Thomas, also persuaded Americans to *drink* oranges: until that time, 1916, they were only eaten. A classic ad headed 'Drink an Orange' began, 'Orange juice – a *delicious* beverage – is healthfulness itself'. A man was hired to invent a juice extractor (shown actual size in the ads) which sold through grocers at 10 cents. More than 3 million were distributed virtually overnight. Hopkins was paid a staggering $185,000 a year.

Ideas can take weeks – or be instantaneous. In the 1960s, a team wrestled for weeks for an idea to illustrate the reliability of the Volkswagen in winter. Eventually they agreed that a snowplough driver would make an excellent spokesman. The breakthrough came a week later when one of the team wondered aloud, 'How does the snowplough driver get to his snowplough?'

More recently, Ian Potter, creative director of FCO, a London agency, recalled the birth of a campaign for Araldite. He was given a brief for five black and white press ads 'to say little more than "this glue can stick anything to anything". I went to see Richard [French, agency chairman] and asked what he thought. He asked what I had in mind. I just turned round and said, "How about sticking a car to the poster?" It was as easy and as hard as that.' The campaign opened with a Ford Cortina stuck to a poster.

Advertising on the agency side is a freebooting profession. There is no recognised way in, no set qualifications. You succeed only by succeeding. Entering advertising is not easy. In a good year, for example, there will be about 120 vacancies in the UK. Competition is intense. Boase Massimi Pollitt claims to receive applications from about one in every thirty-five of the students who graduate from university each year. In the US there is specialist undergraduate training: around ninety colleges in forty-two states offer a programme in advertising, and nearly 5,000 students graduate.

Advertising, however, is one of those areas where employers back hunches and rate samples of work higher than qualifications. Perhaps the highest quality wanted is the sheer determination to get into advertising. 'Advertising is about selling things – anyone entering it ought to be able to sell themselves,' one agency told me. Thus students who parade with sandwich boards or dress up as Superman usually get interviews at least.

J. Walter Thompson, New York, took an unusual recruiting step. It advertised in the *New York Times* inviting would-be copywriters to complete an eight-point copy test. Question 6 said, 'You've heard the story about the man who made a fortune selling refrigerators to Eskimos. In not more than 100 words, how would you sell a telephone to a Trappist monk, who is observing the strict Rule of Silence? (But he can nod acceptance at the end.)' Question 7 went, 'Design/draw two posters. One is for legislating strict gun-control laws. The other is in support of the NRA.'

One big draw is that although advertising may be a tough business it is also a fun business. 'Advertising is the rock 'n' roll of the business world,' said Tom Manahan, of a Boston agency LMS. Fun and success are pursued with equal dedication. Offices are often personalised with fruit machines, juke boxes, cartoon figures, life-size models, fullsize galvanised brightly painted dustbins, jokes (a hat with an axe buried in it), as well as more serious – and expensive – items, like specially designed desks or wall displays of varying kinds of expensive ephemera. Cars are important, both as a part of a pay-and-perks package and as status toys. In the mid 1980s, the most common high-perk car in London was probably the Porsche (various models costing up to £35,000-plus) although there were Ferraris too (up to more than twice that) as well as other high luxury models such as the Aston Martin.

Admen everywhere are regarded, justifiably, as the biggest lunchers of all. They defend the practice – people contacts are so important, it allows them to spread themselves . . . The fact is that in London, for example, it is likely that at least three of the city's most renowned eateries would be up to 75 per cent empty if all the admen walked out: Langans, L'Etoile and the White Tower. One new breed adman, Dave Trott, said contemptuously that advertising is only the third most important thing in many agency men's lives: 'The first two being lunch and dinner.'

There is also, seemingly, enormous effort invested in such areas as organising the best parties and producing the best Christmas cards. Thus Boase Massimi Pollitt throws a Christmas party in Madame Tussauds with 150 staff wearing masks in a likeness of Martin Boase and 150 in the likeness of John Webster, the executive creative director. A creative director at another agency, KMP, is forty, so a helicopter picks him up and takes him to an English seaside resort for a seaside café lunch. Abbott Mead Vickers has a novel idea for its Christmas card – Santa's sleigh being clamped for parking in the wrong place. The photograph, outside the agency's offices, only involves live reindeer and 500 gallons of foam to simulate snow.

Ah, say adland's defenders, all this may be true, but it's only the gloss. What people do not see is the adman working long nights and weekends, dedicated to the clients and the product. What is more, it is frequently added, most who do it are less concerned about the money they earn than about the final ad. And that, indeed, may be true. This is not to say, however, that admen do not care about money. Alfred Politz, a dominant force in advertising research in America in the 1950s and early 1960s, recalled that when he first arrived in the US from Germany to start a new life he asked himself, Which profession makes the most money with the least intelligence? 'The answer was "advertising".' Philip Dusenberry, executive creative director of BBDO, said, 'I have always believed that writing advertisements is the second most profitable form of writing. The first, of course, is ransom notes . . .'

The men at the corporate top in the ad world are far from badly paid. In 1985 Philip Geier of Interpublic earned $1.3 million, Bruce Crawford (BBDO International) $666,500, and Don Johnston (J. Walter Thompson) over $742,000. In the UK, 1987 figures showed the latest earnings of Maurice and Charles Saatchi to be £298,000 each, of Peter Warren (Ogilvy and Mather) £187,000, and Peter Marsh (Allen Brady and Marsh) £182,000. But they are big men in big businesses. It is, perhaps, more interesting to look at pay lower down the scale. In the mid 1980s, big agencies in London were reported paying upwards of £150,000 for top people. In the US, *Adweek* told of a thirty-year-old copy-writer making close to $90,000 who said, 'The phone never stops ringing. I probably get five solid offers a week to jump, and each one contains an exciting compensation package. Agencies will pay almost anything if they want you.' One headhunter alone, Judy Wald, placed over 30 creatives at over $150,000 each plus perks in 1987, notwithstanding the fact that it was a year of redundancies because of a flurry of takeovers.

Perks can range the whole gamut of ingenuity – cars, country club membership, personal expenses, mortgage payments for a country house, children's education and holidays. Stock option schemes and bonuses can become 'golden handcuffs'. A bonus at an agency riding high can apparently be as high as 50 per cent of salary, perhaps a staggering $150,000. Winston Fletcher said, 'You can live off the company by having your food, motoring, travel and flat in town all paid for so that your salary is really pocket-money.'

Some admen will argue that in part the salaries and the perks are compensation not only for a talent shortage, but for the high risks. Stress is rated as high: certainly it is a business of deadlines with rewards for meeting them successfully, retribution for failing to do so. There is also a blurring between work and home, and the strain of having to project much of the time.

Professor Cary Cooper, of the University of Manchester Institute of Science and Technology, conducted a detailed survey into occupational stress. Advertising notched up a score of more than seven on a ten-point stress scale, putting it into the top bracket – although also there were dentistry, mining, the construction industry, acting, police, airline pilots, prison warders and journalism.

Another survey showed that over 90 per cent questioned admitted to drinking way above the recommended 'safe' level (equivalent to eighteen measures of spirit of glasses of wine a week for men or twelve for women). Mrs Denise Larkin, general secretary of the National Advertising Benevolent Society which helps advertising people who are sick or unemployed, said there was a drink pattern: Because a man was working to a deadline he found he had to work overnight. Then he couldn't relax, so he had a drink. The next day he couldn't work, so more drink followed . . . Creative admen may wake up and find they have lost their skills, she said. 'They are very highly strung anyway. The kind of person who makes a good advertising person is also a person given to difficulties when things go wrong. I suppose they have to be prepared to take chances. They are generally risk takers.'

Account losses and agency mergers mean job losses. Mrs Larkin says unemployment is an especial problem because advertising men are used to living well and usually 'spend without accumulating'. She said, 'The moment they are told they are to be promoted, they move on to the next lifestyle – a new house, a new car, private school. One of them told me, "People who live within their means lack ambition." '

Advertising men link age and risk. Advertising, they say, is a young man's business. An anonymous creative head told *Design and Art Direction*, 'It's a dangerous business, for God's sake. As you start pushing forty you figure you have maybe ten years left; no one really knows what happens because agencies are comparatively young.' One of the most striking facts about the advertising scene in London especially is how young much of it is. It is very easy to justify this rationally in terms of ads. Advertising people need to be preoccupied by what is new. It is a business of fads and fashions. That is not meant to be derogatory. Advertising takes and uses from all around it. A young man is more likely to be more attuned.

In 1976, A paper prepared for J. Walter Thompson, London, entitled 'Old Men in Advertising', concluded that:

> it would seem that with few important exceptions older people won't contribute effectively. So they won't enjoy themselves in advertising. Thus it is in an employee's as well as management's interests to recognise that advertising is unlikely to offer many of them a lifetime's career. The prospect of finding a second career is not as horrid as it might seem. Though the specific skills of advertising are of limited use elsewhere, it is an excellent stepping off point for very many other jobs, even at the age of forty or more.

Some argue that when older men leave it is sometimes less because they cannot handle the business any more than that they have 'matured' out of it. They simply find it intellectually intolerable. Shepherd Mead, author of *How to Succeed in Business Without Really Trying*, was creative head of Benton and Bowles in New York until he was forty-one and quit to write fulltime. He said, 'Copywriting is a form of intellectual prostitution. No advertising creative man will stay in advertising when he can afford to get out. Who would write about soap powders when he could be writing his own novel?'[9]

The majority do stay. A large number would, in fact, prefer to write about soap powders than novels. They like the mix of fun and money, thrive on deadlines and applause. They do not think about the final product, except in terms of personal success or failure, and the reactions of their professional peers. It's not so much the end justifying the means (which might be an advertiser justification), but that the means is justified within itself. John Caples, the advertising man who wrote such classics as 'They laughed when I sat down to play the piano', has pointed out that two forces are at work in an adman's prospects: scepticism and the desire to believe. The good adman is content to concentrate his all on overcoming the first and flaming the second.

Nearly eighty years ago, a textbook advised advertising men, 'Above all else, in planning an advertisement that will catch the public, *aim low* . . . the great mass of people, rich or poor, have simple minds, and you must talk to them in a simple way.' Today's advertising man will still do that – but only if he is convinced it will work. Nothing should disguise the fact that glitzy though the advertising scene may be, no matter how pleasant and personable its individuals, what the business is all about is results.

Joe Bensman, a sociologist who spent eight years in an agency, wrote that advertising is not the place for anyone 'kind, gentle, ethical or religious . . . Advertising requires strong defences, toughness, nerve and the willingness to exploit oneself and others.' Or as Jerry della Femina, an agency head himself, put it, 'When you think of advertising, don't think of Rock Hudson manipulating Doris Day. Think of H. R. Haldeman [one of the Watergate conspirators and an ex-adman] trying to screw up some tapes, because that's closest to what large-agency advertising men are about.'

Notes

1 The figures are for 1985, as are others in the book unless stated otherwise. UK figures come from *Campaign* and American from *Advertising Age*.
2 Chandler said, 'Chess is about as elaborate a waste of human intelligence as you could find anywhere outside an advertising agency.'
3 Exactly what it pays is a secret as closely guarded as the minutes of the Soviet Politburo.
4 In the UK, the *Guardian*'s television reviewer wrote, '*A.D.* is in the purest and bubbliest sense of the phrase a soap opera.'
5 The world's largest agency was the Japanese Dentsu, followed by Young and Rubicam, Saatchi and Saatchi Compton Worldwide, Ted Bates Worldwide, J. Walter Thompson Co, Ogilvy and Mather Worldwide, BBDO Worldwide, McCann-Erickson Worldwide, DDB Needham Worldwide and DMB and B. Among holding companies, after Saatchi and Saatchi came the Interpublic Group and then the Omnicom and JWT Groups. Of the top ten holding companies in 1986 five were British, one French, one Australian and only three American.
6 At 2.4 per cent of the Gross National Product, advertising is way ahead of organised crime, which *Fortune* has estimated to be running at 1.1 per cent.
7 The great Creative Age was the 1960s when William Bernbach was creating ads like 'You don't have to be Jewish to love Levy's' with black boys and Indians biting into rye bread, and the famous Volkswagen commercials.
8 There is a sad ending to this story. The Food and Drug Administration objected to, and stopped, the ad, though not until the campaign had run for months and sales had soared.
9 Other writers who have worked in advertising and got out include Sherwood Anderson, John P. Marquand, Eric Ambler and Scott Fitzgerald (whose work included 'We keep you clean in Muscatine', written for a laundry).

Sources

303 'All to sell a carbonated soft drink': Cola drinkers are measured in tens of millions. The magazine *Which?* tested colas on 'fifty discriminating cola drinkers' in 1985, and reported in its January 1986 issue that when given new Coke and Pepsi 'nine testers couldn't tell a difference'.
304 'Mike Detsiny is managing': Article in *Campaign*, 1 August 1986.
307 'By 1985 the average': Association of National Advertisers, New York.
307 'If they spent money': *Sunday Telegraph*, 15 June 1980.

308 'Miner Raymond tells of': *New York Times*, 6 May 1985.

308 'Peter Levelle, head of': *Sunday Telegraph*, 15 June, 1980.

309 'In an attempt to': *Design and Art Direction*, September 1983.

309 'Eighty-seven of America's': Saatchi and Saatchi Compton Worldwide, Review of Advertising Operations 1984.

310 'So does the Dow': *Evening Argus*, Brighton, 20 February 1986.

310 'In its attempt to': *International Herald Tribune*, 15 August 1985.

310 'In spring 1986, Britain's': *The Times*, 3 March 1986.

310 'Even the BBC in': Advertisement in *The Times*, 26 September 1985.

310 'The range of those': *Advertising Age*, 9 September 1985.

310 'The unlikeliest products are': Advertisement in *Defence* magazine, March 1987.

311 'In the three-year period': Spanish Advertising Agencies Association.

312 'In the words of': *Eyes on Tomorrow*.

312 'By the beginning of': *Advertising Age*, 22 June 1981.

314 'Gordon Wade, a management': *Cincinnati Enquirer*, 4 October 1982.

314 'Outside, staff are warned': *Advertising Age*, 21 February 1983.

316 'Five of P & G's': *Advertising Age*, 20 October 1986.

318 'As for individuals': *Financial Times*, 29 May 1986.

318 'In England, Malcolm Parkinson': *Marketing*, 28 July 1983.

318 Figures of agency numbers: US Census Bureau 1984, *Advertising Age*, *Brad Advertiser and Agency List*, January 1987.

319 'Until that time advertising': *The Trouble with Advertising*.

320 'As with the advertisers': *Advertising Age*, 25 May 1987.

320 Lists: *Advertising Age*, 11 May 1987.

323 'In Taiwan, Pepsi's': *Media International*, March 1984.

324 'Erik Elinder argued': Erik Elinder, 'How International can European advertising be?' *Journal of Marketing*, April 1965.

324 'Hallmark Cards, in 1984': *Advertising Age*, 14 May 1984.

325 'If Wall Street is': *Advertising, The Uneasy Persuasion*.

326 'Jay Chiat of Chiat/Day': *Adweek*, 24 January 1983.

327 'As an advertising market': Fuji Bank estimates.

332 'An (anonymous) agency chairman': *Campaign*, 27 February 1987.

332 'Neil Patterson, as creative': *Design and Art Direction*, 10 May 1985.

333 'Bob Pritikin, a San Francisco': *Advertising Age*, 6 September 1982.

333 'In the 1930s, an': Jerry Cowle in *Advertising Age*, 21 March 1983.

334 'More recently, Ian Potter': *Design and Art Direction*, September 1984.

335 'The men at the corporate': *Adweek*, June 1986.

335 'In the UK, 1987': Spicer and Pegler Survey on Agencies in *Campaign*, 2 October 1987.

335 'In the US, *Adweek*': *Adweek*, 3 June 1985.

336 'Winston Fletcher said': *Campaign*, 11 April 1986.

336 'An anonymous creative head': *Design and Art Direction*, 19 April 1984.

337 'In 1976, a paper': Quoted in *Campaign*, 21 May 1976.

337 'Shepherd Mead, author of': *Campaign*, 7 May 1976.

338 'Joe Bensman, a sociologist': *Dollars and Sense*, Macmillan, New York, 1987.

338 'Or as Jerry della Femina': della Femina speaking on Public Television in January 1975.

338 'At 2.4 per cent of': Simon Lloyd, managing director, Foote, Cone and Belding, London.

87

CULTURE JAMMING

Naomi Klein

Source: Naomi Klein, *No Logo: No Space, No Choice, No Jobs, Taking Aim at the Brand Bullies*, London: Flamingo, 2000, pp. 279–309.

Advertising men are indeed very unhappy these days, very nervous, with a kind of apocalyptic expectancy. Often when I have lunched with an agency friend, a half dozen worried copy writers and art directors have accompanied us. Invariably they want to know when the revolution is coming, and where will they get off if it does come.

—Ex-adman James Rorty, *Our Master's Voice*, 1934

It's Sunday morning on the edge of New York's Alphabet City and Jorge Rodriguez de Gerada is perched at the top of a high ladder, ripping the paper off a cigarette billboard. Moments before, the billboard at the corner of Houston and Attorney sported a fun-loving Newport couple jostling over a pretzel. Now it showcases the haunting face of a child, which Rodriguez de Gerada has painted in rust. To finish it off, he pastes up a few hand-torn strips of the old Newport ad, which form a fluorescent green frame around the child's face.

When it's done, the installation looks as the thirty-one-year-old artist had intended: as if years of cigarette, beer and car ads had been scraped away to reveal the rusted backing of the billboard. Burned into the metal is the real commodity of the advertising transaction. "After the ads are taken down," he says, "what is left is the impact on the children in the area, staring at these images."[1]

Unlike some of the growing legion of New York guerrilla artists, Rodriguez de Gerada refuses to slink around at night like a vandal, choosing instead to make his statements in broad daylight. For that matter, he doesn't much like the phrase "guerrilla art," preferring "citizen art" instead. He wants the dialogue he has been having with the city's billboards for more than ten years to be seen as a normal mode of discourse in a democratic society – not as some edgy vanguard act. While he paints and pastes, he wants kids to stop and watch – as they do on this sunny day, just as an old man offers to help support the ladder.

Rodriguez de Gerada even claims to have talked cops out of arresting him on three different occasions. "I say, 'Look, look what's around here, look what's happening. Let me explain to you why I do it.'" He tells the police officer about how poor neighborhoods have a disproportionately high number of billboards selling tobacco and hard liquor products. He talks about how these ads always feature models sailing, skiing or playing golf, making the addictive products they promote particularly glamorous to kids stuck in the ghetto, longing for escape. Unlike the advertisers who pitch and run, he wants his work to be part of a community discussion about the politics of public space.

Rodriguez de Gerada is widely recognized as one of the most skilled and creative founders of culture jamming, the practice of parodying advertisements and hijacking billboards in order to drastically alter their messages. Streets are public spaces, adbusters argue, and since most residents can't afford to counter corporate messages by purchasing their own ads, they should have the right to talk back to images they never asked to see. In recent years, this argument has been bolstered by advertising's mounting aggressiveness in the public domain – the ads discussed in "No Space," painted and projected onto sidewalks; reaching around entire buildings and buses; into schools; onto basketball courts and on the Internet. At the same time, as discussed in "No Choice," the proliferation of the quasi-public "town squares" of malls and superstores has created more and more spaces where commercial messages are the only ones permitted. Adding even greater urgency to their cause is the belief among many jammers that concentration of media ownership has successfully devalued the right to free speech by severing it from the right to be heard.

All at once, these forces are coalescing to create a climate of semiotic Robin Hoodism. A growing number of activists believe the time has come for the public to stop asking that some space be left unsponsored, and to begin seizing it back. Culture jamming baldly rejects the idea that marketing – because it buys its way into our public spaces – must be passively accepted as a one-way information flow.

The most sophisticated culture jams are not stand-alone ad parodies but interceptions – counter-messages that hack into a corporation's own method of communication to send a message starkly at odds with the one that was intended. The process forces the company to foot the bill for its own subversion, either literally, because the company is the one that paid for the billboard, or figuratively, because anytime people mess with a logo, they are tapping into the vast resources spent to make that logo meaningful. Kalle Lasn, editor of Vancouver-based *Adbusters* magazine, uses the martial art of jujitsu as a precise metaphor to explain the mechanics of the jam. "In one simple deft move you slap the giant on its back. We use the momentum of the enemy." It's an image borrowed from Saul Alinsky who, in his activist bible, *Rules for Radicals*, defines "mass political jujitsu" as "utilizing the power of one part of the power structure against another part . . . the superior strength of the Haves become their own undoing."[2] So, by rappelling off the side of a thirty-by-ninety-foot Levi's billboard (the largest in San Francisco) and pasting the face of serial killer Charles Manson over the image, a group of jammers attempts to leave a disruptive message about the labor practices employed to make Levi's jeans. In the statement it left on the scene, the Billboard Liberation Front said they chose Manson's face because the jeans were "Assembled by prisoners in China, sold to penal institutions in the Americas."

The term "culture jamming" was coined in 1984 by the San Francisco audio-collage band Negativland. "The skillfully reworked billboard . . . directs the public viewer to a consideration of the original corporate strategy," a band member states on the album *Jamcon '84*. The jujitsu metaphor isn't as apt for jammers who insist that they aren't inverting ad messages but are rather improving, editing, augmenting or unmasking them. "This is extreme truth in advertising," one billboard artist tells me.[3] A good jam, in other words, is an X-ray of the subconscious of a campaign, uncovering not an opposite meaning but the deeper truth hiding beneath the layers of advertising euphemisms. So, according to these principles, with a slight turn of the imagery knob, the now-retired Joe Camel turns into Joe Chemo, hooked up to an IV machine. That's what's in his future, isn't it? Or Joe is shown about fifteen years younger than his usual swinger self (see image, page 278). Like Baby Smurf, the "Cancer Kid" is cute and cuddly and playing with building blocks instead of sports cars and pool cues. And why not? Before R. J. Reynolds reached a $206 billion settlement with forty-six states, the American government accused the tobacco company of using the cartoon camel to entice children to start smoking – why not go further, the culture jammers ask, and reach out to even younger would-be smokers? Apple computers' "Think Different" campaign of famous figures both living and dead has been the subject of numerous simple hacks: a photograph of Stalin appears with the altered slogan "Think Really Different"; the caption for the ad featuring the Dalai Lama is changed to "Think Disillusioned" and the rainbow Apple logo is morphed into a skull (see image on page 344). My favorite truth-in-advertising campaign is a simple jam on Exxon that appeared just after the 1989 Valdez spill: "Shit Happens. New Exxon," two towering billboards announced to millions of San Francisco commuters.

Attempting to pinpoint the roots of culture jamming is next to impossible, largely because the practice is itself a cutting and pasting of graffiti, modern art, do-it-yourself punk philosophy and age-old pranksterism. And using billboards as an activist canvas isn't a new revolutionary tactic either. San

Francisco's Billboard Liberation Front (responsible for the Exxon and Levi's jams) has been altering ads for twenty years, while Australia's Billboard Utilizing Graffitists Against Unhealthy Promotions (BUG-UP) reached its peak in 1983, causing an unprecedented $1 million worth of damage to tobacco billboards in and around Sydney.

It was Guy Debord and the Situationists, the muses and theorists of the theatrical student uprising of Paris, May 1968, who first articulated the power of a simple *détournement*, defined as an image, message or artifact lifted out of its context to create a new meaning. But though culture jammers borrow liberally from the avant-garde art movements of the past – from Dada and Surrealism to Conceptualism and Situationism – the canvas these art revolutionaries were attacking tended to be the art world and its passive culture of spectatorship, as well as the anti-pleasure ethos of mainstream capitalist society. For many French students in the late sixties, the enemy was the rigidity and conformity of the Company Man; the company itself proved markedly less engaging. So where Situationist Asger Jorn hurled paint at pastoral paintings bought at flea markets, today's culture jammers prefer to hack into corporate advertising and other avenues of corporate speech. And if the culture jammers' messages are more pointedly political than their predecessors', that may be because what were indeed subversive messages in the sixties – "Never Work," "It is Forbidden to Forbid," "Take Your Desires for Reality" – now sound more like Sprite or Nike slogans: Just Feel It. And the "situations" or "happenings" staged by the political pranksters in 1968, though genuinely shocking and disruptive at the time, are the Absolut Vodka ad of 1998 – the one featuring purple-clad art school students storming bars and restaurants banging on bottles.

In 1993, Mark Dery wrote "Culture Jamming: Hacking, Slashing and Sniping in the Empire of Signs," a booklet published by the Open Magazine Pamphlet Series. For Dery, jamming incorporates such eclectic combinations of theater and activism as the Guerrilla Girls, who highlighted the art world's exclusion of female artists by holding demonstrations outside the Whitney Museum in gorilla masks; Joey Skagg, who has pulled off countless successful media hoaxes; and Artfux's execution-in-effigy of arch-Republican Jesse Helms on Capitol Hill. For Dery, culture jamming is anything, essentially, that mixes art, media, parody and the outsider stance. But within these subcultures, there has always been a tension between the forces of the merry prankster and the hard-core revolutionary. Nagging questions re-emerge: are play and pleasure themselves revolutionary acts, as the Situationists might argue? Is screwing up the culture's information flows inherently subversive, as Skagg would hold? Or is the mix of art and politics just a matter of making sure, to paraphrase Emma Goldman, that somebody has hooked up a good sound system at the revolution?

Though culture jamming is an undercurrent that never dries up entirely, there is no doubt that for the last five years it has been in the midst of a

revival, and one focused more on politics than on pranksterism. For a growing number of young activists, adbusting has presented itself as the perfect
tool with which to register disapproval of the multinational corporations
that have so aggressively stalked them as shoppers, and so unceremoniously
dumped them as workers. Influenced by media theorists such as Noam
Chomsky, Edward Herman, Mark Crispin Miller, Robert McChesney and
Ben Bagdikian, all of whom have explored ideas about corporate control
over information flows, the adbusters are writing theory on the streets,
literally deconstructing corporate culture with a waterproof magic marker
and a bucket of wheatpaste.

Jammers span a significant range of backgrounds, from purer-than-thou
Marxist-anarchists who refuse interviews with "the corporate press" to those
like Rodriguez de Gerada who work in the advertising industry by day
(his paying job, ironically, is putting up commercial signs and superstore
window displays) and long to use their skills to send messages they consider
constructive. Besides a fair bit of animosity between these camps, the only
ideology bridging the spectrum of culture jamming is the belief that free
speech is meaningless if the commercial cacophony has risen to the point
that no one can hear you. "I think everyone should have their own billboard, but they don't," says Jack Napier (a pseudonym) of the Billboard
Liberation Front.[4]

On the more radical end of the spectrum, a network of "media collectives" has emerged, decentralized and anarchic, that combine adbusting
with zine publishing, pirate radio, activist video, Internet development
and community activism. Chapters of the collective have popped up in
Tallahassee, Boston, Seattle, Montreal and Winnipeg – often splintering off
into other organizations. In London, where adbusting is called "subverting,"
a new group has been formed, called the UK Subs after the seventies punk
group of the same name. And in the past two years, the real-world jammers
have been joined by a global network of on-line "hacktivists" who carry out
their raids on the Internet, mostly by breaking into corporate Web sites
and leaving their own messages behind.

More mainstream groups have also been getting in on the action. The
U.S. Teamsters have taken quite a shine to the ad jam, using it to build up
support for striking workers in several recent labor disputes. For instance,
Miller Brewing found itself on the receiving end of a similar jam when it
laid off workers at a St. Louis plant. The Teamsters purchased a billboard
that parodied a then current Miller campaign; as *Business Week* reported,
"Instead of two bottles of beer in a snowbank with the tagline 'Two Cold,'
the ad showed two frozen workers in a snowbank labeled 'Too Cold: Miller
canned 88 St. Louis workers.'"[5] As organizer Ron Carver says, "When
you're doing this, you're threatening multimillion-dollar ad campaigns."[6]

One high-profile culture jam arrived in the fall of 1997 when the New
York antitobacco lobby purchased hundreds of rooftop taxi ads to hawk

"Virginia Slime" and "Cancer Country" brand cigarettes. All over Manhattan, as yellow cabs got stuck in gridlock, the jammed ads jostled with the real ones.

"Mutiny on the Corporate Sponsor Ship" – Paper Tiger, 1997 slogan

The rebirth of culture jamming has much to do with newly accessible technologies that have made both the creation and the circulation of ad parodies immeasurably easier. The Internet may be bogged down with brave new forms of branding, as we have seen, but it is also crawling with sites that offer links to culture jammers in cities across North America and Europe, ad parodies for instant downloading and digital versions of original ads, which can be imported directly onto personal desktops or jammed on site. For Rodriguez de Gerada, the true revolution has been in the impact desktop publishing has had on the techniques available to ad hackers. Over the course of the last decade, he says, culture jamming has shifted "from low-tech to medium-tech to high-tech," with scanners and software programs like Photoshop now enabling activists to match colors, fonts and materials precisely. "I know so many different techniques that make it look like the whole ad was reprinted with its new message, as opposed to somebody coming at it with a spray-paint can."

This is a crucial distinction. Where graffiti traditionally seek to leave dissonant tags on the slick face of advertising (or the "pimple on the face of the retouched cover photo of America," to use a Negativland image), Rodriguez de Gerada's messages are designed to mesh with their targets, borrowing visual legitimacy from advertising itself. Many of his "edits" have been so successfully integrated that the altered billboards look like originals, though with a message that takes viewers by surprise. Even the child's face he put up in Alphabet City – not a traditional parody jam – was digitally output on the same kind of adhesive vinyl that advertisers use to seamlessly cover buses and buildings with corporate logos. "The technology allows us to use Madison Avenue's aesthetics against itself," he says. "That is the most important aspect of this new wave of people using this guerrilla tactic, because that's what the MTV generation has become accustomed to – everything's flashy, everything's bright and clean. If you spend time to make it cleaner it will not be dismissed."

But others hold that jamming need not be so high tech. The Toronto performance artist Jubal Brown spread the visual virus for Canada's largest billboard-busting blitz with nothing more than a magic marker. He taught his friends how to distort the already hollowed out faces of fashion models by using a marker to black out their eyes and draw a zipper over their mouths – presto! Instant skull. For the women jammers in particular, "skulling" fitted in neatly with the "truth in advertising" theory: if

301

emaciation is the beauty ideal, why not go all the way with zombie chic – give the advertisers a few supermodels from beyond the grave? For Brown, more nihilist than feminist, skulling was simply a détournement to highlight the cultural poverty of the sponsored life. ("Buy Buy Buy! Die Die Die!" reads Brown's statement displayed in a local Toronto art gallery.) On April Fool's Day, 1997, dozens of people went out on skulling missions, hitting hundreds of billboards on busy Toronto streets (see image, page 344). Their handiwork was reprinted in *Adbusters*, helping to spread skulling to cities across North America.

And nobody is riding the culture-jamming wave as high as *Adbusters*, the self-described "house-organ" of the culture-jamming scene. Editor Kalle Lasn, who speaks exclusively in the magazine's enviro-pop lingo, likes to say that we are a culture "addicted to toxins" that are poisoning our bodies, our "mental environment" and our planet. He believes that adbusting will eventually spark a "paradigm shift" in public consciousness. Published by the Vancouver-based Media Foundation, the magazine started in 1989 with 5,000 copies. It now has a circulation of 35,000 – at least 20,000 copies of which go to the United States. The foundation also produces "uncommercials" for television that accuse the beauty industry of causing eating disorders, attack North American overconsumption, and urge everyone to trade their cars in for bikes. Most television stations in Canada and the U.S. have refused to air the spots, which gives the Media Foundation the perfect excuse to take them to court and use the trials to attract press attention to their vision of more democratic, publicly accessible media.

Culture jamming is enjoying a resurgence, in part because of technological advancements, but also more pertinently, because of the good old rules of supply and demand. Something not far from the surface of the public psyche is delighted to see the icons of corporate power subverted and mocked. There is, in short, a market for it. With commercialism able to overpower the traditional authority of religion, politics and schools, corporations have emerged as the natural targets for all sorts of free-floating rage and rebellion. The new ethos that culture jamming taps into is go-for-the-corporate-jugular. "States have fallen back and corporations have become the new institutions," says Jaggi Singh, a Montreal-based anticorporate activist.[7] "People are just reacting to the iconography of our time." American labor rights activist Trim Bissell goes further, explaining that the thirsty expansion of chains like Starbucks and the aggressive branding of companies like Nike have created a climate ripe for anticorporate attacks. "There are certain corporations which market themselves so aggressively, which are so intent on stamping their image on everybody and every street, that they build up a reservoir of resentment among thinking people," he says. "People resent the destruction of culture and its replacement with these mass-produced corporate logos and slogans. It represents a kind of cultural fascism."[8]

Most of the superbrands are of course well aware that the very imagery that has generated billions for them in sales is likely to create other, unintended, waves within the culture. Well before the anti-Nike campaign began in earnest, CEO Phil Knight presciently observed that "there's a flip side to the emotions we generate and the tremendous well of emotions we live off of. Somehow, emotions imply their opposites and at the level we operate, the reaction is much more than a passing thought."[9] The reaction is also more than the fickle flight of fashion that makes a particular style of hip sneaker suddenly look absurd, or a played-to-death pop song become, overnight, intolerable. At its best, culture jamming homes in on the flip side of those branded emotions, and refocuses them, so that they aren't replaced with a craving for the next fashion or pop sensation but turn, slowly, on the process of branding itself.

It's hard to say how spooked the advertisers are about getting busted. Although the U.S. Association of National Advertisers has no qualms about lobbying police on behalf of its members to crack down on adbusters, they are generally loath to let the charges go to trial. This is probably wise. Even though ad companies try to paint jammers as "vigilante censors" in the media,[10] they know it wouldn't take much for the public to decide that the advertisers are the ones censoring the jammers' creative expressions.

So while most big brand names rush to sue for alleged trademark violations and readily take each other to court for parodying slogans or products (as Nike did when Candies shoes adopted the slogan "Just Screw It"), multinationals are proving markedly less eager to enter into legal battles that will clearly be fought less on legal than on political grounds. "No one wants to be in the limelight because they are the target of community protests or boycotts," one advertising executive told *Advertising Age.*[11] Furthermore, corporations rightly see jammers as rabid attention seekers and have learned to avoid anything that could garner media coverage for their stunts. A case in point came in 1992 when Absolut Vodka threatened to sue *Adbusters* over its "Absolut Nonsense" parody. The company immediately backed down when the magazine went to the press and challenged the distiller to a public debate on the harmful effects of alcohol.

And much to Negativland's surprise, Pepsi's lawyers even refrained from responding to the band's 1997 release, *Dispepsi* – an anti-pop album consisting of hacked, jammed, distorted and disfigured Pepsi jingles. One song mimics the ads by juxtaposing the product's name with a laundry list of random unpleasant images: "I got fired by my boss. Pepsi/ I nailed Jesus to the cross. Pepsi/ ... The ghastly stench of puppy mills. Pepsi" and so on.[12] When asked by *Entertainment Weekly* magazine for its response to the album, the soft-drink giant claimed to think it was "a pretty good listen."[13]

Identity politics goes interactive

There is a connection between the ad fatigue expressed by the jammers and the fierce salvos against media sexism, racism and homophobia that were so much in vogue when I was an undergraduate in the late eighties and early nineties. This connection is perhaps best traced through the evolving relationships that feminists have had with the ad world, particularly since the movement deserves credit for laying the groundwork for many of the current ad critiques. As Susan Douglas notes in *Where the Girls Are*, "Of all the social movements of the 1960s and '70s, none was more explicitly anti-consumerist than the women's movement. Feminists had attacked the ad campaigns for products like Pristeen and Silva Thins, and by rejecting makeup, fashion and the need for spotless floors, repudiated the very need to buy certain products at all."[14] Furthermore, when *Ms.* magazine was relaunched in 1990, the editors took advertiser interference so seriously that they made the unprecedented move of banishing lucrative advertisements from their pages entirely. And the "No Comment" section – a back-page gallery of sexist ads reprinted from other publications – remains one of the highest-profile forums for adbusting.

Many female culture jammers say they first became interested in the machinations of marketing via a "Feminism 101" critique of the beauty industry. Maybe they started by scrawling "feed me" on Calvin Klein ads in bus shelters, as the skateboarding members of the all-high-school Bitch Brigade did. Or maybe they got their hands on a copy of Nomy Lamm's zine, *I'm So Fucking Beautiful*, or they stumbled onto the "Feed the Super Model" interactive game on the official RiotGrrrl Web site. Or maybe, like Toronto's Carly Stasko, they got started through grrrly self-publishing. Twenty-one-year-old Stasko is a one-woman alternative-image factory: her pocket and backpack overflow with ad-jammed stickers, copies of her latest zine and handwritten flyers on the virtues of "guerrilla gardening." And when Stasko is not studying semiotics at the University of Toronto, planting sunflower seeds in abandoned urban lots or making her own media, she's teaching courses at local alternative schools where she shows classes of fourteen-year-olds how they too can cut and paste their own culture jams.

Stasko's interest in marketing began when she realized the degree to which contemporary definitions of female beauty – articulated largely through the media and advertisements – were making her and her peers feel insecure and inadequate. But unlike my generation of young feminists who had dealt with similar revelations largely by calling for censorship and re-education programs, she caught the mid-nineties self-publishing craze. Still in her teens, Stasko began publishing *Uncool*, a photocopied zine crammed with collages of sliced-and-diced quizzes from women's magazines, jammed ads for tampons, manifestos on culture jamming and, in one issue, a full-page ad for Philosophy Barbie. "What came first?" Stasko's Barbie wonders. "The beauty or the myth?" and "If I break a nail, but I'm asleep, is it still a crisis?"

She says that the process of making her own media, adopting the voice of the promoter and hacking into the surface of the ad culture began to weaken advertising's effect on her. "I realized that I can use the same tools the media does to promote my ideas. It took the sting out of the media for me because I saw how easy it was."[15]

Although he is more than ten years older than Stasko, the road that led Rodriguez de Gerada to culture jamming shares some of the same twists. A founding member of the political art troop Artfux, he began adbusting coincident with a wave of black and Latino community organizing against cigarette and alcohol advertising. In 1990, thirty years after the National Association for the Advancement of Colored People first lobbied cigarette companies to use more black models in their ads, a church-based movement began in several American cities that accused these same companies of exploiting black poverty by target-marketing inner cities for their lethal product. In a clear sign of the times, attention had shifted from who was in the ads to the products they sold. Reverend Calvin O. Butts of the Abyssinian Baptist Church in Harlem took his parishioners on billboard-busting blitzes during which they would paint over the cigarette and alcohol advertisements around their church. Other preachers took up the fight in Chicago, Detroit and Dallas.[16]

Reverend Butts's adbusting consisted of reaching up to offending billboards with long-handled paint rollers and whitewashing the ads. It was functional, but Rodriguez de Gerada decided to be more creative: to replace the companies' consumption messages with more persuasive political messages of his own. As a skilled artist, he carefully morphed the faces of cigarette models so they looked rancid and diseased. He replaced the standard Surgeon General's Warning with his own messages: "Struggle General's Warning: Blacks and Latinos are the prime scapegoats for illegal drugs, and the prime targets for legal ones."

Like many other early culture jammers, Rodriguez de Gerada soon extended his critiques beyond tobacco and alcohol ads to include rampant ad bombardment and commercialism in general, and, in many ways, he has the ambitiousness of branding itself to thank for this political evolution. As inner-city kids began stabbing each other for their Nike, Polo, Hilfiger and Nautica gear, it became clear that tobacco and alcohol companies are not the only marketers that prey on poor children's longing for escape. As we have seen, these fashion labels sold disadvantaged kids so successfully on their exaggerated representations of the good life – the country club, the yacht, the superstar celebrity – that logowear has become, in some parts of the Global City, both talisman and weapon. Meanwhile, the young feminists of Carly Stasko's generation whose sense of injustice had been awakened by Naomi Wolf's *Beauty Myth*, and Jean Kilbourne's documentary *Killing Us Softly*, also lived through the feeding frenzies around "alternative," Gen-X, hip-hop and rave culture. In the process, many became vividly aware that marketing affects communities not only by stereotyping them, but also – and equally powerfully – by hyping and chasing after them. This was a tangible shift from one generation of feminists to the next. When *Ms.* went ad-free in 1990, for instance, there was a belief that the corrosive advertising interference from which Gloria Steinem and Robin Morgan were determined to free their publication was a specifically female problem.[17] But as the politics of identity mesh with the burgeoning critique of corporate power, the demand has shifted from reforming problematic ad campaigns to questioning whether advertisers have any legitimate right to invade every nook and cranny of our mental and physical environment: it has become about the disappearance of space and the lack of meaningful choice. Ad culture has demonstrated its remarkable ability to absorb, accommodate and even profit from content critiques. In this context, it has become abundantly clear that the only attack that will actually shake this resilient industry is one leveled not at the pretty people in the pictures, but against the corporations that paid for them.

So for Carly Stasko, marketing has become more an environmental than a gender or self-esteem issue, and her environment is the streets, the university campus and the mass-media culture in which she, as an urbanite, lives her life. "I mean, this is my environment," she says, "and these ads are really directed at me. If these images can affect me, then I can affect them back."

The washroom ad as political catalyst

For many students coming of age in the late nineties, the turning point from focusing on the content of advertising to a preoccupation with the form itself occurred in the most private of places: in their university washrooms, staring at a car ad. The washroom ads first began appearing on North American campuses in 1997 and have been proliferating ever since. As we have already seen in Chapter 5, the administrators who allowed ads to creep onto their campuses told themselves that young people were already so bombarded with commercial messages that a few more wouldn't kill them, and the revenues would help fund valuable programs. But it seems there is such a thing as an ad that breaks the camel's back – and for many students, that was it.

The irony, of course, is that from the advertiser's perspective, niche nirvana had been attained. Short of eyelid implants, ads in college washrooms represent as captive a youth market as there is on earth. But from the students' perspective, there could have been no more literal metaphor for space closing in than an ad for Pizza Pizza or Chrysler Neon staring at them from over a urinal or from the door of a W.C. cubicle. Which is precisely why this misguided branding scheme created the opportunity for hundreds of North American students to take their first tentative steps toward direct anticorporate activism.

Looking back, school officials must see that there is something hilariously misguided about putting ads in private cubicles where students have been known to pull out their pens or eyeliners and scrawl desperate declarations of love, circulate unsubstantiated rumors, carry on the abortion debate and share deep philosophical insights. When the mini-billboards arrived, the bathroom became the first truly safe space in which to talk back to ads. In an instant, the direction of the scrutiny through the one-way glass of the focus group was reversed, and the target market took aim at the people behind the glass. The most creative response came from students at the University of Toronto. A handful of undergraduates landed part-time jobs with the washroom billboard company and kept conveniently losing the custom-made screwdrivers that opened the four hundred plastic frames. Pretty soon, a group calling themselves the Escher Appreciation Society were breaking into the "student-proof" frames and systematically replacing the bathroom ads with prints by Maurits Cornelis Escher. Rather than brushing up on the latest from Chrysler or Molson, students could learn to appreciate the Dutch graphic artist – chosen, the Escherites conceded, because his geometric work photocopies well.

The bathroom ads made it unmistakably clear to a generation of student activists that they don't need cooler, more progressive or more diverse ads – first and foremost, they need ads to shut up once in a while. Debate on campuses began to shift away from an evaluation of the content of ads to the fact that it was becoming impossible to escape from advertising's intrusive gaze.

Of course there are those among the culture jammers whose interest in advertising is less tapped into the new ethos of anti-branding rage and instead has much in common with the morality squads of the political correctness years. At times, *Adbusters* magazine feels like an only slightly hipper version of a Public Service Announcement about saying no to peer pressure or remembering to Reduce, Reuse and Recycle. The magazine is capable of lacerating wit, but its attacks on nicotine, alcohol and fast-food joints can be repetitive and obvious. Jams that change Absolut Vodka to "Absolut Hangover" or Ultra Kool cigarettes to "Utter Fool" cigarettes are enough to turn off would-be supporters who see the magazine crossing a fine line between information-age civil disobedience and puritanical finger-waving. Mark Dery, author of the original culture-jammers' manifesto and a former contributor to the magazine, says the anti-booze, -smoking and -fast-food emphasis reads as just plain patronizing – as if "the masses" cannot be trusted to "police their own desires."[18]

Listening to the marketer within

In a *New Yorker* article entitled "The Big Sellout," author John Seabrook discusses the phenomenon of "the marketer within." He argues persuasively that an emerging generation of artists will not concern themselves with old ethical dilemmas like "selling out" since they are a walking sales pitch for themselves already, intuitively understanding how to produce prepackaged art, to be their own brand. "The artists of the next generation will make their art with an internal marketing barometer already in place. The auteur as marketer, the artist in a suit of his own: the ultimate in vertical integration."[19]

Seabrook is right in his observation that the rhythm of the pitch is hardwired into the synapses of many young artists, but he is mistaken in assuming that the built-in marketing barometer will only be used to seek fame and fortune in the culture industries. As Carly Stasko points out, many people who grew up sold are so attuned to the tempo of marketing that as soon as they read or hear a new slogan, they begin to flip it and play with it in their minds, as she herself does. For Stasko, it is the adbuster that is within, and every ad campaign is a riddle just waiting for the right jam. So the skill Seabrook identifies, which allows artists to write the press bumpf for their own gallery openings and musicians to churn out metaphor-filled bios for their liner notes, is the same quality that makes for a deadly clever culture jammer. The culture jammer is the activist as *anti*marketer, using a childhood filled with Trix commercials, and an adolescence spent spotting the product placement on *Seinfeld*, to mess with a system that once saw itself as a specialized science. Jamie Batsy, a Toronto-area "hacktivist," puts it like this: "Advertisers and other opinion makers are now in a position where they are up against a generation of activists that were watching television before they could walk. This generation wants their brains back and mass media is their home turf."[20]

Culture jammers are drawn to the world of marketing like moths to a flame, and the high-gloss sheen on their work is achieved precisely because they still feel an affection – however deeply ambivalent – for media spectacle and the mechanics of persuasion. "I think a lot of people who are really interested in subverting advertising or studying advertising probably, at one time, wanted to be ad people themselves," says Carrie McLaren, editor of the New York zine *Stay Free!*[21] You can see it in her own ad busts, which are painstakingly seamless in their design and savage in their content. In one issue, a full-page anti-ad shows a beat-up kid face down on the concrete with no shoes on. In the corner of the frame is a hand making away with his Nike sneakers. "Just do it," the slogan says.

Nowhere is the adbuster's ear for the pitch used to fuller effect than in the promotion of adbusting itself, a fact that might explain why culture jamming's truest believers often sound like an odd cross between used-car salesmen and tenured semiotics professors. Second only to Internet hucksters and rappers, adbusters are susceptible to a spiraling bravado and to a level of self-promotion that can be just plain silly. There is much fondness for claiming to be Marshall McLuhan's son, daughter, grandchild or bastard progeny. There is a strong tendency to exaggerate the power of wheatpaste and a damn good joke. And to overstate their own power: one culture-jamming manifesto, for instance, explains that "the billboard artist's goal is to throw a well aimed spanner into the media's gears, bringing the image factory to a shuddering halt."[22]

Adbusters has taken this hard-sell approach to such an extreme that it has raised hackles among rival culture jammers. Particularly galling to its critics is the magazine's line of anticonsumer products that they say has made the magazine less a culture-jamming clearinghouse than a home-shopping network for adbusting accessories. Culture-jammer "tool boxes" are listed for sale: posters, videos, stickers and postcards; most ironically, it used to sell calendars and T-shirts to coincide with Buy Nothing Day, though better sense eventually prevailed. "What comes out is no real alternative to our culture of consumption," Carrie McLaren writes. "Just a different brand." Fellow Vancouver jammers Guerrilla Media (GM) take a more vicious shot at *Adbusters* in the GM inaugural newsletter. "We promise there are no GM calendars, key chains or coffee mugs in the offing. We are, however, still working on those T-shirts that some of you ordered – we're just looking for that perfect sweatshop to produce them."[23]

Marketing the antimarketers

The attacks are much the same as those lobbed at every punk band that signs a record deal and every zine that goes glossy: *Adbusters* has simply become too popular to have much cachet for the radicals who once dusted it off in their local secondhand bookstore like a precious stone. But beyond the standard-issue purism, the question of how best to "market" an antimarketing movement is a uniquely thorny dilemma. There is a sense among some adbusters that culture jamming, like punk itself, must remain something of a porcupine; that to defy its own inevitable commodification, it must keep its protective quills sharp. After the great Alternative and Girl Power™ cash-ins, the very process of naming a trend, or coining a catchphrase, is regarded by some with deep suspicion. "*Adbusters* jumped on it and were ready to claim this movement before it ever really existed," says McLaren, who complains bitterly in her own writing about the "USA Today/MTV-ization" of *Adbusters*. "It's become an advertisement for anti-advertising."[24]

There is another fear underlying this debate, one more confusing for its proponents than the prospect of culture jamming "selling out" to the dictates of marketing. What if, despite all the rhetorical flair its adherents can muster, culture jamming doesn't actually matter? What if there is no jujitsu, only semiotic shadowboxing? Kalle Lasn insists that his magazine has the power to "jolt postmodern society out of its media trance" and that his uncommercials threaten to shake network television to its core. "The television mindscape has been homogenized over the last 30 to 40 years. It's a space that is very safe for commercial messages. So, if you suddenly introduce a note of cognitive dissonance with a spot that says 'Don't buy a car,' or in the middle of a fashion show somebody suddenly says 'What about anorexia?' there's a powerful moment of truth."[25] But the real truth is that, as a culture, we seem to be capable of absorbing limitless amounts of cognitive dissonance on our TV sets. We culture jam manually every time we channel surf – catapulting from the desperate fundraising pleas of the Foster Parent Plan to infomercials for Buns of Steel; from Jerry Springer to Jerry Falwell; from New Country to Marilyn Manson. In these information-numb times, we are beyond being abruptly awakened by a startling image, a sharp juxtaposition or even a fabulously clever détournement.

Jaggi Singh is one activist who has become disillusioned with the jujitsu theory. "When you're jamming, you're sort of playing their game, and I think ultimately that playing field is stacked against us because they can saturate . . . we don't have the resources to do all those billboards; we don't have the resources to buy up all that time, and in a sense, it almost becomes pretty scientific – who can afford these feeds?"

Logo overload

To add further evidence that culture jamming is more drop in the bucket than spanner in the works, marketers are increasingly deciding to join in the fun. When Kalle Lasn says culture jamming has the feeling of "a bit of a fad," he's not exaggerating.[26] It turns out that culture jamming – with its combination of hip-hop attitude, punk anti-authoritarianism and a well of visual gimmicks – has great sales potential.

Yahoo! already has an official culture-jamming site on the Internet, filed under "alternative." At Soho Down & Under on West Broadway in New York, Camden Market in London or any other high street where alterno gear is for sale, you can load up on logo-jammed T-shirts, stickers and badges. Recurring détournements – to use a word that seems suddenly misplaced – include Kraft changed to "Krap," Tide changed to "Jive," Ford changed to "Fucked" and Goodyear changed to "Goodbeer." It's not exactly trenchant social commentary, particularly since the jammed logos appear to be interchangeable with the corporate kitsch of unaltered Dubble Bubble and Tide T-shirts. In the rave scene, logo play is all the rage – in clothing, temporary tattoos, body paint and even ecstasy pills. Ecstasy dealers have taken to branding their tablets with famous logos: there is Big Mac E, Purple Nike Swirl E, X-Files E, and a mixture of uppers and downers called a "Happy Meal." Musician Jeff Renton explains the drug culture's appropriation of corporate logos as a revolt against invasive marketing. "I think it's a matter of: 'You come into our lives with your million-dollar advertising campaigns putting logos in places that make us feel uncomfortable, so we're going to take your logo back and use it in places that make you feel uncomfortable,'" he says.[27]

But after a while, what began as a way to talk back to the ads starts to feel more like evidence of our total colonization by them, and especially because the ad industry is proving that it is capable of cutting off the culture jammers at the pass. Examples of pre-jammed ads include a 1997 Nike campaign that used the slogan "I am not/A target market/I am an athlete" and Sprite's "Image Is Nothing" campaign, featuring a young black man saying that all his life he has been bombarded with media lies telling him that soft drinks will make him a better athlete or more attractive, until he realized that "image is nothing." Diesel jeans, however, has gone furthest in incorporating the political content of adbusting's anticorporate attacks. One of the most popular ways for artists and activists to highlight the inequalities of free-market globalization is by juxtaposing First World icons with Third World scenes: Marlboro Country in the war-torn rubble of Beirut (see image, page 10); an obviously malnourished Haitian girl wearing Mickey Mouse glasses; *Dynasty* playing on a TV set in an African hut; Indonesian students rioting in front of McDonald's arches. The power of these visual critiques of happy one-worldism is precisely what the Diesel clothing company's "Brand O" ad campaign attempts to co-opt. The campaign features ads within ads: a series of billboards flogging a fictional Brand O line of products in a nameless North Korean city. In one, a glamorous skinny blonde is pictured on the side of a bus that is overflowing with frail-looking workers. The ad is selling "Brand O Diet – There's no limit to how thin you can get." Another shows an Asian man huddled under a piece of cardboard. Above him towers a Ken and Barbie Brand O billboard.

Perhaps the point of no return came in 1997 when Mark Hosler of Negativland received a call from the ultra-hip ad agency Wieden & Kennedy asking if the band that coined the term "culture jamming" would do the soundtrack for a new Miller Genuine Draft commercial. The decision to turn down the request and the money was simple enough, but it still sent him spinning. "They utterly failed to grasp that our entire work is essentially in opposition to everything that they are connected to, and it made me really depressed because I had thought that our esthetic couldn't be absorbed into marketing," Hosler says.[28] Another rude awakening came when Hosler first saw Sprite's "Obey Your Thirst" campaign. "That commercial was a hair's breadth away from a song on our [*Dispepsi*] record. It was surreal. It's not just the fringe that's getting absorbed now – that's always happened. What's getting absorbed now is the idea that there's no opposition left, that any resistance is futile."[29]

311

I'm not so sure. Yes, some marketers have found a way to distill culture jamming into a particularly edgy kind of nonlinear advertising, and there is no doubt that Madison Avenue's embrace of the techniques of adbusting has succeeded in moving product off the superstore shelves. Since Diesel began its aggressively ironic "Reasons for Living" and "Brand O" campaigns in the U.S., sales have gone from $2 million to $23 million in four years,[30] and the Sprite "Image Is Nothing" campaign is credited with a 35 percent rise in sales in just three years.[31] That said, the success of these individual campaigns has done nothing to disarm the antimarketing rage that fueled adbusting in the first place. In fact, it may be having the opposite effect.

Ground zero of the cool hunt

The prospect of young people turning against the hype of advertising and defining themselves against the big brands is a continuous threat coming from cool-hunting agencies like Sputnik, that infamous team of professional diary readers and generational snoops. "Intellectual crews," as Sputnik calls thinking young people, are aware and resentful of how useful they are to the marketers:

> They understand that mammoth corporations now seek their approval to continually deliver goods that will translate to megasales in the mainstream. Their stance of being intellectual says to each other, and to themselves, and most importantly to marketers – who spend innumerable dollars for in-your-face this-is-what-you-need advertisements – that they cannot be bought or fooled anymore by the hype. Being a head means that you won't sell out and be told what to wear, what to buy, what to eat or how to speak by anyone (or anything) other than yourself.[32]

But while the Sputnik writers inform their corporate readers about the radical ideas on the street, they appear to think that though these ideas will dramatically influence how young people will party, dress and talk, they will magically have no effect whatsoever on how young people will behave as political beings.

After they sound the alarm, the hunters always reassure their readers that all this anticorporate stuff is actually a meaningless pose that can be worked around with a hipper, edgier campaign. In other words, anticorporate rage is no more meaningful a street trend than a mild preference for the color orange. The happy underlying premise of the cool hunters' reports is that despite all the punk-rock talk, there is no belief that is a true belief and there are no rebels who cannot be tamed with an ad campaign or by a street promoter who *really speaks to them*. The unquestioned assumption is that there is no end point in this style cycle. There will always be new spaces to colonize – whether physical or mental – and there will always be an ad that will be able to penetrate the latest strain of consumer cynicism. Nothing new is taking place, the hunters tell each other: marketers have always extracted symbols and signs from the resistance movements of their day.

What they don't say is that previous waves of youth resistance were focused primarily on such foes as "the establishment," the government, the patriarchy and the military-industrial complex. Culture jamming is different – its rage encompasses the very type of marketing that the cool hunters and their clients are engaging in as they try to figure out how to use anti-marketing rage to sell products. The big brands' new ads must incorporate a youth cynicism not about products as status symbols, or about mass homogenization, but about multinational brands themselves as tireless culture vultures.

The admen and adwomen have met this new challenge without changing their course. They are busily hunting down and reselling the edge, just as they have always done, which is why Wieden & Kennedy thought there was nothing strange about asking Negativland to shill for Miller. After all, it was Wieden & Kennedy, a boutique ad agency based in Portland, Oregon, that made Nike a feminist sneaker. It was W&K who dreamed up the postindustrial alienation marketing plan for Coke's OK Cola; W&K who gave the world the immortal plaid-clad assertion that the Subaru Impreza was "like punk rock"; and it was W&K who brought Miller Beer into the age of irony. Masters at pitting the individual against various incarnations of mass-market bogeymen, Wieden & Kennedy sold cars to people who hated car ads, shoes to people who loathed image, soft drinks to the Prozac Nation and, most of all, ads to people who were "not a target market."

The agency was founded by two self-styled "beatnik artists," Dan Wieden and David Kennedy, whose technique, it seems, for quieting their own nagging fears that they were selling out has consistently been to drag the ideas and icons of the counterculture with them into the ad world. A quick tour through the agency's body of work is nothing short of a counterculture reunion – Woodstock meets the Beats meets Warhol's Factory. After putting Lou Reed in a Honda spot in the mid-eighties, W&K used the Beatles anthem "Revolution" in one Nike commercial, then carted out John Lennon's "Instant Karma" for another. They also paid proto-rock-and-roller Bo Diddley to do the "Bo Knows" Nike spots, and filmmaker Spike Lee to do an entire series of Air Jordan ads. W&K even got Jean-Luc Godard to direct a European Nike commercial. There were still more counter-cultural artifacts lying around: they stuck William Burroughs's face in a mini-TV-set in another Nike commercial and designed a campaign, nixed by Subaru before it made it to air, that used Jack Kerouac's *On the Road* as the voice-over text for an SVX commercial.

After making its name on the willingness of the avant-garde to set its price for the right mix of irony and dollars, W&K can hardly be blamed for thinking that culture jammers would also be thrilled to take part in the postmodern fun of a self-aware ad campaign. But the backlash against the brands, of which culture jamming is only one part, isn't about vague notions of alternativeness battling the mainstream. It has to do with the specific issues that have been the subject of this book so far: the loss of public space, corporate censorship and unethical labor practices, to name but three – issues less easily digested than tasty morsels like Girl Power and grunge.

Which is why Wieden & Kennedy hit a wall when they asked Negativland to mix for Miller, and why that was only the first in a string of defeats for the agency. The British political pop-band Chumbawamba turned down a $1.5 million contract that would have allowed Nike to use its hit song "Tub-thumping" in a World Cup spot. Abstract notions about staying indie were not at issue (the band did allow the song to be used in the soundtrack for *Home Alone 3*); at the center of their rejection was Nike's use of sweat-shop labor. "It took everybody in the room under 30 seconds to say no," said band member Alice Nutter.[33] The political poet Martin Espada also got a call from one of Nike's smaller agencies, inviting him to take part in the "Nike Poetry Slam." If he accepted, he would be paid $2,500 and his poem would be read in a thirty-second commercial during the 1998 Winter Olympics in Nagano. Espada turned the agency down flat, offering up a host of reasons and ending with this one: "Ultimately, however, I am reject-ing your offer as a protest against the brutal labor practices of the company. I will not associate myself with a company that engages in the well-documented exploitation of workers in sweatshops."[34] The rudest awakening came with Wieden & Kennedy's cleverest of schemes: in May 1999, with labor scandals still hanging over the swoosh, the agency approached Ralph Nader – the consumer-rights movement's most powerful leader and a folk hero for his attacks on multinational corporations – and asked him to do a Nike ad. The idea was simple: Nader would get $25,000 for holding up an Air 120 sneaker and saying, "Another shameless attempt by Nike to sell shoes." A letter sent to Nader's office from Nike headquarters explained that "what we are asking is for Ralph, as the country's most prominent consumer advocate, to take a light-hearted jab at us. This is a very Nike-like thing to do in our ads." Nader, never known for being light of heart, would only say, "Look at the gall of these guys."[35]

It was indeed a very Nike-like thing to do. Ads co-opt out of reflex – they do so because consuming is what consumer culture does. Madison Avenue is generally not too picky about what it will swallow, it doesn't avoid poison directed against itself but rather, as Wieden & Kennedy have shown, chomps down on whatever it finds along the path as it looks for the new "edge." The scenario that it appears unwilling to consider is that its admen and adwomen, the perennial teenage followers, may finally be following their target market off a cliff.

Adbusting in the thirties: "become a toucher upper!"

Of course the ad industry has disarmed backlashes before – from women complaining of sexism, gays claiming invisibility, ethnic minorities tired of gross caricatures. And that's not all. In the 1950s and again in the 1970s, Western consumers became obsessed with the idea that they were being fooled by advertisers through the covert use of subliminal techniques. In 1957, Vance Packard published the runaway best-seller *The Hidden Persuaders*, which shocked Americans with allegations that social scientists were packing advertisements with messages invisible to the human eye. The issue re-emerged in 1973, when Wilson Bryan Key published *Subliminal Seduction*, a study of the lascivious messages tucked away in ice cubes. Key was so transported by his discovery that he made such bold claims as "the subliminal promise to anyone buying Gilbey's gin is simply a good old-fashioned sexual orgy."[36]

But all these antimarketing spasms had one thing in common: they focused exclusively on the content and techniques of advertising. These critics didn't want to be subliminally manipulated – and they *did* want African Americans in their cigarette ads and gays and lesbians selling jeans. Because the concerns were so specific, they were relatively easy for the ad world to address or absorb. For instance, the charge of hidden messages harbored in ice cubes, and other carefully cast shadows, spawned an irony-laden advertising subgenre that design historians Ellen Luton and J. Abbot Miller term "meta-subliminal" – ads that parody the charge that ads send secret messages. In 1990, Absolut Vodka launched the "Absolut Subliminal" campaign which showed a glass of vodka on the rocks with the word "absolut" clearly screened into the ice cubes. Seagram's and Tanqueray gin followed with their own subliminal in-jokes, as did the cast of *Saturday Night Live* with the recurring character Subliminal Man.

The critiques of advertising that have traditionally come out of academe have been equally unthreatening, though for different reasons. Most such criticism focuses not on the effects of marketing on public space, cultural freedom and democracy, but rather on ads' persuasive powers over seemingly clueless people. For the most part, marketing theory concentrates on the way ads implant false desires in the consuming public – making us buy things that are bad for us, pollute the planet or impoverish our souls. "Advertising," as George Orwell once said, "is the rattling of a stick inside a swill bucket." When such is the theorist's opinion of the public, it is no wonder that there is little potential for redemption in most media criticism: this sorry populace will never be in possession of the critical tools it needs to formulate a political response to marketing mania and media synergy.

The future is even bleaker for those academics who use advertising criticism for a thinly veiled attack on "consumer culture." As James Twitchell writes in *Adcult USA*, most advertising criticism reeks of contempt for the people who "want – ugh! – things."[37] Such a theory can never hope to form the intellectual foundation of an actual resistance movement against the branded life, since genuine political empowerment cannot be reconciled with a belief system that regards the public as a bunch of ad-fed cattle, held captive under commercial culture's hypnotic spell. What's the point of going through the trouble of trying to knock down the fence? Everyone knows the branded cows will just stand there looking dumb and chewing cud.

Interestingly, the last time that there was a successful attack on the practice of advertising – rather than a disagreement on its content or techniques – was during the Great Depression. In the 1930s the very idea of the happy, stable consumer society portrayed in advertising provoked a wave of resentment from the millions of Americans who found themselves on the outside of the dream of prosperity. An anti-advertising movement emerged that attacked ads not for faulty imagery but as the most public face of a deeply faulty economic system. People weren't incensed by the pictures in the ads, but rather by the cruelty of the obviously false promise that they represented – the lie of the American Dream that the happy consumer lifestyle was accessible to all. In the late twenties, and through the thirties, the frivolous promises of the ad world made for stomach-wrenching juxtapositions with the casualties of economic collapse, setting the stage for an unparalleled wave of consumer activism.

There was a short-lived magazine published in New York called *The Ballyhoo*, a sort of Depression-era *Adbusters*. In the wake of the 1929 stock-market crash, *The Ballyhoo* arrived as a cynical new voice, viciously mocking the "creative psychiatry" of cigarette and mouthwash ads, as well as the outright quackery used to sell all kinds of potions and lotions.[38] *The Ballyhoo* was an instant success, reaching a circulation of more than 1.5 million in 1931. James Rorty, a 1920s Mad Ave adman turned revolutionary socialist, explained the new magazine's appeal: "Whereas the stock in trade of the ordinary mass or class consumer magazine is reader-confidence in advertising, the stock in trade of *Ballyhoo* was reader-disgust with advertising, and with high-pressure salesmanship in general. . . . *Ballyhoo*, in turn, parasites on the grotesque, bloated body of advertising."[39]

Ballyhoo's culture jams include "Scramel" cigarettes ("they're so fresh they're insulting"), or the line of "69 different Zilch creams: What the well greased girls will wear. Absolutely indispensable (Ask any dispensary)." The editors encouraged readers to move beyond their snickers and go out and bust bothersome billboards themselves. A fake ad for the "Twitch Toucher Upper School" shows a drawing of a woman who has just painted a mustache on a glamorous cigarette model. The caption reads, "Become a Toucher Upper!" and goes on to say: "If you long to mess up advertisement: if your heart cries out to paint pipes in the mouths of beautiful ladies, try this 10-second test NOW! Our graduates make their marks all over the world!

Good Toucher Uppers are always in demand" (see image on page 278). The magazine also created fake products to skewer the hypocrisy of the Hoover administration, like the "Lady Pipperal Bedsheet De Luxe" – made extra long to snugly fit on park benches when you become homeless. Or the "smilette" – two hooks that clamp on to either side of the mouth and force a happy expression. "Smile away the Depression! Smile us into Prosperity!"

The hard-core culture jammers of the era were not the *Ballyhoo* humorists, however, but photographers like Walker Evans, Dorothea Lange and Margaret Bourke-White. These political documentarians latched on to the hypocrisies of ad campaigns such as the National Association of Manufacturers' "There's No Way Like the American Way" by highlighting the harsh visual contrasts between the ads and the surrounding landscape. A popular technique was photographing billboards with slogans like "World's Highest Standard of Living" in their actual habitat: hanging surreally over breadlines and tenements. The manic grinning models piled into the family sedan were clearly blind to the tattered masses and squalid conditions below. The photographers of the era also scrupulously documented the fragility of the capitalist system by picturing fallen businessmen holding up "Will Work for Food" signs in the shadow of looming Coke billboards and peeling hoardings.

In 1934, advertisers began to use self-parody to deal with the mounting criticism they faced, a tactic that some saw as proof of the industry's state of disrepair. "It is contended by the broadcasters, and doubtless also by the movie producers, that this burlesque sales promotion takes the curse out of sales talk, and this is probably true to a degree," writes Rorty of the self-mockery. "But the prevalence of the trend gives rise to certain ominous suspicions . . . When the burlesque comedian mounts the pulpit of the Church of Advertising, it may be legitimately suspected that the edifice is doomed; that it will shortly be torn down or converted to secular uses."[40]

Of course the edifice survived, though not unscathed. New Deal politicians, under pressure from a wide range of populist movements, imposed lasting reforms on the industry. The adbusters and social documentary photographers were part of a massive grassroots public revolt against big business that included the farmers' uprising against the proliferation of supermarket chains, the establishing of consumer purchasing cooperatives, the rapid expansion of a network of trade unions and a crackdown on garment industry sweatshops (which had seen the ranks of the two U.S. garment workers' unions swell from 40,000 in 1931 to more than 300,000 in 1933). Most of all, the early ad critics were intimately linked to the burgeoning consumer movement that had been catalyzed by *One Hundred Million Guinea Pigs: Dangers in Everyday Foods, Drugs and Cosmetics* (1993), by F. J. Schlink and Arthur Kallet, and *Your Money's Worth: A Study in the Waste of the Consumer Dollar* (1927), written by Stuart Chase and F. J. Schlink. These books presented exhaustive catalogs of the way regular folks were getting lied to, cheated, poisoned and ripped off by America's captains of industry. The authors founded Consumer Research (later splintered off into the Consumers Union), which served both as an independent product-testing laboratory and a political group that lobbied the government for better grading and labeling of products. The CR believed objective testing and truthful labeling could make marketing so irrelevant it would become obsolete. According to Chase and Schlink's logic, if consumers had access to careful scientific research that compared the relative merits of the products on the market, everyone would simply make measured, rational decisions about what to buy. The advertisers, of course, were beside themselves, and terrified of the following F. J. Schlink had built up on the college campuses and among the New York intelligentsia. As adman C. B. Larrabee noted in 1934, "Some forty or fifty thousand persons won't so much as buy a box of dog biscuits unless F. J. gives his 'O. K.' . . . obviously they think most advertisers are dishonest, double-dealing shysters."[41]

Schlink and Chase's rationalist utopia of Spock-like consumerism never came to fruition, but their lobbying did force governments around the world to move to outlaw blatantly false claims in advertising, to establish quality standards for consumer goods, and to become actively involved in the grading and labeling of them. And the *Consumers Union Reports* is still the buyer's bible in America, though it long ago severed its ties to other social movements.

It is worth noting that the modern-day ad world's most extreme attempts to co-opt anticorporate rage have fed directly off images pioneered by the Depression-era documentary photographers. Diesel's Brand O is almost a direct replica of Margaret Bourke-White's "American Way" billboard series, both in style and composition. And when the Bank of Montreal ran an ad campaign in Canada in the late nineties, at the height of a popular backlash against soaring bank profits, it used images that recalled Walker Evans's photographs of 1930s businessmen holding up those "Will Work for Food" signs. The bank's campaign consisted of a series of grainy black-and-white photographs of ragged-looking people holding signs that asked, "Will I ever own my own home?" and "Are we going to be okay?" One sign simply read, "The little guy is on his own." The television spots blasted Depression-era gospel and ragtime over eerie industrial images of abandoned freight trains and dusty towns.

In other words, when the time came to fight fire with fire, the advertisers raced back to an era when they were never more loathed and only a world war could save them. It seems that this kind of psychic shock – a clothing company using the very images that have scarred the clothing industry; a bank trading on anti-bank rage – is the only technique left that will get the attention of us ad-resistant roaches. And this may well be true, from a marketing point of view, but there is also a larger context that reaches beyond imagery: Diesel produces many of its garments in Indonesia and other parts of the Far East, profiting from the very disparities illustrated in its clever Brand O ads. In fact, part of the edginess of the campaign is the clear sense that the company is flirting with a Nike-style public-relations meltdown. So far, the Diesel brand does not have a wide enough market reach to feel the full force of having its images slingshot back at its body corporate, but the bigger the company gets – and it is getting bigger every year – the more vulnerable it becomes.

That was the lesson in the responses to the Bank of Montreal's "Sign of the Times" campaign. The bank's use of powerful images of economic collapse at exactly the same time that it announced record profits of $986 million (up in 1998 to $1.3 billion) inspired a spontaneous wave of adbusting. The simple imagery of the campaign – people holding up angry signs – was easy for the bank's critics to replicate with parodies that skewered the bank's exorbitant service fees, its inaccessible loans officers and the closing of branches in low-income neighborhoods (after all, the bank's technique had been stolen from the activists in the first place). Everyone got in on the action: lone jammers, CBC television's satirical show *This Hour Has 22 Minutes, The Globe and Mail's Report on Business Magazine*, and independent video collectives.

Clearly, these ad campaigns are tapping into powerful emotions. But by playing on sentiments that are already directed against them – for example, public resentment at profiteering banks or widening economic disparities – the process of co-optation runs the very real risk of amplifying the backlash, not disarming it. Above all, imagery appropriation appears to radicalize culture jammers and other anticorporate activists – a "co-opt this!" stance develops that becomes even harder to diffuse. For instance, when Chrysler ran a campaign of pre-jammed Neon ads (the one that added a faux aerosol "p," changing "Hi" to "Hip"), it inspired the Billboard Liberation Front to go on its biggest tear in years. The BLF defaced dozens of Bay Area Neon billboards by further altering "Hip" to "Hype," and adding, for good measure, a skull and crossbones. "We can't sit by while these companies co-opt our means of communication," Jack Napier said. "Besides . . . they're tacky."

Perhaps the gravest miscalculation on the part of both markets and media is the insistence on seeing culture jamming solely as harmless satire, a game that exists in isolation from a genuine political movement or ideology. Certainly for some jammers, parody is perceived, in rather grandiose fashion, as a powerful end in itself. But for many more, as we will see in the next chapters, it is simply a new tool for packaging anticorporate salvos, one that is more effective than most at breaking through the media barrage. And as we will also see, adbusters are currently at work on many different fronts: the people scaling billboards are frequently the same ones who are organizing against the Multilateral Agreement on Investment, staging protests on the streets of Geneva against the World Trade Organization and occupying

319

banks to protest against the profits they are making from student debts. Adbusting is not an end in itself. It is simply a tool – one among many – that is being used, loaned and borrowed in a much broader political movement against the branded life.

Notes

1 Personal interview.
2 Saul D. Alinsky, *Rules for Radicals: A Pragmatic Primer for Realistic Radicals* (Random House: New York, 1971), 152.
3 Personal interview. Many adbusters I interviewed chose to remain anonymous.
4 Personal interview.
5 Mary Kuntz, "Is Nothing Sacred," *Business Week*, 18 May 1998, 130–37.
6 Ibid.
7 Personal interview.
8 Personal interview.
9 Katz, *Just Do It*, 39.
10 *New York Times*, 4 April 1990, B1. DeWitt F. Helm Jr., president of the Association of National Advertisers, called the whitewashing over cigarette and alcohol ads by church groups "vigilante censorship."
11 Alison Fahey, "Outdoor Feels the Drought," *Advertising Age*, 6 August 1990, 3.
12 "The Greatest Taste Around," *Dispepsi*, Negativland, 1997.
13 "Soda Pop," *Entertainment Weekly*, 26 September 1997.
14 Susan J. Douglas, *Where the Girls Are* (Times Books: New York, 1994), 227.
15 Personal interview.
16 Stephanie Strom, "Billboard Owners Switching, Not Fighting," *New York Times*, 4 April 1990, B1.
17 Steinem, "Sex, Lies & Advertising."
18 Personal interview.
19 John Seabrook, "The Big Sellout," *New Yorker*, 20 & 27 October 1997, 182–95.
20 Bob Paquin, "E-Guerrillas in the Mist," *Ottawa Citizen*, 26 October 1998.
21 Personal interview.
22 Manifesto produced by Earth First! in Brighton, England.
23 *Guerrilla Shots* 1, no. 1.
24 Carrie McLaren, "Advertising the Uncommercial," *Escandola*, published by Matador Records, November 1995.
25 Jim Boothroyd, "ABC Opens the Door," *Adbusters*, Winter 1998, 53–54.
26 Personal interview.
27 Mitchel Raphael, "Corporate Perversion," *Toronto Star*, 7 February 1998, M1.
28 Doug Saunders, "One Person's Audio Debris Is Another's Is Another's Musical Treasure," *Globe and Mail*, 25 September 1997, C5.
29 Barnaby Marshall, "Negativland: Mark Hosler on the Ad Assault," *Shift* on-line, 22.
30 *Time*, 17 November 1997.
31 *Advertising Age*, 18 November 1996.
32 Lopiano-Misdom and De Luca, *Street Trends*, 27–28.
33 "Anarchy in the U.K.," *Times* (London), 16 May 1998.
34 Martin Espada, *Zapata's Disciple* (Boston: South End Press, 1998).
35 "Nader Nixes Nike $25K Run," *Washington Post*, 13 May 1999.
36 Wilson Bryan Key, *Subliminal Seduction* (New York: Penguin, 1973), 7.

37 James Twitchell, *Adcult USA: The Triumph of Advertising in American Culture* (New York: Columbia University Press, 1996), 12.
38 The term "creative psychiatry" comes from a speech made by Columbia journalism professor Walter B. Pitkin to the 1933 convention of the Association of National Advertisers.
39 Rorty, *Our Master's Voice*, 382–83.
40 Ibid.
41 C. B. Larrabee, "Mr. Schlink," *Printer's Ink*, 11 January 1934, 10.

88

GLOBAL TEENS GROWING INDIFFERENT TO BRAND AMERICA

Adbusters

Source: Adbusters (2006), http://adbusters.org/the_magazine/66/Global_Teens_Growing_Indifferent_to_Brand_America.html

In case you missed the memo, the Stars and Stripes have seen better days.

Even before George W. Bush's theatrical "Mission Accomplished" cameo aboard the USS Abraham Lincoln, brand visionaries had already set out on their grave task of sorting through the marketing ramifications of a president gone wild. Their collective conclusion would prove inevitable: if you want to insulate yourself against the USA's rapidly tarnishing global image, you'd better stop wrapping your brands in the Red, White and Blue.

Three years later, the tumult has quieted. Far from indicating a reversal of America's fortunes, however, the relative calm has more to do with grim resignation. "America" – the brand, the idea, the dream – just doesn't move product like it used to.

A marketing study released early this year puts a pretty savage point on the dilemma. Based on research conducted in the summer of 2005, Chicago branding agency Energy BBDD ranked the "likeability" of 54 globally-marketed brands amongst 13 to 18 years olds from a baker's dozen of countries, including the United States.

Of the big brands with roots in the USA, just five – Nike, Colgate, Coca-Cola, M&Ms and Kodak – made it into the top ten. Contrast this with ten years ago, when a comparable study conducted by D'Arcy Masius Benton & Bowles discovered near-total supremacy of US brands over the much-desired teen demographic, capturing eight of the top ten "likeability" slots.

It's clear that name recognition is not to blame for the decline. In the new study, McDonald's ranked second for name recognition, just behind Coca-Cola, yet plunged to #32 when ranked according to likeability.

10 MOST LIKED BRANDS BY TEENS WORLDWIDE		
RANK	**2005**	**1995**
1	SONY	COCA-COLA
2	NOKIA	SONY
3	ADIDAS	ADIDAS
4	NIKE	NIKE
5	COLGATE	PEPSI
6	NESTLE	KODAK
7	CADBURY	COLGATE
8	COCA-COLA	DISNEY
9	M&MS	M&MS
10	KODAK	REEBOK

Disney and Pepsi suffered the same fate, placing #9 and #3 for recognition, respectively, yet not even breaking the top twenty for likeability.

"An association with the US seemed to be a drag on the likeability of brands, despite high logo recognition," noted Chip Walker, executive vice president at Energy BBDO, in a January interview with *Women's Wear Daily*. "There seems to be a great ambivalence towards America among global teens."

While none of this spells out-and-out doom for US brands, being forced to stop drinking from the poisoned well has left marketers scrambling to uncover new formulas for generating teen cool.

Of the US entries in the current top ten, Nike has perhaps been the most aggressive in shedding its mantle of Americana in favor of "localizing" itself across the world. Hence the ongoing Joga Bonito (Play Beautiful) campaign, featuring the likes of Brazilian footballer Ronaldinho Gaúcho and the retired French icon Eric Cantona. Hence, also, Nike's move to acquire other brands that already enjoy local caché – as with Canadian hockey-equipment manufacturer Bauer, now Nike Bauer – or its new, $43 million sponsorship deal with India's national cricket team.

In a roundabout way, then, it may be tempting to prophesy that the Brand America crisis could ultimately be a boon to those US brands that have been coasting on borrowed cool, obliging them to fabricate more resilient, bespoke identities that are better suited to emerging markets.

Tempting, yes, but likely also a tad hasty, given another major finding of the Energy BBDO study. "Marketers face big trouble," note the study's authors, "62 percent of global teens are apathetic about marketing and advertising. That is, they are not anti-brand, but perhaps more dangerously, they just don't care – don't care about wearing brand logos, don't believe advertising, and feel there is too much advertising in the world."

This isn't just a small matter of a few errant kids. The global teen market is huge and growing – in 2002, worth approximately $170 billion in the States alone. More trenchantly, adolescence is regarded as the ideal moment to begin cultivating "positive consideration" and brand loyalty, right at the moment when kids begin to make independent purchasing decisions. No wonder, then, that the specter of a disinterested, brand-apathetic teen is to a marketer what root rot is to a gardener: a sign of horrible, "dangerous" things to come

Clayton Dach

Comments:

I for one, speaking as a 17 year old, can understand being completely indifferent to brands. I work for minimum wage, and what I do with my money is stongly weighted on price as well as smart consumerism. I think this habit will only be solidified as I grow older. Why save my money for an overpriced piece of designer clothing made in a sweatshop when I can buy cheaper, higher quality goods from a local source?
Vance

I would love to think that US branding is on its way out, however, branding has proven to reinvent itself time and time again. Has anyone else ever heard of consumers being compared to roaches? Eventually, the consumer is so oversaturated with advertising that the cooperations will just continue to find more and more invasive ways to spray the consumer with their poison. If we are not careful, we will all end up living corporately sponsored lives. A gross exaggeration of what is slowly happening.
Hilde

I understand how teenage apathy could deteriorate the profits of various brand names. However, is not a move away from exasperated consumerism and American domination a positive thing? If teenagers are buying what they like and what is functional and attracts them despite the brand name isn't market competition becoming more legitimate and less blind?
Sara

I totally agree, you've hit the nail right on the head with the hammer.
Nathan

It is sad but true. After spending 17 years in the US, I came back to Pakistan. During my teen days, everyone wanted to go to the US for

education but now 90% want to go to UK or Australia. If you ask them why, most of the time there is same answer. Culturally US has gone backwards and they have alienated themselves.
Usman

I think one of the ways that brands will gain ground is through likability. Volkswagen did it when I was younger and still does it (I'm 19, btw). They use casual language and make it seem like they aren't trying too hard to get you. Apple is doing the same thing. They focus on their casual dialogue. I could go on about good ads and bad ads, but the way to capture the attention of a teen is not to make the same old ad. It has to be really funny or unique in a way that goes against what we see as lifeless company advertising. I'd happily brand myself with Apple but you wouldn't catch me dead in Abercrombie. DIY too is becoming more mainstream. Thrift stores, stickers, and skateboarders. Kodak has a nostalgia factor I think. It doesn't try too hard. Trying too hard is unnattractive.
Justin Ridgley

Hey, I'm a teenager. I sympathize with this article and find it to be true from presonal experience.
Elder

Many Americans already live branded lives: their clothing, personal grooming products, automobiles, and even speech habits (vocabulary, phrasing, etc.) and dietary practices are influenced heavily by what they see on television. How many times have I heard "talk to the hand," "take it to the next level," and "b□een there, done that, got the t-shirt," all of which appear to be the common tongue of talk show hosts like Oprah, etc?
Jon Koppenhoefer

Emerging economies must be made aware of the power of marketing. It must be stressed that gobbling up any designer garbage thrown their way does not a happy person make.
Peter

Colgate? Can anyone explain that?
CPT

I know things are different in China. Young people like big brands much more than others. Megalopolis culture holds that one lives better than other people through "excellence" brands.
Zhaisi

We've been ruled by a government that works for big corporations as Coca-Cola, Walmart, Nike, Levis, Exxon, etc. So that means that the

government does not believe in social education because they only need cheap workers and free natural resources for their big corps. Here the Secretary of Public Education SEP does not cover the empire of mass-media education that has made us Mexicans just big dumb consumers of the USA's brands. If we let in another PAN government, we are going to be condemned to work for U.S. MAQUILAS, because this democracy is just a mask of this neocolonization of big corps ruled by terrorist countries that bribe people like FELIPE CALDERON.
Bernarda Prez.

I like how Colgate is on the top list. When you go to a school like mine, you would never guess it.
Nicholas

I find myself hating many of the brands on that list. I've found that brands with recognition, like Sony and the like, skimp on any kind of quality in their products. Liking a big brand doesn't set you apart from anyone and create individuality, but finding a little no-name with great products gives you identity.
Garrett

The truth is, even though American brands are falling out of favor, European and Asian consumerist brands will just pick up the slack. The news is an indicator of the decline in America's appeal – but it is not warming news about the reduction of consumerism.
E.J.

I thnk there is a growing conciousness about the global situation and I see it first hand in Kansas City, Missouri, where more and more people are staring to shop and buy local products.
Libby

Corporations suck. Cooperate!
Canadian Teen

I'm a teen and I have a question: why is Colgate on the list?
The States is now fraught with Old Age ideals, a president obsessed with violence and self-grandeur and brands that don't have universal appeal. It's a sad time for American marketing.
Candi

Maybe the decline in U.S. global influence is due to the trend to bash the U.S. It's now cool to call the U.S. names like ☐ "bully" or "powerhungry," especially by Americans. Why have others stopped liking us? Maybe because we have, also.

Jake
CTP – because nothing beats a shiny American smile!

X-Geronimo

I bet I can guess why Colgate is high on the list. I think it's because of the tooth whitening stuff. But yeah, I've always disliked wearing stuff with brandnames on display I just don't find it very stylish and the thinking that things are cooler just because what brand they are. I still don't have an Ipod, or a cell phone. But I don't really care! I get them when I need them, or have enough money. Also, ditto on the comment about how brands trying too hard is unattractive. I saw a commercial for Nike in the movies and it was about getting more air. Like i'm gonna fly if I wear those.

BLF

Although these componies are all about the profit, they rule the earth. They're becoming more powerful than the goverments and more important. The amount of jobs and stability they provide for not just America but other countries is amazing. I hate to say it but it's a two-sided coin. Anyways, Adbusters is becoming just another medium to create an image. And by they way who runs these large huge selfish companies. O, I know, the hippies and beats who traded their music and freedom in for cash. Where have the young outspoken kids of the '60s and '70s gone? O wait, that was just another image. Money rules all!

Matt

Well one approach marketers have taken in response to possible teen brand apathy is to start earlier. More and more, childrer, some as young as two or three years old, are being marketed to – cultivated to brand loyalty. And, frighteningly, these kids have few, if any, defenses against marketing appeals. If SpongeBob tells them to love PopTarts, they're gonna love 'em and perhaps always love 'em till the day they die. Once that childhood association with happiness and satisfaction is there, it may never go away.

Lisa

The US is easy to blame. But this is a global phenomenon.

Nurd on a Computer

Some states in India just banned Coke and Pepsi products because they contain pesticides, 24x higher than the agreed limit. This will accelerate their brand deterioration outside of the US.

Chad

I completely agree on the strong anti-American trend with teens at the moment, but I think that most teens do not really think about which country the company they are buying from is rooted. Although this does exclude some of the largest companies that are very well known for having US roots (e.g. Nike, McDonalds, Coca-Cola, etc.).

Frank

My only hope is that this growing disinterest in brand names will increase a focus on the manner in which these products are made as deciding factors in choosing which companies to be loyal to.
Connor

Colgate, the toothpaste anyone?
Phill

I think brands should focus on quality and customer service rather than advertising. It builds loyalty and loyalty is the biggest seller.
Erin

Teenagers are mindless drones only doing what the next one is doing. This will never change.
Giaour

I just bought a german-made car. When I think German, I think Nazi – I can't help it. All those years of public education where I was forced to watch documentaries on the Holocaust. So I was thinking, if I lived outside of the US, and I went to buy a coke, would I think Nazi and still buy the coke?
Rachel

I have to disagree with the previous comment. This is one of my first visits to this site and viewing generalizations such as this one anger me greatly. I ask Giaour where the revolutions in mans' history have started? I have a hint: places of education, universities, populated with mostly . . . YOUNG PEOPLE. If the revolutions themselves didn't start there, chances are the idea did. Teenagers are the same as adults, likely better in the sense that they have not come to grips with the control of corporations. Think of all the adults that commute to the metropolitan centers to fill their 8–5 jobs, earn their pay, buy mid-range cars, dress in the same stuff (suits and ties, etc.) What is more drone to you, a bunch of business men in bowler hats or a bunch of teenagers trying to find their way in the world?
Sean

Rachel, the coke you buy is still going to an awful dictator and regime – BUSH.
Sean

Business men of course – especially the ones in bowlers. I am impressed even more after this visit (my first to the site) with the clarity and intelligence that TEENS have posted on this topic. I've never bought into brands, and their advertisements are becoming more abrasive, confusing and ineffective. I'm glad there are adolescents seeing these ads for the moneysucking campaigns they are.
Joe

Let's not generalize now.
K.S.

I agree with Matt, everything becomes an image that can sell. Even Adbusters. This WHOLE anti-corparate image has been done – does anyone remember the beat poets or punks? EVERYTHING is for sale and not just from the U.S.
Melissa

I have to agree with the last comment – this is an image too, so what happens after you guys bring the corporations to their knees?
Trevor

This is merely the evolution or 'de-evolution' depending on the PERSPECTIVE of a nation which was built specifically for capitalist gain. It's true, America in all its glory was bought and paid for by profiteering British interests a long time ago. America IS, always HAS BEEN, and always WILL BE a place where corporate and monetary interests rule. Without this, America ceases to be what it is. Without this, America has no influence, no power, no teeth. By this point, advertising has such a hold on everyone who doesn't outright reject it from conception. Schools have their trendy clicks, which are a precursor for trendy businessmen/women. The statusquo here in America is impressed upon us before we are old enough to recognize it. American life itself is crafted around savvy business practices. Corporate influence and advertisement isn't becoming confusing and ineffective, it's becoming more and more transparent. It's getting to the point that if your average American wanted to cut that out of their life, the result would be a complete redefining of the world around you. It's one extreme to the next. The mind of the young is a battlefield that corporations spend millions trying to understand, for the purpose of exploitation and commercial gain. Why else would corporations focus such massive amounts of resources on marketing and advertising to young audiences? If the teen brain isn't already taken by consumerism and corporate interest, then why would there be mass campaigns focused directly at it? Because a teenager is a perfect consumer! The peer pressure concept has been totally exploited by corporate gain. Everytime I watch a commercial I think of the moneysucking campaign that it is. This doesn't do anything for me, or anything to fight consumerism. A good ad campaign creates the market for the product long before the product is even introduced. I wouldn't be one bit surprised to find out that Adbusters was a clever campaign enginered to capitalize on people's ideas of rejecting the corporate beast. So don't anyone be too impressed with the young minds here that seem to reject consumerism and corporate interest. After all, what else would they say once they're here?
Glaston

Yes, this whole anticorporate thing has been done by the beat poets and the punks and countless other people. And yet the corporations are still running the world. They are still filling our minds with insidious commercials, still getting us to buy their products. If we do not try to be anticorporate, what are we going to do? Become corporate? Stop caring and stop worrying about it? Give into the apathy? Are you so cynical that you think this is just an anticorporate image that has no meaning and campus talking on their cell phones, listening to their Ipods, adjusting the straps of their Dooney and Burk purses, oblivious to everything around them, lost in a mediated trance. I have taught college students who were so apathetic that they could not find one single topic they were passionate about for their persuasive essays. These kids are turning into drones. Something needs to be done. Don't be so cynical.
Angel Lynne

This article is really interesting, and I can see it's true from my own experience. Here in Brazil, when I was younger (I'm 17 now) all my friends used to wear big logo t-shirts or American flag accessories; you could see it everywhere. But now, it's like most of us are angry with U.S., and all the shit its president does. However, it's impossible for me not to agree that brands still rule the world, rule yours and my country. American brands will, unfortunately, come to find its way out.
Gabi

Why is Media Literacy not a required class in highschool? Is there anything that we can do collectivly to change this?
Toronto Canvas

Marketing will stay one step ahead, until education trumps. Right now you have the wealthy predominantly white purchasing the Abercrombie/ American Eagle/etc, where the rich want to dress like they are poor. Then you have the poor predominantly Black/Hispanic spending as much money as possible to appear rich, keeping the tags on clothes, buying the most lavish items possible. It's all a game of what do you NOT have and simply informing you that you are NOT something/ someone drives you to desire it.
Paul

I wish it was a required course too! I did an advertising unit with my freshman college students, and we examined the underlying messages in advertisements. Many were surprised to find that every ad is based on a psychological appeal, and some were critical, saying things like "it's just an ad; quit overanalyzing." At the very least a media literacy class would teach kids to analyze the images they see, and not to buy into everything the corporations tell them. I think if this was a required

course, we would see less debt spending and far less fights/killings over the latest Nike shoes.
Angellynne

Although I agree that the American name and the brands that go with it are facing a decline from the Glory Days, I think that it is also important to consider that most consumers have become more purchase savvy. Research has shown that people want to buy things that have a purpose or a cause, such as a new Vodka drink that's main advertising campaing is saving Panthers in the Rainforest. McDonalds and Pepsi may not have made the list due to how much publicity there has been recently due to how unhealthy they are. Coca-Cola, the largest seller of bottled water (Dasani), has not faced such harsh reprimands. I don't know all the facts or marketing trends, but I'm suggesting that there is more here than America being unpopular and am willing to go so far as to say that just maybe people are spending their dollars more wisely.
Peace Love Green

I think that people are just too tired of ads and brands. I live in Greece and if only one can imagine how obviously the media and corps seem to be falling apart, one could easily understand why things have turned out this way. For example, younger people have been totally alienated from TV because of the huge ad packs during TV shows. People are just getting more and more tired of this. It doesn't make sense. It seems like the industry commits suicide or the marketing deps are so pressured that they've been drained to the max. No fresh ideas, absolutely stupid commercials based on sex, cheap word games and power. Teenagers are out of this psyche at a point of total indifference. Social factors have a big piece on this pie also. Here in Greece, people are obliterated by banking – aggressive marketing, loans, credit cards.
Kostas (Graphic Designer)

I believe that people are basically branded as soon as they are a few weeks old. It is common knowledge that parents always want the best for their children, so when they are born they buy the best of every-thing and spoil the kids. It actually is really difficult to reverse the thoughts and consumerism of teenagers in high school. It is a never ending battle for teens in school because they all want to fit in, they all want to be liked and admired, so they go to Abercrombie & Fitch, Hollister, Aeropostal, etc. because that's where the cool kids shop and if they can be cool from wearing those clothes, then surely all the rest can too. At least that's is how it seems to be at my high school.

God take a look at yourselfs, i bet sittig at your desk writing these coments on your branded computer woops thought brands were the devil,
Andy

The US brand names seem to have themselves deeply rooted in consumerist markets. They buy up the small brands that are struggling to keep afloat. The CocaCola company buys up small beverage companies to make up their empire. I feel sorry for all those small international companies who have to make a 'deal with the devil' to stay profitable. If this continues do you think the world's wealth will belong to those on the 'top ten' chart? PS. Toronto Canvas, I think if people want to learn about Media Studies they'd take the course. And you can only take Media Studies in grade 12? And that's when people are worrying about University applications.
Monika Lemke

Thank God.
The Aromas Kid

The fact that children are too apathetic to care about what brand they are buying is not exactly all together good at all. Our apathetic society feeds off and depends on these companies to experience feelings such as excitement, love, thrills, through movies, xbox, following stereotypes of people living these emotions through style which is created by the companies, and so on. So sure the kids don't care what brand as long as it gives them the thrills that their boring lives could never provide to them, and of course there will allways be companies to do this.
Em

I wish I could get away from it all.
Dylanger

Hey, what about ipod? It's head and shoulders above Sony anyday.
ipod

The thing with this B☐rand America is the fact that it creates this desire and dependency that is hard to break. They stupify their campaigns so that the teens are more drawn in. Just look the movies and TV shows out now: it's all commedy but stupid comedy. Keep in mind these corporations don't make their money off of intelligent people. Just the young vunerable and stupid are the ones who are swept up in the machine. Kids should be taught reasoning in schools as well as tolerance and autonomy. As soon as a teen gives up his or her independence it's very easy to spoonfeed them anything and have it stick. The adolescent mind is like clay: very impressionable and easy to mold to your likeness. Dependancy has become a tradition; within dependancy their lies fear; fear kills initiative and makes the mind dull and narrow.
Josh

The toothpaste market is a goldmine, just waiting to be exploited; what are there two known brands colgate and macleens. Too bad I don't

have a toothpaste factory of my own. I'm glad to find that countless teenage feelgood movies about following your own beat have finally let the message sink in. Huzzahs for independant and advertising apathetic teens everywhere. Go forth and spend at the best value stores possible! Or conversely dont spend without necessity! 62%, that's great; other 38% hey, get over it, brand doens't mean jack.
Jess

Note: Comments must be approved before being posted, and may be edited for length and clarity. Irrelevant and inappropriate comments will be deleted outright. If you have any comments or concerns about this process, feel free to email websubmissions[at]adbusters[dot]org.

INDEX

Adbusters **IV** 307–10
adjectival compounds **I** 308–9
adjective **I** 308
adulterous narratives **III** 202–5
advertisements: cost of making
IV 259–60; rhetorical interventions,
as **III** 192
advertising: combining products
in use, and **III** 146–8; covert
communications in **II** 175–84;
creation of *see* creation of
advertising; development of *see*
development of advertising; history
of **I** 36–8; language and motive, and
I 217–24; object of study, as **I** 2–5;
public relations compared **IV** 14–18;
reasons for studying **I** 289–91; testing
limits of conventional **III** 173–91
advertising agencies **IV** 270–92;
account men **IV** 287; 'creative
shootout' **IV** 285; development
IV 275; dirty tricks **IV** 286–7; global
advertising in China, and **II** 189–90;
internationalisation **IV** 277–8; length
of relationship with clients **IV** 286–7;
linking age and risk **IV** 292–3;
mega-agencies **IV** 276; new business
IV 284–5; occupational stress **IV** 292;
parties **IV** 290–1; payment **IV** 291;
perks **IV** 292; qualifications **IV** 290;
Saatchi brothers **IV** 277; staff
IV 273–4; 'suits' **IV** 287
advertising and communications
I 54–7; controlling minority and
expectant majority **I** 56; coexistence
of new technology and old social
forms **I** 54; newspapers **I** 54–5, 57;
public policy **I** 55; social failure, and

I 55–6; submission **I** 55, 57; 'young
market' **I** 57
advertising and consumerism **I** 211–22
advertising and society **IV** 222–9;
benefit to society, whether **IV** 229;
brutal persuaders **IV** 225–6;
children **IV** 226–7; demon
advertising **IV** 222–3; environment
IV 227–8; ethnic problem **IV** 228–9;
mirroring society **IV** 223–4;
pollution **IV** 227–8; prostitution of
the arts **IV** 227; servant or seducer,
whether **IV** 224–5; visions of
organised conspiracy **IV** 222–3
advertising and the modulation of
narcissism **III** 192–207; adulterous
narratives **III** 202–3; adultery
III 192–207; advertisements as
rhetorical interventions **III** 192;
ambiguous texts **III** 196; bi-polar self
III 197; coherent disposition of self
III 198; fantasy life **III** 205; Heinz
Kohut **III** 197–8; 'maintenance of
self' **III** 198; narcissism **III** 197;
narcissistic libido **III** 197–8;
oppositions in imagery **III** 194–5;
organisation and expression of
competing conflictual qualities
and values **III** 200; Peugeot 306
III 199–200; reader's dilemma
III 195–8; readerships **III** 201–2;
reading dilemmas **III** 193–5; Renault
Laguna **III** 202–3; textual concerns
III 195; Volkswagen Passat **III** 203–5
advertising as an object of study:
appeal of **I** 2–5
advertising in power **I** 46–8; new media
I 47; statistics 1935 **I** 46–7

334